Account Title	Number
Preferred Stock	510
Paid-In Capital in Excess of Par–Preferred	511
Stock Subscribed–Preferred	512
Common Stock	520
Paid-In Capital in Excess of Par–Common	521
Paid-In Capital in Excess of Stated Value–Common	522
Stock Subscribed–Common	523
Stock Dividend Distributable	525
Paid-In Capital-Stock Dividend	530
Paid-In Capital–Treasury Stock Transactions	531
Paid-In Capital–Retirement of Stock	532
Minority Interest	540
Retained Earnings	550
Retained Earnings Appropriated	551
Unrealized Gain (Loss) from Available-for-Sale Securities	560
Accumulated Translation Adjustment	562
Treasury Stock	564
Dividends	598
Income Summary	599

REVENUES

Revenue	600
Sales	602
Fee Revenue	604
Parking Revenue	606
Repairs Revenue	608
Rent Revenue	610
Cash Sales	612
Credit Sales	614
Interest Revenue	616
Dividends Revenue	618
Miscellaneous Revenue	620
Sales Returns and Allowances	622
Sales Discounts	624
Income from Subsidiary	630

EXPENSES

Advertising Expense	700
Bond Issue Expense	701
Cash Over or Short	702
Cleaning Supplies Expense	703
Cost of Goods Sold	704
Depletion Expense	706
Depreciation Expense–Building	708
Depreciation Expense–Delivery Equipment	710
Depreciation Expense–Equipment	712
Depreciation Expense–Equipment Under Capital Lease	713
Depreciation Expense–Land Improvements	714
Depreciation Expense–Office Equipment	716
Employer Payroll Expense	718
Franchise Amortization Expense	720
Fuel Expense	722
Goodwill Amortization Expense	724
Income Tax Expense	726
Insurance Expense	728
Interest Expense	730
Laboratory Expense	732
Licenses Expense	733

Account Title	Number
Maintenan…	
Maintenan…	
Miscellaneous Expense	738
Office Supplies Expense	740
Organization Costs Amortization Expense	742
Parts Expense	744
Patent Amortization Expense	746
Pension Expense	748
Professional Fees Expense	750
Property Tax Expense	752
Purchases	754
Purchases Discounts	756
Purchases Discounts Lost	758
Purchases Returns and Allowances	760
Rent Expense	762
Research and Development Expense	764
Sales Commissions Expense	766
Sales Expense	768
Sales Supplies Expense	770
Sick Pay Expense	772
Supplies Expense	774
Telephone Expense	775
Transportation-In	776
Uncollectible Accounts Expense	778
Utilities Expense	780
Vacation Pay Expense	782
Wages and Salaries Expense	784

GAINS AND LOSSES

Gains

Exchange Gain	800
Gain from Disposal	802
Gain from Retirement of Debt	804
Gain from Sale of Equipment	806
Gain from Sale of Investments	808
Gain from Sale of Property	810
Gain (Loss) from Realization	815
Unrealized Gain (Loss) from Investments	820

Losses

Exchange Loss	850
Loss from Damaged Inventory	852
Loss from Decline in Market Value of Merchandise Inventory	853
Loss from Disposal	854
Loss from Inventory Shortage	856
Loss from Sale of Equipment	858
Loss from Sale of Investments	860
Loss from Sale of Mineral Deposits	861
Loss from Sale of Property	862

MANUFACTURING ACCOUNTS

Manufacturing Overhead	900
Material Price Variance	905
Material Quantity Variance	910
Labor Efficiency Variance	915
Labor Rate Variance	920
Controllable Overhead Variance	925
Overhead Volume Variance	930

INTRODUCTION TO
MANAGERIAL ACCOUNTING

JIAMBALVO MAY McDONALD

JAMES JIAMBALVO, PhD, CPA
Chair, Department of Accounting
University of Washington

ROBERT G. MAY, PhD
KPMG Peat Marwick Centennial Professor of Accounting
Associate Dean, College of Business Administration and
Graduate School of Business
The University of Texas at Austin

CHARLES L. McDONALD, PhD, CPA
Associate Professor and Director,
Center for Accounting Research and Professional Education
University of Florida

SOUTH-WESTERN College Publishing
An International Thomson Publishing Company

AB88AA2
Copyright © 1995
by South-Western Publishing Co.
Cincinnati, Ohio

I(T)P
International Thomson Publishing
South-Western College Publishing is an ITP Company.
The ITP trademark is used under license

ALL RIGHTS RESERVED
The text of this publication, or any part thereof, may not be reproduced or transmitted in any form or by any means, electronic or mechanical, including photocopying, recording, storage in an information retrieval system, or otherwise, without prior written permission of the publisher.

Sponsoring Editor: David L. Shaut
Developmental Editor: Minta Berry
Production Editor: Mark Sears
Production House: Berry Publication Services
Cover Design: Bruce Design
Internal Design: Lesiak/Crampton Design
Photographer, Chapter Openers: Kessler Photography
Photo Editor: Jennifer Mayhall
Marketing Manager: Michael O'Brien

Credits:
   993   David Joel/Tony StoneImages/MacNeal Hospital

ISBN: 0-538-84499-X
   2 3 4 5 6 7 VH 0 9 8 7 6 5
Printed in the United States of America

Library of Congress Cataloging-in-Publication Data
The complete version of the text is catalogued as follows:

May, Robert G.
   Accounting / Robert G. May, James Jiambalvo, Charles L. McDonald.
      p.   cm.
   Includes bibliographical references and index.
   ISBN 0-538-83062-X
      1. Accounting.   I. Jiambalvo, James   . II. McDonald,
   Charles L.   . III. Title.
   HF5635.M452 1995
   657—dc20   94-31231
                                                                  CIP

DEDICATION

To our families

James Jiambalvo
Robert G. May
Charles L. McDonald

PREFACE

According to the Accounting Education Change Commission (AECC):

> The primary objective of the first course in accounting is for students to learn about accounting as an information development and communication function that supports economic decision-making. The knowledge and skills provided by the first course in accounting should facilitate subsequent learning even if the student takes no additional academic work in accounting or directly related disciplines. For example, the course should help students perform financial analysis; derive information for personal or organization decisions; and understand business, governmental, and other organizational entities.[1]

Introduction to Managerial Accounting directly addresses the AECC's recommendations in the following ways:

1. A decision-making focus is evident in every chapter.
2. Accounting is discussed in a way that provides insight into how businesses and other organizations function.

This text is suitable for a one-quarter course covering principles of managerial accounting. Material is presented in sufficient depth so that students who aspire to major in accounting will have more than adequate preparation for additional accounting courses. However, the text is aimed primarily at the majority of students who will major in other disciplines. The text stresses basic principles and presents analytical tools in contexts that students will find appealing. Students will appreciate the clear prose, helpful graphics, and emphasis on decision making.

Decision-Making Focus

Each chapter opens with a brief, believable story about a decision maker facing a realistic business decision or dilemma. In the body of the chapter, we introduce accounting information related to the decision maker's problem. By the end of the chapter, we close the loop, describing and illustrating financial analyses that specifically address the decision maker's concerns. The scenarios provide a context that aids understanding of the material, and they emphasize the role of accounting information in economic decision making.

Most students who study managerial accounting will go on to become business managers, rather than accountants. As managers, they will need to plan operations, evaluate subordinates, and make a variety of decisions using managerial accounting information and techniques. Consistent with a focus on business majors, rather than accounting majors, as the users of this text, we decided to expand the coverage of certain managerial accounting topics, and to reduce coverage of some of the more procedural topics. For example, recognizing that activity based costing is a critical element of managerial accounting, this topic is covered in both the chapter on job-order costing, Chapter 21, and in the chap-

---

[1]Accounting Education Change Commission, *The First Course in Accounting*, Position Statement No. Two, (June 1992).

ter on cost allocation, Chapter 24. Process costing, however, is a somewhat "technical" topic in that the ideas are easily mastered but specific procedures are quite complex. To reduce technical complexity, we present the relatively simple weighted-average approach and ignore the more complex FIFO approach.

Analyzing, Thinking, and Communicating

Throughout this text, we emphasize decision making and thinking about problems in a rich business context. The thinking-in-context emphasis is reinforced in the end-of-chapter materials. At the end of each chapter are a set of Critical Thinking and Communicating cases. They range from thought-provoking ethical situations, to scenarios that promote critical thinking about the limitations of accounting and the motives of managers who choose accounting methods, to cases requiring the analysis and interpretation of financial statements. In most cases, a substantial writing exercise is required or implied. The following icons are used to identify the cases:

Decision Case

Ethical Dilemmas

Financial Analysis Case

Communication Case

Supplementary Material for the Instructor

Solutions Manual The comprehensive manual contains solutions to questions, exercises, and problems. Suggested solutions and key points of discussion are provided for all cases. All exercises and problems are correlated to the appropriate learning objectives and time estimates are provided for all problems. The manual is also available in electronic media.

Solution Transparencies The solutions to exercises and problems are available on transparency for ease of classroom presentation.

Test Bank A printed test bank includes true/false, multiple choice, and problem materials for all chapters. All items are correlated to the appropriate learning objectives. The level of difficulty for the items is also identified.

MicroExam 4.0 Computerized Test Bank The test bank is available in a MicroExam version. All items that appear in the print test bank are available electronically. Among the features of the electronic version are the ability to customize the test, the ability to prepare multiple versions of the same questions, and the ability to add or edit questions and problems.

Videos *The Role of Management Accounting in the Production Process* features management accounting at work in high-profit companies. *GE Lighting Systems: Continuous Flow Manufacturing* studies employees producing products in both conventional and advanced manufacturing environments.

Supplementary Material for the Student

Working Papers Appropriate forms for students to use in solving end-of-chapter problems are available.

Study Guide A study guide is available. The study guide provides discussion and exercises for each chapter in learning objective order.

Acknowledgements

Throughout the text, relevant professional statements of the Financial Accounting Standards Board and other authoritative publications are discussed, quoted, or footnoted. We are indebted to the American Institute of Certified Public Accountants, the Financial Accounting Standards Board, the American Accounting Association, and the Institute of Management Accountants for material from their publications.

During the development of this text, many individuals contributed significant insights and provided guidance to us as we wrote and refined the text. We especially thank Bruce Koch, John Beegle, and David Coffee for their time and effort in assisting with the content development and review of the end of chapter material. We are also grateful for the assistance of Steven Rice in the preparation of the tax appendix.

We sincerely appreciate the efforts of all who have contributed to the final product. The following faculty served as reviewers and class testers during the project:

James Abbott	Broome Community College
Michael Adkins	Lexington Community College
Rainer Albright	The University of Alabama
Herman Andress	Santa Fe Community College
Sue Atkinson	Tarleton State University
Debra Barbeau	Southern Illinois University at Carbondale
Donald J. Barnett	California State University–Dominguez Hills
Homer L. Bates	University of North Florida
Susan Shannon Bates	Boise State University
Anne Connell Baucom	University of North Carolina–Charlotte
Kathleen Bindon	University of Alabama
Dorothy Binger	Tallahassee Community College
Sallie Branscom	Virginia Western Community College
Ronald P. Brooker	Phoenix College
Howard Bryan	Santa Rosa Junior College
James I. Bryant	Catonsville Community College
Carol Buchl	Northern Michigan University
Leon Button	Scottsdale Community College
David Bydalek	Mesa Community College
Eric Carlson	Kean College of New Jersey
Charles F. Chanter	Grand Rapids Junior College
Michael C. Chester	Norfolk State University
C. David Coffee	Western Carolina University
Kenneth L. Coffey	Johnson County Community College
A. Carter Cogle	Southside Virginia Community College
Judith Considine	Rutgers University
Grace M. Conway	Adelphi University
Judith M. Cook	Grossmont College
Tomas Cooper	Parkland College
Fredonna Cox	Eastern Kentucky University
Alan E. Davis	Philadelphia Community College
Paul L. Donohue	Delaware County Community College
Joseph G. Doser	Truckee Meadows Community College
Lola A. Dudley	Eastern Illinois University
Dean Edmiston	Emporia State University
Randy Edwards	Appalachian State University
John A. Elfrink	Southeast Missouri State University
David Fetyko	Kent State University
Carl J. Fisher	Foothill College

R. Leigh Frackelton, Jr.	Mary Washington College
Joseph Gallo	Cuyahoga Community College–Metro Campus
Helen Gernon	University of Oregon
Shirley Glass	Macomb Community College–South
Robert F. Godfrey	Marshall University
Maxwell P. Godwin	Southwest Texas State University
Harold Goedde	North Carolina A & T University
William D. Goodman	Bluefield State College
Donald J. Griffin	Cayuga Community College
Joyce Griffin	Kansas City Kansas Community College
Donald D. Gusarson	Cabrillo College
William T. Hall, Sr.	Fayetteville Technical Community College
Linda Herrington	Community College of Allegheny County
George Holdren	University of Nebraska
Cynthia L. Holloway	Tarrant County Junior College–Northeast
Patty Holmes	Des Moines Area Community College
Anita V. Hope	Tarrant County Junior College–Northeast
George Ihorn	El Paso Community College
Randy Johnston	Penn State University
Brent Joyce	Virginia Highlands Community College
Bruce Koch	University of North Texas
Edward Krohn	Miami-Dade Community College
Michael Layne	Nassau Community College
Marcella Y. Lecky	The University of Southwestern Louisiana
Albert Y. Lew	Wright State University
Norbert Lindskog	Harold Washington College
Johanna D. Lyle	Kansas State University
Thomas Lynch	Hocking Technical College
Rene Manes	The Florida State University
Ken Mark	Kansas City Kansas Community College
Thomas J. McCoy	Middlesex County College
William McFarland	Illinois Central College
Maria Trini U. Melcher	California State University–Fullerton
Phillip Mills	Miami-Dade Community College–South Campus
Thomas P. Moncada	Eastern Illinois University
Paula Morris	Kennesaw State College
C. Lynn Murray	Florida Community College–South Campus
M. Salah Negm	Prince George's Community College
Cletus O'Drobinak	South Suburban College
Leslie Oakes	Rutgers University
Frances Aileen Ormiston	Mesa Community College
John Overton	University of New Hampshire
John Palipchak	Penn State–Beaver Campus
Lynn M. Paluska	Nassau Community College
Joseph S. Patterson	DeKalb Community College–South Campus
Deborah Dianne Payne	Roosevelt University
A. George Petrie	University of Texas–Pan American
Rose Marie Pilcher	Richland College
Sharyll A.B. Plato	Central State University–Oklahoma
Norma C. Powell	Bryant College
Barbara Powers	Wytheville Community College
Robert D. Reid	Germanna Community College
Reg Rezac	Texas Women's University
Carla Lemley Rich	Pensacola Junior College
Juan Rivera	University of Notre Dame
Lawrence A. Roman	Cuyahoga Community College–Eastern
David L. Rozelle	Western Michigan University
Leo Ruggle	Mankato State University
Pearl B. Sandelman	De Anza College
Wallace James Satchell	St. Philip's Community College
John Schryver	Bentley College
Robbie Sheffy	Tarrant County Junior College
Michael T. Stein	Rutgers University
John R. Stewart	University of Northern Colorado
Linda Sugarman	University of Akron

Thomas Sullivan	Quincy College
Lisa Tahlier	North Carolina Wesleyan College
Greg Thom	Parkland College
Ingrid R. Torsay	DeKalb Community College–Central Campus
Charles L. Vawter	Glendale Community College
Vicki S. Vorell	Cuyahoga Community College–Western
DuWayne M. Wacker	University of North Dakota
Lori A. Wahila	Broome Community College
Al Walczak	Linn-Benton Community College
Thomas C. Waller	University of Houston–Clear Lake
Sharon Walters	Morehead State University
Peter R. Wilson	New York University
Frank Zattich	Lincoln Land Community College
Karl M. Zehms	University of Wisconsin–Green Bay

ABOUT THE AUTHORS

James Jiambalvo is a Professor of Accounting at the University of Washington. He received undergraduate and masters degrees from the University of Illinois and the Ph.D. degree from The Ohio State University. Professor Jiambalvo has published articles in a number of top accounting journals including *The Accounting Review*, *Contemporary Accounting Research*, the *Journal of Accounting and Economics*, and the *Journal of Accounting Research*. He has also served on the editorial boards of *Auditing: A Journal of Practice and Theory*, *Contemporary Accounting Research*, the *Journal of Management Accounting Research*, and he is a past associate editor of *The Accounting Review*. Professor Jiambalvo is a CPA and he has been recognized at the University of Washington with the Burlington Northern Faculty Achievement Award.

Robert G. May is the KPMG Peat Marwick Centennial Professor of Accounting at The University of Texas at Austin and Associate Dean for Academic Affairs. He has also held appointments at the University of Washington and at Stanford University. He received his Ph.D. from Michigan State University.

Professor May has published articles in scholarly journals and was co-winner of the 1976 AICPA Notable Contribution to the Accounting Literature Award. He has served as Associate Editor of *The Accounting Review*. He has coauthored three textbooks: *A New Introduction to Financial Accounting*, *A Brief Introduction to Managerial and Social Uses of Accounting*, and *Evaluating Business Ventures*. He is the co-developer of SCAD, a Simulated Case for Audit Decisions, under a grant from Price Waterhouse Foundation and developer of Variables Sampling Education Support Software (VSESS) under a grant from Coopers & Lybrand Foundation.

Professor May has taught a variety of graduate and undergraduate courses in accounting. He received teaching awards at the University of Washington and at the University of Texas. He was co-recipient of the American Accounting Association Innovation in Accounting Education Award in 1991 and 1993. Professor May has had public accounting experience and is active in the American Accounting Association.

Charles L. McDonald is Associate Professor and Director of the Center for Accounting Research and Professional Education of the Fisher School of Accounting at the University of Florida. He received a Ph.D. in accounting from Michigan State University. Articles by Professor McDonald have appeared in *The Accounting Review*, *Accounting Horizons*, *Corporate Accounting*, and the *Journal of Business Research*. Professor McDonald is a CPA and a member of the American Accounting Association, American Institute of Certified Public Accountants, and the Florida Institute of Certified Public Accountants. He has served on numerous committees of those organizations including the Financial Accounting Standards Committee of the AAA and is currently a member of the Accounting Standards Executive Committee of the AICPA.

CONTENTS IN BRIEF

MANAGERIAL ACCOUNTING *831*

- **20** Managerial Accounting and Cost Information *832*
- **21** Job-Order Costing and Changes in the Manufacturing Environment *864*
- **22** Process Costing *902*
- **23** Cost-Volume-Profit Relationships *934*
- **24** Cost Allocation and Activity-Based Costing *978*
- **25** Budgetary Planning and Control *1022*
- **26** Standard Costs and Variance Analysis *1052*
- **27** Cost Information and Management Decisions *1080*
- **28** Capital Budgeting Decisions *1106*
- **29** Control of Decentralized Organizations *1134*
- **APPENDIX A** Present and Future Value Tables *1165*
- Glossary *1169*
- Index *1182*

CONTENTS

MANAGERIAL ACCOUNTING *831*

20 MANAGERIAL ACCOUNTING AND COST INFORMATION *832*

Introduction to Managerial Accounting *834*
  Planning and Evaluation 834 ■ Decision Making 836 ■ Difference Between Financial and Managerial Accounting 837 ■ Similarities Between Financial and Managerial Accounting 838

Emphasis on Cost Information *838*

Cost Classifications for Manufacturing Firms *839*
  Manufacturing Costs 839 ■ Nonmanufacturing Costs 840 ■ Product and Period Costs 841

Balance Sheet Presentation of Product Costs *841*

Flow of Product Costs in Accounts *842*

Income Statement Presentation of Product Costs *843*
  Comparison of Financial Statements of Merchandising and Manufacturing Firms 845

Cost of Services *846*

Cost Classifications for Planning, Evaluation, and Decision Making *846*
  Variable and Fixed Costs 846 ■ Direct and Indirect Costs 848 ■ Controllable and Noncontrollable Costs 848

21 JOB-ORDER COSTING AND CHANGES IN THE MANUFACTURING ENVIRONMENT *864*

Use of Product Cost Information *866*
  Financial Reporting and Product Costs 866 ■ Managerial Decision Making and Product Costs 866

Types of Costing Systems *866*
  Job-Order Costing Systems 867 ■ Process Costing Systems 867

Overview of Job Cost and Financial Statement Accounts *867*

Job-Order Costing System *869*
  Direct Material Cost 869 ■ Direct Labor Cost 870 ■ Manufacturing Overhead 871

Flow of Costs in Work in Process Inventory, Finished Goods Inventory, and Cost of Goods Sold *873*

Allocating Overhead to Jobs *873*
  Overhead Allocation Rates 873 ■ Selecting an Overhead Allocation Base 874 ■ Activity-Based Costing (ABC) and Multiple Overhead Rates 874 ■ Predetermined Overhead Rates 877 ■ Eliminating Over- or Underapplied Overhead 878

XV

Changes in the Manufacturing Environment and Product Costing Systems *879*
  Just-in-Time (JIT) Manufacturing 880 ▪ Computer-Controlled Manufacturing 880 ▪ Flexible Manufacturing Systems 881 ▪ Total Quality Management 881

Revisiting the Eastern Electric Example *882*

22 PROCESS COSTING *902*

Difference Between Job-Order and Process Costing Systems *904*

Product and Cost Flows *904*
  Product Flows Through Departments 904 ▪ Cost Flows Through Accounts 905

Calculating Unit Cost *907*
  Equivalent Units 908 ▪ Cost per Equivalent Unit 908

Calculating and Applying Cost per Equivalent Unit: Mixing Department Example *909*
  Cost Transferred Out 910 ▪ Ending Work in Process 910

Production Cost Report *911*
  Reconciliation of Units 911 ▪ Reconciliation of Costs 911

Basic Steps in Process Costing *911*

Answering Stacy's Question *913*

Transferred-In Cost *913*

Transferred-In Cost: Packaging Department Example *913*

23 COST-VOLUME-PROFIT RELATIONSHIPS *934*

Common Cost Behavior Patterns *936*
  Variable Costs 936 ▪ Fixed Costs 937 ▪ Mixed Costs 937

Cost Estimation Methods *939*
  Account Analysis 939 ▪ Scattergraph Approach 941 ▪ High-Low Method 941 ▪ Regression Analysis 944 ▪ The Relevant Range 944

Cost-Volume-Profit Analysis *945*
  Break-Even Point 945 ▪ Profit Equation 946 ▪ Margin of Safety 947 ▪ Contribution Margin 947 ▪ Contribution Margin Ratio 947 ▪ "What If" Analysis 948

Multiproduct Analysis *949*
  Contribution Margin Approach 949 ▪ Contribution Margin Ratio Approach 949

Assumptions in C-V-P Analysis *951*
  Union Skate Company 951

Appendix 23-A: Variable and Full Costing *953*

24 COST ALLOCATION AND ACTIVITY-BASED COSTING *978*

Purposes of Cost Allocation *980*
  To Provide Information for Decision Making 980 ▪ To Provide "Full Cost" Information 981 ▪ To Reduce Frivolous Use of Common Resources 981 ▪ To Encourage Evaluation of Services 982

Process of Cost Allocation *980*
  Determining the Cost Objectives 982 ▪ Forming Cost Pools 983 ▪ Selecting an Allocation Base and Allocating Costs 984

Allocating Service Department Costs *985*
  Direct Method of Allocating Service Department Costs 985 ■ *Sequential Method of Allocating Service Department Costs 986*

Allocating Joint Costs *989*

Problems with Cost Allocation *991*
  Responsibility Accounting and Controllable Costs 991 ■ *Arbitrary Allocations 992* ■ *Unitized Fixed Costs and Lump-Sum Allocations 994* ■ *The Problem of Too Few Cost Pools 995*

Activity-Based Costing *997*
  The Problem of Using Only Measures of Production Volume to Allocate Overhead 997 ■ *The ABC Approach 998* ■ *Relating Cost Pools to Products Using Cost Drivers 998* ■ *Comprehensive Example of the ABC Approach 999* ■ *Different Costs for Different Purposes 1003*

25 BUDGETARY PLANNING AND CONTROL *1022*

Use of Budgets in Planning and Control *1024*
  Planning 1024 ■ *Control 1024*

Developing the Budget *1024*
  Budget Time Period 1025 ■ *Zero Base Budgeting 1025*

The Master Budget *1025*
  Sales Budget 1026 ■ *Production Budget 1026* ■ *Direct Material Purchases Budget 1027* ■ *Direct Labor Budget 1028* ■ *Manufacturing Overhead Budget 1029* ■ *Selling and Administrative Expense Budget 1029* ■ *Budgeted Income Statement 1029* ■ *Capital Acquisitions Budget 1031* ■ *Cash Receipts and Disbursements Budget 1031* ■ *Budgeted Balance Sheet 1034*

Use of Computers in the Budget Planning Process *1035*

Budgetary Control *1035*
  Static and Flexible Budgets 1036

Investigating Budget Variances *1037*

Conflict in Planning and Control Uses of Budgets *1038*

Evaluation, Measurement, and Management Behavior *1038*

The Preston Manufacturing Company Case *1039*

26 STANDARD COSTS AND VARIANCE ANALYSIS *1052*

Standard Costs and Budgets *1054*

Development of Standard Costs *1055*

Ideal and Attainable Standards *1055*

General Approach to Variance Analysis *1056*

Material Variances *1057*
  Material Price Variance 1057 ■ *Material Quantity Variance 1057* ■ *Reconciling the Material Price and Quantity Variances to the Total Material Variance 1057*

Direct Labor Variances *1058*
  Labor Rate Variance 1058 ■ *Labor Efficiency Variance 1058* ■ *Reconciling the Labor Efficiency and Labor Rate Variances to the Total Labor Variance 1059*

Overhead Variances *1059*
   Overhead Volume Variance 1059 ■ *Controllable Overhead Variance 1061* ■ *Reconciling the Overhead Volume Variance and the Controllable Overhead Variance to the Total Overhead Variance 1061*

Comprehensive Example *1061*
   Material Variances 1063 ■ *Labor Variances 1064* ■ *Overhead Variances 1064*

Investigation of Standard Cost Variances *1065*
   Management by Exception 1066 ■ *"Favorable" Variances May Be Unfavorable 1066*

Responsibility Accounting and Variances *1067*

Recording Standard Costs in Accounts *1067*
   Recording Material Costs 1067 ■ *Recording Labor Cost 1068* ■ *Recording Manufacturing Overhead 1068* ■ *Recording Finished Goods 1069* ■ *Recording Cost of Goods Sold 1069*

Closing Variance Accounts *1069*

27 COST INFORMATION AND MANAGEMENT DECISIONS *1080*

Differential Costs and Revenues *1082*
   Additional Processing Decision 1082 ■ *Make or Buy Decisions 1083* ■ *Dropping a Product Line 1087*

Summary of Differential, Avoidable, Sunk, and Opportunity Costs *1089*

Decisions Involving Production Constraints *1090*

Pricing Decisions *1092*
   Full Cost Pricing 1092 ■ *Contribution Approach to Pricing 1092*

Qualitative Consideration in Decision Analysis *1094*

28 CAPITAL BUDGETING DECISIONS *1106*

Capital Budgeting Decisions *1108*

Evaluating Investment Opportunities Time Value of Money Approaches *1109*
   The Net Present Value Method 1109 ■ *The Internal Rate of Return Method 1111* ■ *Summary of Net Present Value and Internal Rate of Return 1112*

Estimating the Required Rate of Return *1113*

Further Consideration of Cash Flows *1113*
   Cash Flows, Taxes, and the Depreciation Income Tax Shield 1114 ■ *Adjusting Cash Flows for Inflation 1115*

Simplified Approaches to Capital Budgeting *1116*
   Payback Period Method 1116 ■ *Accounting Rate of Return 1117*

Conflict Between Performance Evaluation and Capital Budgeting *1118*

Island Air Revisited *1122*

Appendix 28-A: The Internal Rate of Return with Unequal Cash Flows *1123*

29 CONTROL OF DECENTRALIZED ORGANIZATIONS *1134*

Why Firms Decentralize *1136*
   Disadvantages of Decentralization 1138

Responsibility Accounting and Decentralization *1139*

Cost Centers, Profit Centers, and Investment Centers *1140*
   Cost Centers 1140 ■ *Profit Centers 1141* ■ *Investment Centers 1141*

Evaluating Investment Centers *1142*
  Return on Investment 1142 ■ *Evaluating Investment Centers and Managers with ROI 1143* ■ *Problems with Using ROI 1143* ■ *Residual Income 1145*

Transfer Pricing *1147*
  Opportunity Costs and Transfer Prices 1147 ■ *Market Price as the Transfer Price 1148* ■ *Market Price and Opportunity Cost 1148* ■ *Variable Costs as the Transfer Price 1150* ■ *Full Cost Plus Profit as the Transfer Price 1151* ■ *Negotiated Transfer Prices 1152* ■ *Service Centers Turned Into Profit Centers with Transfer Prices 1152* ■ *Transfer Prices and Income Taxes in an International Context 1153*

APPENDIX A PRESENT AND FUTURE VALUE TABLES *1165*

Glossary *1169*

Index *1182*

MANAGERIAL ACCOUNTING

CHAPTER 20

Managerial Accounting and Cost Information

You may someday manage a department store, an advertising agency, or an automobile manufacturing plant. As a manager you will have to plan operations, evaluate subordinates, and make a variety of decisions using accounting information. In some cases you will find accounting information from the balance sheet, the income statement, the statement of retained earnings, and the statement of cash flows to be useful. However, much of the information in these statements is more relevant to *external* users of accounting information such as stockholders, creditors, and government agencies. In addition, you will need information prepared specifically for *internal* users of accounting information such as firm managers. This type of information is referred to as managerial accounting information.

Previous chapters introduced financial accounting which stresses accounting concepts and procedures that relate to preparing reports for external users of accounting information. In comparison, **managerial accounting** stresses accounting concepts and procedures needed to prepare reports for internal users of accounting information. The remainder of this book is devoted to the subject of managerial accounting. This chapter on managerial accounting provides an overview and illustrates the role of managerial accounting in planning, evaluation, and decision making. The chapter also introduces a number of cost terms and concepts that are critical to the understanding of managerial accounting.

LEARNING OBJECTIVES

1. State the primary goal of managerial accounting.
2. Describe how budgets are used to plan and how performance reports are used to evaluate.
3. Distinguish between manufacturing and nonmanufacturing costs and between product and period costs.
4. Describe the flow of product costs in a manufacturing firm's accounts.
5. Distinguish between fixed and variable costs, direct and indirect costs, and controllable and noncontrollable costs.

INTRODUCTION TO MANAGERIAL ACCOUNTING

LO 1 State the primary goal of managerial accounting.

The primary goal of managerial accounting is to provide information that helps managers plan and evaluate company activities and make business decisions. Providing information for *planning, evaluation, and decision making* is the purpose of managerial accounting.

Planning and Evaluation

LO 2 Describe how budgets are used to plan and how performance reports are used to evaluate.

Planning is a key activity for all companies. A plan provides financial direction much like a road map provides directions and distances to specific locations. A map helps you avoid wrong turns and wasted time; likewise, a financial plan guides a company toward its objectives. With such a plan, employees focus on company goals and follow the most efficient route to achieve them Plans also aid evaluation. Managers can compare actual results to planned results and decide if corrective action is necessary. If actual results differ from those in the plan, then the company may not have followed the plan properly or the plan itself may have been deficient.

Illustration 20-1 presents the major steps in the planning and evaluation process. Managers take actions to implement the plan. Their actions lead to results that are compared to those of the original plan. Based on this evaluation, managers take necessary corrective action. Corrective action may consist of training employees to do a better job, changing a production process, or even firing a manager who is responsible for deviating from the plan. It may also consist of revising an unrealistic plan.

Budgets for Planning. Managerial accountants prepare financial plans called **budgets**. A wide variety of budgets may be prepared. For example, a *profit budget* indicates planned income; a *cash flow budget* planned cash inflows and outflows; and a *production budget* the planned quantity of production and the expected cost.

Consider the production budget for Marie's Pie Company. In the coming year, the company plans to produce 200,000 pies. The company estimates it will use $225,000 of ingredients and pay factory workers $200,000. It also expects to pay $25,000 for rent, incur $20,000 of depreciation of equipment, and pay $15,000 for other costs. The production cost budget presented in Illustration 20-2 summarizes this information.

The production cost budget informs the managers of Marie's Pie Company how many pies the company intends to produce and what the needed

CHAPTER 20 MANAGERIAL ACCOUNTING AND COST INFORMATION

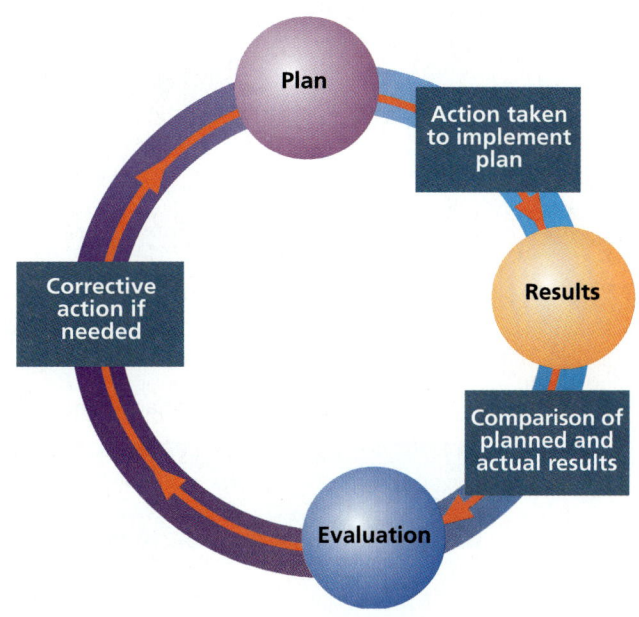

ILLUSTRATION 20-1 Planning and Evaluation Process

resources will cost. With this information, managers can implement the plan. For example, managers must purchase ingredients sufficient to produce 200,000 pies.

ILLUSTRATION 20-2 Production Cost Budget

Marie's Pie Company Budgeted Production Costs For the Year Ended December 31, 19X1	
Budgeted production	200,000 pies
Production costs:	
Ingredient cost	$225,000
Labor cost	200,000
Rent	25,000
Depreciation	20,000
Other	15,000
Total budgeted production costs	$485,000

Performance Reports for Evaluation. Besides communicating company plans to managers, budgets are used to *evaluate* how well managers have implemented the plans. The evaluation compares the budget with actual results. The report comparing actual and budgeted performance is a **performance report**. If actual results are consistent with the budget, managerial performance is judged to be acceptable. If actual results deviate significantly from the budget, however, it is necessary to determine if the deviation is the result of good or bad managerial performance. By identifying good and poor performance, the company can maintain control of its operations. Managers who perform exceptionally well should be rewarded to encourage further high levels of job performance. The poor performance of other managers should be corrected.

Suppose that during 19X1, Marie's Pie Company actually produced 200,000 pies and incurred the following costs:

Ingredient cost	$265,000
Labor cost	195,000
Rent	25,000
Depreciation	20,000
Other	14,000
Total production cost	$519,000

A performance report comparing these actual costs to the budgeted costs is presented in Illustration 20-3.

ILLUSTRATION 20-3 Performance Report

Marie's Pie Company
Performance Report, Production Costs
For the Year Ended December 31, 19X1

	Budget	Actual	Budget minus Actual
Production	200,000 pies	200,000 pies	
Production costs:			
Ingredient cost	$225,000	$265,000	$(40,000)
Labor cost	200,000	195,000	5,000
Rent	25,000	25,000	0
Depreciation	20,000	20,000	0
Other	15,000	14,000	1,000
Total production costs	$485,000	$519,000	$(34,000)

Typically, performance reports indicate only those areas that should be investigated. They do not provide definitive information on performance. For example, the performance report presented in Illustration 20-3 indicates that something may be amiss in the control of ingredient cost. Actual costs are $40,000 more than budgeted. There are many potential reasons why the cost is greater than the amount budgeted. Perhaps the price of fruit or sugar increased. Perhaps an oven malfunction resulted in wasted ingredients. Such explanations must be investigated before taking appropriate corrective action. While performance reports may not provide definitive answers, they are still extremely useful. Managers can use them to "flag" areas that need closer attention and to avoid areas that are under control. It would not seem necessary, for example, to investigate labor, rent, depreciation, or other costs since these costs are either equal to or relatively close to the planned level of cost. Typically, managers follow the principle of **management by exception** when using performance reports. Management by exception means they investigate departures from the plan that appear to be exceptional; they do not investigate minor departures from the plan.

Decision Making

In addition to providing information for planning and evaluation, managerial accounting information helps managers make nonroutine decisions, which address problems that do not occur regularly. For example, should the firm add a new product? Should it drop an existing product? Should it manufacture a component used in assembling its major product or contract with another company to produce the component? What price should the firm charge for a new product? While ways to solve these problems exist, the necessary cost information is not always readily available. In these cases, the managerial accountant must develop the needed information.

Differences Between Financial and Managerial Accounting

Important differences exist between financial and managerial accounting. In contrast to financial accounting, managerial accounting

1. Is directed at internal rather than external users of accounting information.
2. May deviate from GAAP.
3. May present more detailed information.
4. May present more nonmonetary information.
5. Places more emphasis on the future.

Internal Versus External Users. As already discussed, financial accounting is aimed primarily at external users of accounting information while managerial accounting is aimed primarily at internal users. External users such as investors, creditors, and government agencies need information to make investment, lending, and regulation decisions. Thus, their information needs differ from those of internal managers who need information for routine planning and evaluation of the firm's internal operations and for making a number of other less routine decisions.

Need to Use GAAP. Much of financial accounting information is required. The Securities and Exchange Commission (SEC) requires large, publicly traded companies to prepare reports in accordance with GAAP. Even companies that are not under the jurisdiction of the SEC prepare financial accounting information in accordance with GAAP to satisfy creditors. Managerial accounting, on the other hand, is completely optional. It stresses information that is *useful* to internal managers for planning, evaluation, and decision making. If a managerial accountant believes that deviating from GAAP will provide more useful information to internal managers, GAAP should not be followed.

Detail of Information. Financial accounting presents information in a highly summarized form. Net income, for example, is presented for the company as a whole. To run a company, however, managers need the more detailed information that the managerial accountant can supply. For example, managers need information about the cost of operating individual departments, in addition to the cost of operating the company as a whole.

Emphasis on Nonmonetary Information. Both managerial and financial accounting reports generally contain monetary information. Managerial accounting reports can also contain a substantial amount of nonmonetary information. The quantity of material consumed in production, the number of hours worked by the office staff, and the number of units produced are examples of important nonmonetary data that appear in managerial accounting reports.

Emphasis on the Future. Financial accounting is primarily concerned with presenting the results of past transactions. Managerial accounting, on the other hand, places considerable emphasis on the future. As indicated previously, one of the primary purposes of managerial accounting is planning. Thus, managerial accounting information often involves estimates of the costs and benefits of future transactions.

Similarities Between Financial and Managerial Accounting

We do not want to overstate the differences between financial accounting and managerial accounting in terms of their respective user groups. Financial accounting reports are aimed *primarily* at external users, and managerial accounting reports are aimed *primarily* at internal users. However, managers also make significant use of financial accounting reports, and external users occasionally request financial information that is generally considered appropriate for internal users. For example, creditors may ask management to provide them with detailed cash flow projections.

EMPHASIS ON COST INFORMATION

Consider the following questions that a manager may need to address.

Planning What will our material *cost* be next month if we increase production by 20 percent?

Evaluation Did the night-shift supervisor do a good job of controlling labor *costs* last month?

Decision Making Does the labor *cost* savings justify purchasing a computer-controlled assembly line?

To answer these and other important questions, managers must understand a number of cost terms and concepts. The remainder of this chapter considers the classification of costs for manufacturing firms, the use of cost information by service organizations, and cost classifications in planning, evaluation, and decision making.

INSIGHTS INTO ETHICS

Bob Jakes is the chief financial officer of Suncamp Corporation. Last week he had lunch with one of the major shareholders of the company, Bruce Kemper, who is considering buying additional shares from other shareholders. Kemper indicated that while he was generally pleased with the company's performance, he had reservations about how the company plans to deal with increased foreign competition. Bob, of course, has access to all company information, including budgets for new product development and advertising campaigns. Bob knows this information, if shared with Kemper, will convince him that the company is well positioned for the coming year. Also, it will demonstrate to Kemper that Bob is "on top of" his important financial planning responsibilities. In his position as a major shareholder, Kemper could recommend Bob for the position of president, a position that will open in the next year following the current president's retirement.

Should Bob disclose how Suncamp Corporation plans to deal with increased foreign competition? What do you think most managers would do if they were in Bob's position?

COST CLASSIFICATIONS FOR MANUFACTURING FIRMS

LO 3
Distinguish between manufacturing and nonmanufacturing costs and between product and period costs.

Determining the cost of items a merchandising firm purchases from a supplier is relatively easy. The cost of the items is the purchase cost net of returns, allowances, and discounts plus related shipping costs. Determining the cost of items a manufacturing firm produces is more complex. Using both labor and machinery, a manufacturing firm converts raw materials into finished goods. Complexity arises because the costs of the resources used in production must be assigned to units produced. Merchandising and manufacturing firms are compared in Illustration 20-4. This section discusses the broad classification of manufacturing and nonmanufacturing costs. These classifications are based on whether the costs are associated with the production of goods. It also discusses product and period cost classifications that are related to the timing of expensing costs.

ILLUSTRATION 20-4 Comparison of Merchandising and Manufacturing Firms

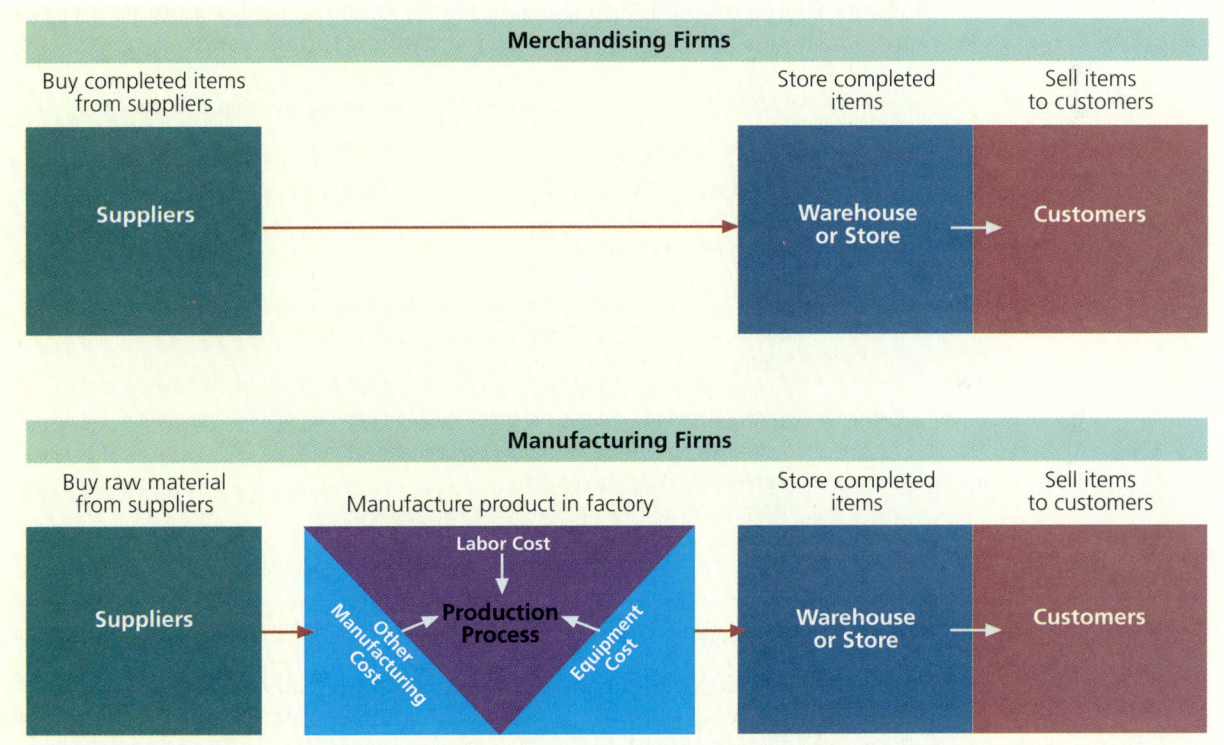

Manufacturing Costs

Manufacturing costs include all those associated with the production of goods. They include three cost categories: direct material, direct labor, and manufacturing overhead.

Direct Material. **Direct material** includes the cost of all materials and parts that are directly traced to items produced. For The Wooden Boat Company, a manufacturer of rowboats, direct material includes the cost of wood and fittings. Tracing these costs directly to individual boats is easy. Direct material probably does not include the cost of minor materials such as glue and nails. While such minor material costs could be traced to a particular boat, it probably is not worth the time to do so. Materials that are not directly traced to a product are referred to as **indirect materials**.

Direct Labor. **Direct labor** includes the cost of labor that is directly traced to items produced. The Wooden Boat Company's direct labor would include the labor cost of the workers directly involved in constructing a rowboat. It probably does not include the cost of managers or supervisors. Although it is theoretically possible to trace the time each supervisor spends on a particular boat, it is generally not worthwhile to do so. Labor costs that are not traced directly to products produced are referred to as **indirect labor costs**.

Manufacturing Overhead. **Manufacturing overhead** includes the costs of all manufacturing activities other than direct material and direct labor. It includes indirect material, indirect labor, and a wide variety of other cost items. For the Wooden Boat Company example, manufacturing overhead includes the costs of glue, nails, salaries of supervisors, depreciation of tools, depreciation of the building where manufacturing takes place, utilities, and a number of other items. Illustration 20-5 lists some common manufacturing overhead costs.

ILLUSTRATION 20-5 Common Manufacturing Overhead Costs

Indirect factory labor
Indirect material
Overtime premium
Night-shift premium
Vacation and holiday pay for factory workers
Social Security and Medicare taxes for factory workers
Health insurance for factory workers
Power, heat, and light in the factory
Depreciation of factory equipment
Depreciation of plant
Insurance on plant and factory equipment
Repair of factory equipment
Maintenance of factory building and grounds
Property taxes related to the factory

Nonmanufacturing Costs

Nonmanufacturing costs can be defined simply as all costs that are not associated with the production of goods. Nonmanufacturing costs typically include selling and general and administrative costs.

Selling Costs. Selling costs include all those associated with securing and filling customer orders. Thus, selling costs include advertising, sales personnel salaries, depreciation of automobiles and office equipment the sales force uses and costs of storing and shipping finished goods.

General and Administrative Costs. General and administrative costs include all those associated with the firm's general management. Thus, general and administrative costs include the salaries of the company president and accounting personnel, depreciation of the general office building, depreciation of office equipment general managers use, and the cost of supplies clerical employees use.

In many cases, a cost is classified by its use rather than by its specific nature. Consider janitorial costs. Janitorial costs associated with maintaining a production area are classified as a manufacturing cost (specifically, manufacturing overhead). On the other hand, janitorial costs associated with maintaining the general office building are classified as a nonmanufacturing cost (specifically, general and administrative cost).

Product and Period Costs

A distinction is made in regard to the timing of when costs are recognized as expenses. Product costs are identified with goods produced and expensed when goods are sold. Period costs are identified with accounting periods and expensed in the period incurred.

Product Costs. **Product costs** are those assigned to goods produced. Thus, product costs and manufacturing costs are terms that are often used interchangeably. Both include direct material, direct labor, and manufacturing overhead. Product costs are considered an asset (inventory) until the finished goods are sold. When the goods are sold, the product costs are expensed. This ensures a proper matching of revenue with the costs necessary to produce it. Direct labor cost incurred in 19X1 to produce goods sold in 19X2 becomes an expense in 19X2, the year of the sale when revenues are recognized.

Period Costs. **Period costs** are costs identified with accounting periods rather than with goods produced. Selling and general and administrative costs (nonmanufacturing costs) are period costs. We recognize period costs as expenses in the period incurred. Rent paid on an *office building* is a period cost and becomes an expense in the period incurred. In contrast, the rent paid on a *factory building* is a product cost and becomes an expense when goods are sold. Differences between product and period costs are summarized in Illustration 20-6.

ILLUSTRATION 20-6 Relationship Among Cost Categories

	Type of Cost	When Expensed
	Product Cost	
Manufacturing Costs	Direct material Direct labor Manufacturing overhead	Expensed when goods are sold
	Period Cost	
Nonmanufacturing Costs	Selling cost General and administrative cost	Expensed in period they are incurred

BALANCE SHEET PRESENTATION OF PRODUCT COSTS

Product costs may appear on the balance sheet as assets in three inventory accounts: raw materials, work in process, and finished goods. **Raw Materials Inventory** includes the cost of materials on hand that are used to produce a company's products. Returning to the Wooden Boat Company, wood and fittings are included in Raw Materials Inventory. **Work in Process Inventory** is the inventory account for the cost of goods that are only partially completed. For example, if at the end of the year The Wooden Boat Company has one partially completed boat, the cost of all direct labor, direct material, and manufacturing overhead incurred to bring the boat to its current state of partial completion would be included in Work in Process Inventory. **Finished Goods Inventory** is the account for the cost of all items that are complete and ready to sell. If, at the end of the year, The Wooden Boat Company has two boats that are completed and ready to sell, Finished Goods Inventory would include the cost of all direct material, direct labor, and manufacturing overhead incurred to bring the boats to their finished state. A simplified balance sheet showing the three inventory accounts is presented in Illustration 20-7.

ILLUSTRATION 20-7 Balance Sheet Presentation of Inventory Accounts

The Wooden Boat Company
Balance Sheet
For Year Ended December 31, 19X1

Assets			Liabilities and Stockholders' Equity	
Cash		$ 1,000	Accounts payable	$ 1,000
Accounts receivable		2,000	Notes payable	2,000
Inventory:			Long-term debt	2,000
Raw materials	$2,000		Common stock	5,000
Work in process	3,000		Retained earnings	8,000
Finished goods	4,000	9,000		
Equipment (net)		6,000	Total liabilities and	
Total assets		$18,000	stockholders' equity	$18,000

LO 4
Describe the flow of product costs in a manufacturing firm's accounts.

FLOW OF PRODUCT COSTS IN ACCOUNTS

In an accounting system, product costs flow from one inventory account to another. Illustration 20-8 demonstrates the flow of product costs in the accounts.

The cost of *direct* material used reduces the Raw Material Inventory account and increases Work in Process Inventory. *Indirect* material used, however, is not added directly to Work in Process Inventory—it is accumulated in Manufacturing Overhead. The amount of direct labor used increases Work in Process Inventory, but indirect labor is not added directly to Work in Process Inventory. Instead, like indirect material, it is accumulated in Manufacturing Overhead. The cost accumulated in Manufacturing Overhead, which includes indirect material, indirect labor, and a variety of other overhead costs, is also added to Work in Process Inventory.

Once items are finished, the cost of the completed items is transferred from Work in Process Inventory and into Finished Goods Inventory. The cost of items completed is referred to as **cost of goods manufactured**. When the completed items are sold, the cost of the items sold is transferred from Finished Goods Inventory into Cost of Goods Sold.

ILLUSTRATION 20-8 Flow of Product Costs in Accounts

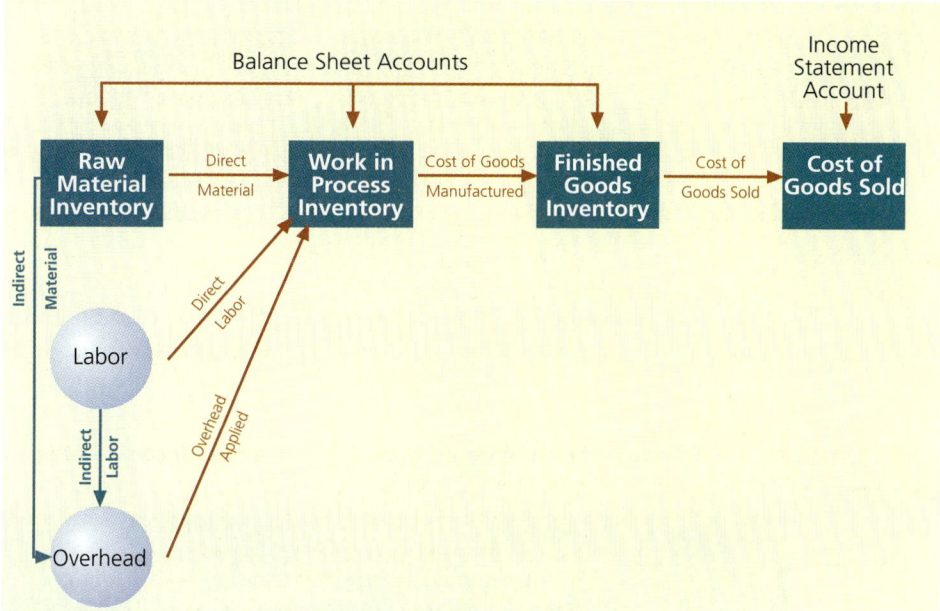

INCOME STATEMENT PRESENTATION OF PRODUCT COSTS

When finished goods are sold, the cost of the inventory sold is considered an expense and must be removed from inventory and charged to cost of goods sold. This provides a matching of revenue (sales dollars) with the cost of producing the revenue (the cost of goods sold). Before cost of goods sold can be calculated, however, we must first calculate cost of goods manufactured. Recall that cost of goods manufactured is the cost associated with all goods completed during a period. Cost of goods manufactured can be calculated using a simple formula. It is equal to the beginning balance in Work in Process Inventory plus current manufacturing costs (direct material, direct labor, and manufacturing overhead incurred in the current period) minus the ending balance in Work in Process Inventory.

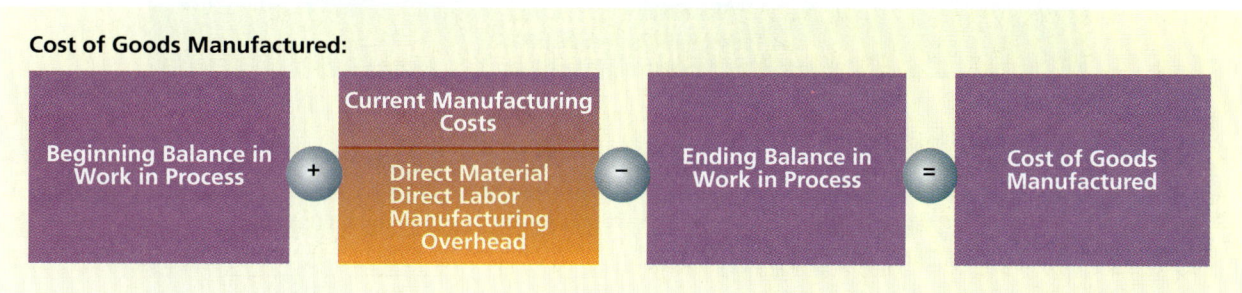

Once cost of goods manufactured is known, cost of goods sold can also be calculated using a simple formula. It is equal to the beginning balance in Finished Goods Inventory plus cost of goods manufactured minus the ending balance in Finished Goods Inventory.

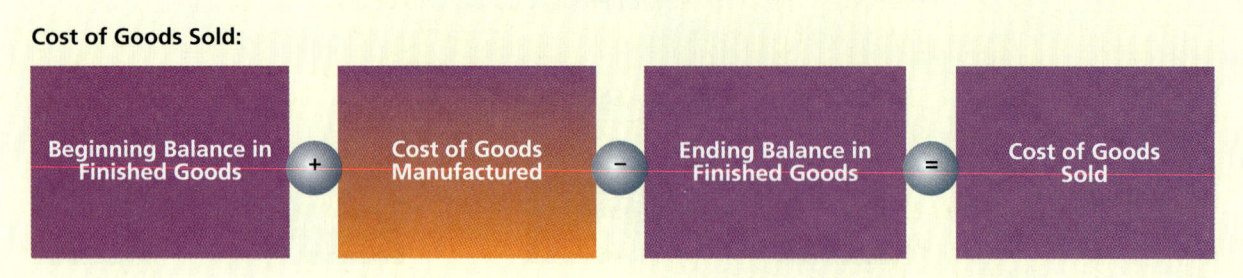

Illustration 20-9 presents a schedule of cost of goods manufactured and a simplified income statement showing cost of goods sold for the Wooden Boat

ILLUSTRATION 20-9 Schedule of Cost of Goods Manufactured and an Income Statement Showing Cost of Goods Sold

The Wooden Boat Company
Schedule of Cost of Goods Manufactured
For the Year Ended December 31, 19X1

Beginning balance in work in process			$ 2,000
Add current manufacturing costs:			
Direct material:			
Beginning balance	$10,000		
Purchases	20,000		
Ending balance	(5,000)	$25,000	
Direct labor		15,000	
Manufacturing overhead:			
Heat, light, and power	$ 1,000		
Depreciation of equipment	15,000		
Other	5,000	21,000	61,000
Total			$63,000
Less: Ending balance in work in process			3,000
Cost of goods manufactured			$60,000

The Wooden Boat Company
Income Statement
For the Year Ended December 31, 19X1

Sales		$150,000
Less cost of goods sold:		
Beginning finished goods	$20,000	
Add: Cost of goods manufactured	60,000	
Cost of goods available for sale	$80,000	
Less: Ending finished goods	4,000	76,000
Gross profit		$74,000
Less nonmanufacturing expenses:		
Selling expenses	$ 3,000	
General and administrative expenses	52,000	55,000
Net income		$19,000

Company. Note that in the schedule of cost of goods manufactured, the calculation of direct material cost is indicated (beginning balance, plus purchases, minus ending balance). Also, note that in the income statement, the sum of the beginning balance in finished goods plus cost of goods manufactured is referred to as the **cost of goods available for sale**.

Comparison of Financial Statements of Merchandising and Manufacturing Firms

The financial statements of a merchandising firm differ from those of a manufacturing firm. The main differences relate to the inventory accounts and cost of goods sold. Illustration 20-10 shows that the typical merchandising firm has a single inventory account—Merchandise Inventory. A manufacturing firm, on the other hand, has three inventory accounts: Raw Materials Inventory, Work in Process Inventory, and Finished Goods Inventory. Also, note that while cost of goods sold in a merchandising firm includes only the net cost of items purchased from suppliers, cost of goods sold in a manufacturing firm includes direct material, direct labor, and manufacturing overhead.

ILLUSTRATION 20-10 Comparison of Merchandising and Manufacturing Firms

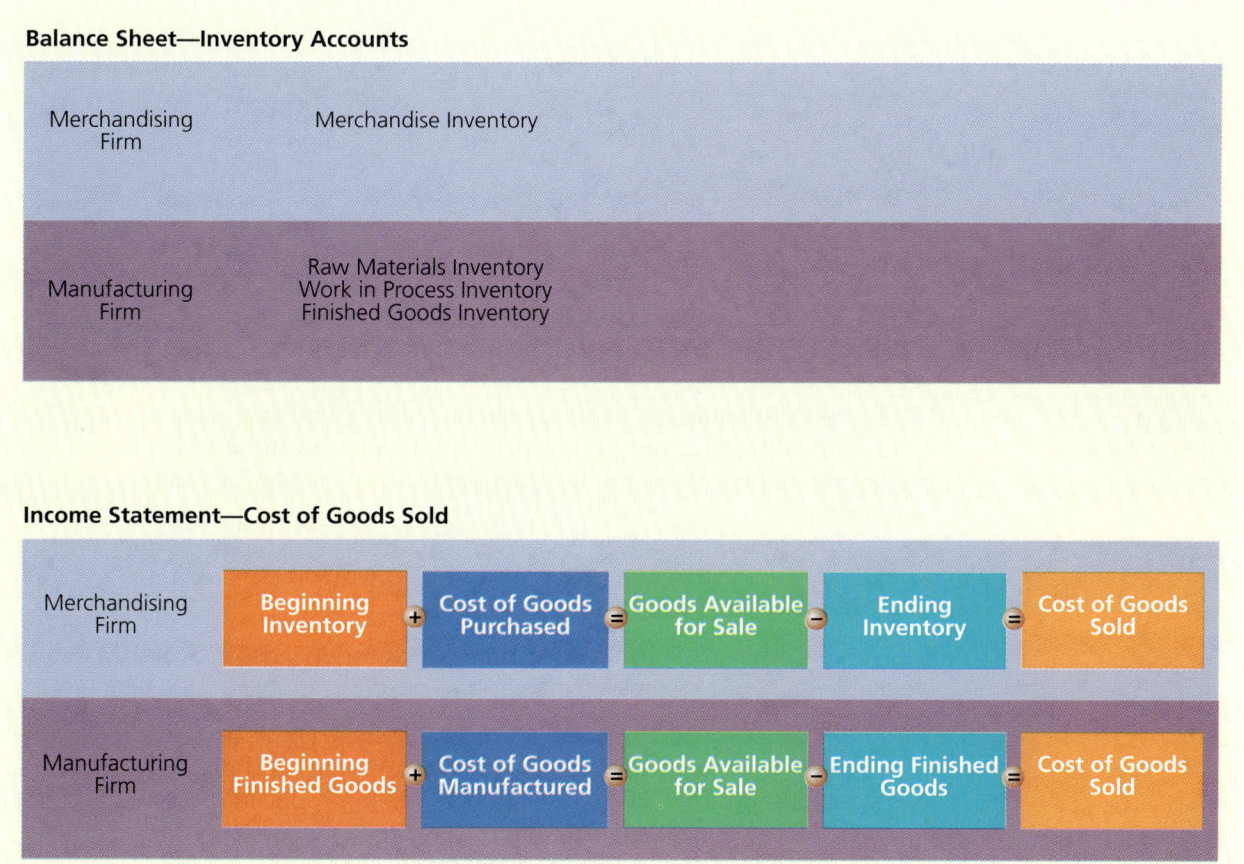

COST OF SERVICES

Just as accountants at manufacturing firms are asked to determine product costs, accountants at service companies are asked to determine the costs of various service activities. A bank may want to know the cost of processing customer checks, a firm of certified public accountants may want to know the cost of performing an audit or a hospital may want to know the cost of an x-ray. Managerial accounting procedures can provide this information. Suppose, for example, the owner of Lakeside Bicycle Shop wants to know the average cost, excluding parts, of repairing bicycles in the month of June for purposes of setting repair prices. The report presented in Illustration 20-11 provides the desired cost information.

ILLUSTRATION 20-11 Cost of Repair Services

Lakeside Bicycle Shop Cost of Repair Services For Year Month of June 19X1	
Repair salaries	$2,800
Supplies	500
Depreciation of tools	200
Miscellaneous costs	100
Total repair costs	$3,600
Number of repairs	240
Average cost per repair	$15
Number of labor hours	180
Average cost per labor hour	$20

COST CLASSIFICATIONS FOR PLANNING, EVALUATION, AND DECISION MAKING

LO 5
Distinguish between fixed and variable costs, direct and indirect costs, and controllable and noncontrollable.

Earlier, we distinguished between manufacturing and nonmanufacturing costs and between product and period costs. In addition to these cost terms, a number of cost classifications are also important for planning, evaluation, and decision making.

Variable and Fixed Costs

The classification of a cost as variable or fixed depends on whether the cost changes or remains the same in relation to business activity.

Variable Costs. **Variable costs** are those that increase or decrease in response to increases or decreases in business activity. Material and direct labor are variable costs because they fluctuate with changes in production (business activity). Suppose the Redmond Manufacturing Company incurred the following variable costs in the prior month when production was 1,000 units:

	1,000 Units	Cost per Unit
Variable costs:		
Direct material	$25,000	$25
Direct labor	50,000	50
Power costs	5,000	5
Total variable cost	$80,000	$80

How much cost should the company plan on for the current month if production is expected to increase by 10 percent to 1,100 units? Assuming the costs change in proportion to changes in activity, if production increases by 10 percent, the cost would be expected to increase by 10 percent. Thus, direct material should increase to $27,500; direct labor to $55,000; and power to $5,500.

	1,100 Units	Cost per Unit
Variable costs:		
Direct material	$27,500	$25
Direct labor	55,000	50
Power costs	5,500	5
Total variable cost	$88,000	$80

Note that while the *total variable cost* increases from $80,000 to $88,000 when production changes from 1,000 to 1,100 units, the *variable cost per unit* does not change. It remains $80 per unit. With an $80 per unit variable cost, variable cost (in total) increases by $8,000 (i.e., $80 x 100) when production increases by 100 units.

Fixed Costs. **Fixed costs** are those that do not change when there are changes in business activity. Depreciation, rent, and insurance are costs that typically do not change with changes in business activity. Suppose that in the prior month, Redmond Manufacturing Company incurred $6,000 of fixed costs, including $2,000 of depreciation, $3,000 of rent, and $1,000 of insurance. If the Redmond Manufacturing Company increases production to 1,100 units in the current month, the levels of depreciation, rent cost, and insurance cost incurred should remain the same as when production was only 1,000 units. However, with fixed costs, the cost per unit does change when there are changes in production. When production increases, the constant amount of fixed cost is spread over a larger number of units. This drives down the fixed cost per unit. With an increase in production from 1,000 to 1,100 units, *total fixed cost* remains at $6,000. Note, however, that *fixed cost per unit* decreases from $6 per unit to $5.46 per unit.

	Prior Month		Current Month	
	1,000 Units	Cost Per Unit	1,100 Units	Cost Per Unit
Fixed costs:				
Depreciation	$2,000	$2	$2,000	$1.82
Rent	3,000	3	3,000	2.73
Insurance	1,000	1	1,000	.91
Total fixed cost	$6,000	$6	$6,000	$5.46

Direct and Indirect Costs

A **direct cost** is one that is directly traceable to a product, activity, or department. **Indirect costs** are those that either cannot be directly traced to a product, activity, or department, or are not worth tracing. As discussed above, indirect product costs are referred to as manufacturing overhead. The distinction between a direct and an indirect cost depends on the object of the cost tracing. For example, The General Manufacturing Company has production facilities in Memphis and Houston and incurs separate insurance costs for each facility. The insurance cost related to the Memphis facility is obviously a direct cost of the Memphis plant. However, the insurance cost is an indirect cost of the individual products produced in the Memphis plant because *direct* tracing of the insurance cost to each product is not possible. This situation is presented in Illustration 20-12.

ILLUSTRATION 20-12 Insurance as Both a Direct and Indirect Cost

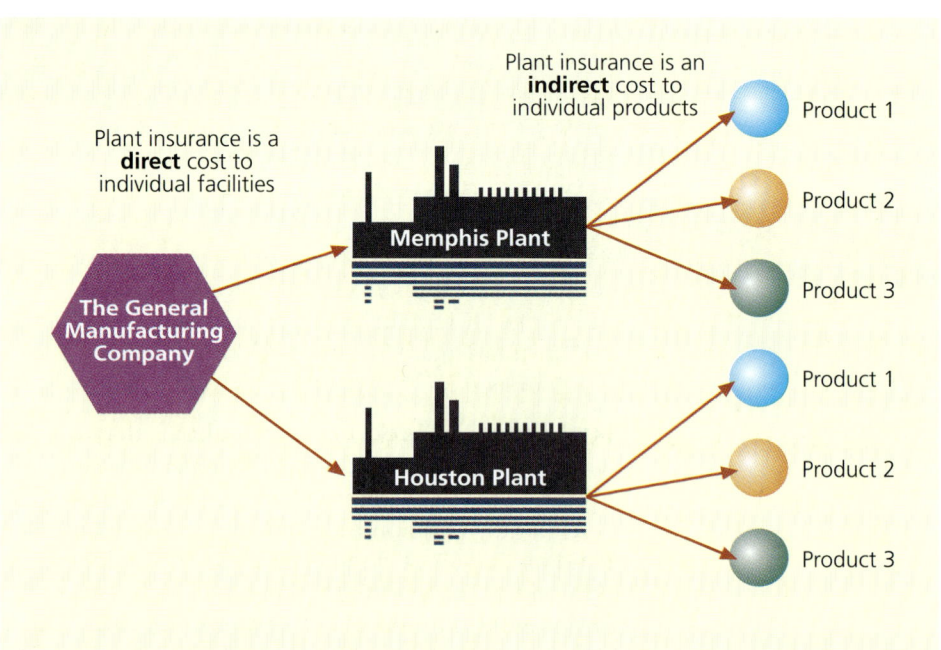

Controllable and Noncontrollable Costs

A manager can influence a **controllable cost** but cannot influence a **noncontrollable cost**. The distinction between controllable and noncontrollable costs is especially important when evaluating manager performance. Managers should not be evaluated unfavorably if a cost not under their control increases.

As an example of controllable and noncontrollable costs, consider a plant supervisor. This individual influences labor and material costs by scheduling workers and assuring an efficient production process. Thus, labor and material costs are a supervisor's controllable costs. However, the supervisor cannot determine insurance for a plant. A plant manager or an insurance specialist makes decisions regarding insurance. Therefore, insurance cost is a supervisor's noncontrollable cost but a plant manager's or an insurance specialist's controllable cost.

SUMMARY

State the primary goal of managerial accounting. The primary goal of managerial accounting is to provide information that helps managers plan and evaluate company activities and make business decisions.

Describe how budgets are used to plan and how performance reports are used to evaluate. Managerial accountants prepare financial plans referred to as budgets. These plans help employees understand company goals and follow the most efficient route to achieve them. Performance reports compare actual performance to the budget. Actual results that deviate significantly from the plan signal the need to determine the cause of the deviation.

Distinguish between manufacturing and nonmanufacturing costs and between product and period costs. Manufacturing costs include all those associated with the production of goods. They include direct material, direct labor, and manufacturing overhead. Nonmanufacturing costs are all those not associated with the production of goods. Selling and general and administrative costs are nonmanufacturing costs. Costs can also be classified as either product costs or period costs. Product costs are identical to manufacturing costs and include direct labor, direct material, and manufacturing overhead. Period costs, on the other hand, are expensed in the period they are incurred. Period costs include both selling and general and administrative costs, which are also referred to as nonmanufacturing costs.

Describe the flow of product costs in a manufacturing firm's accounts. As they are incurred, product costs are assigned to Work in Process Inventory. When the items in work in process are completed, the cost of the completed items is removed from Work in Process Inventory and added to Finished Goods Inventory. When the finished goods are sold, the cost of the items sold is removed from Finished Goods Inventory and added to Cost of Goods Sold. Thus, product costs become an expense when completed items are sold.

Distinguish between fixed and variable costs, direct and indirect costs, and controllable and noncontrollable costs. Variable costs are those that increase or decrease in response to changes in business activity. Fixed costs remain constant when there are changes in business activity. Direct costs are those that are directly traceable to a product, activity, or department. Indirect costs either cannot be directly traced or they are not worth tracing. Controllable costs are those a manager can influence. On the other hand, a cost that a manager cannot influence is a noncontrollable cost.

REVIEW PROBLEM

The management of Cutter Saw Blade Company is reviewing the results of operations for the calendar year 19X2, for the purpose of evaluating the efficiency of their operations and the performance of their factory supervisor. The review is also the first step in preparing the manufacturing budget for the 19X3 operating year. The company accountant prepared the following information for the production of saw blades.

Cutter Saw Blade Company
Manufacturing Activity
For the Year Ended December 31, 19X2

	Budgeted	Actual
Production (units)	250,000	250,000
Production costs:		
Direct material	$ 375,000	$ 385,000
Direct labor	500,000	535,000
Indirect material	75,000	72,000
Indirect labor	300,000	320,000
Payroll taxes	57,500	60,700
Heat, light, & power	80,000	78,000
Depreciation on plant assets	50,000	50,000
Insurance & taxes	20,000	21,000
Total production costs	$1,457,500	$1,521,700

The manager knew the causes of some of the differences between budgeted and actual costs were due to the following items:

1. The cost of raw materials went up 5 percent on May 1.
2. The new three-year labor contract, signed July 1, 19X2, increased the hourly rate for direct labor from $10 per hour to $12 per hour and for indirect labor from $6 per hour to $7 per hour.
3. Property taxes increased in July 19X2, while the 5 year insurance policy continued at the same rate.

REQUIRED:

a. Prepare a performance report for 19X2 by adding a variance column (difference between budget and actual) to the Manufacturing Activity Report.
b. Calculate a budgeted unit cost and the actual unit cost for saw blades during 19X2.
c. Evaluate the variances identified in the performance report.

SOLUTION:

(a) *Prepare a performance report.*

Cutter Saw Blade Company
Performance Report, Production Costs
For the Year Ended December 31, 19X2

	Budgeted	Actual	Budget Minus Actual
Production (units)	250,000	250,000	0
Production costs:			
Direct material	$ 375,000	$ 385,000	$(10,000)
Direct labor	500,000	535,000	(35,000)
Indirect material	75,000	72,000	3,000
Indirect labor	300,000	320,000	(20,000)
Payroll taxes	57,500	60,700	(3,200)
Heat, light, & power	80,000	78,000	2,000
Depreciation on plant assets	50,000	50,000	0
Insurance & taxes	20,000	21,000	(1,000)
Total production cost	$1,457,500	$1,521,700	$(64,200)

(b) *Calculate budgeted and actual unit costs.*

Budgeted cost per unit:

$1,457,500 ÷ 250,000 = $5.83 per unit

Actual cost per unit: $1,521,700 ÷ 250,000 = $6.09 per unit

(c) *Evaluate the variances found in a.*

1. The production activity variance of zero indicates that production for the year equals the level planned.
2. The direct material cost variance is unfavorable. However, when the increase in the cost of material is considered, the expected cost of the material is $385,938 [(375,000 x 5/12) + (375,000 x 7/12 x 1.05)]. Therefore, what at first appears unfavorable becomes slightly favorable when examined more carefully. This could imply that management was effective in controlling material usage or it could relate to effective purchasing.
3. The direct labor cost variance is unfavorable. The increase in the labor rate in the middle of the year from $10 to $12 per hour gives an expected cost of the direct labor of $550,000 [(500,000 x 6/12) + (500,000 x 6/12 x 12/10)]. This means that the actual cost of $535,000 is less than expected in light of the wage increase and is actually favorable by $15,000. Management was apparently effective in controlling labor.
4. The indirect material variance is $3,000 favorable. This implies either control over material use or effective purchasing, or both.
5. The indirect labor variance is $20,000 unfavorable. The increase in the wage rate in the middle of the year from $6 to $7 per hour gives an expected cost for the indirect labor of $325,000 [(300,000 x 6/12) + (300,000 x 6/12 x 7/6)]. This means that the actual cost of $320,000 is less than would be expected in light of the wage increase.
6. The payroll taxes variance is $3,200 unfavorable. It was budgeted at 7.1875% (57,500 ÷ 800,000) for direct labor plus indirect labor. It would have been expected to be $62,891 [(550,000 + 325,000) x .071875)] in light of the wage increases in mid-year and is actually favorable by $2,191 (62,891 − 60,700).
7. The heat, light, & power variance is $2,000 favorable. This may be due to less demand for heat or air conditioning due to weather or it may be the result of management's actions to reduce the use of electrical power.
8. The depreciation of plant assets variance is zero, implying that there were no changes in the plant asset holdings during the year.
9. The insurance & taxes variance is $1,000 unfavorable. The July 19X2 increase in property taxes could explain part or all of this variance.

KEY TERMS

budgets, *834*
controllable cost, *848*
cost of goods available for sale, *845*
cost of goods manufactured, *842*
direct cost, *848*
direct material, *839*
finished goods inventory, *842*
fixed costs, *847*
indirect costs, *848*
indirect labor costs, *840*
indirect materials, *840*
management by exception, *836*
managerial accounting, *833*
manufacturing costs, *839*
manufacturing overhead, *840*
noncontrollable cost, *848*
nonmanufacturing costs, *840*
performance report, *835*
period costs, *841*
product costs, *841*
raw materials inventory, *841*
variable costs, *846*
work in process inventory, *842*

SELF-QUIZ

LO 1 1. The primary goal of managerial accounting is to:
   a. Provide information for potential and current investors in the company.
   b. Provide information for both current and prospective investors as well as for creditors.
   c. Provide information for current and prospective investors, current and prospective creditors, and for the several taxing agencies.
   d. Provide information for planning, evaluation, and decision making.

LO 1 2. Match the following terms with the management activities described below.
LO 2
   ___ a. Planning
   ___ b. Evaluation
   ___ c. Decision Making
   (1) This management activity involves the process of reviewing all the available data relative to a pressing question which requires a decision between alternative actions. This activity may involve routine operating items or one-time major choices.
   (2) This management activity provides both direction for the firm and a defined goal against which performance may be measured.
   (3) This activity relates actual results with planned outcomes as a basis for corrective action.

LO 2 3. Which of the following statements about budgets is incorrect?
   a. Budgets may be expressed in dollars, quantities, or both.
   b. Budgets may reflect projected revenues, projected expenses, projected cash flows, or projected quantities of inputs or outputs.
   c. Budgets must be prepared in accordance with GAAP.
   d. Budgets are used both for planning and for evaluating performance.

LO 2 4. Which of the following is not a basic element of a performance report?
   a. Assets, liabilities, and owner's equity.
   b. Budget data for the period.
   c. Actual cost results for the period.
   d. Variances of actual cost data from budget data.

LO 1 5. Which of the following statements is incorrect?
LO 2
   a. Managerial accounting statements do not necessarily comply with GAAP.
   b. Financial accounting statements normally reflect more detail than would be found in managerial accounting statements.
   c. Managerial accounting statements emphasize future activities and future costs.
   d. Financial accounting data is directed primarily at external users rather than internal users.

LO 3 6. Which of the following is not a manufacturing cost?
   a. Raw materials
   b. Freight out
   c. Direct labor
   d. Manufacturing overhead

LO 3 7. Which of the following inventory accounts found in the general ledger of a manufacturing firm would be equivalent to the Merchandise Inventory account of a retail establishment?
   a. Supplies Inventory
   b. Raw Materials Inventory
   c. Work in Process Inventory
   d. Finished Goods Inventory

LO 3 8. Which of the following does not describe direct materials in a manufacturing environment?
   a. Identifiable in the product
   b. Not material in amount
   c. Traceable to the product
   d. Material in amount

LO 3 9. Which of the following activities best represents direct labor in a manufacturing environment?
   a. Moving the product from one work station to another.
   b. Cleaning up around the machinery.
   c. Delivering raw materials to the work stations.
   d. Welding a component to the product.

LO 3 10. List three expenses that could be properly classified as manufacturing overhead.

LO 3 11. List three nonmanufacturing costs normally classified as selling expenses.

LO 3 12. List three nonmanufacturing costs normally classified as administrative expenses.

LO 3 13. Which of the following costs would be classified as a product cost?
   a. Transportation out
   b. Insurance expense—administrative
   c. Direct materials
   d. Sales salaries
   e. None of the above

LO 3 14. Which of the following costs would be classified as a period cost?
   a. Direct labor
   b. Indirect labor
   c. Direct materials
   d. Sales salaries

CHAPTER 20 MANAGERIAL ACCOUNTING AND COST INFORMATION 853

LO 3 15. Which of the following accounts would not appear in a balance sheet?
a. Raw Materials Inventory
b. Work in Process Inventory
c. Cost of Goods Sold
d. Finished Goods Inventory

LO 4 16. Which of the following reduces the work in process inventory account?
a. Cost of goods sold
b. Cost of goods manufactured
c. Cost of direct materials used
d. Cost of direct labor put into production

LO 4 17. The calculation of cost of goods manufactured does not include:
a. Work in process inventory, beginning
b. Cost of goods sold
c. Work in process inventory, ending
d. Direct materials
e. None of the above

LO 5 18. The total amount of _____ cost varies with changes in activity while the total amount of _____ cost remains unchanged with changes in activity.

LO 5 19. _____ costs are directly traceable to a product, activity, or department while _____ costs are not.

LO 5 20. A cost is _____ if a particular manager can influence it and _____ if he or she cannot.

SOLUTIONS TO SELF-QUIZ
1. d   2. a. (2) b. (3) c. (1)   3. c   4. a   5. b   6. b   7. d   8. b   9. d   10. Indirect materials, indirect labor, depreciation on factory plant and equipment (Note: Other examples are shown in the list in Table 20-5 on page 840).   11. Sales salaries and commissions, freight out, advertising (Note: Other sales expenses are shown on page 840).   12. Salaries of accounting personnel, salaries of administrative personnel, bad debt expense (Note: Administrative expenses are shown on page 840.)
13. c   14. d   15. c   16. b   17. b   18. variable, fixed   19. direct, indirect   20. controllable, noncontrollable

---

QUESTIONS

Q20-1 Discuss the purpose of managerial reports.

Q20-2 Briefly describe the planning and evaluation process.

Q20-3 Explain how budgets serve both the planning and evaluation process.

Q20-4 Describe the elements of a performance report and explain how it is useful to management.

Q20-5 How do managerial accounting reports differ from financial accounting reports?

Q20-6 Do GAAP-based financial statements serve the needs of both the external users and the internal users equally well? Discuss.

Q20-7 What kinds of non-monetary information might typically be found in managerial accounting reports?

Q20-8 Do managers normally use GAAP-based financial statements in performing their managerial functions? Discuss.

Q20-9 Explain what is meant by the statement: "Managerial accounting looks forward in time while financial accounting looks backward in time."

Q20-10 Are all material costs entered into production classified as direct materials? Explain.

Q20-11 Distinguish between direct labor and indirect labor.

Q20-12 List five costs which would typically be found in a manufacturing overhead account.

Q20-13 Explain the term *nonmanufacturing costs* and list the two general types of nonmanufacturing costs.

Q20-14 Define the term *product costs* and explain how product costs differ from period costs.

Q20-15 When are product costs charged to expense?

Q20-16 Explain how the costs of production flow through the accounting records.

Q20-17 How do the costs of a merchandising business differ from the costs of a manufacturing business?

Q20-18 Discuss how cost of service information may be used in a nonmanufacturing business.

Q20-19 Explain why fixed costs are called "fixed" and variable costs are called "variable."

Q20-20 Why are certain traceable costs not treated as direct costs?

EXERCISES

LO 1,2

E20-1 Managerial Accounting, Budgets, Performance Reports Match the following terms with the definitions that appear below.

___ a. Budgets
___ b. Evaluation
___ c. Planning
___ d. Decision making
___ e. Performance reports
___ f. Management by exception

(1) Looking forward in time to map out the activities that should take place to move the firm toward its objectives.
(2) Outputs of the planning process that will normally be monetary in nature but which may include nonmonetary data as well.
(3) Managements' review of the company's activities, on an after-the-fact basis, to see if the results are appropriate in light of the plans.
(4) One of management's main functions for which accountants may prepare a variety of reports to help management select between alternatives.
(5) The direction of management's attention to items that seem to be out of control or offer opportunities for benefits, minimizing management's time on activities under control.
(6) Show the actual results of the activities of a business and the planned results for comparative purposes by management.

LO 2

E20-2 Budgets Which of the following statements related to budgets are true? Explain why the false statements are not true.

a. Budgets are written plans, prepared by management, for the purpose of guiding future business activity.
b. Budgets may be expressed in dollars, in quantities such as pounds of materials or hours of direct labor, or both.
c. Budgets must be prepared in accordance with GAAP.
d. Budgets may be prepared for periods of less than a year, i.e., a week, month, or quarter.
e. The mandated use of budgets insures that some planning will take place but they have no value after the planning process is completed.
f. Budgets are useful to communicate the objectives and goals of the business.

LO 2

E20-3 Performance Reports Which of the following statements related to performance reports are true? Explain why the false statements are not true.

a. Performance reports provide a comparison of actual performance with planned performance.
b. Unfavorable variances in a performance report would indicate that the responsible manager did not exercise adequate control over his or her area of authority.
c. Performance reports should only be prepared annually.
d. Performance reports are prepared according to Generally Accepted Accounting Principles.

LO 3

E20-4 Manufacturing Costs Match the managerial accounting terms with the definitions shown on the next page.

___ a. Direct materials
___ b. Indirect materials
___ c. Direct labor
___ d. Indirect labor
___ e. Manufacturing overhead
___ f. Work in process

(1) All costs of production other than direct materials and direct labor.
(2) Those materials that are essential in the production of a firm's product but which either are not traceable to the product or are not in the product in material amounts.
(3) The costs associated with products that have entered the production process but which have not yet been completed.
(4) The costs of labor that are directly traceable to the product.
(5) Those materials that are essential in the production of a firm's products which are traceable to the products.
(6) The costs of labor that are essential to the production process but which cannot be directly traced to the product.

LO 3

E20-5 Manufacturing Costs The three elements of manufacturing costs are (1) direct materials, (2) direct labor, and (3) manufacturing overhead. Define each of the three terms and include three examples of overhead costs in the definition of manufacturing overhead.

LO 3

E20-6 Manufacturing Costs and Nonmanufacturing Costs Identify each of the following accounts as direct material (*DM*); direct labor (*DL*); manufacturing overhead (*MOH*); selling expense (*SE*); or administrative expense (*AE*).

___ a. Supervisors' salaries
___ b. Machine operators' salaries
___ c. Factory supplies used
___ d. Depreciation on machinery
___ e. Office supplies used
___ f. Raw materials used that are traced to products
___ g. Sales office electricity
___ h. Sales salaries
___ i. Factory rent
___ j. Freight out
___ k. Advertising
___ l. Factory electricity
___ m. Freight in
___ n. Office overhead

LO 3

E20-7 Product and Period Costs Indicate which of the following statements regarding product and period costs are true and which are false and explain why the false statements are incorrect.

a. Product costs are includable in the cost of inventory of a firm prior to the sale of the items to which they relate.
b. Period costs are expensed in the period in which the goods produced are sold.
c. Product costs are expensed in the period in which they are incurred.
d. Period costs are matched with revenue on a period basis rather than on a product basis.
e. Product costs may include costs which expire over time rather than being directly traceable to the product.
f. All product costs are traceable to the product directly and involve material amounts.

LO 4   **E20-8**   **Flow of Product Costs**   Product costing involves the accumulation of the production-related costs temporarily in one inventory account and then transferring costs to another inventory account upon completion.

a. The first inventory account is _____.
b. The second inventory account is _____.
c. Which inventory account of a manufacturer is essentially equivalent to the merchandise inventory account of a retailer or wholesaler?

LO 4   **E20-9**   **Flow of Product Costs**   Which of the following statements are correct with regard to product cost flows? Explain why each incorrect statement is wrong.

a. Direct labor cost is added to the work in process account.
b. Manufacturing overhead cost includes selling and administrative expenses.
c. Materials issued into production increase Raw Materials Inventory and reduce Work in Process Inventory.
d. Delivery expense is an item includable in manufacturing overhead.
e. The cost of goods manufactured is the total of the additions to the work in process account.
f. The cost of units sold during the period increase Finished Goods Inventory and decrease Cost of Goods Sold.
g. Indirect labor and indirect materials are both part of manufacturing overhead.
h. The depreciation on factory equipment is a period cost because depreciation occurs relative to the passage of time.

LO 5   **E20-10**   **Cost Classifications**   Identify each of the following statements as being related to fixed costs or to variable costs.

a. A cost that varies in total with changes in the activity level.
b. A cost that varies on a per unit basis with changes in the activity level.
c. A cost that remains fixed per unit with changes in the activity level.
d. A cost that remains fixed in total with changes in the activity level.

LO 5   **E20-11**   **Identifying Costs**   Indicate whether each of the following costs is: (1) *Fixed* or *Variable*, and (2) *Direct* or *Indirect*.

a. Direct labor
b. Direct material
c. Factory supplies
d. Factory rent
e. Depreciation—machinery
f. Utilities expense

LO 5   **E20-12**   **Identifying Costs**   Explain how a cost can be controllable at one administrative level and noncontrollable at another administrative level.

PROBLEM SET A

LO 1,2   **P20-1A**   **Budgets in Managerial Accounting**   Ye Olde Forge makes hand-wrought iron mailbox posts which are marketed through monthly ads in three national magazines. The following production cost budget was prepared for 19X3.

CHAPTER 20 MANAGERIAL ACCOUNTING AND COST INFORMATION

Ye Olde Forge
Budgeted Production Costs
For the Year Ended December 31, 19X3

Budgeted production	10,000 posts
Iron bar stock (direct material, variable)	$ 8,000
Direct labor (variable)	24,000
Fuel and flux (indirect material, variable)	3,600
Building rent (fixed)	12,000
Depreciation on forge and tools (fixed)	4,800
Utilities & other expenses (variable)	2,400
Total budgeted production costs	$54,800

REQUIRED:

Answer the following:
a. What is the budgeted cost of each mailbox post?
b. Use the budget information as a basis and prepare a new budget for a revised production output of 15,000 posts.
c. What is the budgeted cost of each mailbox post at the 15,000-unit production level?
d. Why is the new budgeted cost for each mail box post in part c less than under the budget in part a?

LO 2

P20-2A **Performance Reports** Crystal Line Co. manufactures a water filter insert that removes sediment and other small particles from residential water systems. The insert fits most brands of water filters currently available and can be washed and reused several times. It is marketed through several chain drug stores. The budget data and operating results shown below and on the next page are for the month of May 19X6.

REQUIRED:

a. Prepare a performance report. (Use Illustration 20-3 as a guide.)
b. Explain why the fixed costs did not generate a variance.
c. What might explain the unfavorable variances in the variable costs?
d. Does the high dollar amount of unfavorable variance indicate that management has a cost control problem?

Crystal Line Company
Budgeted Production Costs
For the Month Ended May 31, 19X6

Budgeted production (units)	20,000
Production costs:	
Direct materials (variable)	$ 80,000
Direct labor (variable)	40,000
Indirect materials (variable)	20,000
Utilities (variable)	2,000
Factory rent (fixed)	4,000
Depreciation on equipment (fixed)	8,000
Total budgeted production costs	$154,000

Crystal Line Company
Actual Production Costs
For the Month Ended May 31, 19X6

Actual production (units)	30,000
Production costs:	
Direct materials	$120,000
Direct labor	65,000
Indirect materials	29,000
Utilities	3,000
Factory rent	4,000
Depreciation on equipment	8,000
Total actual production costs	$229,000

LO 3,4

P20-3A Manufacturing and Nonmanufacturing Costs, Financial Statements The following selected data are from the records of Accountants Paper Products, Inc., for the month of February 19X3. They manufacture columnar pads and sell them directly to CPAs using direct mail advertising.

Advertising expense	$ 3,600
Factory payroll (70% direct labor)	20,000
Factory supplies used	3,000
Factory taxes	900
Factory utilities	400
Finished goods inventory (2/1/X3)	8,200
Finished goods inventory (2/28/X3)	5,200
Freight in	1,200
Freight out	2,400
Insurance expense (80% to factory)	500
Office salaries	2,400
President's salary	4,800
Raw materials inventory (2/1/X3)	3,700
Raw materials inventory (2/28/X3)	4,400
Raw material purchases (February)	13,200
Sales	92,600
Sales salaries	4,000
Factory supervisor's salary	2,400
Work in process inventory (2/1/X3)	3,800
Work in process inventory (2/28/X3)	2,800

REQUIRED:

a. Prepare a schedule of cost of goods manufactured for February 19X3, following Illustration 20-9 in the chapter.
b. Prepare an income statement for February 19X3.

LO 4

P20-4A Product Cost Flows Dyno Electric Company builds a small electric motor which is used as a component in the production of medical equipment by their customers. It is a very high-quality motor that is designed to operate for extended periods at variable speeds, with an unusually long time between failures. Special high-tech machines are used to wind the copper wire on the armatures and to wind the field coils. The armature shafts and the motor cases are purchased ready for use. The following information is available from the April 19X5 accounting records. Note that 80% of the motors produced during the period were sold.

Purchase of copper wire (25 spools)	$ 12,500
Ending inventory of copper wire	7,500
Beginning inventory of copper wire	0
Purchases of armature shafts	8,500
Ending inventory of armature shafts	700
Beginning inventory of armature shafts	1,200
Purchases of motor cases	3,000
Ending inventory of motor cases	800
Beginning inventory of motor cases	400
Direct labor costs	22,000
Overhead costs incurred and charged to production this period	33,000
Beginning inventory of work in process	2,000
Ending inventory of work in process	3,000
Beginning inventory of finished goods	16,000

REQUIRED:

a. Prepare T-accounts for Inventory of Copper Wire, Inventory of Armature Shafts, Inventory of Motor Cases, Inventory of Production Supplies, Manufacturing Overhead, Work in Process Inventory, Finished Goods Inventory, and Cost of Goods Sold.
b. Enter the given amounts as appropriate in the T-accounts to reflect the flow of product costs in the accounts of the firm.
c. Prepare a schedule of cost of goods manufactured.

LO 3,5 **P20-5A Classification of Costs** The costs shown in the following schedule are typical of a manufacturing environment.

Costs	a	b	c	d	e
1. Direct materials	___	___	___	___	___
2. Freight out	___	___	___	___	___
3. Freight in	___	___	___	___	___
4. Depreciation on equipment	___	___	___	___	___
5. Office salaries	___	___	___	___	___
6. Interest expense	___	___	___	___	___
7. Supervisors' salaries	___	___	___	___	___
8. Factory utilities	___	___	___	___	___
9. Office supplies	___	___	___	___	___
10. Factory supplies	___	___	___	___	___

REQUIRED:

Complete the schedule to classify the costs as:
a. Manufacturing or Nonmanufacturing (*Mfg* or *Non*)
b. Product or Period (*Pro* or *Per*)
c. Fixed or Variable as to production or sales (*Fix* or *Var*)
d. Direct or Indirect as to the product (*Dir* or *Ind*)
e. Controllable or Noncontrollable (*Con* or *NoC*) at the production department level.

LO 2,3,5 **P20-6A Evaluation, Cost Identification, and Control** The following data are from the general ledger and other records of the Highlander Pillow Corporation for the month ended June 19X4.

	Budget	Actual
Production quantities (pillows)	6,000	6,000
Polyfoam used (direct material)	$6,000	$6,200
Pillow ticking used (direct material)	$1,000	$900
Direct labor	$8,200	$8,300
Factory insurance	$750	$750

	Budget	Actual
Indirect labor	$4,100	$4,150
Indirect materials	$600	$700
Depreciation on factory machinery	$2,400	$2,400
Depreciation on factory buildings	$1,800	$1,800
Interest expense	$750	$775
Sales salaries	$1,600	$1,600

REQUIRED:

Identify the variances (differences between budget and actual) for each production cost and indicate at what managerial level (production supervisor, plant manager, or company president) you would expect control over the cost to exist. Explain your choice of the managerial level selected.

PROBLEM SET B

LO 1,2

P20-1B   Managerial Accounting and Budgets Flexi-mold Company, of South Hampton, Virginia, produces a line of flexible molds for ceramic shops. These are sold domestically and abroad. The only direct material is a rubber-like plastic which results in a mold that can be reused many times. They are planning on producing 30,000 molds during 19X8. The direct material is expected to cost $1.50 per mold. The labor requirement, all direct, is 1⁄4 hour of labor per mold at $8.00 per hour. Utilities average $.40 per mold and supplies are expected to cost $.24 per mold. Depreciation is expected to be $8,000 per year for machinery and $12,000 per year for the factory building. The factory insurance premium is contracted at $2,400 for the year.

REQUIRED:

a. Develop the 19X8 production budget and expected unit cost for the Flexi-mold Company.
b. Calculate the per unit cost of molds.
c. Calculate the per unit cost of molds if the production volume were 25% higher.

LO 2

P20-2B   Performance Reports Daly Book Binding Company does high-quality book binding for limited edition art books. The following budget and actual manufacturing data are for the month of August 19X9.

	Budget	Actual
Books bound	100	100
Bindery materials	$2,500	$2,600
Bindery labor	5,000	4,800
Utilities	150	75
Insurance	75	75
Depreciation expense	200	200
Rent	250	250

REQUIRED:

a. Prepare a performance report for Daly Book Binding Company, using Illustration 20-3 as a guide.
b. Discuss probable causes for each of the variances.
c. Why do some of the costs have no variances?
d. How should management react to the variances?

LO 3,4

P20-3B **Cost Classifications** Celtic Production Co. manufactures cabers (similar to small telephone poles) which are used for the caber toss at Scottish games around the world. They use spruce logs, purchased from suppliers in several western states, as their raw material. The cabers must be of uniform size and weight and require a considerable amount of hand labor in their production. The following information was taken from the records of Celtic Production Co. for the month of March 19X7.

Finished goods inventory, 3/1/X7	$12,000
Accounts payable	14,000
Factory supervision	4,000
Direct labor	30,000
Factory insurance	250
Factory depreciation	500
President's salary	5,000
Sales commissions	1,200
Sales revenue	93,000
Raw material inventory, 3/1/X7	400
Material purchases	16,750
Raw material inventory, 3/31/X7	800
Factory utilities	2,000
Factory supplies used	600
Work in process inventory, 3/1/X7	1,200
Work in process inventory, 3/31/X7	1,000
Sales salaries	3,600
Office salaries	2,400
Taxes on plant	300
Office insurance (one-third to sales)	300
Finished goods inventory, 3/31/X7	10,500

REQUIRED:

a. Prepare a schedule of cost of goods manufactured for the month ended March 31, 19X7.
b. Prepare an income statement for the month ended March 31, 19X7, classifying the selling expenses and administrative expenses in separate groups.

LO 4

P20-4B **Product Cost Flows** Vista Lighting Products Company produces a motion sensitive, automatic, external light fixture which is popular as both a residential and commercial lighting device. Ninety percent of the October production was sold during the month. The following information is available for operations during the month of October 19X6.

Fixture parts inventory, 10/1/X6	$11,500
Fixture parts inventory, 10/31/X6	9,500
Purchases of fixture parts	68,000
Work in process inventory, 10/1/X6	22,500
Work in process inventory, 10/31/X6	20,000
Finished goods inventory, 10/1/X6	16,000
Finished goods inventory, 10/31/X6	29,300
Direct labor costs	12,000
Indirect labor costs	6,000
Factory supplies used	14,500
Utilities expense—factory	1,100
Depreciation on machinery and factory buildings	22,000
Factory insurance	900
Factory supervision	4,000

REQUIRED:

a. Prepare T-accounts for Fixture Parts Inventory, Work in Process Inventory, Finished Goods Inventory, Manufacturing Overhead, and Cost of Goods Sold.
b. Enter the given amounts as appropriate in the T-accounts to reflect the flow of product costs for the month of October 19X6.
c. Prepare a schedule of cost of goods manufactured.

LO 3,5

P20-5B Classification of Costs The costs shown in the following schedule are typical of a manufacturing environment.

Costs	a	b	c	d	e
1. Administrative salaries	___	___	___	___	___
2. Direct material cost	___	___	___	___	___
3. Depreciation of plant assets	___	___	___	___	___
4. Depreciation of office equipment	___	___	___	___	___
5. Freight out	___	___	___	___	___
6. Plant utility costs	___	___	___	___	___
7. Cost of goods sold	___	___	___	___	___
8. Indirect labor cost	___	___	___	___	___
9. Factory insurance	___	___	___	___	___
10. Sales commissions	___	___	___	___	___

REQUIRED:

Complete the schedule to classify the costs as:
a. Manufacturing or Nonmanufacturing (*Mfg* or *Non*)
b. Product or Period (*Pro* or *Per*)
c. Fixed or Variable as to production or sales (*Fix* or *Var*)
d. Direct or Indirect as to the product (*Dir* or *Ind*)
e. Controllable or Noncontrollable (*Con* or *NoC*) at the production department level.

LO 2,3,5

P20-6B Performance Evaluation, Cost Identification, and Control You are in the process of preparing a performance report and a new budget for the Cabinet Corner, a manufacturer of bathroom base cabinets for mobile homes. The budgeted and actual production data for 19X7 are shown below:

	Budget	Actual
Production quantities (units)	4,000	4,000
Production costs:		
Cabinet plywood used	$ 32,000	$ 33,000
Direct labor	36,000	35,800
Indirect labor	18,000	21,000
Glue, nails and screws	4,200	4,450
Plant utilities	1,800	1,950
Insurance	2,400	2,500
Depreciation on plant assets	4,600	4,600
Supervision	20,000	20,000
Total production costs	$119,000	$123,300

REQUIRED:

Identify the variances (differences between budget and actual) for each production cost and indicate the managerial level (production supervisor, plant manager, or company president) at which you would expect to find control over the cost to exist. Explain your choices.

CRITICAL THINKING AND COMMUNICATING

C20-1 A spokesperson for a large U.S. auto maker made a statement in 1971 that the cost of the base model of one of their popular compact cars was $1,850. At the time the suggested retail price, before freight and dealer preparation, was $1,919. Around that same time, a union official involved in the negotiation of a labor contract with the auto maker made a public statement suggesting that the cost of producing that particular model was about $1,200.

REQUIRED:

a. Discuss how two responsible individuals could cite such different cost figures.
b. Do you feel, from the information presented, that one of the individuals was citing an incorrect cost? Discuss.

C20-2 A senior accounting professor at State University asked his students the following question on an exam: "Can depreciation expense be carried on the balance sheet as an asset?"

REQUIRED:

Provide a response to the question.

CHAPTER 21

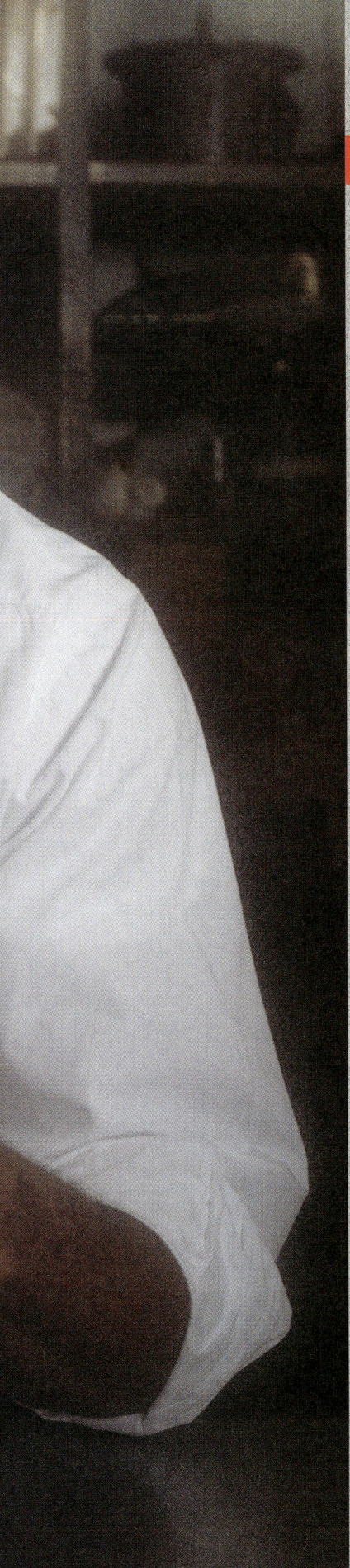

Job-Order Costing and Changes in the Manufacturing Environment

Ryan Spence, Ph.D., has recently designed a highly adjustable surgical table. To develop a prototype for marketing to hospitals, he needs several components, including five custom-built electric motors. Spence asks Eastern Electric to manufacture the motors and Eastern is interested because, based on projected demand, it knows Spence may ultimately order 10,000 motors per year. Eastern also knows Spence cannot afford to pay a high price for the motors at this stage and offers to sell them for just 10 percent over cost. But, how can Eastern determine the cost of the motors? For this determination, Eastern will use a **product costing system**, which is an integrated set of documents, ledgers, accounts, and accounting procedures used to measure and record the cost of manufactured products.[1]

In this chapter, we present a particular type of product costing system referred to as a job-order costing system. Most product costing systems develop product cost information that reflects the total cost of manufacturing a product. Because the product cost information is comprehensive (including both fixed and variable manufacturing costs), it is often referred to as **full cost** information.

In this chapter, we also address changes in the manufacturing environment and how these changes help companies survive in a competitive global economy. Management accountants need to keep abreast of these changes, which affect the type and amount of costs and, to some extent, the design of the product costing system.

---

[1]Product costing systems are also referred to as *cost accounting systems*.

LEARNING OBJECTIVES

1. Discuss the types of product costing systems.
2. Explain the relationship between the cost of jobs and Work in Process Inventory, Finished Goods Inventory, and Cost of Goods Sold.
3. Describe how direct material, direct labor, and manufacturing overhead are traced to jobs.
4. Explain how a predetermined overhead rate is used to apply overhead to jobs.
5. Discuss the accounting treatment of the difference between actual overhead and overhead allocated to jobs using a predetermined rate.
6. Discuss changes in the manufacturing environment of U.S. companies and how they affect product costing.

USE OF PRODUCT COST INFORMATION

Product cost information is used for a variety of purposes. Two of its most common uses are in financial reporting and in managerial decision making.

Financial Reporting and Product Costs

Manufacturing companies need product cost information to prepare financial statements in accordance with GAAP. To be consistent with GAAP, the inventory balance on the balance sheet must accurately reflect the cost of producing the goods that remain in inventory at the end of the accounting period. Also, the cost of goods sold amount presented on the income statement must accurately reflect the cost of the items sold during the accounting period. Because product cost information is necessary for external financial reporting, all manufacturing companies must have some type of product costing system. These systems generally produce full cost information, which GAAP requires.

Managerial Decision Making and Product Costs

Product cost information also is needed for a variety of managerial decisions. For example, Eastern Electric needs product cost information for its pricing decision. Sometimes the product cost information needed for management decision making is different from that produced for external financial reports. For external financial reports, product cost information mixes both fixed and variable manufacturing costs. Many internal management decisions, however, require information with separate fixed and variable cost components. The information needed for management decisions will be examined in detail later in the text. For now, you should simply understand that product cost information produced for external reporting purposes may not be appropriate for management decisions unless it is modified or adjusted.

LO 1
Discuss the types of product costing systems.

TYPES OF COSTING SYSTEMS

There are two major product costing systems: job-order and process. Which system to use depends on the type of manufacturing.

Job-Order Costing Systems

Companies that use a job-order costing system generally produce individual products or batches of unique products. This is the case when a company manufactures goods to a customer's specifications. A **job** is an individual product or batch for which a company needs cost information. When the items that make up the job are completed and sold, the company can match the cost of the job with the revenue it produced and obtain an appropriate measure of gross profit. Companies using job-order costing systems include construction companies, equipment and tool producers, ship building companies, and printing companies.

Process Costing Systems

In contrast, companies using a process costing system generally produce large quantities of identical items that pass through uniform and continuous production operations. Costs are accumulated by each operation, and the unit cost of items produced is determined by dividing the costs of the production operations by the number of identical items produced.

$$\text{Unit Cost of Items Produced} = \frac{\text{Total Cost of Production}}{\text{Total Number of Units Produced}}$$

In a process costing system, costs are not traced to specific items produced since each item is identical. It is sufficient to assign to each item its average unit cost of production. Companies using process costing systems include producers of metals, chemicals, paints, and plastics.

OVERVIEW OF JOB COST AND FINANCIAL STATEMENT ACCOUNTS

LO 2 Explain the relationship between the cost of jobs and Work in Process Inventory, Finished Goods Inventory, and Cost of Goods Sold.

As previously discussed, product costs include three items: direct material, direct labor, and manufacturing overhead. In a job-order costing system, the cost of a job is the sum of these three cost items. Thus, a job-order system must be able to trace these costs to specific jobs. (See Illustration 21-1.)

ILLUSTRATION 21-1 Relating Product Costs to Jobs

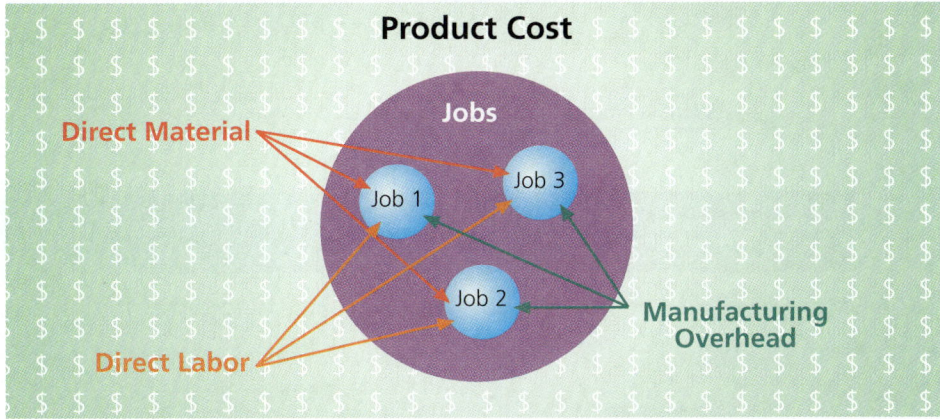

Also, recall that product costs are reflected in Work in Process Inventory and Finished Goods Inventory on the balance sheet and in Cost of Goods Sold on the income statement. In a job-order costing system, Work in Process Inventory will include the cost of all jobs that are currently being worked on (i.e., those that are in process). Finished Goods Inventory will include the cost of all jobs that are completed but not yet sold. Cost of Goods sold will include the cost of all jobs that are sold during the accounting period. (See Illustration 21-2.)

ILLUSTRATION 21-2 Job Costs and Financial Statement Accounts

Work in Process Inventory	Finished Goods Inventory	Cost of Goods Sold
Cost of jobs being worked on	Cost of jobs completed but not yet sold	Cost of jobs sold

Costs flow through a job-order costing system based on the status of jobs. First, direct material, direct labor, and manufacturing overhead costs related to jobs being worked on are added to Work in Process Inventory. When specific jobs are completed, the costs of those jobs (referred to as the costs of goods manufactured) are deducted from Work in Process Inventory and added to Finished Goods Inventory. When specific jobs are sold, the costs of those jobs are removed from Finished Goods Inventory and added to Cost of Goods Sold. These cost flows are indicated in Illustration 21-3.

As you read the following discussion, remember these components of a job-order costing system:

1. The items making up the costs of a job (direct material, direct labor, and manufacturing overhead).
2. The way the status of jobs triggers the flow of costs through the accounts (Work in Process Inventory, Finished Goods Inventory, and Cost of Goods Sold). These are the basic structural elements that we build on in our discussion of job-order costing system procedures.

ILLUSTRATION 21-3 Flow of Costs in a Job-Order Costing System

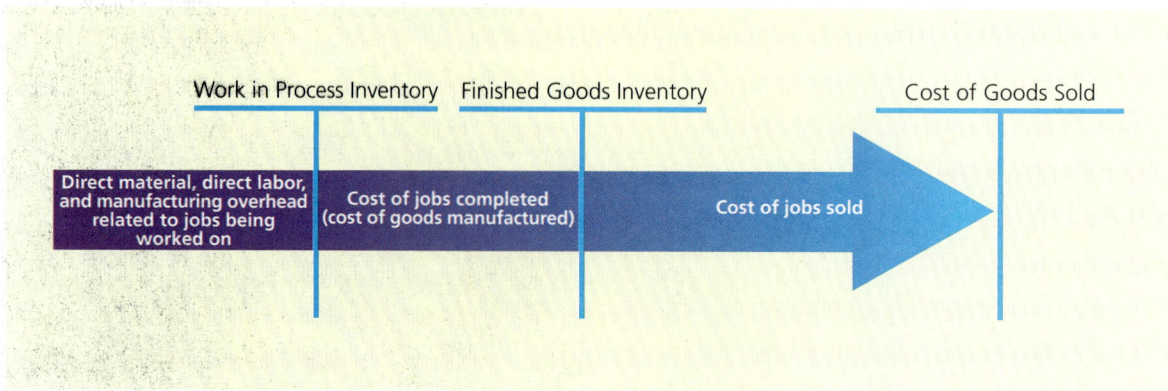

JOB-ORDER COSTING SYSTEM

LO 3 Describe how direct material, direct labor, and manufacturing overhead are traced to jobs.

A company begins its job-order costing operations when it decides to produce a specific product for a customer's order or for stock. For example, an electric motor manufacturer receives an order for five custom-designed motors, a print shop receives an order for 20,000 spring catalogs from a clothing manufacturer, or a residential construction company receives an order to build a summer home. If the company decides to accept the order, it prepares a **job cost sheet**, a form used to accumulate the cost of producing the item or items ordered (i.e., the cost of the job). An example of a job cost sheet is presented in Illustration 21-4. How specific numbers are entered on the job cost sheet will be explained later. For now, simply note that the job cost sheet contains detailed information on the three categories of product costs: direct material, direct labor, and manufacturing overhead.

ILLUSTRATION 21-4 Job Cost Sheet

EasternElectric
25 E. Hill Street, Columbus, Ohio 43268

Job number 2574 Date needed 3/20 Date started 3/12 Date completed 3/16
Customer Spence Development Company, 628 Meridian, Columbus, OH 43205-1182
Description Five compact motors for use in medical equipment

	Direct Material		Direct Labor			Manufacturing Overhead
Date	Requisition Number	Cost	Labor Report Number	Hours	Cost	$16.25 per direct labor hour
3/12	7556	238.53	108	14	163.50	227.50
3/13	7642	5,480.30	109	22	250.25	357.50
3/14	7731	325.67	110	26	287.63	422.50
3/15	7805	1,683.50	111	43	485.60	698.75
3/16	7860	750.90	112	41	562.82	666.25
	Total	8,478.90	Total	146	1,749.80	Total 2,372.50

Cost summary:
Direct Material	$ 8,478.90
Direct Labor	1,749.80
Manufacturing Overhead	2,372.50
Total	$12,601.20

Direct Material Cost

A **material requisition form** (Illustration 21-5) is used to request the release of materials from a company's storage. The form lists the type, quantity, and cost of material, as well as the number of the job requiring the materials. Because the form includes the job number, it can be used to trace material cost to specific jobs. Requiring a supervisor's signature helps prevent the unauthorized issuance of material.

Each material requisition form is listed in summary form on the job cost sheet. For example, on material requisition form number 7556, presented in

Illustration 21-5, the total cost of items requested amounts to $238.53. When these items are released from storage, the total cost is posted to the job cost sheet (see Illustration 21-4) and cross-referenced by the material requisition number.

ILLUSTRATION 21-5 Material Requisition Form

Eastern*Electric*

Material Requisition Number __7556__   Job Number __2574__   Date __3/12__

Item	Quantity	Unit Cost	Total
A2763	2	10.25	$ 20.50
A5438	10	12.04	120.40
D3760	1	80.10	80.10
D3658	1	17.53	17.53
		Total	$238.53

Approved by: *K. Dawson*

When a company purchases materials, it includes their costs in the raw materials inventory account. Removing materials from storage for a specific job decreases Raw Materials Inventory and increases Work in Process Inventory. Periodically (daily, weekly, or monthly), the company calculates and records in the general journal the total cost of materials issued to jobs. Suppose a company purchases $60,000 of materials and issues $50,000 of materials to specific jobs. The entries to record these transactions are:

(Date)	Raw Materials Inventory	60,000	
	Accounts Payable		60,000
	To record purchase of raw materials.		
(Date)	Work in Process Inventory	50,000	
	Raw Materials Inventory		50,000
	To record requisition of raw materials.		

Direct Labor Cost

In a job-order costing system, workers complete **time tickets** (also called *job tickets* or *work tickets*) to keep track of the amount of time spent on each job (Illustration 21-6). If many workers are assigned a particular job, individual time tickets may not be posted directly to job cost sheets since that would produce too much detail. Illustration 21-7 presents a daily labor cost summary by job. As you can see, Number 687 is just one of the tickets completed and submitted for Job 2574 on March 12. Time ticket 687 might represent 3 hours spent wiring motors, while time ticket 689 might represent 6 hours spent assembling components. On March 12, a total of 14 hours were spent on Job 2574 and cost $163.50. The total labor cost traced to Job 2574 ($163.50) is the amount posted to the job cost sheet. (See Illustration 21-4.)

Periodically, the amount of direct labor cost attributed to current jobs must be debited to Work in Process Inventory. Suppose a company incurs $30,000 of direct labor cost. The appropriate journal entry is:

(Date)	Work in Process Inventory	30,000	
	Wages and Salaries Payable		30,000
	To record direct labor cost.		

ILLUSTRATION 21-6 Labor Time Ticket

Eastern *Electric*

Date __3/12__

Time Ticket Number __687__ Employee Number __7843__ Grade __3__

Job	Time Start	Time Stop	Total Hours
2574	2:00 p.m.	5:00 p.m.	3.00

ILLUSTRATION 21-7 Daily Labor Cost Summary

Eastern *Electric*

Daily Labor Report Number: 108   Date: 3/12

Job	Time Ticket	Hours	Grade	Rate	Cost
2574	687	3.00	3	12.50	$ 37.50
2574	689	6.00	3	12.50	75.00
2574	690	2.50	2	11.80	29.50
2574	693	2.50	1	8.60	21.50
		14.00			$ 163.50
2580	688	5.00	3	12.50	$ 62.50
2580	692	6.00	3	12.50	75.00
2580	737	1.00	2	11.80	11.80
		12.00			$ 149.30

Various Additional Labor Charges by Job $2,254.50

Total Daily Labor Cost $2,567.30

Manufacturing Overhead

So far, we have traced raw materials and direct labor costs to jobs. The final and most complex cost component to trace is manufacturing overhead, which we will discuss in a general way before going into more detail later in the chapter.

Manufacturing overhead costs cannot be traced directly to goods produced. Thus an alternative method of assigning overhead costs to jobs is needed. The basic approach involves assigning overhead to jobs based on some common characteristic that jobs share, such as direct labor hours or cost. The common characteristic is referred to as an allocation base. Once an allocation base is selected, an **overhead allocation rate** can be developed by dividing estimated overhead costs by the estimated quantity of the allocation base. The terms *allocation base* and *overhead allocation rate* will be discussed further later in this chapter. Suppose Eastern Electric anticipates $325,000 of manufacturing overhead and 20,000 labor hours during the year. With these estimates, it calculates and assigns $16.25 of overhead for every direct labor hour worked ($325,000 ÷ 20,000). Of course, the more labor hours a job requires, the more overhead will be assigned to it. The amount of overhead assigned to jobs is referred to as **overhead applied**. Note that in Illustration 21-4, overhead is assigned to jobs on the basis of labor hours. With an overhead rate of $16.25 and 146 labor hours, $2,372.50 of manufacturing overhead is assigned to Job 2574.

Recording manufacturing overhead is a two-step process. First, when a company incurs actual overhead costs, it debits these costs to Manufacturing Overhead. Second, in applying overhead to jobs, the company credits Manufacturing Overhead and debits Work in Process Inventory.

Step 1. Overhead costs include depreciation, utilities, and a variety of other costs. Therefore, the credit side of the entry to record manufacturing overhead can include a large number of accounts. Suppose a company incurs $10,000 of depreciation, $1,000 of utilities cost, and $55,000 of various other overhead costs that we will not specify for the sake of brevity. The journal entry to record these costs is:

(Date)	Manufacturing Overhead	66,000	
	Accumulated Depreciation		10,000
	Utilities Payable		1,000
	Various other accounts		55,000
	To record overhead costs incurred.		

Step 2. The company periodically calculates the total amount of estimated overhead costs applied to jobs and makes an entry to credit Manufacturing Overhead and debit Work in Process Inventory. Suppose $60,000 of overhead is applied to jobs. The journal entry is:

(Date)	Work in Process Inventory	60,000	
	Manufacturing Overhead		60,000
	To record overhead costs applied to jobs.		

Tracing Costs to Jobs: A Summary Material requisition forms are used to trace direct material costs to jobs while time tickets are used to trace direct labor costs to jobs. Since manufacturing overhead costs cannot be directly traced to jobs, they are indirectly traced by using an overhead rate multiplied by each job's measure of the allocation base. Illustration 21-8 summarizes the methods used to trace manufacturing costs to jobs.

ILLUSTRATION 21-8 How Manufacturing Costs Are Traced to Jobs

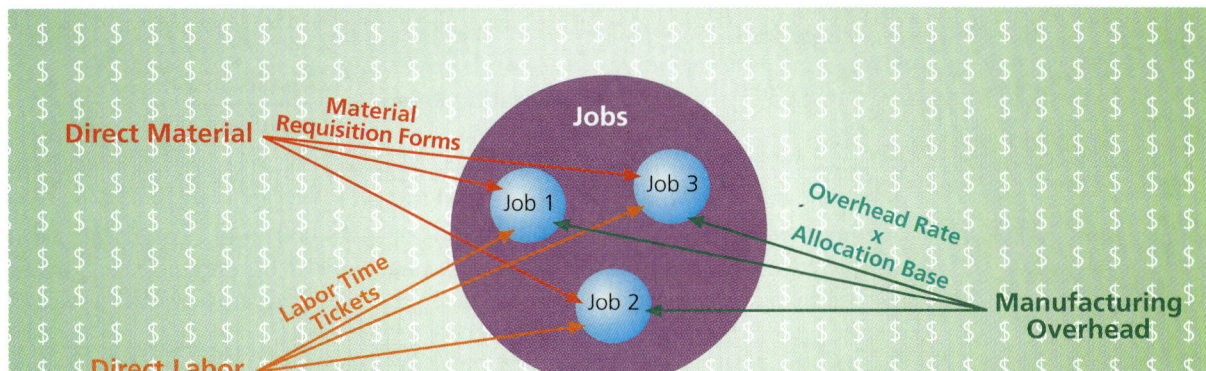

FLOW OF COSTS IN WORK IN PROCESS INVENTORY, FINISHED GOODS INVENTORY, AND COST OF GOODS SOLD

When a company begins work on a job, it records production costs in Work in Process Inventory using journal entries such as those illustrated earlier. When jobs are completed, the company reduces Work in Process Inventory by the cost of the completed jobs and increases Finished Goods Inventory by the same amount. When the company sells completed jobs it reduces Finished Goods Inventory by the cost of the completed jobs sold and increases Cost of Goods Sold. Suppose the cost of jobs completed is $80,000 and the cost of jobs sold is $70,000. The journal entries are:

(Date)	Finished Goods Inventory	80,000	
	Work in Process Inventory		80,000
	To record cost of jobs completed.		
(Date)	Cost of Goods Sold	70,000	
	Finished Goods Inventory		70,000
	To record cost of goods sold expense.		

ALLOCATING OVERHEAD TO JOBS

We have seen how direct material, direct labor, and manufacturing overhead are accumulated in a job-order costing system. However, the process of assigning manufacturing overhead to specific jobs and recording overhead in the accounts, referred to as **overhead allocation**, needs to be examined in more detail.

Overhead Allocation Rates

Because overhead costs are related only indirectly to jobs being produced, a company must develop some means of allocating or assigning overhead costs to current jobs. It does so by means of an overhead allocation rate. The rate is calculated as the ratio of overhead costs to activity. Common measures of activity include direct labor hours, direct labor cost, machine hours, and direct material cost. You will recall that the measure of these activities is referred to as the allocation base.

$$\text{Overhead Allocation Rate} = \frac{\text{Overhead Cost}}{\text{Activity}}$$

Suppose a company had $50,000 of overhead cost and used 10,000 labor hours during the year. In this example, the company can calculate an average *actual* overhead cost per labor hour of $5 ($50,000 ÷ 10,000) and can assign overhead to jobs based on the amount of labor hours worked on each job. For example, if a particular job required 100 labor hours, the company would assign it an overhead allocation of $500 (100 x $5).

Selecting an Overhead Allocation Base

The measure of activity (the denominator in the equation shown above) used to calculate an overhead rate is the **allocation base**. The allocation base is used to spread the overhead among various jobs, all of which have some quantity of activity associated with them. In choosing among alternative allocation bases (such as direct labor hours, direct labor cost, machine hours, and direct material cost), keep in mind that jobs with greater quantities of an allocation base will receive larger allocations of overhead. For example, suppose machine hours are used as an allocation base and an overhead rate is calculated as $10 per machine hour. If one job uses 40 machine hours and another job uses 20 machine hours, the first job will receive an allocation of $400 and the second job will receive an allocation of only $200. This would be appropriate if greater activity, as measured by machine time, requires the firm to incur more overhead cost.

The allocation base a company uses should be strongly associated with its overhead cost. That is, increases in overhead cost should coincide with increases in the allocation base. If increases in overhead are more closely associated with increases in machine hours rather than labor hours, the company should allocate overhead on the basis of machine hours. In selecting the allocation base, a company should consider whether the production process is labor intensive or machine intensive. If an operation is labor intensive (i.e., large quantities of labor are used to produce most jobs), then direct labor hours or direct labor cost might be a reasonable allocation base. If an operation is highly mechanized, then machine hours might be a reasonable allocation base.

Activity-Based Costing (ABC) and Multiple Overhead Rates

Many companies allocate overhead to jobs using a single overhead rate with an allocation base of direct labor. However, overhead costs are caused by a variety of factors; allocating costs just on the basis of labor, or any single allocation base, may seriously distort product costs. **Activity-based costing (ABC)** is a method of assigning overhead costs to products using a number of different allocation bases. In the ABC approach, the company first identifies the major activities that create overhead costs and then groups these costs into so-called **cost pools**. By dividing the amount of each cost pool by a measure of its corresponding activity (referred to as a **cost driver**), the company calculates multiple overhead rates. The company then assigns overhead to a product based on how much of each activity (cost driver) it caused.

Illustration 21-9 presents examples of typical cost pools and cost drivers. In the traditional approach to allocation, the allocation base or cost driver is a measure of production volume, such as direct labor or machine hours. In the ABC approach, the cost drivers include activities that are not necessarily related to production volume. Since many costs are not dependent on production volume, the ABC approach is more accurate. For example, consider the cost driver *number of setups*. *Setups* are activities involved in organizing and adjusting equipment in preparation for a production run. In the ABC approach, two products that require the same number of setups will receive the same allocation of setup cost. This is not the case when overhead is allocated only on the basis of a measure of production volume such as direct labor. If one of the products is a high-volume product, then it will have more labor and receive a greater allocation of setup cost than a low-volume product that requires little labor—even if both products require one setup.

ILLUSTRATION 21-9 Examples of Cost Pools and Cost Drivers

Cost Pools	Cost Drivers
Cost of setting up equipment	Number of setups
Material ordering costs	Number of purchase orders
Material receiving costs	Number of shipments received
Cost of electricity	Number of machine hours
Health insurance for workers	Number of workers

A simplified example with only two products and two cost pools illustrates how ABC results in more accurate cost information. Suppose the Wilson Manufacturing Company Produces two products, A and B, and has two major cost pools. The first cost pool is $600,000, and the related driver is labor cost. The second cost pool is $400,000, and the related driver is number of setups.

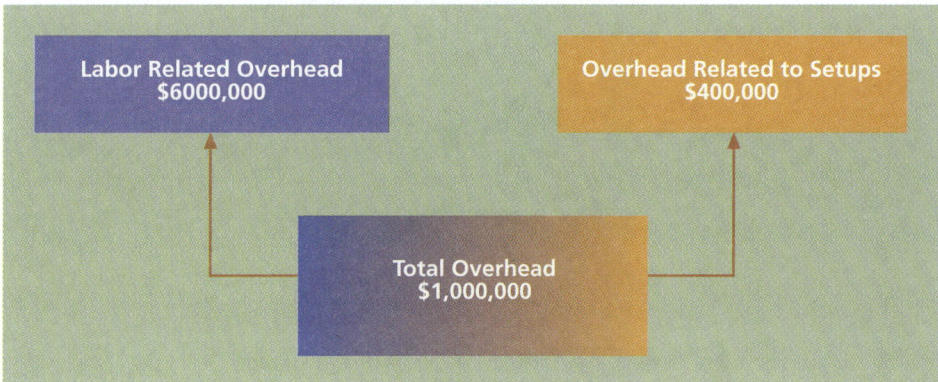

In the current year, Wilson Manufacturing expects $200,000 of labor and 40 setups. Product A, a high-volume product with annual production of 40,000 units, requires $150,000 of labor and 20 setups. Product B, a low-volume product with annual production of only 1,000 units, requires only $50,000 of labor but, as with Product A, also requires 20 setups.

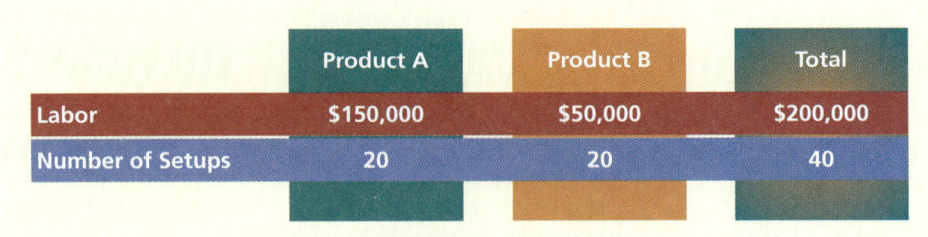

How much cost will Wilson Manufacturing assign to Products A and B if it uses an ABC system with labor and setups as the cost drivers? The analysis required to answer this question is presented in Illustration 21-10. The overhead rate for labor-related costs is $3 per dollar of labor ($600,000 overhead ÷ $200,000 labor). The overhead rate for setup-related costs is $10,000 per setup ($400,000 overhead ÷ 40 setups). With these overhead rates, Wilson assigns Product A $650,000 of total overhead ($450,000 of labor-related overhead and $200,000 of setup-related overhead) and product B $350,000 of total overhead ($150,000 of labor-related overhead and $200,000 of setup-related overhead).

ILLUSTRATION 21-10 Simplified Example Comparing ABC and Traditional Approaches to Allocation

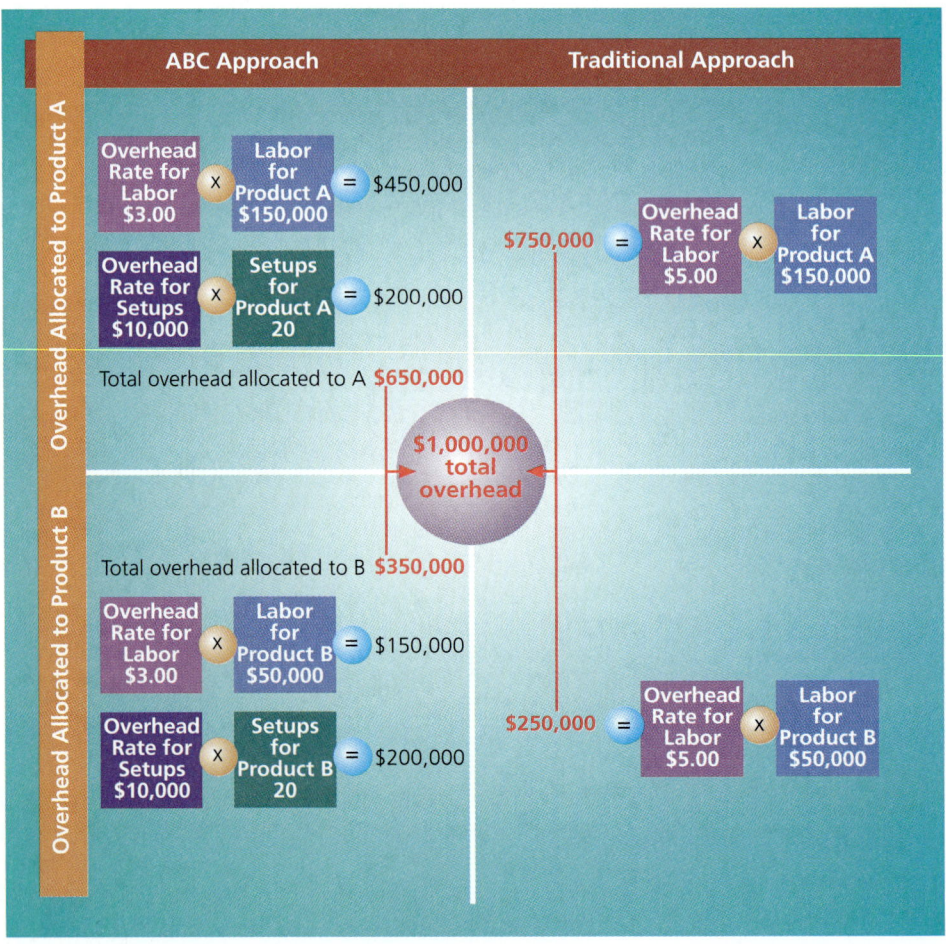

Since costs are allocated based on the factors that actually caused them, allocations under the ABC approach can be more accurate. Compare in Illustration 21-10 the allocations under ABC with those Products A and B would receive if overhead was allocated by taking a traditional approach with labor cost as the allocation base. Under the traditional approach, the overhead rate would be $5 per dollar of labor ($1,000,000 of total overhead ÷ $200,000 of total labor). Product A would thus receive an allocation of $750,000 and Product B an allocation of $250,000.

Note that when only a single allocation base (labor cost) is used, Product A receives a much larger allocation ($750,000 versus $650,000 using ABC). The reason: Product A, a high-volume product, uses a lot of labor, which is the only allocation base for overhead. However, this allocation is not accurate. Much of overhead is due to setting up the production lines. Product A requires no more setups than Product B and should, therefore, receive the same allocation of these costs. The ABC approach recognizes this important fact. With more accurate product cost information, managers can make better product pricing decisions. For example, managers might decide to decrease the price of Product A and increase the price of Product B.

In the real world, overhead costs are due to a variety of different factors; thus, they should be allocated using a number of different allocation bases or cost drivers. How many cost pools and cost drivers should a company use? The managerial accountant must make a cost/benefit tradeoff. The more cost pools and cost drivers used, the more accurate the product cost information. However, recordkeeping costs increase with the number of different allocation bases; beyond a certain point, the recordkeeping cost will exceed the benefit of more accurate information.

While multiple allocation rates generally should be used, you will see several examples in this chapter and elsewhere in the text where overhead costs are allocated using only a single allocation base such as labor hours, labor cost, or machine hours. This is done for simplicity, not because it is good practice in the real world.

Predetermined Overhead Rates

LO 4
Explain how a predetermined overhead rate is used to apply overhead to jobs.

Companies can develop overhead rates by dividing *actual* overhead by the *actual* level of the allocation base. Most companies do not follow this practice, however, because total actual overhead cost and the total actual level of the allocation base are not known until the end of the accounting period. It is impossible to determine the actual overhead rate until the end of the accounting period. However, until this rate is developed, no overhead can be applied to jobs. Companies want to know the cost of jobs before their accounting periods end. In many cases, the price companies charge for a job depends on its cost. Thus, companies need an immediate cost figure to determine the price to charge a customer and to determine the profitability of jobs.

Typically, overhead rates are based on *estimates* of overhead cost and *estimates* of the level of the allocation base rather than on *actual* costs and quantities. Overhead rates calculated by estimation are referred to as **predetermined overhead rates**. Once the estimated overhead cost and estimated allocation base are established, the company can calculate the predetermined overhead rate by dividing the estimated overhead by the estimated level of the allocation base.

$$\text{Predetermined Overhead Rate} = \frac{\text{Estimated Total Overhead Cost}}{\text{Estimated Level of Allocation Base}}$$

Consider our example of Eastern Electric. Management estimates that $325,000 of total manufacturing overhead will be incurred in the coming year and that 20,000 labor hours will be required. Thus, the predetermined overhead rate is $16.25 per labor hour ($325,000 ÷ 20,000), and a job requiring 100 direct labor hours to complete would be allocated $1,625 of overhead (i.e., $16.25 x 100 labor hours).

The estimated or budgeted overhead cost and the estimated level of the allocation base generally are estimated for a year so that the overhead allocation rate stays the same from month to month. If a shorter period such as one month were used, the overhead rate would fluctuate from month to month, causing identical jobs produced in different months to have different costs. This results because some overhead charges only occur in certain months. For example, in summer months a company may incur extra power costs because the plant is air-conditioned. Another reason for fluctuations in a shorter period of time is that overhead includes both variable and fixed cost items. When *expected* levels of the allocation base decrease, the *expected* amount of variable overhead also decreases. However, the expected amount of fixed overhead does not decrease. Thus, the overhead rate is likely to be higher in slower months.

Eliminating Over- or Underapplied Overhead

LO 5
Discuss the accounting treatment of the difference between actual overhead and overhead allocated to jobs using a predetermined rate.

As indicated earlier, recording manufacturing overhead is a two-step process. First, the company accumulates *actual* costs of various overhead items in the manufacturing overhead account. Second, the company applies overhead to individual jobs using the predetermined overhead rate. This increases Work in Process Inventory and decreases Manufacturing Overhead. Thus, a company makes two types of entries to the manufacturing overhead account: the debit entries record actual overhead costs incurred; the credit entries record the amount of overhead applied to jobs in process.

Manufacturing Overhead	
Actual Overhead Costs Incurred	Overhead Costs Applied to Jobs

Unless the estimates for overhead and the level of the allocation base equal their actual amounts, the amount of overhead a company applies to jobs using a predetermined overhead rate will not equal actual overhead cost incurred. Because estimates are seldom perfectly accurate, there is likely to be a difference between the debits to Manufacturing Overhead (recording actual overhead costs) and the credits to Manufacturing Overhead (recording the amount of overhead applied to jobs using the predetermined overhead rate). The difference is referred to as **underapplied overhead** if actual overhead is greater than the amount of overhead applied, or as **overapplied overhead** if actual overhead is less than the amount applied. At the end of the accounting period, the amount of under- or overapplied overhead is equal to the balance in Manufacturing Overhead and the company must close the account eliminating the balance. If the company has done a reasonable job of estimating its predetermined overhead rate, the amount of over- or underapplied overhead will not be large. In this case, the company simply would close the account and adjust Cost of Goods Sold. For example, suppose a company had $50,000 of actual overhead and applied $48,000 to jobs using a predetermined overhead rate. In this case, overhead is underapplied by $2,000, the debit balance in the manufacturing overhead account. To close the account, the company makes the following journal entry:

(Date)	Cost of Goods Sold	2,000	
	Manufacturing Overhead		2,000
	To close out Manufacturing Overhead and eliminate underapplied overhead.		

Theoretically, the company should apportion the amount of under- or overapplied overhead among Work in Process Inventory, Finished Goods Inventory, and Cost of Goods Sold. This follows from the fact that use of a predetermined rate results in job costs that differ from their actual costs by the amount of over- or underapplied overhead. Because the costs of jobs are reflected in Work in Process Inventory, Finished Goods Inventory, and Cost of Goods Sold, the company should adjust all these accounts to reflect actual overhead costs. Apportioning costs among Work in Process Inventory, Finished Goods Inventory, and Cost of Goods Sold can be accomplished based on the relative cost recorded in these accounts. For example, suppose a company has Work in Process Inventory of $10,000, Finished Goods Inventory of $10,000, Cost of Goods Sold of $20,000, and underapplied overhead of $2,000. The apportionment rate would be $.05 for each dollar in the accounts (i.e., $2,000 ÷ $40,000). Thus, Work in Process Inventory would receive $500; Finished Goods Inventory, $500; and Cost of Goods Sold, $1,000. The company would make the following journal entry:

(Date)	Work in Process Inventory	500	
	Finished Goods Inventory	500	
	Cost of Goods Sold	1,000	
	Manufacturing Overhead		2,000
	To apportion underapplied overhead.		

Whether the amount of over- or underapplied overhead is applied to Cost of Goods Sold or apportioned among Work in Process Inventory, Finished Goods Inventory, and Cost of Goods Sold depends on the dollar value of over- or underapplied overhead. If the amount is immaterial, it is sufficient for practical purposes for the company to simply debit (for underapplied overhead) or credit (for overapplied overhead) the amount to Cost of Goods Sold. If the amount is material, the company should apportion it among Work in Process Inventory, Finished Goods Inventory, and Cost of Goods Sold.

CHANGES IN THE MANUFACTURING ENVIRONMENT AND PRODUCT COSTING SYSTEMS

LO 6 Discuss changes in the manufacturing environment of U.S. companies and how they affect product costing.

In the last two decades, U.S. companies have experienced stiff foreign competition. To compete effectively in a global economy, many U.S. manufacturers have made fundamental changes in their operations and business philosophies. These changes in the manufacturing environment affect the types of costs that are incurred and, to some extent, the way the costs are recorded in the product costing system. We will discuss four of the major changes: just-in-time manufacturing, computer-controlled manufacturing, flexible manufacturing systems, and total quality management.

Just-in-Time (JIT) Manufacturing

Many U.S. and Japanese companies use an innovative manufacturing system variously referred to as a **just-in-time (JIT) system**, a Kanban system, or a zero-inventory production system (ZIPS). One important goal of such manufacturing systems is to minimize inventories of raw materials and work in process. Companies with JIT systems make arrangements with suppliers to deliver materials just before they are needed in the production process. Also, when products need to be manufactured on multiple production lines (e.g., a product may need to be manufactured on a production line that involves welding before moving on to a production line that involves machining), production on one line is scheduled so that operations are completed just in time to meet the requirements of the next production line. With such a system, work in process inventory does not build up and clog the factory floor.

Survey data indicate that approximately 13 percent of U.S. companies have adopted JIT systems.[2] Dramatic improvements in manufacturing performance have been reported. Some companies report 90 percent reductions in production lead time, 90 percent reductions in work in process, and 80 percent reductions in space required for production.

The approach to product costing when JIT systems are adopted can be quite different from the job-order costing systems described in this chapter. For example, some companies have combined the raw materials inventory and work in process inventory accounts into a new account called Raw-and-in-Process (RIP). When a company uses the RIP account, Work in Process Inventory is not tracked since the balance (held down by the JIT approach to minimizing inventory) is not material. Detailed information on the way product costing systems are adapted to JIT, Kanban, or ZIPS can be found in most cost accounting texts.

Computer-Controlled Manufacturing

Another major change: more and more companies are using highly automated **computer-controlled manufacturing systems**. Using computers to control equipment, including robots, generally increases the flexibility and accuracy of the production process. While state-of-the-art equipment and computer-controlled systems may help U.S. firms meet the challenge of global competition, they also have a significant effect on the composition of product costs. Survey data indicate that, on average, product costs consist of 53 percent material, 15 percent direct labor, and 32 percent overhead.[3] However, some highly automated companies such as Hewlett Packard report that direct labor accounts for as little as 3 percent of total production costs.[4] Decreasing labor costs are causing many companies to reconsider their overhead allocation bases. Currently, the most commonly used allocation bases for assigning overhead to jobs are direct labor hours and direct labor cost. However, in highly mechanized companies where direct labor is a small part of total manufacturing costs, using labor as an allocation base generally is not appropriate. Investing in state-of-the-art equipment also changes the company's mix of fixed and variable

---

[2] See R. A. Howell, J. D. Brown, S. R. Soucy, and A. H. Seed, III, *Management Accounting in the New Manufacturing Environment*, (National Association of Accountants, 1987), p. 126.

[3] Howell, et al., op. cit., p. 39.

[4] See B. R. Neumann, and P. R. Jaouen, "Kanban, Zips and Cost Accounting: A Case Study," *Journal of Accountancy* (August, 1986), pp.133–138.

costs. When equipment is substituted for labor, fixed costs generally increase and variable costs decrease.

Flexible Manufacturing Systems

Many companies hope to gain a competitive advantage by developing **flexible manufacturing systems**. Such systems, which generally are highly automated and often involve computer-controlled equipment, are configured so that machines easily can be adjusted to produce a number of different products or variations of standard products. With a flexible manufacturing system, companies easily can respond to custom orders. Flexible manufacturing systems also improve delivery times on orders and allow companies to introduce new products quickly.

Flexible manufacturing can be costly. In many cases, it requires a substantial investment in equipment and software to coordinate computer-controlled production processes. Additionally, more white-collar workers such as engineers may be needed. In 1985, General Electric Company developed a "factory of the future" with a flexible manufacturing system for $52 million. To justify this investment, the plant has to keep its machines working at substantially higher activity levels. In spite of the high cost, expenditures on flexible manufacturing systems are growing rapidly.[5]

Flexible manufacturing systems also impact product costing since costs must be traced to each of the potentially large number of custom products. However, the additional effort in accounting for custom products will not be significant if computerized accounting systems are used.

Total Quality Management

To survive in an increasingly competitive environment, firms realize they must produce high-quality products. An increasing number of companies have instituted **total quality management (TQM)** programs to insure high-quality products and efficient production processes. Currently, no generally agreed-upon "right" way to institute a TQM program exists. However, most companies with TQM develop philosophies that stress listening to the needs of customers, making products right the first time and reducing defective products that must be reworked, and encouraging workers to improve their production processes continuously. Indeed, some TQM programs are referred to as Continuous Quality Improvement programs. At Marlow Industries, a manufacturer of thermoelectric cooling devices, workers sign a Quality Pledge that reads: "I pledge to make a constant, conscious effort to do my job right today, better tomorrow, recognizing that my individual contribution is critical to the success of Marlow Industries."[6]

The results of an effective TQM program can be impressive. At Sundstrand Data Control, a manufacturer of electronic instruments, statistics show that its TQM program has reduced rework on some instrument production lines by 66 percent and has reduced scrap costs by 60 percent. Its cycle time (the time it

---

[5] See Mark Trumball "Manufacturing in Small Batches," *Christian Science Monitor*, Vol. 83, No. 186, (August 20, 1991), Sec. 1, p. 8.

[6] "Charting a New Course: Marlow Industries Sets Its Sights on Quality and Shoots for the Coveted Baldrige on the Way," *Dallas Business Journal*, Vol. 15, Issue 4, September 27, 1991, Sec. 1, p. 15.

takes to produce a product from beginning to end) also has decreased by 90 percent.[7]

How does TQM affect product costing systems? Strong advocates would argue that unless there is TQM, there is no need for product costing since companies without TQM will not survive! Undoubtedly, there is some truth to this position. To survive, companies must have high-quality products. Additionally, TQM affects product costing by reducing the need for tracking the cost of scrap and rework related to each job. If TQM is able to reduce these costs to an insignificant level, the benefit of tracking the costs far outweighs the cost to the accounting system.[8]

We have touched on some of the significant changes in the environment of manufacturing firms. Our purpose has been to make sure you have a basic understanding of the setting in which management accountants calculate product costs. Management accountants must "speak the language" of top management and operating personnel if they want to have a significant impact on important decisions. Increasingly, the language includes references to TQM, flexible manufacturing, computer-controlled manufacturing, and JIT. These topics are discussed in much more detail in courses in operations management and production. If you plan on a career in management accounting, study of these topics should be a priority.

REVISITING THE EASTERN ELECTRIC EXAMPLE

At the start of the chapter, we presented a scenario where Eastern Electric agreed to sell Ryan Spence five motors for 10 percent over cost. Now you know

INSIGHTS INTO ETHICS

Andover Equipment Company manufactures compressors for both private companies and the Department of Defense. The compressors produced for the Department of Defense require more than average labor because of the hand finishing needed to insure that the units will function under extreme conditions. For example, the model 240 compressor normally requires 10 machine hours and 4 labor hours to produce. The model produced for the Department of Defense (model 240B) requires 10 machine hours and 6 labor hours.

Brad Stevens, the cost accountant for Andover, proposes that the company change its overhead allocation base from machine hours to labor hours. The result of this change will be that compressors produced for the Department of Defense will show a substantially higher cost than compressors produced for the general public. Brad thinks this is a good idea because the compressors sold to the Department of Defense are sold on a cost-plus basis. That is, the selling price is a fixed markup over cost.

Discuss the appropriateness of using the allocation system to justify charging higher prices to the Department of Defense.

---

[7]Steve Wilhelm, "Quality Program Keeps Spreading at Sundstrand," *Puget Sound Business Journal*, Vol. 11, Issue 52 (May 13, 1991), Sec. 1, p. 17.

[8]We should point out that many service firms such as banks, insurance companies, and hospitals have adopted the TQM programs initially developed by manufacturers. TQM is especially popular in the health-care field.

how Eastern could use a job-order costing system to determine its cost and the price to charge Spence. The job cost sheet for the example was presented in Illustration 21-4. Total cost was $12,601.20. The selling price, therefore, will be $13,861.32.

Total cost of five motors	$12,601.20
Plus markup of 10 percent	1,260.12
Selling price	$13,861.32

If Spence's product "takes off," Eastern Electric most likely will renegotiate the selling price of the motors—a 10 percent markup is generally considered to be low. Also, Eastern will be able to continue using its product costing system to analyze the profitability of future orders.

SUMMARY

Discuss the types of product costing systems. There are two types of product costing systems: job-order systems and process costing systems. Companies using job-order systems generally produce individual products or batches of products that are unique. Companies using process costing systems generally produce large quantities of identical items in a continuous production operation.

Explain the relationship between the cost of jobs and Work in Process Inventory, Finished Goods Inventory, and Cost of Goods Sold. Work in Process Inventory includes the cost of all jobs currently being worked on. Finished Goods Inventory includes the cost of all jobs that are completed but not yet sold. Cost of Goods Sold includes the cost of all jobs that are sold during the accounting period.

Describe how direct material, direct labor, and manufacturing overhead are traced to jobs. Job cost sheets track the direct material, direct labor, and manufacturing overhead cost of each job. Direct material cost is traced to jobs by means of material requisition forms. Direct labor is traced to jobs by means of labor time tickets. Manufacturing overhead is applied to jobs using an overhead rate.

Explain how a predetermined overhead rate is used to apply overhead to jobs. Most companies apply overhead to jobs using a predetermined, rather than an actual, overhead rate. Actual overhead cannot be determined until the end of the accounting period, and companies cannot wait until the end of the period before applying overhead to jobs.

Discuss the accounting treatment of the difference between actual overhead and overhead allocated to jobs using a predetermined rate. If the amount of overhead applied to inventory does not equal actual overhead, the company must apportion the difference among Work in Process Inventory, Finished Goods Inventory, and Cost of Goods Sold. This adjusts the accounts to reflect actual overhead costs. If the amount of under- or overapplied overhead is immaterial, the company can close it to Cost of Goods Sold.

Discuss changes in the manufacturing environment of U.S. companies and how they affect product costing. U.S. companies are facing stiff competition from foreign manufacturers. In response, many companies have adopted manufacturing systems that minimize inventories of raw materials and work in process. Also, many companies are developing total quality management programs and are becoming highly automated. Generally, highly automated companies should not use labor hours or labor cost as an overhead allocation base because labor is a relatively small part of their product cost.

REVIEW PROBLEM

Andre's Cabinetry Shop, Incorporated, manufactures and installs a wide variety of household cabinets built to customers' design from top quality lumber. The prices of the cabinets vary with the cost of woods selected by the customers and the complexity of the design.

Andre started with an investment of $30,000 in equipment and a building rented four years ago for $3,600 per year. The equipment has an estimated useful life of 24 years with no expected salvage value. 19X2 costs included: utilities, $1,200; maintenance, $600; shop supplies, $1,800; paint and varnish, $800; and insurance and taxes, $2,750. All of these costs are considered to be production costs and are assigned to jobs as overhead.

Job 524 was the only job in process at the end of 19X2. It had been charged with direct materials of $800, direct labor of $1,200, and overhead of $500, using an overhead allocation rate of 25 percent of direct costs (direct material plus direct labor). Costs are not expected to change in 19X3.

Andre works an average of 2,400 hours per year, and is paid at $20 per hour. The major difference in the jobs is the time required to build the designs.

Additional information is as follows:

1. Andre feels that his overhead allocation rate needs to be adjusted as he is not getting a reasonable share of the more expensive jobs he bids on.
2. During January 19X3, Andre completed Job 524, adding direct material costing $600 and 20 labor hours. Two other jobs, numbers 525 and 526, were started and completed. All completed jobs were installed and billed at cost plus 10%. Jobs 527 and 528 were started but not completed. Information related to jobs for January is as follows:

	525	526	527	528
Direct material	$1,100	$750	$900	$600
Direct labor cost	1,000	700	500	600
Direct labor hours	50	35	25	30

REQUIRED:

a. Select an appropriate overhead allocation base and calculate an overhead application rate for use in 19X3.
b. What is the total cost that will appear on the job cost sheets for Jobs 524 through 528 at the end of January 19X3?
c. Prepare summary journal entries to record the issuance of the materials to the jobs, to charge the jobs with the direct labor involved, and to apply the manufacturing overhead using the overhead rate determined above.
d. Prepare T-accounts for Work in Process Inventory, Finished Goods Inventory, and Cost of Goods Sold, including the beginning and ending balances of the accounts.
e. Reconcile Work in Process Inventory and Cost of Goods Sold balances with the totals on the appropriate job cost sheets.

CHAPTER 21 JOB-ORDER COSTING AND CHANGES IN THE MANUFACTURING ENVIRONMENT

SOLUTION:

Planning and Organizing Your Work
1. Costs making up manufacturing overhead are primarily related to labor hours and space utilization. Material cost does not seem to be a causal factor. Labor hours may be a better base.
2. Apply overhead to the jobs completed, including Job 524, and to jobs in process.

(a) *Select an appropriate overhead allocation base.*

Andre's expected overhead in 19X3 is:

Depreciation of equipment ($30,000 ÷ 24)	$ 1,250
Rent	3,600
Utilities	1,200
Maintenance	600
Shop supplies	1,800
Paint and varnish	800
Insurance and property taxes	2,750
Total expected overhead	$12,000

$$\frac{\text{Expected Overhead Cost}}{\text{Expected Direct Labor Hours}} = \frac{\$12,000}{2,400} = \$5.00 \text{ per Direct Labor Hour}$$

Direct labor hours were selected as the appropriate basis for the application of manufacturing overhead to the jobs because the major difference in the jobs was related to the number of labor hours worked. There should be a strong relationship between the total overhead cost incurred and the number of direct labor hours worked.

(b) *Prepare job cost sheets.*

Job 524	
Beg. Bal.	2,500
DM	600
DL	400
OH	100
End. Bal.	3,600

Job 525	
DM	1,100
DL	1,000
OH	250
Bal.	2,350

Job 526	
DM	750
DL	700
OH	175
Bal.	1,625

Job 527	
DM	900
DL	500
OH	125
Bal.	1,525

Job 528	
DM	600
DL	600
OH	150
Bal.	1,350

(c) *Prepare summary journal entries.*

Work in Process Inventory	3,950	
Raw Materials Inventory		3,950
To record material requisitions as follows:		

Job 524	$ 600			
Job 525	1,100			
Job 526	750			
Job 527	900			
Job 528	600			
	$3,950			

Work in Process Inventory 3,200
    Wages and Salaries Payable 3,200
To record labor time tickets as follows:
    Job 524 20 hours @ $20 $ 400
    Job 525 50 hours @ $20   1,000
    Job 526 35 hours @ $20   700
    Job 527 25 hours @ $20   500
    Job 528 30 hours @ $20   600
                                  $3,200

Work in Process Inventory 800
    Manufacturing Overhead 800
To apply overhead to jobs as follows:
    Job 524   20 hours @ $5.00 $ 100
    Job 525   50 hours @ 5.00   250
    Job 526   35 hours @ 5.00   175
    Job 527   25 hours @ 5.00   125
    Job 528   30 hours @ 5.00   150
                                  $ 800

(d) *Prepare T-accounts.*

Work in Process Inventory

Bal.	2,500	Job 524	3,600
Jan. Dir. Mat.	3,950	Job 525	2,350
Dir. Lab.	3,200	Job 526	1,625
Appl. OH	800		
Bal.	2,875		

Finished Goods

Bal.	0	Job 524	3,600
Job 524	3,600	Job 525	2,350
Job 525	2,350	Job 526	1,625
Job 526	1,625		
Bal.	0		

Cost of Goods Sold

Job 524	3,600	
Job 525	2,350	
Job 526	1,625	
Bal.	7,575	

(e) *Reconciliation of account balances and job cost sheets.*

Andre's Cabinetry Shop, Incorporated
Reconciliation of Job Cost Sheets to Work in Process Inventory
January 31, 19X3

Job 527	$1,525
Job 528	1,350
Total Work in Process Inventory	$2,875

Andre's Cabinetry Shop, Incorporated
Reconciliation of Job Cost Sheets to Cost of Goods Sold
January 31, 19X3

Job 524	$3,600
Job 525	2,350
Job 526	1,625
Total cost of goods sold	$7,575

KEY TERMS

activity-based costing (ABC), *874*
allocation base, *874*
computer-controlled manufacturing systems, *880*
cost driver, *874*
cost pools, *874*
flexible manufacturing systems, *881*
full cost, *865*
job, *867*
job cost sheet, *869*
just-in-time (JIT) system, *880*
material requisition form, *869*
predetermined overhead rates, *877*
product costing system, *865*
overapplied overhead, *878*
overhead allocation, *873*
overhead allocation rate, *872*
overhead applied, *872*
time tickets, *870*
total quality management (TQM), *881*
underapplied overhead, *878*

SELF-QUIZ

LO 1 1. Two common types of product costing systems are _____ _____ _____ and _____ _____.

LO 1 2. Product cost information is used for _____ _____ and _____ _____ _____.

LO 1 3. GAAP reporting of inventories in financial statements requires the use of _____ _____.

LO 1 4. The components of a product costing system include which of the following?
a. Documents and ledgers
b. Sales invoices
c. Accounts and accounting procedures
d. a and b only
e. a and c only

LO 1 5. The best example of an entity using a job-order costing system would be:
a. Textile production
b. Concrete block production
c. Petroleum refining
d. Antique automobile restoration
e. None of the above

LO 1 6. Full costing includes which of the following in the determination of product cost?
a. Only variable costs of production
b. Only fixed costs of production
c. Direct fixed and variable costs of production
d. All fixed and variable costs of production
e. None of the above

LO 1 7. Product costs are necessary to report:
a. Production efficiency in the annual report
b. Product cost in inventory on the balance sheet
c. Product cost in cost of goods sold on the income statement
d. a and b only
e. b and c only

LO 1 8. The two most common uses of product cost information are for:
a. Financial reporting and managerial decision making
b. Controlling product quantity and quality
c. Setting management goals and objectives
d. Evaluation of management control skills
e. None of the above

LO 2 9. The costs of all jobs still in process will be found in the _____ _____ _____ account.

LO 2 10. The costs of all jobs completed and not yet sold will be found in the _____ _____ _____ account.

LO 2 11. The costs of all jobs completed and sold this period will be found in the _____ _____ _____ _____ account.

LO 3 12. A _____ _____ _____ _____ is used to accumulate the labor hours worked on each job from the time tickets.

LO 4 13. The overhead application rate is determined from:

a. Estimated overhead costs ÷ estimated activity base
b. Actual overhead costs ÷ estimated activity base
c. Estimated overhead costs ÷ actual activity base
d. Actual overhead costs ÷ actual activity base

LO 4 14. Three common activity bases are _____ _____ _____, _____ _____ _____, and _____ _____.

LO 4 15. A _____ _____ is a major activity used in activity-based costing (ABC) as the basis for assigning costs to a cost pool.

LO 4 16. _____ _____ _____ tends to provide more accurate allocation of costs and better information for decision making.

LO 5 17. Under- or overapplied overhead is theoretically allocated to _____ _____ _____ _____, _____ _____ _____, and _____ _____ _____ _____ unless the amounts are not material in amount.

LO 5 18. When under- or overapplied overhead is not material in amount, it is assigned to _____ _____ _____ _____.

LO 6 19. Total quality management (TQM) involves all of the following except:
a. Listening to customers and their needs
b. Very close supervision of all employees
c. "Get it right the first time" philosophy
d. Encouraging workers' continuous improvement.

SOLUTIONS TO SELF-QUIZ
1. job order costing, process costing   2. financial reporting, managerial decision making   3. full costing   4. e   5. d
6. d   7. e   8. a   9. work in process inventory   10. finished goods inventory   11. cost of goods sold
12. daily labor cost summary   13. a   14. direct labor hours, direct labor cost, machine hours   15. cost driver
16. Activity-based costing   17. Work in Process Inventory, Finished Goods Inventory, and Cost of Goods Sold   18. Cost of Goods Sold   19. b

---

QUESTIONS

Q21-1 Is a product costing system necessary for a manufacturing company? Discuss.

Q21-2 What product costs are properly included in inventory according to Generally Accepted Accounting Principles (GAAP)?

Q21-3 Explain how product cost information is used in external financial reports.

Q21-4 Discuss how product cost information is used by management for internal purposes.

Q21-5 Identify the two most common types of product costing systems and discuss the manufacturing environment conducive to each system.

Q21-6 Identify the form used to withdraw materials from the storeroom for the production of a job and the information normally shown on that form.

Q21-7 What is the purpose of a job cost sheet and what information does it include?

Q21-8 What information is normally shown on a time ticket?

Q21-9 How can a large number of labor time tickets be handled efficiently?

Q21-10 Discuss the relationship between the job cost sheets and the work in process inventory account found in the general ledger.

Q21-11 Explain the rationale for applying overhead using a predetermined application rate instead of applying actual overhead to jobs.

Q21-12 Compare the traceability of costs in a job-order costing system and a process costing system.

Q21-13 Describe the content of the work in process inventory account, the finished goods inventory account, and the cost of goods sold account in a job-order costing system.

Q21-14 Describe the development of an overhead allocation rate.

Q21-15 Identify an important characteristic of a good overhead allocation base. Explain.

Q21-16 Trace the flow of costs through a job-order costing system from inception to the financial statements.

Q21-17 The manufacturing overhead account is debited for actual costs and is credited for the estimated overhead amounts applied to production. It is unlikely that the two amounts will be exactly equal, leaving a balance in the account at the end of the period. What is the difference between these two amounts called and how is it disposed of?

Q21-18 In modern, capital-intensive, production facilities, new approaches to manufacturing systems have reduced the proportion of direct labor cost to total production cost significantly. Discuss the effect this might have on the selection of an allocation base for the application of overhead.

EXERCISES

LO 1

E21-1 Product Costing Systems For the list of product manufacturers below, indicate whether a job-order cost system (*JO*) or a process cost system (*P*) would be most appropriate.
___ a. Drink bottler
___ b. Pharmaceutical firm
___ c. Appliance manufacturer
___ d. Home builder
___ e. Printing shop
___ f. Ship builder

LO 2

E21-2 Cost System Accounts in Job-Order Costing Place a YES beside the general ledger accounts utilized as inventory-related accounts in a job-order cost system and a NO by those which are not.
___ a. Raw Materials Inventory
___ b. Wages and Salaries Payable
___ c. General and Administrative Expenses
___ d. Work in Process Inventory
___ e. Finished Goods Inventory
___ f. Merchandise Inventory
___ g. Cost of Goods Sold
___ h. Manufacturing Overhead

LO 3

E21-3 Direct Materials in Job-Order Costing Five material requisitions were received by the materials storeroom of the Saint Louis Foundry during the first week of 19X4. M.R. 101-C was for direct materials for Job 1501, $750.00. M.R. 102-C was for direct materials issued to Job 1502, $550.00. M.R. 103-C was for indirect materials issued to the factory supervisor $110.00. M.R. 104-C was for direct materials issued to Job 1501, $450.00. M.R. 105-C was for direct materials issued to Job 1503, $600.00.

REQUIRED:

Prepare a summary journal entry to record the issuance of these materials. Calculate the amount of direct materials assigned to each job.

LO 3

E21-4 Direct Labor in Job-Order Costing Wolk Products Company had the following labor time tickets for the month of February 19X3.

Ticket Number	Employee Number	Pay Rate	Hours Worked	Job Number
2101	011	$ 8.00	120	201
2102	008	15.00	80	201
2103	011	8.00	40	202
2104	008	15.00	30	203
2105	008	15.00	50	204

REQUIRED:

a. Summarize the labor time tickets and prepare a journal entry to record the direct labor for the month.
b. Calculate the amount of direct labor assigned to each job.

LO 3,4

E21-5 Overhead Allocation Bases The Muffler Repair Shop expects to incur total overhead of $24,000 during 19X6. They have 5 employees who each work 2,000 hours per year. Two of the employees earn $8 per hour and three earn $7 per hour. The only machines in the shop are three automobile lifts which together are used a total of 1600 hours per year and a gas welder which is used an average of 200 hours per year. Each job is billed for the materials, direct labor, and overhead, plus 20 percent of the total cost.

REQUIRED:

Calculate overhead allocation rates based on direct labor hours, direct labor cost, and automobile lift hours.

LO 2,3,4

E21-6 Job-Order Costing Terminology Match the following cost accounting terms with the definitions shown below.

___ a. Full costing
___ b. Allocation base
___ c. Job cost sheet
___ d. Labor time ticket
___ e. Overhead allocation
___ f. Underapplied overhead
___ g. Overapplied overhead

(1) The systematic assignment of overhead costs to production, through the work in process inventory account, at a predetermined rate.
(2) A written record of time spent on a particular job by an individual worker.
(3) A measure of activity, highly correlated with overhead cost, which is used as the denominator in establishing an overhead allocation rate.
(4) A form used to accumulate the direct and indirect costs of production. It serves as a subsidiary ledger for Work in Process Inventory.
(5) A cost method which includes in product cost both the variable and fixed costs associated with the production process.
(6) A debit balance in Manufacturing Overhead remaining after all overhead applications to Work in Process Inventory have been made.
(7) A credit balance in Manufacturing Overhead remaining after all overhead applications to Work in Process Inventory have been made.

LO 4

E21-7 Manufacturing Overhead in Job-Order Costing Franklin Machine Shop does a variety of automotive machine work for local repair businesses. The machinery used is a major cost factor in overhead and Franklin applies overhead on a machine hour basis. The average job requires less than one day and several jobs are completed each day.

REQUIRED:

Discuss why a predetermined overhead rate might be preferred by Franklin Machine Shop as opposed to applying actual overhead costs. Consider whether the use of two overhead rates, one based on labor hours and one based on machine hours, might provide more accurate costing.

LO 4,5

E21-8 Allocating Manufacturing Overhead to Jobs Crankey Fabricators provided the following data for 19X1:

Expected annual direct labor hours	20,000
Expected annual direct labor cost	$250,000
Expected machine hours	15,000
Expected material cost for the year	$400,000
Expected overhead	$300,000

REQUIRED:

a. Prepare a computation of 19X1 overhead allocation rates using each of the four possible bases shown.
b. Determine the cost the following job (number 253) under each of the four overhead allocation rates.

Direct materials	$2,500
Direct labor (140 hours @ $11.00)	1,540
Machine hours used	100

LO 2,3,4

E21-9 Job Cost Sheets Renko Company is a steel fabricator. Prepare a job cost sheet for Job 300, consisting of the production of 900 welded steel basement supports for Mickey Deeb Construction Company. The overhead is applied on the basis of direct labor hours, using a predetermined overhead rate of $15. The direct costs associated with Job 300 are: direct materials, $3,000; direct labor, 150 hours at $9.50 per hour. Use Illustration 21-4 in the text as an example. The job was started May 4, due May 21, and completed May 14.

LO 4

E21-10 Predetermined Overhead Rates Arra Saunooke has operated a welding shop for a number of years, and the business always has generated ample cash to live on. Most jobs have been small and the charges made have been cash amounts set arbitrarily considering the needs of the customers and their ability to pay. This year, when calculating the year's profits, Arra has determined that net income amounted to only about $4.00 per hour for the hours worked. You have suggested that a job-cost system would allow Arra to better understand his costs and price his work accordingly. Additional information is as follows:

Hours worked totaled 2,100. The utility bills for the shop amounted to $2,800. Welding rods and other supplies cost $4,650. The equipment in the shop cost $25,000 three years ago and has an estimated life of 10 years and no salvage value. The building was built 6 years ago at a cost of $44,000 and has an estimated life of 20 years with no residual value. Both the building and equipment are depreciated on a straight-line basis. Direct materials used last year totaled $26,500.

REQUIRED:

Determine an appropriate overhead rate to be used.

LO 5

E21-11 Under- and Overapplied Manufacturing Overhead Quest Manufacturing uses a job-order costing system. The account balances at the end of the period for the product-cost-related accounts are:

Raw Materials Inventory	$20,000
Work in Process Inventory	40,000
Finished Goods Inventory	60,000
Cost of Goods Sold	80,000
Manufacturing Overhead	9,000 (credit)

REQUIRED:

Prepare the journal entries to close the manufacturing overhead account assuming the overapplied amount is material.

LO 2,3 E21-12 **Tracing Production Inputs to Jobs** Smith's Body Shop does collision damage repair and painting of automobiles and small trucks. Smith's billings reflect a markup of 15% over job cost.

During August 19X7, Smith bid $2,300 for the repair of a severely damaged automobile. He purchased replacement parts from a junkyard for $325 and a front windshield from Hour Glass Co. for $225. He bought the paint and hardener at Taylor's for $135. The job required six hours labor to strip the auto interior, seven hours of cutting and welding, two hours to replace the rear wiring (using the old harness), six hours of sanding and priming, five hours to re-install the interior, one hour to replace the windshield and eight hours to paint, trim and finish the job. Labor is paid at $24 per hour. Overhead is applied at $15 per labor hour. Apex Insurance company was billed directly for the job.

REQUIRED:

Prepare a job cost sheet for the repair job. Use the above information to prepare the journal entries to record the repair job in the accounting records of Smith's Body Shop. Prepare all entries through the recognition of revenue from the job.

PROBLEM SET A

LO 2, 3 P21-1A **Tracing Production Costs to Jobs** Waterford Metal Shop makes a variety of parts for other manufacturers on an order basis. The following job cost sheets reflect the activity for the week ending October 15, 19X3. There was no beginning work in process inventory at the start of the week.

For: Regis Products			**Job** 302
Quantity: 300	**Item:** 713-R		
Number	Direct Material	Direct Labor	Applied Overhead
MR22	$1,200		
L116		$900	
L118		750	
Completed 10/13/X3			$825

For: White Sheetmetal			**Job** 303
Quantity: 1000	**Item:** 880-C		
Number	Direct Material	Direct Labor	Applied Overhead
MR23	$2,800		
L119		$1,800	
Completed 10/15/X3			$900

For: Quinto Primo Co.			**Job** 304
Quantity: 2,500	**Item:** 4992-D		
Number	Direct Material	Direct Labor	Applied Overhead
MR25	$1,450		
L117		$2,200	
MR27	1,220	850	
L120			
Completed 10/15/X3			$1,525

For: Mixweld, Inc.			**Job** 305
Quantity: 4200	**Item:** 1020		
Number	Direct Material	Direct Labor	Applied Overhead
MR26	$960		
L121		$410	$205

For: Brink Brakes			**Job** 306
Quantity: 200	**Item:** 2650		
Number	Direct Material	Direct Labor	Applied Overhead
MR28	$750		
L122		$500	$250

REQUIRED:

a. Reconstruct the journal entries in summary form to record the issuance of direct materials, to record direct labor, and to apply overhead for the week.
b. Prepare the journal entry to record the completion of Jobs 302 – 304.
c. Compute the balance in Work in Process Inventory and reconcile this balance with the job cost sheets.

LO 3,4

P21-2A Calculating Predetermined Overhead Rates Wilkes Manufacturing Company, a maker of furniture frames for furniture manufacturers, is reviewing the application of overhead in its job-order costing system. The expected activity levels for 19X3 are:

Direct material costs	$ 542,000
Direct labor hours	104,000
Direct labor cost	$1,248,000
Machine hours	2,080,000

Overhead expected for 19X3 includes:

Indirect material	$ 68,000
Indirect labor	624,000
Utility expense	48,000
Depreciation of equipment	140,000
Depreciation of factory building	24,000
Payroll taxes	140,000
Property and liability insurance	48,000
Total expected manufacturing overhead	$1,092,000

Most of the indirect labor is related to operating and maintaining machinery.

REQUIRED:

a. Determine the overhead application rate under each of the allocation bases for which you have information.
b. Select the overhead allocation base that you would recommend and justify your selection in one paragraph.

LO 3,4

P21-3A Job Costs Under Different Overhead Rates Highland Innovative Parts Co. manufactures parts to order for antique automobiles. Highland has a complete foundry and metal shop and makes everything from fenders to engine blocks. Each customer order is treated as a separate job. They currently have two jobs, 1523 and 1524, which are complete except for the application of overhead. They want to know what each job's cost would be under three different overhead application rates: (1) direct labor cost, (2) direct labor hours, and (3) machine hours. Projections for 19X3 are as follows:

Direct labor cost $120,000
Direct labor hours   8,000
Machine hours   5,000
Overhead costs $ 86,000

Depreciation on machinery and equipment accounts for 75 percent of the overhead costs.

The job cost sheets show the following:

	Job 1523	Job 1524
Direct material	$ 855	$1,650
Direct labor	$1,020	$1,020
Direct labor hours	85	68
Machine hours	100	200

REQUIRED:

a. Determine the overhead application rate under three suggested allocation bases.
b. Calculate the cost of Job 1523 and Job 1524 using each of the three bases.
c. Discuss which allocation base appears preferable.

LO 5

P21-4A   Under- or Overapplied Overhead   Atrium Door and Window Company produces metal doors and windows to order for architects. At the end of their accounting period, March 31, 19X3, their account balances reflected the following:

Raw Materials Inventory, 3/31/X3	$ 84,000
Work in Process Inventory, 3/31/X3	42,000
Finished Goods Inventory, 3/31/X3	84,000
Cost of Goods Sold (March)	290,000
Manufacturing Overhead	24,000 (credit)

REQUIRED:

a. Determine the adjusted balances of the above accounts if the balance of Manufacturing Overhead is considered material in amount.
b. Determine the adjusted balances of the above accounts if the balance of Manufacturing Overhead is considered immaterial in amount.

LO 2,3,4,5

P21-5A   Inventory Accounts and Cost of Goods Sold under Job-Order Costing   The following T-accounts represent transactions of the Seagrave Equipment Company, builders of large industrial machinery. During the month of October 19X8, Job 101 was completed and transferred to finished goods, Jobs 102 and 103 were started, completed, and transferred to finished goods, and Job 104 was started but incomplete by the end of the month.

Raw Materials Inventory				Work in Process Inventory		
Bal.	21,000		79,000	Bal.	32,000	232,000
	88,000		11,000		79,000	
					96,000	
					48,000	

Accounts Payable				Finished Goods Inventory		
			88,000	Bal.	38,500	105,500
					232,000	

Manufacturing Overhead				Cost of Goods Sold		
	11,000		48,000		105,500	
	28,000					
	4,000					
	2,500					

CHAPTER 21 JOB-ORDER COSTING AND CHANGES IN THE MANUFACTURING ENVIRONMENT

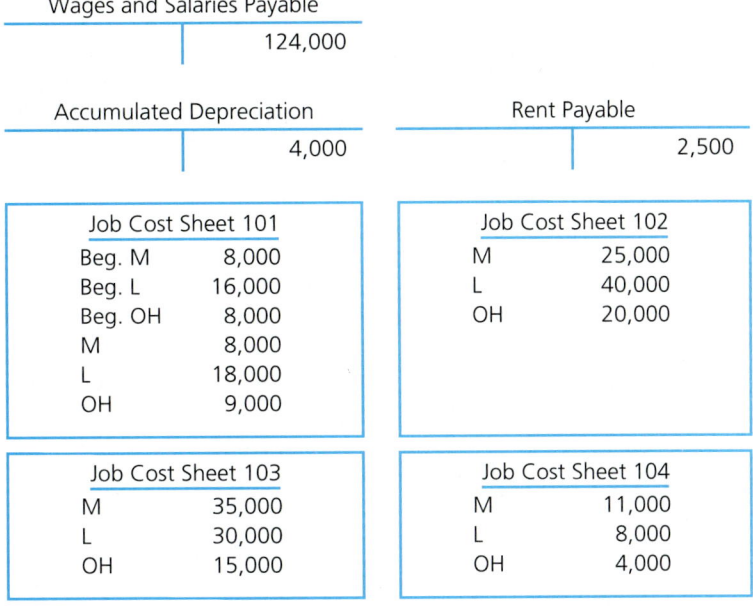

REQUIRED:

a. Prepare the journal entries, with explanations for the information shown in the T-accounts.
b. Determine the probable base used for the application of manufacturing overhead.
c. Given that the amount of the estimated overhead for the year was $552,000, calculate the activity level estimated for the allocation base.

LO 2,3,5   **P21-6A**   **Comprehensive Job-Order Costing Problem**   Candy Cane Confectioners produce special orders of sugar candies and chocolates for several large airlines. During November 19X9, they purchased on credit 1,800 pounds of confectioners sugar @ $90 per cwt, (hundred weight), 2,000 pounds of granulated sugar @ $70 per cwt, 800 pounds of chocolate @ $300 per cwt, and 200 pounds of caramel @ $120 per cwt from Atlanta Confectionery Supply. In addition, they purchased for cash 60 dozen eggs @ $.70 per dozen and 80 pounds of paraffin @ $.60 per pound from PMG Food Supply. The beginning balances in the job-order costing accounts were:

Raw Materials Inventory	$2,400
Work in Process Inventory	6,400
Finished Goods Inventory	8,600

The ending balances in the job-order costing accounts were:

Raw Materials Inventory	$3,200
Work in Process Inventory	4,800
Finished Goods Inventory	5,400

Direct labor cost $3,600 for 450 hours, indirect labor cost $1,800, utilities were billed at $340, rent paid was $600, and other overhead costs paid in cash totaled $4,800. Manufacturing overhead is applied at $15 per direct labor hour. Sales during the period were $25,682 and selling and administrative expenses were $8,000. Assume both were cash transactions.

REQUIRED:

a. Journalize the month's activity.
b. Post the entries in T-accounts.
c. Prepare an income statement for the month of November 19X9.

PROBLEM SET B

LO 1,2,3

P21-1B Job-Order Costing Inventory Accounts and Cost of Goods Sold Emoric Die Company manufactures cutting dies for the shoe industry in St. Louis. Each set of dies is specifically designed to the customers' templates. During the first week in May 19X3, six orders were received from customers. They were assigned job numbers 1406-1411. The following transactions occurred during the first week of May.

May 3 Received shipment of steel from Granite City Steel, fob destination, $4,800, 2/10, net/30.
   3 Received and paid for factory supplies from Millard supply, $2,100.
   3 Issued materials into production per materials requisitions as follows:

Job No.	Direct Materials	Indirect Materials	Factory Supplies
1406	$ 560		
1407	730		
1408	1,480		
1409	540		
1410	370		
1411	285		
Totals	$3,965	$799	$350

May 7 The labor time ticket summary reflected the following costs for the week:

Job No.	Direct Labor	Indirect Labor	Supervision
1406	$1,420		
1407	1,840		
1408	3,220		
1409	1,200		
1410	720		
1411	560		
Totals	$8,960	$6,400	$1,400

May 7 Overhead was applied to all jobs in process at 180 percent of direct labor cost.
   7 Jobs 1406, 1407, 1408, and 1409 were completed and transferred to finished goods, Jobs 1410 and 1411 were still in process at the end of the week.
   7 Jobs 1406, 1407, 1408, and 1409 were shipped to the customers and billed at 150 percent of total job cost.

REQUIRED:

a. Prepare the journal entries to record the above transactions.
b. Post the transactions to T-accounts.

LO 3,4

P21-2B Calculating Predetermined Overhead Rates Martin Machine Works manufactures automobile accessories. Management is studying its costing system to determine if their current overhead application procedure is appropriate for their products. Martin estimates the following for 19X9:

Direct material cost	$ 800,000
Direct labor cost	200,000
Manufacturing overhead	400,000
Total production cost	$1,400,000

The details of manufacturing overhead are as follows:

Indirect material	$ 50,000
Indirect labor	300,000
Depreciation of equipment	40,000
Other costs	10,000
Total manufacturing overhead	$400,000

Most of the indirect labor is related to ordering and moving material.

REQUIRED:

a. Determine the overhead application rate under each of the allocation bases for which you have information.
b. Select the overhead application base that you would recommend and justify your selection in one paragraph.

LO 3,4 **P21-3B** **Different Overhead Application Rates for Job-Order Costing**

1. Millikan Company has expected manufacturing overhead consisting of:

Indirect material	$ 25,000
Indirect labor	40,000
Depreciation of machinery	100,000
Depreciation of building	20,000
Repair and maintenance on machinery	125,000
Utilities and taxes	35,000

They expect to use 15,000 direct labor hours at a cost of $330,000 and 10,000 machine hours during the year.

2. Acme Shoe Company has expected overhead costs of $1,200,000. The majority of the overhead costs are incurred providing production support to the direct labor force. The direct labor rates vary from $10 to $20 per hour for employees depending on the complexity of their task. Acme projects direct labor costs of $1,000,000 and 60,000 direct labor hours. The more complex tasks require proportionally more support than do the less complex tasks.

3. Moultre Metal Works fabricates steel on order. There exists a strong relationship between the weight of the materials handled and the overhead support required. Moultre expects production to require 280 tons of materials costing $280,000 in 19X3. They expect to incur $60,000 of direct labor costs, 6,000 direct labor hours, and overhead of $120,000.

REQUIRED:

a. Determine appropriate overhead allocation bases for each of the independent cases above.
b. Justify the selection of each allocation base.
c. Calculate the overhead application rate in each case.

LO 5 **P21-4B** **Under- or Overapplied Overhead** Ranger Custom Boots had total revenue of $120,000 for 19X3 with cost of goods sold of $50,000, administrative expenses of $24,000, and selling expenses of $12,000, before allocating a debit balance in the manufacturing overhead account of $22,000. The account balances are:

Raw Materials Inventory	$24,000
Work in Process Inventory	60,000
Finished Goods Inventory	30,000

REQUIRED:

a. Calculate net income treating the difference in the manufacturing overhead account as immaterial.

b. Calculate net income treating the difference in the manufacturing overhead account as material.
c. Discuss the significance of the alternative treatments.

LO 2,3,4,5

P21-5B **Job-Order Costing Systems** The following T-accounts represent one week of transactions in a typical large job shop.

Raw Materials Inventory			Insurance Payable	
Bal. 25,000	15,000			100
	5,000			

Work in Process Inventory			Finished Goods Inventory	
Bal. 15,000	55,000	Bal. 55,000	45,000
25,000				
25,000				

Manufacturing Overhead			Accumulated Depreciation	
5,000	25,000			14,000
10,000				
14,000				
900				
100				

Utilities Payable			Accounts Payable	
	900			25,000

Cost of Goods Sold			Wages and Salaries Payable	
45,000				35,000

REQUIRED:

a. Identify each of the several transactions from the ledger accounts and prepare a journal entry with an explanation for each. There were no beginning balances in the inventories.
b. Prepare the journal entry to close the under- or overapplied manufacturing overhead if:
   1. The difference is not deemed material.
   2. The difference is deemed material.

LO 2,3,4,5,6

P21-6B **Accounting for a Job-Order Cost System** Ellie Ford and Marti Wilson have both retired after 30 years in the food industry. Having been active for so many years, they found retirement boring and began catering wedding receptions on a limited basis. The primary costs involved in setting up in business included the purchase of appropriate linens, $1,000; two complete silver services (high quality silver plate), $800; glass plates and cups, $1,200; and cake decorating tools and accessories, $400. It is expected that all of the above equipment will last 10 years with no salvage value. They do all of the food preparation in their apartment and found that in an average month the utility bill is $100 higher than when they did not cater. All baking and cooking supplies are treated as direct materials and the only other cost incurred is liability insurance at $1,200 per year. All direct materials are purchased at a local grocery for cash, and they pay themselves an hourly wage of $25 per hour.

During the month of June, they catered 5 weddings.

CHAPTER 21 JOB-ORDER COSTING AND CHANGES IN THE MANUFACTURING ENVIRONMENT   **899**

	Direct Materials	Labor Hours
Boroski wedding	$ 350	20
Miller wedding	700	35
Walker wedding	425	18
Redfern wedding	1,500	80
Litchford wedding	550	28

The overhead allocation base is labor hours based on an estimated 1,000 hours per year, and the billings are at 120 percent of job cost. Overhead allocations and markups are rounded to the nearest dollar.

REQUIRED:

a. Journalize the month's activities.
b. Post the entries in T-accounts for Work In Process and Cost of Goods Sold.
c. Prepare the job cost sheets for each of the five June catering jobs.
d. Prepare a partial income statement (just through gross margin) for the month of June.

CRITICAL THINKING AND COMMUNICATING

C21-1 Two companies, A and B, manufacture identical products and use job-order costing systems. The materials handled by A and B are extremely heavy. While A uses a considerable amount of labor to move and process materials, B has recently automated. Thus, B has substituted a considerable amount of machinery for most of the direct labor that they formerly employed. The following information relates to the two companies:

Items Listed in Manufacturing Overhead	(A)	(B)
Indirect materials	$ 22,800	$ 22,000
Indirect labor	56,100	39,000
Depreciation on plant & equipment	22,200	122,800
Material handling costs	123,500	2,200
Supervision	18,000	9,000
Factory insurance	4,800	20,000
Factory property taxes	9,600	38,000
Payroll taxes	25,000	16,000
Utility expense	18,000	31,000
Total overhead costs	$300,000	$300,000
Direct material cost	$200,000	$200,000
Direct labor cost	$160,000	$ 80,000
Direct labor hours	16,000	8,000
Machine hours	10,000	20,000

REQUIRED:

Decide on an appropriate overhead application rate for each of the two companies and prepare a memo justifying the rate selected.

C21-2 Wall Well Drillers have been drilling domestic water supply wells for three years. Ed and Denise Wall, the owners, have accounted for all revenues and expenses properly from a tax standpoint but have simply closed the books once each year to determine profitability. They have priced their drilling based on $8.00 per foot, which is a rate they heard was prevalent in several nearby communities. Due to the mountainous terrain in their county they have found that some wells take much longer to drill than others and feel that there has to be a better way to price their work than simply by the foot. They ask you what could be done to better determine the cost of wells drilled in different areas of the county so they could price more appropriately and earn a fair return on each well drilled. You suggest that a job-order costing system would collect the type of information they need. Denise explains that she and Ed have to meet with two potential customers and ask if you can prepare a written explanation of how they could collect the cost information by job and mail your report to them. You agree.

REQUIRED:

Write the letter and explain job-order costing to Ed and Denise Wall in terms of their well drilling operation.

CHAPTER 22

Process Costing

Stacy Brannen was just finishing a plant tour at Kent Chemical Company's Midwest plant. Only two weeks ago, she had graduated from State University in mechanical engineering. Now, she was nearing the end of her first day on the job at Kent. The assistant plant manager, Bill Merton, conducted the tour and pointed out the steps involved in processing paints, stains, and wood preservatives. While the tour concentrated on the equipment used in the production processes, Stacy found herself wondering how the cost of products was determined. "Bill, can you give me a rough idea of how you calculate product costs?" she asked. "I noticed, for example, that to end up with a gallon of wood preservative ready to ship, both mixing and packaging operations must be performed. With labor, material, and overhead added in these separate operations, is tracing costs to wood preservative a difficult job?"

"Well," Bill replied, "let's see if we can catch Walter Hunt before he goes home for the night. He's the plant controller, and no one can do a better job than Walt of explaining how product costing is done at Kent Chemical."

Kent Chemical Company uses a process costing system. Companies that produce large numbers of homogeneous items—such as paints, plastics, cereals, cosmetics, and metals—in a continuous production process commonly use process costing. Thus, well-known companies like DuPont, the Quaker Oats Company, and the Ralston Purina Company use process costing. In this chapter, we introduce you to the essential elements of a process costing system.

> **LEARNING OBJECTIVES**
>
> 1. Describe product flows through departments and record cost flows in accounts.
> 2. Discuss the concept of equivalent units.
> 3. Calculate the cost per equivalent unit.
> 4. Calculate the cost of goods completed and the ending work in process balance in a processing department.
> 5. Describe a production cost report.

DIFFERENCE BETWEEN JOB-ORDER AND PROCESS COSTING SYSTEMS

Manufacturing firms use one of two primary systems to calculate the cost of inventory: a job-order system or a process costing system. In a job-order system, each unique product or batch is a "job" for which the company needs cost information. Therefore, manufacturing costs are traced to specific jobs. When jobs are completed, the firm removes the cost of the jobs from Work in Process Inventory and debits it to Finished Goods Inventory. When it sells the completed jobs, the firm removes the cost of the jobs from Finished Goods Inventory and debits it to Cost of Goods Sold.

Process costing, on the other hand, is essentially a system of averaging. Dividing production costs by the total number of homogeneous items produced results in an average unit cost. When items are completed, multiplying the number of units completed by the average unit cost determines the cost the firm removes from Work in Process Inventory and debits to Finished Goods Inventory. When items are sold, multiplying the number of units sold by the average unit cost determines the cost the firm removes from Finished Goods Inventory and debits to Cost of Goods Sold. Illustration 22-1 compares job-order and process costing systems.

PRODUCT AND COST FLOWS

LO 1
Describe product flows through departments and record cost flows in accounts.

Just as a product passes through several departments before it is completed, costs flow through several accounts before the firm can record the cost of the product in Finished Goods Inventory.

Product Flows Through Departments

In the typical production operation of process costing companies, the product must pass through two or more departments. The Kent Chemical Company, for example, manufactures wood preservative in two departments: Mixing and Packaging. After the mixing department blends chemical materials, it transfers the liquid preservative to the packaging department where it is placed in metal containers of various sizes.

Materials, labor, and overhead are added at different stages in each processing department. Generally, identifying the stage when materials enter the pro-

ILLUSTRATION 22-1 Comparison of Job-Order and Process Costing Systems

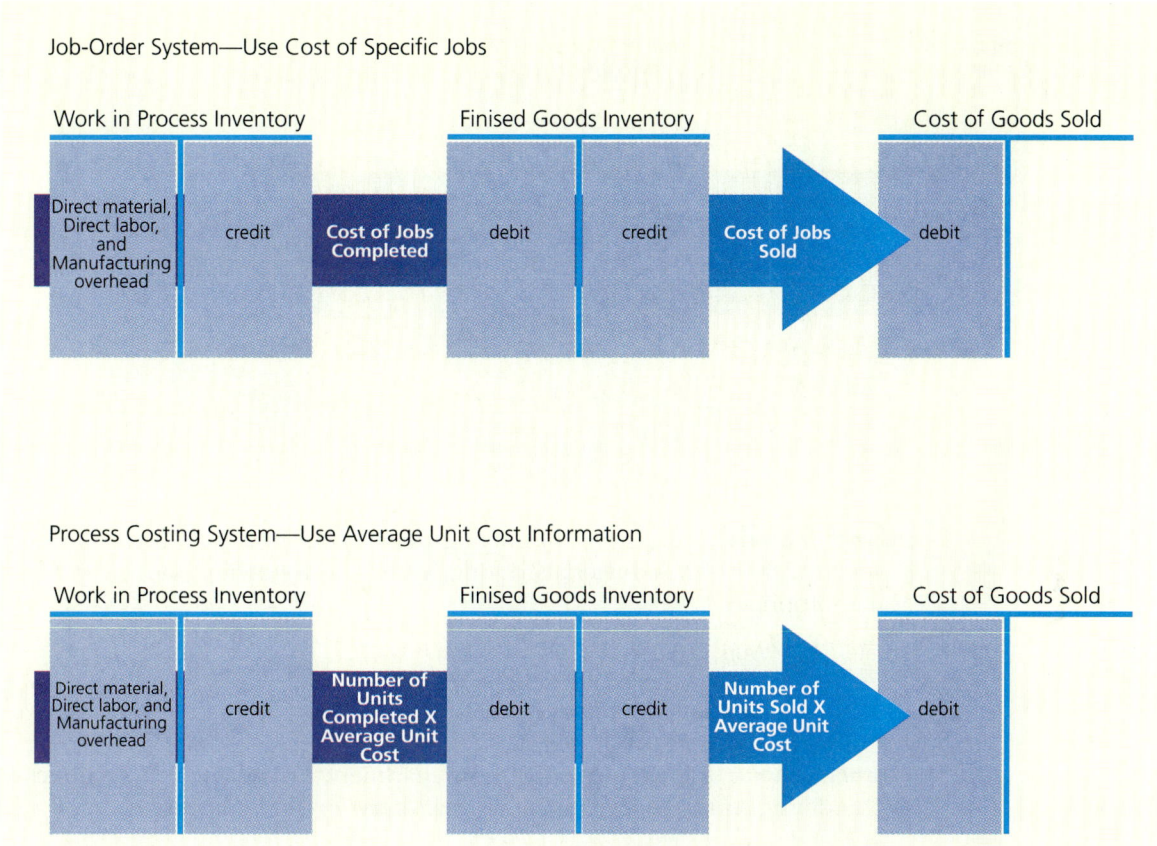

duction process is easy. The mixing department adds chemical materials at the start of the process. Determining exactly when labor and overhead are added to the process is more difficult. Labor and overhead are often grouped together and are referred to as **conversion costs**. Conversion costs are often assumed to be added evenly throughout the process. Illustration 22-2 shows how items flow through the two processing departments and how costs are incurred. As indicated, materials enter both processing departments at the start. However, conversion costs (labor and overhead) are assumed to enter each of the processes evenly.

Cost Flows Through Accounts

The product costs accumulated in a process costing system are essentially the same costs considered in job-order costing: direct material, direct labor, and manufacturing overhead. Additionally, a processing department may have a cost called **transferred-in cost**. This is the cost a prior processing department incurs and transfers to the next processing department. Each processing department accumulates product costs in a separate departmental work in process inventory account. The sum of the departmental work in process inventory accounts is the amount in Work in Process Inventory for the whole company. The following journal entries record product costs in a process costing system and illustrate the flow of costs between processing departments.

ILLUSTRATION 22-2 Flow of Items Through Processing Departments

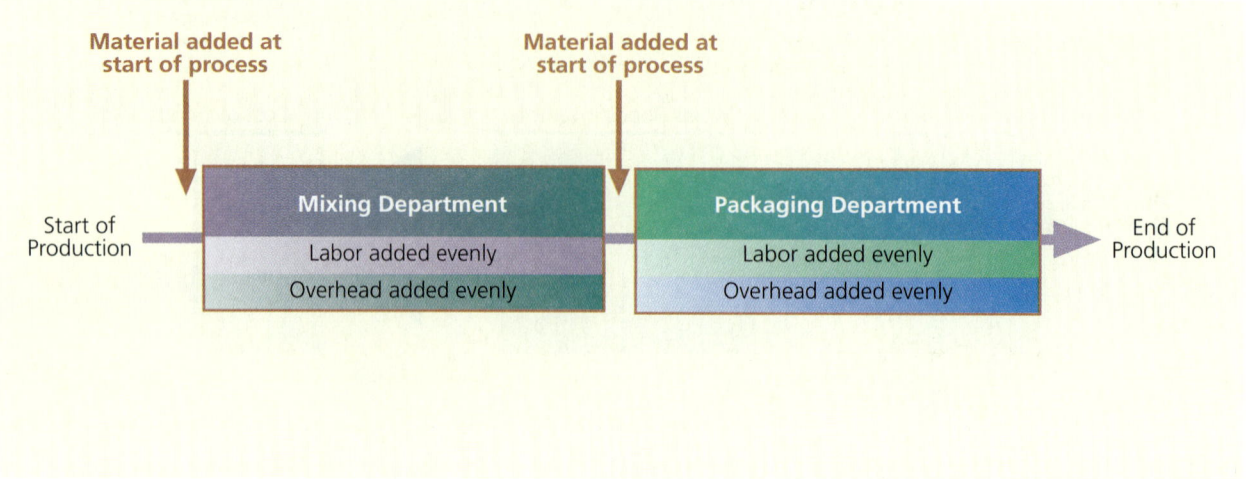

Direct Material. Suppose the mixing department of Kent Chemical Company uses $142,000 of raw materials during April. The following journal entry would be appropriate:

(Date)	Work in Process Inventory, Mixing	142,000	
	Raw Materials Inventory		142,000
	To record use of raw material.		

Direct Labor. Suppose the mixing department incurs $62,200 of direct labor costs during April. The following journal entry would be appropriate:

(Date)	Work in Process Inventory, Mixing	62,200	
	Wages and Salaries Payable		62,200
	To record direct labor cost.		

Manufacturing Overhead. To assign overhead to products in a process costing system, a company may use either actual overhead costs or a predetermined overhead rate. Unless the amount of overhead cost and the level of production are fairly constant from month to month, using actual overhead costs results in substantial fluctuations in the unit cost of goods produced. For this reason, most companies use a predetermined overhead rate. Suppose that at the start of the year, the mixing department estimates it will incur $2,160,000 of overhead cost and $720,000 of direct labor cost. Using direct labor as an allocation base, the department calculates a predetermined overhead rate of $3 for each dollar of direct labor cost. Assuming the department incurs $62,200 of direct labor cost in the month of April, it would assign $186,600 of overhead to Work in Process Inventory that month.

(Date)	Work in Process Inventory, Mixing	186,600	
	Manufacturing Overhead		186,600
	To record manufacturing overhead applied to Work in Process Inventory.		

Transferred-in Cost. When one processing department completes its work, it transfers the items to the next department along with the related cost (referred to as *transferred-in cost*.) Suppose that during April, the mixing department

INSIGHTS INTO ACCOUNTING

HYBRID COSTING SYSTEMS

In many cases, product costing systems combine aspects of both process and job-order costing. Such a hybrid system is used by Kunde Estate Winery, a small wine producer in California's Sonoma Valley. At Kunde Estate Winery, costs are accumulated by various production processes as in a process costing system. The processes include crushing, fermenting, tank aging, barrel aging, and bottling. However, each lot of wine in a given vintage may be processed somewhat differently, requiring each lot to be treated as a separate job as in a job-order costing system.

Source: John Y. Lee and Brian Gray, "Kunde Estate Winery: A Case Study in Cost Accounting," CMA Magazine, Vol. 67, Issue 3 (April 1993): 15–19.

completes units with a cost of $360,000. It transfers the completed units to the packaging department and the related cost becomes a transferred-in cost to Packaging. The journal entry to record the transfer is:

(Date)	Work in Process Inventory, Packaging	360,000	
	Work in Process Inventory, Mixing		360,000
	To record transfer of units from Mixing to Packaging.		

The flow of costs between the departmental work in process inventory accounts is presented in Illustration 22-3.

ILLUSTRATION 22-3 Flow of Costs Between Processing Departments

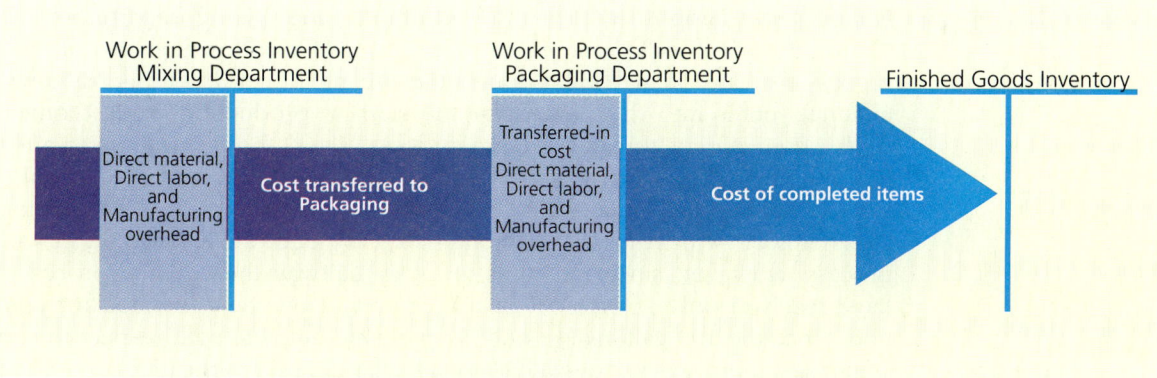

CALCULATING UNIT COST

We have said that process costing is essentially a system of averaging. This section shows how to calculate an average unit cost in a process costing system.[1] First, however, we must explain an essential concept in process costing—the concept of equivalent units.

---

[1] The approach we take is the so-called weighted-average method. Other approaches such as the FIFO method are possible but are not covered here.

LO 2
Discuss the concept of equivalent units.

Equivalent Units

In a process costing system, the number of partially completed units in work in process are expressed in terms of an equivalent number of whole units. When the units are converted to a comparable number of completed units, they are referred to as **equivalent units**. In Illustration 22-4, if 100 units in work in process are 50 percent completed, then they are equivalent to 50 completed units (100 x 50%).

ILLUSTRATION 22-4 How Equivalent Units Are Calculated

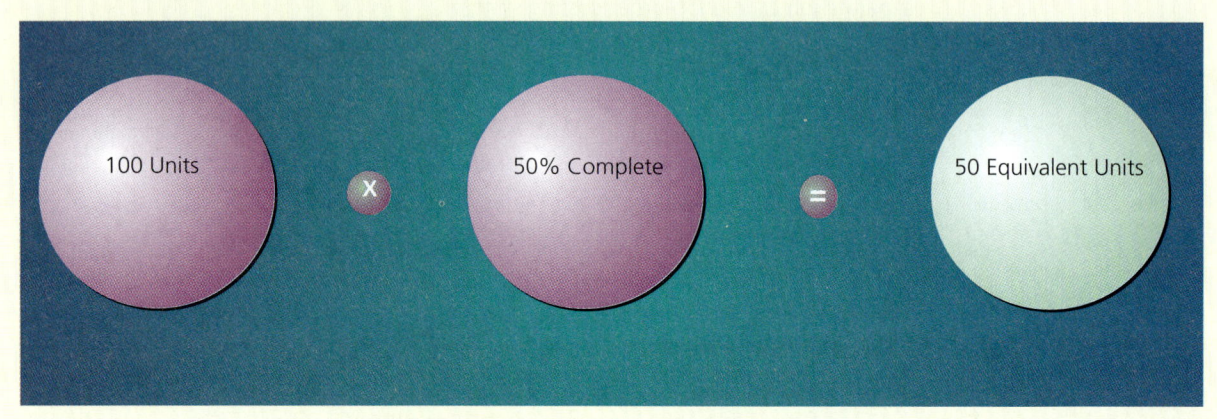

The number of equivalent units in work in process may be different for material and conversion costs as shown in Illustration 22-5. The reason is that material and conversion costs enter the production process at different times. For example, suppose that at the end of July, the mixing department at Kent Chemical has 100 gallons (units of production) of wood preservative in work in process that are 50 percent through the mixing process. Further, assume that materials enter into the process at the start of production, while conversion costs enter evenly throughout the process. Even though the units are only halfway through the process, they have received 100 percent of material since material was added immediately at the start of the process. (See Illustration 22-2.) Therefore, with respect to material cost, 100 equivalent units are in work in process. However, since the units are only halfway through the process, they have received only 50 percent of the labor and overhead needed for completion. Since the 100 gallons are only 50 percent complete with respect to conversion costs, there are 50 equivalent units for labor and overhead.

LO 3
Calculate the cost per equivalent unit.

Cost per Equivalent Unit

The unit cost in a process costing system is often referred to as a **cost per equivalent unit**. The formula for the unit cost calculation is:

$$\text{Cost per Equivalent Unit} = \frac{\text{Cost in Beginning WIP} + \text{Cost Incurred in Current Period}}{\text{Units Completed} + \text{Equivalent Units in Ending WIP}}$$

The numerator contains the cost in beginning work in process plus the cost incurred in the current period. This is the total cost that a processing department is responsible for each period. The total cost is divided by the units com-

ILLUSTRATION 22-5 Differences in Equivalent Units for Material and Conversion Costs (Assuming Material Added at Start of Process)

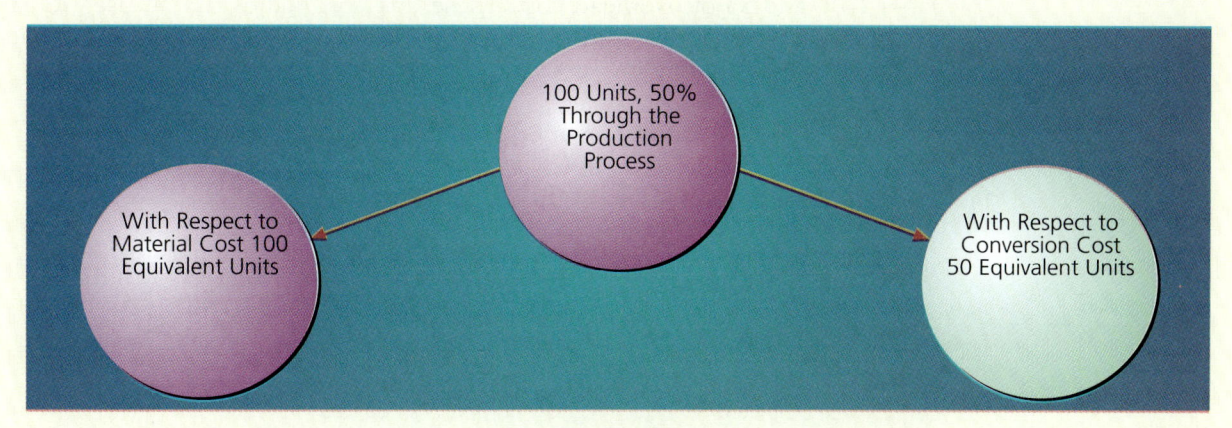

pleted plus the equivalent units in ending work in process. Thus, a cost per equivalent unit amount spreads the cost at the start of the period and the cost incurred during the period over the units in process at the end of the period and the units completed.

LO 4
Calculate the cost of goods completed and the ending work in process balance in a processing department.

CALCULATING AND APPLYING COST PER EQUIVALENT UNIT: MIXING DEPARTMENT EXAMPLE

The cost per equivalent unit calculations for the mixing department of Kent Chemical Company follow. At the start of April, the mixing department has on hand beginning work in process inventory consisting of 10,000 gallons of wood preservative that are 80 percent complete. During the month, 70,000 gallons are started, 60,000 are completed, and 20,000 are on hand at the end of April that are 50 percent complete with respect to conversion costs. The cost in beginning work in process consists of $18,000 of material cost, $7,800 of labor cost, and $23,400 of overhead cost. During April, the mixing department incurs $142,000 of material cost and $62,200 of labor cost. Since the mixing department's predetermined overhead rate is $3 for each dollar of labor cost, it applies $186,600 of overhead to production during the month.

The cost per equivalent unit calculations for the mixing department are presented in Illustration 22-6. The cost of material includes the $18,000 in beginning work in process and the $142,000 of material cost incurred during April. The total of $160,000 is divided by the sum of the number of units completed (60,000 gallons) and the equivalent units in ending work in process (20,000 gallons). Dividing total cost by the total number of units yields a cost per equivalent unit for materials of $2.

Note that there are 20,000 units on hand at the end of April that are only 50 percent through the mixing process. However, since material enters at the start of the mixing process, the 20,000 units are 100% complete with respect to material cost. Thus, there are 20,000 equivalent units in ending work in process for materials. However, for both labor and overhead, the 20,000 units on hand are only 50 percent complete, so they correspond to only 10,000 equivalent units. The total cost per equivalent unit is $6, consisting of $2 of material cost, $1 of labor cost, and $3 of overhead cost. These unit cost figures can be used to calculate the cost of goods completed and transferred out of the mixing department and the cost of ending work in process.

ILLUSTRATION 22-6 Calculation of Cost per Equivalent Unit—Mixing Department

	Material	Labor	Overhead	Total
Cost:				
Beginning WIP	$ 18,000	$ 7,800	$ 23,400	$ 49,200
Cost incurred during April	142,000	62,200	186,600	390,800
Total (a)	$160,000	$70,000	$210,000	$440,000
Units:				
Units completed	60,000	60,000	60,000	
Equivalent units, ending WIP	20,000	10,000	10,000	
Total (b)	80,000	70,000	70,000	
Cost per equivalent unit (a ÷ b)	$2 +	$1 +	$3 =	$6

Cost Transferred Out

The mixing department completed 60,000 gallons during April and transferred them to the packaging department. The unit cost is $6. Therefore, $360,000 of cost is related to the units completed and transferred. The journal entry at the end of April to record the transfer was presented earlier, but we repeat it here:

(Date)	Work in Process Inventory, Packaging	360,000	
	Work in Process Inventory, Mixing		360,000
	To record transfer of units from Mixing to Packaging.		

Ending Work in Process

The Mixing Department's ending balance in Work in Process Inventory is $80,000. This balance is made up of 20,000 equivalent units for material at $2 per equivalent unit, 10,000 equivalent units for labor at $1, and 10,000 equivalent units for overhead at $3.

Ending Balance in Work in Process Inventory, Mixing	
Material (20,000 equiv. units at $2)	$40,000
Labor (10,000 equiv. units at $1)	10,000
Overhead (10,000 equiv. units at $3)	30,000
Total	$80,000

The T-account for Work in Process Inventory summarizes the cost activity for the mixing department, resulting in the $80,000 ending balance.

	Work in Process Inventory, Mixing			
	Beginning balance	49,200		
Costs added → Material		142,000	Cost transferred out	360,000
Labor		62,200		
Overhead		186,600		
	Ending balance	80,000		

LO 5
Describe a production cost report.

PRODUCTION COST REPORT

A **production cost report**, an end-of-the-month report for a process costing system, provides reconciliations of units and costs as well as the details of the cost per equivalent unit calculations. A production cost report for the mixing department of Kent Chemical Company is provided in Illustration 22-7. The unit cost calculations in the production report are identical to the ones just presented. We will concentrate now on the reconciliations of units and costs.

Reconciliation of Units

Assuming no units are lost (due to evaporation, damage, or theft), the number of units in beginning work in process inventory plus the number of units started during the period should be equal to the number of units completed plus the number of units in work in process at the end of the period. For the mixing department, 10,000 units were in beginning inventory, and 70,000 units were started during the period. This means that 80,000 units must be accounted for. Since 60,000 units were completed and 20,000 units are in work in process at the end of the period, all of the units are accounted for.

Reconciliation of Costs

For each period, the total cost that must be accounted for is the sum of the costs in beginning Work in Process Inventory and the costs incurred during the period. In the mixing department, this amounts to $440,000. The cost must be either transferred out with the completed units or remain in ending work in process inventory. The amount transferred out is $360,000, and the amount in ending work in process inventory is $80,000. Since they sum to $440,000, the total amount of cost is accounted for.

BASIC STEPS IN PROCESS COSTING

Unless process cost problems are approached in a systematic way, it is easy to get lost in the calculations. Here is a summary of the basic steps we have presented above. As you can see, each of the steps is performed when the production cost report is prepared.

Step 1 Account for the number of physical units. The number of units at the start of the period plus the number of units started during the period should equal the number of units completed plus the number of units in ending work in process.

ILLUSTRATION 22-7 Production Cost Report, Mixing Department

Production Cost Report
Mixing Department
April 19X1

Step 1

Quantity Reconciliation:

Units in beg. WIP (100% material, 80% conversion costs)	10,000
Units started during April	70,000
Units to account for	80,000
Units completed and transferred to Packaging	60,000
Units in ending WIP (100% material, 50% conversion costs)	20,000
Units accounted for	80,000

Step 2

Cost Per Equivalent Unit Calculation:

	Material	Labor	Overhead	Total
Cost:				
Beginning WIP	$ 18,000	$ 7,800	$ 23,400	$ 49,200
Costs incurred during April	142,000	62,200	186,600	390,800
Total	$160,000	$70,000	$210,000	$440,000
Units:				
Units completed	60,000	60,000	60,000	
Equivalent units, ending WIP	20,000	10,000	10,000	
Total	80,000	70,000	70,000	
Cost per equivalent unit	$2 +	$1 +	$3 =	$6

Step 4

Cost Reconciliation:

Total cost to account for	$440,000

Step 3

Cost of completed units transferred to Packaging (60,000 × $6)		$360,000
Cost of ending WIP:		
Material (20,000 equivalent units × $2)	$40,000	
Labor (10,000 equivalent units × $1)	10,000	
Overhead (10,000 equivalent units × $3)	30,000	80,000
Total cost accounted for		$440,000

Step 2 Calculate the cost per equivalent unit for material, labor, and overhead. Remember that cost (numerator in the calculation) includes both beginning costs and costs incurred during the period. The number of equivalent units (denominator in the calculation) includes both the number of units completed and the number of equivalent units in ending work in process.

Step 3 Assign cost to items completed and items in ending work in process. The cost of items completed is simply the product of the total cost per equivalent unit and the number of units completed. The cost of items in work in process is the sum of the products of equivalent units in process and cost per equivalent unit for material, labor, and overhead.

Step 4 Account for the amount of product cost. The cost of beginning inventory plus the costs incurred during the period should equal the amount of cost assigned to completed items plus the amount of cost assigned to items in ending work in process.

ANSWERING STACY'S QUESTION

Recall that in the scenario at the start of the chapter, Stacy Brannen asked how Kent Chemical Company calculates the cost of products such as wood preservative. At this point, you should be able to answer a similar question. Essentially, material, labor, and overhead costs are accumulated in each processing department. In each department, the cost per equivalent unit is calculated for material, labor, and overhead (Step 2). Then, the costs per equivalent unit are used to determine the cost of items completed and the cost of ending work in process (Step 3).

TRANSFERRED-IN COST

As noted earlier, companies using process costing systems generally use several processes to produce their product. When one processing department completes items, it transfers the cost of the completed units to the next processing department. This procedure is repeated until the units are completed in the last process. At that point, the firm transfers the cost of the items to Finished Goods Inventory. The method of dealing with cost transfers is presented in the following example of the packaging department of Kent Chemical Company. To calculate product costs in the packaging department, we will use the same procedures already used to calculate product costs in the mixing department. Thereby, you are provided with another opportunity to enhance your understanding of the procedures.

TRANSFERRED-IN COST: PACKAGING DEPARTMENT EXAMPLE

In working through the packaging department example, examine the information provided in the production cost report for the packaging department (Illustration 22-8). At the start of April, the packaging department has 15,000 gallons that are 50 percent through the packaging operation. During the month of April, the department receives 60,000 gallons from the mixing department. There are now 75,000 gallons to account for. At the end of April, 5,000 gallons are 40 percent complete, and 70,000 gallons are completed and transferred to finished goods, which accounts for the total of 75,000 gallons. Reconciling the physical number of units is the first of the four steps in solving a process costing problem and is shown in the Quantity Reconciliation section of the production cost report (Illustration 22-8).

The second step is to calculate the cost per equivalent unit. The beginning balance in work in process includes $10,500 of material cost, $4,500 of labor, $9,000 of overhead, and $92,250 of cost transferred-in from the mixing department. In addition, the packaging department incurred $49,500 of material cost, $27,900 of labor cost, $55,800 of overhead, and $360,000 of cost transferred-in from the mixing department during the month of April. The costs are divided by the number of completed units plus the equivalent units in ending work in

ILLUSTRATION 22-8 Production Cost Report, Packaging Department

Production Cost Report
Packaging Department
April 19X1

Quantity Reconciliation:

Units in beg. WIP (100% material, 50% conversion costs)	15,000
Units received from Mixing during April	60,000
Units to account for	75,000
Units completed and transferred to Finished Goods	70,000
Units in ending WIP (100% material, 40% conversion costs)	5,000
Units accounted for	75,000

Cost Per Equivalent Unit Calculation:

	Material	Labor	Overhead	Trans.-in	Total
Cost:					
Beginning WIP	$10,500	$ 4,500	$ 9,000	$ 92,250	$116,250
Costs incurred during April	49,500	27,900	55,800	360,000	493,200
Total	$60,000	$32,400	$64,800	$452,250	$609,450
Units:					
Units completed	70,000	70,000	70,000	70,000	
Equivalent units, ending WIP	5,000	2,000	2,000	5,000	
Total	75,000	72,000	72,000	75,000	
Cost per equivalent unit	$0.80 +	$0.45 +	$0.90 +	$6.03 =	$8.18

Cost Reconciliation:

Total cost to account for		$609,450
Cost of completed units transferred to Finished Goods (70,000 × $8.18)		$572,600
Cost of ending WIP:		
Material (5,000 equivalent units × $0.80)	$ 4,000	
Labor (2,000 equivalent units × $0.45)	900	
Overhead (2,000 equivalent units × $0.90)	1,800	
Transferred-in (5,000 equivalent units × $6.03)	30,150	36,850
Total cost accounted for		$609,450

process for each cost category. As the production cost report shows, this yields cost per equivalent unit values of $.80 for material, $.45 for labor, $.90 for overhead, and $6.03 for transferred-in cost. Because it has not been covered in the previous example, note especially the calculation of cost per equivalent unit for transferred-in cost. The sum of transferred-in cost in beginning work in process ($92,250) plus the transferred-in cost during April ($360,000) is the numerator of the calculation ($452,250). The denominator (75,000 units) is the sum of the units completed (70,000) plus the equivalent units in ending work in process

(5,000). The result is a cost per equivalent unit for transferred-in cost of $6.03. One aspect of the calculation may be confusing: the equivalent units in ending work in process. The 5,000 units in process at the end of April are only 40 percent through the packaging process. However, these units are 100 percent complete with respect to transferred-in cost since they were transferred in with all of the mixing department cost that they will receive. Therefore, there are 5,000 equivalent units in ending work in process with respect to transferred-in cost.

The third step in solving the process costing problem is to assign cost to items completed and items in ending work in process. The cost of the completed items is $572,600. As indicated in the production cost report, this is computed as the cost per equivalent unit ($8.18) times the number of units completed (70,000). Once the packaging department completes the units, Kent includes the cost of both the mixing operation and the packaging operation in the units transferred to finished goods. The entry to record the transfer is:

(Date)	Finished Goods Inventory	572,600	
	Work in Process Inventory, Packaging		572,600
	To record cost of units completed and transferred to Finished Goods Inventory.		

The cost of ending work in process is composed of material, labor, overhead, and transferred-in cost. For each cost category, the equivalent units in ending work in process is multiplied by the cost per equivalent unit. As indicated in the production cost report, the sum of the cost categories is the ending balance of $36,850.

The fourth, and final, step is to account for the amount of product cost. The cost of beginning inventory ($116,250) plus the amount of costs incurred during the period ($493,200) is the total cost that must be accounted for ($609,450). As indicated in the production cost report, this is accounted for by the cost of the completed items ($572,600) plus the cost of ending work in process ($36,850).

SUMMARY

Describe product flows through departments and record cost flows in accounts. Companies that produce large numbers of identical items use process costing systems to accumulate the cost of inventory. Typically, companies use several distinct processes to produce the items. When units are completed in one process, the cost of the units is transferred to the next process. This procedure is repeated until the units are completed in the last process. Along with transferred-in costs, each process may add its own material, labor, and overhead cost.

Discuss the concept of an equivalent unit. Units in work in process are not equal to fully completed units. Therefore, these partially completed units are expressed in terms of equivalent whole units.

Calculate the cost per equivalent unit. Process costing is essentially a system of averaging. The average cost is referred to as the cost per equivalent unit. It equals the sum of beginning work in process costs and current period costs divided by the sum of units completed and equivalent units in ending work in process.

Calculate the cost of goods completed and the ending work in process balance in a processing department. To calculate the cost of completed items, the total

INSIGHTS INTO ETHICS

Right after graduation, Carol Owens began working in the cost accounting department of Aktron Chemical Company. She's been employed by the company for five months and is beginning to feel comfortable with her job. Last week she completed a production cost report for the month of January, which assumed that the 10,000 units in process at the end of the month were 10 percent complete with respect to labor and overhead. The plant engineer in charge of production provided the 10 percent estimate. Her supervisor, Otis Atkins, reviewed the report and asked her to redo the analysis using a completion percentage of 80 percent. He explained that the engineers are often careless in estimating completion percentages, and he believed his figure was more accurate. However, he did not tell Carol how he determined his estimate. Further, Carol knows that the effect of this change will be to shift more cost to work in process and less cost to the finished units. Since the finished units will be sold in February, their lower cost will tend to boost net income during a month that is typically a low income month for the company.

What should Carol do? Should she confront her supervisor and ask him to justify the 80 percent figure?

cost per equivalent unit is multiplied by the number of units completed. To calculate the cost of units in work in process, the number of equivalent units in process is multiplied by the cost per equivalent unit separately for each cost category (i.e., material, labor, overhead, and transferred-in cost). This is necessary because the units in work in process at the end of the period may be completed to different degrees with respect to each of these costs.

Describe a production cost report. A production cost report provides a reconciliation of units in beginning inventory and units started to units in ending inventory and units completed. It also provides a reconciliation of costs in beginning inventory and costs added during the period to costs in ending inventory and costs transferred out.

REVIEW PROBLEM

Omega Files Company manufactures a single, five-drawer file cabinet for accounting and legal offices. They have 15-inch wide drawers and are insulated for fire survival of two hours. The production occurs in two departments, Forming and Assembly & Painting. The metal materials for the cabinets are introduced into production as the beginning step in the forming department.

The first process consists of cutting and forming cabinet housing and drawer parts from sheet metal, which is acquired in 50-yard rolls. The drawer rails and slide latches are stamped out of a heavier gauge steel alloy.

The completed parts are transferred to Assembly & Painting where the drawers and cabinets are assembled and painted, and the fire insulation and locking mechanisms are added. As units are transferred into the assembly & painting department from the forming department, the appropriate materials to complete those units are immediately issued to the assembly & painting department.

The completed units are transferred to a finished goods warehouse. The following information is available for April 19X3:

CHAPTER 22 PROCESS COSTING

Unit Information:	Forming Dept.	Assembly & Painting Dept.
Beginning WIP Inventory, 4/1/X3:		
(100% material, 40% conversion costs)	750	
(100% material, 60% conversion costs)		1,000
Units started into production during April	6,000	
Units transferred in during April		?
Ending WIP inventory 4/30/X3:		
(100% material, 50% conversion costs)	600	
(100% material, 75% conversion costs)		800

Note: Transferred-in units are always 100% complete as to prior department costs. It is normally assumed that there are no spoiled or lost units unless specified.

Cost Information:	Forming Dept.	Assembly & Painting Dept.
Beginning WIP:		
Direct materials	$ 60,000	$ 20,000
Direct labor	6,000	36,000
Manufacturing overhead applied	6,000	12,000
Transferred-in costs	N/A	120,000
Total beginning WIP	$ 72,000	$188,000
Costs added during the period:		
Direct materials	$480,000	$123,000
Direct labor	123,000	381,000
Manufacturing overhead applied	123,000	127,000
Transferred-in costs	N/A	?
Total costs added during the period	$726,000	?

REQUIRED:

a. Prepare a production cost report for April for each of the departments.
b. Prepare journal entries to record the April transactions of the Forming Department.
c. Prepare journal entries to record the April transactions of the Assembly & Painting Department.

SOLUTION:

(a) *Prepare production cost reports.*

Production Cost Report
Forming Department
April 19X3

Quantity Reconciliation:	
Units in beginning WIP	750
Units started during April	6,000
Units to account for	6,750
Units completed and transferred to Assembly & Painting	6,150
Units in ending WIP (100% material, 50% conversion costs)	600
Units accounted for	6,750

Cost Per Equivalent Unit Calculation:

Cost:	Material	Labor	Overhead	Total
Beginning WIP	$ 60,000	$ 6,000	$ 6,000	$ 72,000
Costs incurred during April	480,000	123,000	123,000	726,000
Total	$540,000	$129,000	$129,000	$798,000

Units:	Direct Material	Direct Labor	Mfg. Overhead
Units completed	6,150	6,150	6,150
Equivalent units, ending WIP	600	300	300
Total	6,750	6,450	6,450

Cost per equivalent unit $80   + $20   + $20   = $120

Cost Reconciliation:

Total cost to account for	$798,000
Cost of completed units transferred to Assembly & Painting (6,150 units x $120)	$738,000
Cost of ending WIP:	
Material (600 equivalent units x $80) $48,000	
Labor (300 equivalent units x $20) 6,000	
Overhead (300 equivalent units x $20) 6,000	60,000
Total cost accounted for	$798,000

Production Cost Report
Assembly & Painting Department
April 19X3

Quantity Reconciliation:

Units in beginning WIP	1,000
Units received from Forming during April	6,150
Units to account for	7,150
Units completed and transferred to Finished Goods	6,350
Units in ending WIP (100% material, 75% conversion costs)	800
Units accounted for	7,150

Cost Per Equivalent Unit Calculation:

Cost:	Material	Labor	Overhead	Trans.-In	Total
Beginning WIP	$ 20,000	$ 36,000	$ 12,000	$120,000	$ 188,000
Costs incurred during April	123,000	381,000	127,000	738,000	1,369,000
Total	$143,000	$417,000	$139,000	$858,000	$1,557,000

Units:				
Units completed	6,350	6,350	6,350	6,350
Equivalent units, ending WIP	800	600	600	800
Total	7,150	6,950	6,950	7,150

Cost per equivalent unit	$20	+	$60	+	$20	+	$120	=	$220

Cost Reconciliation:

Total cost to account for		$1,557,000
Cost of completed units transferred to Finished Goods (6,350 units x $220)		$1,397,000
Cost of ending WIP:		
Material (800 equivalent units x $20)	$16,000	
Labor (600 equivalent units x $60)	36,000	
Overhead (600 equivalent units x $20)	12,000	
Transferred-in (800 equivalent units x $120)	96,000	160,000
Total cost accounted for		$1,557,000

(b) *Prepare journal entries for the forming department.*

These entries can be reconstructed from the information in the production cost report for the department for April.

(1)	Work in Process Inventory, Forming	726,000	
	Raw Materials Inventory		480,000
	Wages and Salaries Payable		123,000
	Manufacturing Overhead		123,000
	To record inputs to production for April.		
(2)	Work in Process Inventory, Assembly & Painting	738,000	
	Work in Process Inventory, Forming		738,000
	To record transfer of costs from Forming to Assembly & Painting.		

(c) *Prepare journal entries for the assembly & painting department.*

These entries can be reconstructed from the information in the April production cost report for the department.

(1)	Work in Process Inventory, Assembly & Painting	631,000	
	Raw Materials Inventory		123,000
	Wages and Salaries Payable		381,000
	Manufacturing Overhead		127,000
	To record inputs to production for April. (Note: the entry for the costs transferred in from Forming has been made in entry b.(2) above.)		
(2)	Finished Goods Inventory	1,397,000	
	Work in Process Inventory, Assembly & Painting		1,397,000
	To record cost of units completed and transferred to Finished Goods Inventory.		

KEY TERMS

conversion costs, *905*
cost per equivalent unit, *908*
equivalent units, *908*
production cost report, *911*
transferred-in costs, *905*

SELF QUIZ

LO 1 1. Indicate which of the following characteristics are associated with a process costing system. (Yes/No)
  ___ a. Heterogeneous products
  ___ b. Homogeneous products
  ___ c. Continuous production
  ___ d. Discontinuous production
  ___ e. Costs are traced to jobs
  ___ f. Costs are traced to processing departments

LO 1 2. The best example of a business requiring a process cost system would be a(n):
  a. Custom cabinet shop.
  b. Antique furniture restorer.
  c. Soap manufacturer.
  d. Home builder.
  e. Automobile repair shop.

LO 1 3. The costs in a process cost system are traced to:
  a. Specific jobs.
  b. Specific customers.
  c. Specific company administrators.
  d. Specific production departments.
  e. None of the above.

LO 1 4. The transfer of indirect materials into production would include a debit to:
  a. Materials Inventory
  b. Manufacturing Overhead
  c. Work in Process Inventory
  d. Finished Goods Inventory

LO 1 5. Match the following cost accounting terms with the definitions shown below.
  ___ a. Conversion costs
  ___ b. Equivalent units of production
  ___ c. Transferred-in costs
  ___ d. Cost per equivalent unit
  (1) The costs associated with units received from a preceding department within the company for further processing.
  (2) The unit cost in a process costing system.
  (3) The costs associated with changing units of direct materials into finished products; they include both direct labor and manufacturing overhead.
  (4) Hypothetical units of output, which assume that a number of partially completed units may reasonably be treated as a proportionally smaller number of completed units with respect to any factor of production, i.e., direct materials, direct labor, etc., when calculating average unit cost in a process costing system.

LO 1 6. Determine the amount of conversion cost in the following list of costs.
  1. Direct material $25,000
  2. Direct labor 35,000
  3. Manufacturing overhead 45,000
  4. Selling expenses 10,000
  5. Administrative expenses 50,000

LO 1 7. When units completed in one processing department are received by another department for further processing, the related costs are called _____ _____ by the receiving department, and debited to the _____ _____ _____ of the receiving department.

LO 2 **LO 3** 8. If raw material A is introduced into a production department at the beginning of the production process, which statement is correct about the equivalent units of production respect to material A?
  a. All the units in the department are 100% complete as to materials.
  b. All the units in the department are on the average 50% complete as to materials.
  c. Equivalent units of materials is not a function of when the materials are entered into the process.
  d. All of the above statements are incorrect.

LO 2 **LO 3** 9. If raw material B is introduced into a production department at the very end of the production process as they are transferred to the next department, what statement can you make about the equivalent units of product in the ending work in process inventory account with respect to material B?
  a. All of the units in work in process are complete with respect to material B.
  b. All of the units in work in process are on average 50% complete as to material B.
  c. Equivalent units of materials is not a function of when the materials are entered into the process.
  d. All of the above statements are incorrect.

LO 1 10. A transfer of production goods from the first producing department to the second producing department would include a:
  a. Debit to Finished Goods Inventory.
  b. Debit to Cost of Goods Sold.
  c. Debit to Work in Process, Department One.
  d. Debit to Work in Process, Department Two.

LO 1 11. The application of manufacturing overhead to work in process would include which of the following?
  a. A debit to Manufacturing Overhead.
  b. A credit to Manufacturing Overhead.
  c. A credit to Work in Process Inventory.
  d. A debit to Finished Goods Inventory.

LO 5 12. The Quantity Reconciliation portion of a production cost report includes all of the following except:

a. Beginning units in process.
b. Ending units in process.
c. Units started and completed during the period.
d. Units completed and transferred out.
e. Units started during the period.

LO 5 13. The units as shown in the Quantity Reconciliation portion of a production cost report are:
a. Equivalent units of production.
b. Units without regard to stage of completion.
c. Units complete as to materials.
d. Units complete as to prime costs.

LO 3 14. The elements in the cost per equivalent unit calculation include all of the following except:
a. Cost of goods sold.
b. Total costs for each input.
c. Equivalent units for each input.
d. Unit cost for each input.

LO 2 15. The number of equivalent units of production for an input are:
LO 3
a. The number of units placed into production and completed during the period.
b. The number of units placed into production during the period.
c. The comparable number of whole units.
d. None of the above.

LO 2 16. A company has beginning work in process of 10,000 units, 60% complete as to conversion costs. They start 50,000 units during the period and have 20,000 in ending work in process, 30% complete as to conversion cost. The denominator in the cost per equivalent unit calculation for conversion is:
a. 56,000.
b. 46,000.
c. 40,000.
d. 64,000.

LO 2 17. Transferred-in costs are:
LO 3
a. Always recalculated by the receiving department.
LO 4
b. Not considered further by the receiving department.
LO 5
c. Related to 100% complete equivalent units.
d. None of the above.

LO 2 18. Transferred-in costs occur in:
LO 3
a. All production departments.
LO 4
b. The first and last production departments.
LO 5
c. All production departments after the first.
d. None of the above is correct.

LO 5 19. Production cost reports are:
a. Essential external financial reports.
b. Essential internal financial reports.
c. Useful to management but not essential.
d. None of the above.

LO 2 20. A key to solving process costing problems is:
LO 5
a. Tracing costs to individual jobs.
b. Calculating equivalent units of production.
c. Having only one work in process inventory account.
d. None of the above.

SOLUTIONS TO SELF-QUIZ
1. Answers b, c, and f, are Yes   answers a, d, and e, are No (job-order costing)   2. c   3. d   4. b   5. a. (3) b. (4) c. (1) d. (2)   6. $80,000   7. transferred-in costs, work in process   8. a   9. d   10. d   11. b   12. c   13. b   14. a   15. c   16. b   17. c   18. c   19. b   20. b

QUESTIONS

Q22-1 What are the two primary systems used by manufacturing firms to calculate production costs?

Q22-2 Identify the fundamental difference in the assignment of costs in a process costing system and a job-order costing system.

Q22-3 The accounts used to track the flow of costs through either a job-order cost system or a process costing system are essentially the same, except that a process system may have a separate work in process account for each department. Explain how the flow of costs through the ledger accounts differs between the two systems.

Q22-4 Discuss the relationship between product flows and cost flows in a process costing manufacturing environment.

Q22-5 What factors must be considered in calculating equivalent units of work in process for direct materials when the direct materials are introduced into a production process at some point other than at the beginning of the process?

Q22-6 Costs are transferred into departments subsequent to the first department in a process costing system. Discuss how these costs are treated by the receiving departments.

Q22-7 Explain the concept of "equivalent units."

Q22-8 Why are units often in a different stage of completion with respect to raw materials and conversion costs?

Q22-9 Why do we usually calculate separate equivalent units in work in process for materials, labor, and manufacturing overhead?

Q22-10 What items of production cost make up the "costs to account for" in a production cost report?

Q22-11 Identify where the "costs to account for" on a production cost report would appear in the financial statements at the end of the period.

Q22-12 Discuss what is accomplished by preparing a reconciliation of the physical units as a part of the production cost report.

Q22-13 How does the production cost report provide the information for recording costs transferred out of a department?

Q22-14 A work in process inventory account has no beginning balance. 1,000 units are introduced into production, 900 units are completed and transferred out, and 100 units are in process at the end of the period. Is it logical to assume that 10% of the costs in the work in process account should be assigned to the ending balance in Work in Process Inventory? Discuss.

Q22-15 Do transferred-in costs occur in all departments of a manufacturer using a process costing system? Explain.

EXERCISES

LO 1

E22-1 Flow of Process Costs Through Accounts Wilton Mfg. Co. produces one product in a single department on a process basis. Present the following information as it would appear in Wilton's ledger. Use T-accounts.

Production Dept.

WIP, 5/1/X5		$ 13,800
Costs added during May:		
Direct material	$26,500	
Direct labor	34,000	
Manufacturing overhead	68,000	128,500
WIP, 5/31/X5		11,800

LO 1

E22-2 Flow of Process Costs Through Accounts Chiapa Corporation uses a process costing system with only one work in process inventory account and completed its first year of manufacturing operations on December 31, 19X8. The cost of completed goods transferred to the finished goods warehouse during the period was $138,000. Direct material purchases totaled $45,000 with $5,000 remaining in ending inventory. Overhead applied to production during the year was $55,000.

REQUIRED:

Use T-accounts to determine the amount of direct labor used during the period assuming the ending Work in Process Inventory balance was $15,000.

CHAPTER 22 PROCESS COSTING

LO 2 **E22-3** **Equivalent Units** A company has 25 units of product in beginning work in process which are 100% complete as to materials and 40% complete as to direct labor and manufacturing overhead. During the period, 150 additional units of product are started into production and at the end of the period 40 units are still in ending work in process, 100% complete as to materials, and 60% complete as to direct labor and manufacturing overhead.

REQUIRED:

Calculate the denominator to be used in determining the cost per equivalent unit for direct materials, direct labor, and manufacturing overhead.

LO 2 **E22-4** **Equivalent Units** Department B, which had no beginning work in process, received 25,000 units from Department A during the period. There were 5,000 of those units still in work in process at the end of the period.

REQUIRED:

What is the denominator Department B would use in calculating its cost per equivalent unit for transferred in cost?

LO 2 **E22-5** **Calculation of Equivalent Units** Arapaho Toy Company produces one model of a doll in a single department. The month ended with 500 dolls in process 80% complete as to direct materials and 50% complete as to conversion costs. 27,000 dolls were transferred to finished goods during the month and 25,000 were started during the month. The beginning inventory was 60% complete as to direct materials and 40% complete as to conversion costs.

REQUIRED:

Determine the denominators to be used in the calculations of cost per equivalent unit for materials and conversion costs.

LO 2 **E22-6** **Calculation of Equivalent Units** Marlin Reel Company produces heavy duty saltwater fishing reels in two departments, Stamping and Assembly. During 19X4, 2,800 reels were completed and shipped to customers. There were no beginning inventories in either department. The stamping department had an ending inventory of 420 units, 100% complete as to direct materials and 50% complete as to conversion costs. They started 3,500 units into production during the period. The ending inventory of the assembly department was 100% complete as to transferred-in costs and direct materials, and 60% complete as to conversion costs.

REQUIRED:

Determine the denominators to be used in the calculations of cost per equivalent units for the cost items in each department.

LO 3 **E22-7** **Cost per Equivalent Unit** The beginning balance in Work in Process Inventory at Maco Manufacturing included $4,000 for direct labor. During the period, $50,000 of direct labor costs were incurred. During the period, 8,000 units were completed, and 2,000 units, 50% complete with respect to direct labor, remained in work in process.

REQUIRED:

Calculate the cost per equivalent unit for direct labor.

LO 2,3,4 **E22-8** **Cost per Equivalent Unit, Costs Transferred Out** Bimini Beach Wear manufactures one popular model swimsuit in a single production department. All materials are added at the beginning of the process. 5,000 units were started into production during May. 2,000 units were in beginning work in process (100% DM, 80% CC) and 1,000 units were in ending work in process (100% DM, 60% CC). The May production costs were:

	Direct Materials	Conversion Costs
Beginning work in process	$ 6,000	$ 6,400
Costs added in May	15,000	20,000

REQUIRED:

Compute the cost per equivalent unit for May and the cost transferred to Finished Goods Inventory.

LO 4

E22-9 Costing Ending Work in Process Wachovia Parts Co. had 2,400 units in ending work in process at May 31. The units are 100% complete with respect to materials and 40% complete with respect to conversion costs. Their equivalent units of production and costs for May were:

	Cost per Equivalent Unit
Direct materials	$6
Direct labor	$2
Manufacturing overhead	$1

REQUIRED:

Calculate the cost of the ending work in process inventory at May 31.

LO 4

E22-10 Costing for Goods Completed and Ending Work in Process Howell Hang-Gliders produces a single model, HM24, in a process system. At the end of October 19X7, there were four gliders in process, 60% complete as to labor and overhead. Eighty percent of the materials are added at the beginning of production and the other twenty percent is added immediately before transfer to the finished goods warehouse. Eighty-five gliders were completed during the month. Assume that direct materials cost per equivalent unit during October was $250 and the conversion cost per equivalent unit was $400.

REQUIRED:

Determine the cost of the ending work in process inventory and the cost transferred to Finished Goods Inventory.

LO 5

E22-11 Production Cost Report for a Single Department Firm Dolphin Products Company manufactures swimfins in a single department. Use the following information to prepare a production cost report for Dolphin.

	Units
WIP, October 1, 19X9	
(100% D.M., 80% D.L., 60% MOH)	800
Units started into production in October	2,600
WIP, October 31, 19X9	
(100% D.M., 60% D.L., 40% MOH)	600
Cost Data:	
Beginning WIP:	
Direct material (100%)	$3,200
Direct labor	1,920
Manufacturing overhead	960

Costs added during October:
Direct material	$11,080
Direct labor	7,876
Manufacturing overhead	5,728

LO 5

E22-12 Production Cost Reports With Two Departments Beta Products produces school desk tops which are sold for further manufacturing use. Production occurs in two departments, Cutting and Laminating. There were no beginning inventories in either department.

REQUIRED:

Prepare a January production cost report for each department using the following unit information for January 19X8.

Unit information:	Cutting	Laminating
Started into production	12,000	
Transferred in		11,500
Ending WIP (100% direct materials, 80% conversion cost in each department.)	?	500
Cost entering production in January 19X8:	*Cutting*	*Laminating*
Direct materials	$24,000	$17,250
Direct labor	17,850	18,240
Applied overhead	8,925	9,120

PROBLEM SET A

LO 1

P22-1A Product Cost Flows Whitmor Bag produces a heavy kraft paper mailing package in a single department for the U.S. Postal Service. Activity for February 19X6, resulted in the production and shipment of 30,000 packaging bags at a cost of $.60 per bag. The cost consisted of 30% material cost, 50% labor cost, and 20% manufacturing overhead. There were no beginning or ending inventories of raw material, work in process, or finished goods. Whitmor uses a process costing system with a single work in process inventory account.

REQUIRED:

Trace the product costs through Whitmor's accounts with journal entries.

LO 1

P22-2A Flow of Process Costs through Departments and Accounts Apex Manufacturing produces a single homogeneous product in a continuous process which involves two departments. The following cost information was available for the two departments for March 19X4:

	Dept. I	Dept. II
WIP, 3/1/X4	$ 0	$ 0
Costs added during March:		
Direct material	14,000	6,000
Direct labor	4,000	10,000
Manufacturing overhead applied	28,000	18,000
Transferred-in costs	N/A	45,200
WIP, 3/31/X4	800	12,400

REQUIRED:

Trace the costs for Apex through the accounts by preparing the accounting entries directly into T-accounts to record the issue of direct materials, the cost of direct labor (paid in cash), the application of manufacturing overhead, and the transfer of the costs associated with completed products, for both departments.

LO 2,3,4 **P22-3A** **Equivalent Units, Cost per Equivalent Unit, and Valuation of Ending Work in Process Inventory for a Single Department Manufacturer** Marquita Manufacturing produces one type of air filter for use in jet aircraft in a single department. Parts are added at many points throughout the heavily automated process. August 19X2, production began with 600 filters in work in process, 80% complete as to materials and 70% complete as to conversion costs. During the month, an additional 3,200 units were started into process. Eight hundred filters were still incomplete at the end of the month, which were on average 60% complete as to materials and 50% complete as to conversion costs.

Department cost information for August:

	Beginning Work in Process	Added in August
Raw materials	$48,000	$317,400
Direct labor	12,600	94,500
Manufacturing overhead	84,000	590,900

REQUIRED:

In the format used in a production cost report:
a. Calculate the cost per equivalent unit for each of the three factors of production and in total.
b. Calculate the costs remaining in Work in Process Inventory on August 31, 19X2.
c. Discuss possible reasons as to why the cost of manufacturing overhead is high relative to the other two inputs.

LO 2,3,4 **P22-4A** **Equivalent Units, Cost per Equivalent Unit, and Cost of Goods Completed for Two Departments** Classi-Craft, Ltd. builds a high quality ski-board that it markets in the southeastern U.S. at $125. During March 19X0, information about inventory production to be sold in the summer market was as follows:

Unit information:

	Laminating	Finishing
Beginning WIP	2,000	3,000
Started into production	12,000	
Transferred-in		?
Ending WIP (100% DM, 60% DL, 60% MOH in each department)	1,800	1,500

Costs in beginning WIP, March 1, 19X0:

	Laminating	Finishing
Direct material	$80,000	$ 30,000
Direct labor	42,000	42,000
Manufacturing overhead	36,000	36,000
Transferred-in costs	N/A	300,000

Costs incurred in March 19X0:

	Laminating	Finishing
Direct materials	$480,000	$152,400
Direct labor	356,400	381,400
Manufacturing overhead	362,400	299,800
Transferred-in costs	N/A	?

REQUIRED:

a. Calculate the cost per equivalent unit for each of the two departments during the month of March.

b. Calculate the costs assigned to the units transferred to the finishing department from the laminating department during March and prepare the journal entry to record the transfer.
c. Calculate the costs assigned to the units transferred from the finishing department to Finished Goods Inventory during March and prepare the journal entry to record the transfer.

LO 3,4,5

P22-5A **Production Cost Report for One Department** Lo-tech is a laminator of cross-country skis. The production process is primarily highly skilled hand labor working with high quality hardwoods. Work in process is always large because each pair of skis is in process for three to three and one-half months. Each craftsperson must allow considerable time for drying adhesives in lamination as well as between coats of the high-gloss finish.

September 19X1 began with 3,000 units in process which were on average 60% complete as to direct materials and conversion costs. Four thousand units were started in process during the month and ending inventory consisted of 5,000 units which were on average 50% complete as to direct materials and conversion costs.

Cost information:

	Beginning Work in Process	Costs Added in September
Direct material	$144,000	$216,000
Direct labor	288,000	432,000
Manufacturing overhead	36,000	54,000

REQUIRED:

a. Prepare a production cost report for Lo-Tech for the month of September 19X1.
b. Prepare the journal entry to show the transfer of the units completed during September.

LO 3,4,5

P22-6A **Production Cost Report for Two Departments** Bellrite Statuary manufactures bronzed statues in two departments, Casting and Finishing. Materials are added at the start of the production process in each department while direct labor and manufacturing overhead are incurred evenly over the processes. Information for production activity and related costs for July 19X3 include:

Unit information:

	Casting Dept.	Finishing Dept.
Beginning WIP	1,000	800
Started during July	24,000	?
Ending WIP:		
(55% complete as to conversion)	1,100	
(80% complete as to conversion)		1,000

Cost information:

	Casting Dept.	Finishing Dept.
Beginning WIP:		
Direct material	$30,000	$ 8,000
Direct labor	22,500	4,000
Manufacturing overhead	11,250	2,000
Transferred-in costs		59,200

	Casting Dept.	Finishing Dept.
Costs added in July 19X3:		
Direct material	$745,000	$246,410
Direct labor	688,145	216,500
Manufacturing overhead	331,820	122,950

REQUIRED:

Prepare a production cost report for each of the two departments for July 19X3.

PROBLEM SET B

LO 1

P22-1B **Product Cost Flows** Alamo Corp. manufactures a model of the famous Texas shrine from which it takes its name. They are sold as souvenirs at the historic site. Activity for February 19X5 resulted in the production of 5,000 models at a cost of $1.20 each. The cost consisted of 45% direct material cost, 45% direct labor cost, and 10% manufacturing overhead. There were no units in the work in process or finished goods at the beginning or at the end of the month and there was no beginning or ending balance in the raw materials inventory account. Eighty percent of the units were sold during the month. Alamo uses a process costing system with a single work in process inventory account.

REQUIRED:

Use the above information to reconstruct journal entries related to production for February.

LO 1

P22-2B **Flow of Process Costs through Departments and Accounts** Toren Chemical Company produces a single product in two departments. The following costs relate to April 19X7.

	Dept. I	Dept. II
WIP, 4/1/X7	$ 26,000	$ 46,000
Costs added during April:		
Direct material	180,000	80,000
Direct labor	45,000	55,000
Manufacturing overhead	230,000	110,000
Transferred-in costs	N/A	?
WIP, 4/30/X7	0	36,000

REQUIRED:

Trace the April costs for Toren through the accounts by posting entries directly into T-accounts to record the issue of direct materials, the cost of direct labor (paid in cash), the application of manufacturing overhead, and the transfer of the costs associated with completed products, for both departments.

LO 2,3,4

P22-3B **Equivalent Units and Cost per Equivalent Units, Transferred Cost and Ending Work in Process for One Department** Chip's Chips, a producer of jumbo bags of potato chips, began the month of August 19X9, with 5,000 units in process that were 100% complete as to materials and 60% complete as to labor and overhead. They started 25,000 units into production during the month of which 4,000 remained in ending inventory 80% complete as to materials and 40% complete as to conversion costs. The costs included:

Beginning WIP:
Direct materials	$ 4,000
Direct labor	1,050
Manufacturing overhead	2,100

Costs added during the period:
Direct materials	$22,280
Direct labor	9,990
Manufacturing overhead	11,700

REQUIRED:

a. Calculate the cost per equivalent unit for each element of production cost and the total cost per equivalent unit for the month of August.
b. Calculate the cost of the units transferred to Finished Goods Inventory during August.
c. Calculate the cost of Work in Process Inventory at the end of August.

LO 2,3,4   P22-4B **Equivalent Units, Cost per Equivalent Unit, and Cost of Goods Completed for Two Departments** Production information is shown below for the Corinth Column Company for August 19X8. Corinth manufactures decorative columns used in residential construction. The columns are produced in two departments, Cutting and Assembly. The cutting department saws the eight identical parts for each column and routes interlocking slots on each side. The assembly department assembles and glues the eight sides and routes decorative patterns on the completed column. The units are delivered unfinished as some contractors prefer to paint them while others use a stain finish.

Unit information:

	Cutting	Assembly
Beginning WIP	200	300
Started into production	1,000	
Transferred-in		?
Ending WIP:		
(100% DM, 60% DL, 60% MOH)	100	
(80% DL, 80% MOH)		200

Costs in beginning WIP, August 1, 19X8:

	Cutting	Assembly
Direct material	$10,000	N/A
Direct labor	4,700	$ 3,660
Manufacturing overhead	3,550	2,600
Transferred-in costs	N/A	36,000

Costs incurred in August 19X8:

	Cutting	Assembly
Direct materials	$50,000	N/A
Direct labor	41,700	$37,140
Manufacturing overhead	31,250	24,600
Transferred-in costs	N/A	?

REQUIRED:

a. Calculate the cost per equivalent unit for each of the departments during the month of August.
b. Calculate the costs assigned to the units transferred to the assembly department from the cutting department during August and prepare the journal entry to record the transfer.
c. Calculate the costs assigned to the units transferred from the assembly department to Finished Goods Inventory during August and prepare the journal entry to record the transfer.

LO 3,4,5 **P22-5B** **Production Cost Report for One Department** Ferrous Fabricators manufactures steel studs for residential construction from steel sheets. The steel sheet material is cut, punched, and folded in a single department using heavy machinery with a minimum of labor. The steel is brought into the production department directly from the trucks which deliver it as it is needed. The work in process inventory is kept relatively small at all times. The finished studs are loaded directly into the customers' trucks for shipment from the production department. No inventories of raw materials or finished goods are kept on hand. Consequently, the only manufacturing accounts used are Work in Process Inventory and Cost of Goods Sold.

The plant operated three weeks in December 19X6, closing for the holidays during the last week.

There were 500 units in process which were 100% complete as to direct material and 60% complete as to conversion costs. Thirty-six thousand units were started in process during the month and ending inventory consisted of 100 units which were 100% complete as to direct materials and 50% complete as to conversion costs.

Cost information:

	Beginning Work in Process	Costs Added in December
Direct material	$350	$25,200
Direct labor	32	3,613
Manufacturing overhead	96	10,839

REQUIRED:

a. Prepare a production cost report for Ferrous for the month of December 19X6.
b. Prepare the journal entry to show the transfer of the units completed during December.

LO 3,4,5 **P22-6B** **Production Cost Report for Two Departments** HydraProducts, Inc., produces a sports beverage in two departments: Blending and Bottling. In each department, material is added at the start of the process while labor and overhead are assumed to be incurred evenly throughout the process.

The following costs were incurred during April 19X4:

Unit information:	Mixing	Bottling
Beginning WIP	1,000	2,000
Started during April	100,000	?
Ending WIP		
(50% complete for conversion costs)	11,000	4,000
Cost information:	**Mixing**	**Bottling**
Beginning WIP:		
Direct material	$ 500	$ 400
Direct labor	400	200
Manufacturing overhead	200	100
Transferred-in cost	N/A	1,000
Costs added in April 19X4:		
Direct material	$60,000	$40,000
Direct labor	50,000	22,000
Manufacturing overhead	25,000	11,000
Transferred-in cost	N/A	?

REQUIRED:

Prepare a production cost report for each of the two departments of HydraProducts for April 19X4.

CRITICAL THINKING AND COMMUNICATING

C22-1 Vermont Production Company has been operating successfully for several years in the manufacture and sale of folding boat seats. The seats are marketed to both manufacturers of boats and as after-market products for boat owners. The manufacturing costs in the first of its two production departments, Framing, have increased noticeably over the first six months of 19X2. The costs in the second department, Upholstery, have remained relatively constant except for the costs transferred in from the framing department. The following costs per equivalent unit were incurred in the framing department during the period.

Framing Department Cost per Equivalent Unit:

	Direct Material	Direct Labor	Mfg. Overhead	Total Cost
January 19X2	$46.20	$24.00	$12.00	$82.20
February 19X2	45.10	24.40	12.20	81.70
March 19X2	46.05	24.70	12.35	83.10
April 19X2	46.25	25.80	12.90	84.95
May 19X2	46.40	26.40	13.20	86.00
June 19X2	46.50	27.70	13.85	88.05

There have been no changes in the design of the production process or in the production layout. Output has remained constant per month over the period as has the number of direct labor hours worked. Material price increases have been very low. The labor contract, which includes a provision for time and one-half pay for overtime, is still in force through October 19X2, with the wage rate constant. The overapplied manufacturing overhead figure has increased each month throughout the six-month period. This has not occurred in the prior years.

REQUIRED:

a. Comment on the manufacturing overhead applied during the period. Consider what has caused the increase and what might be observed concerning the application base.
b. Comment on the change in the cost per equivalent unit for labor. Discuss a possible cause and an approach for management to seek a solution.
c. Comment on the change in the material cost during the period.

C22-2 Thermo Chemical, a company that produces paint stripper, is considering ways to treat the costs of "wasted units." At the start of December, there were 150,000 gallons in beginning work in process. During December, 600,000 gallons were started. Of the 750,000 units to account for, 150,000 gallons remained in process at the end of December. These units were 100% complete with respect to material and 20% complete with respect to conversion costs. 300,000 gallons were completed during April and, unfortunately, 300,000 gallons were wasted due to worker error. On two separate occasions, incorrect quantities of chemicals were added and batches of paint stripper were ruined.

Top management at Thermo has suggested that the cost associated with the production errors should be buried in the cost of the units completed and the units in process. This would result in cost of units completed of $1,528,182 and cost of ending work in process of $292,818 calculated as shown on the following page.

REQUIRED:

Assume you are the controller. Write a brief memo to Milton Stone, CEO at Thermo Chemical, commenting on the appropriateness of the proposed approach.

Thermo Chemical
Production Cost Report
December 19X1

Quantity Reconciliation:

Units in beginning WIP	150,000
Units started	600,000
Units to account for	750,000
Units completed	300,000
Units in ending WIP (100% material, 20% conversion costs)	150,000
Wasted units	300,000
Units accounted for	750,000

Cost Per Equivalent Unit Calculation:

Cost:	Material	Labor	Overhead	Total
Beginning WIP	$105,000	$ 45,000	$ 90,000	$ 240,000
Cost incurred during April	420,000	387,000	774,000	1,581,000
Total	$525,000	$432,000	$864,000	$1,821,000
Units:				
Units completed	300,000	300,000	300,000	
Equivalent units, ending WIP	150,000	30,000	30,000	
Total	450,000	330,000	330,000	

Cost per equivalent unit $1.16667 + $1.30909 + $2.61818 = $5.09394

Cost Reconciliation:

Total cost to account for		$1,821,000
Cost of completed units transferred to finished goods ($300,000 x $5.09394)		$1,528,182
Cost of ending WIP:		
Material (150,000 equivalent units x $1.16667)	$175,000	
Labor (30,000 equivalent units x $1.30909)	39,273	
Overhead (30,000 equivalent units x $2.61818)	78,545	292,818
Total cost accounted for		$1,821,000

CHAPTER 23

Cost-Volume-Profit Relationships

Mary Stuart, vice president of marketing for Union Skate Company, anticipates the company can increase sales of its deluxe in-line skates by 1,000 pairs if it launches an advertising campaign costing $80,000. The skates sell for $150 per pair. In the past year, the company produced and sold 20,000 pairs at a total cost of $2,940,000. Thus, last year's volume was 20,000 pairs; revenue, $3,000,000; costs, $2,940,000; and profit related to this model, $60,000. Should Union Skate launch the advertising campaign? The answer depends on how cost and profit will change in response to the 1,000-unit increase in volume.

Mary knows that advertising costs and revenues will increase by $80,000 and $150,000 (1,000 x $150), respectively. If no other costs change (i.e., all other costs are fixed), additional profits will be $70,000 ($150,000 – $80,000). This means profits would more than double as a result of the advertising. However, Mary believes some other costs will increase in response to the increase in volume. Suppose the costs are completely variable and increase in proportion to increases in volume. Last year, costs were $2,940,000 for 20,000 pairs of skates or $147 per pair. Thus, costs might be expected to increase by $147,000 if Union Skates produces and sells 1,000 additional pairs. Together with the $80,000 advertising cost, total costs will increase by $227,000. Since revenue will only increase by $150,000, profits would decrease by $77,000 as a result of the advertising campaign. Thus, if costs are completely variable, Mary should recommend that the advertising campaign not be implemented.

	Assume All Costs Fixed	Assume All Costs Variable
Additional revenue	$150,000	$150,000
Additional costs:		
Advertising	80,000	80,000
Other	0	147,000
Total additional costs	$ 80,000	$227,000
Effect on profit	$ 70,000	$ 77,000

Mary knows that neither analysis is appropriate because the costs of manufacturing the skates are neither 100 percent fixed nor 100 percent variable. How can she determine how costs and profit change in response to changes in volume? The method managerial accountants use to understand how costs and profits change when a company's volume changes is referred to as **cost-volume-profit (C-V-P) analysis**. In this chapter, we develop the tools to analyze cost-volume-profit relationships. These tools will help you solve the type of problem Mary faces.

> **LEARNING OBJECTIVES**
> 1. Identify the common cost behavior patterns.
> 2. Estimate the relationship between cost and activity using account analysis, the high-low method, and scattergraphs.
> 3. Perform cost-volume-profit analysis for single products.
> 4. Perform cost-volume-profit analysis for multiple products.
> 5. Discuss differences between variable and full costing (Appendix 23-A).
> 6. Discuss how income will differ between variable and full costing when the number of units produced does not equal the number of units sold (Appendix 23-A).

COMMON COST BEHAVIOR PATTERNS

LO 1 Identify the common cost behavior patterns.

To perform C-V-P analysis, you need to know how costs behave when volume changes. In this section, some common patterns are presented. While these patterns may not provide exact descriptions of how costs behave in response to changes in volume or activity, they are reasonable approximations. The common cost behavior patterns discussed are *variable costs*, *fixed costs*, and *mixed costs*. Variable and fixed costs were briefly introduced earlier in the text. A more complete discussion is provided here.

Variable Costs

Variable costs are those that change in response to changes in volume or activity. Managerial accountants typically assume that variable costs change *in proportion* to changes in activity. Thus, if activity increases by 10 percent, then variable costs will also increase by 10 percent. Some common variable costs are direct and indirect materials, direct labor, energy, and sales commissions. Exactly how activity should be measured in analyzing a variable cost depends on the situation. At McDonald's restaurants, food costs vary with the number of customers served. At United Airlines, fuel costs vary with the number of miles flown. In these situations, number of customers and number of miles are good measures of activity.

Suppose Union Skate Company's variable costs equal $100 per pair of skates. In this case, total variable costs at a production level of 5,000 pairs (the measure of activity) are equal to $500,000 ($100 × 5,000), while total variable costs at 25,000 pairs are equal to $2,500,000 ($100 × 25,000). A graph of the relationship between total variable costs and production is provided in Illustration 23-1. Note that while total variable costs increase with production, variable costs per pair remain at $100.

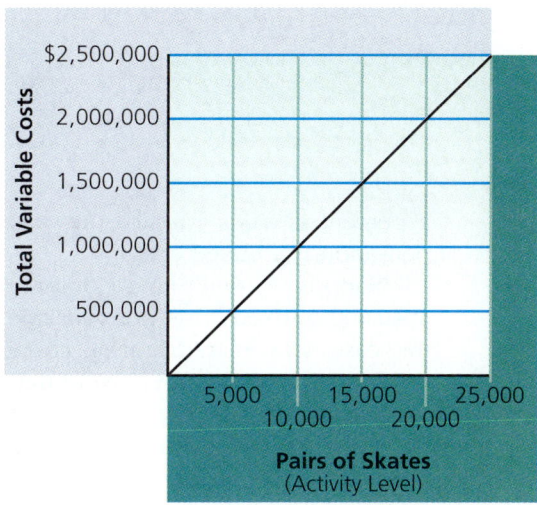

ILLUSTRATION 23-1 Variable Cost Behavior

Fixed Costs

Fixed costs are those that do not change in response to changes in activity levels. Some typical fixed costs are depreciation, supervisory salaries, and building maintenance. Suppose Union Skate Company's fixed costs per year are $940,000. A graph of the relationship between fixed costs and production is provided in Illustration 23-2. Irrespective of the number of skates produced, the amount of total fixed costs remains at $940,000. However, the amount of fixed costs per pair does change with changes in the level of activity. When activity increases, the amount of fixed costs per pair decreases because the fixed costs are spread over more units. For example, at 5,000 pairs of skates, the fixed costs per pair are $188 ($940,000 ÷ 5,000), while at 25,000 pairs, the fixed costs per pair are only $37.60 ($940,000 ÷ 25,000).

Mixed Costs

Mixed costs are those that contain both variable cost and fixed cost elements. These costs are sometimes referred to as *semivariable costs*. Accountants often work with cost information that results from summing fixed and variable cost items. For example, total production cost is composed of material, labor, and both fixed and variable overhead cost items. Therefore, total production cost is a mixed cost. Some individual costs are also mixed costs. For example, a salesperson may be paid $30,000 per year (fixed amount) plus commissions equal to

ILLUSTRATION 23-2 Fixed Cost Behavior

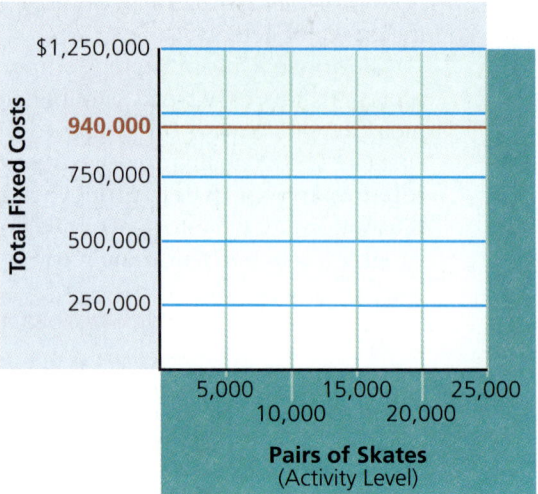

1 percent of sales (variable amount). In this case, the salesperson's total compensation is a mixed cost.

Suppose Union Skate Company's total manufacturing cost is composed of $940,000 of fixed costs per year and $100 of variable costs per pair of skates. In this case, total manufacturing cost is a mixed cost. A graph of the cost is presented in Illustration 23-3. Note that the total cost line intersects the vertical axis at $940,000 (just below the $1,000,000 point). This is the amount of fixed costs per year. From this point, total cost increases by $100 for every pair of skates produced. Thus, at 25,000 pairs the total cost is $3,440,000, or $940,000 of fixed costs and $2,500,000 of variable costs ($100 × 25,000).

ILLUSTRATION 23-3 Mixed Cost Behavior

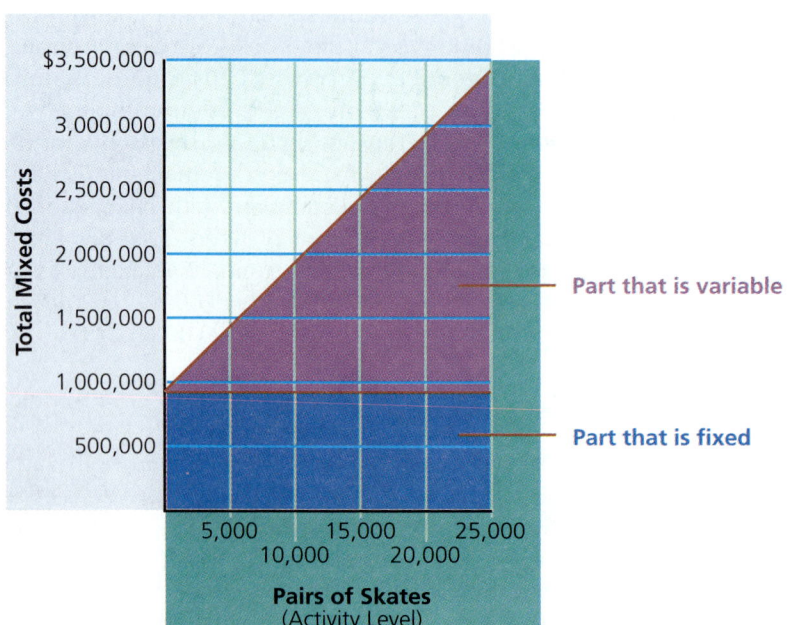

COST ESTIMATION METHODS

LO 2
Estimate the relationship between cost and activity using account analysis, the high-low method, and scattergraphs.

To predict how much cost a company will incur at various activity levels, the managerial accountant must know how much of the total cost is fixed and how much is variable. In many cases, cost information is not broken down into fixed and variable cost components. Therefore, the accountant must know how to estimate fixed and variable costs from available information. In this section, we present four techniques for estimating the amount of fixed and variable costs: account analysis, scattergraph approach, high-low method, and regression analysis.

Account Analysis

One of the most common approaches to estimating fixed and variable costs, **account analysis** requires that the accountant use his or her professional judgment to classify cost accounts as either fixed or variable. The total of the costs classified as variable can be divided by a measure of activity to calculate the variable costs per unit of activity. The total of the costs classified as fixed provides the estimate of fixed costs. Return to the Union Skate Company example. For the past year, the cost of producing 20,000 pairs of deluxe in-line skates was $2,940,000. Account analysis would require a detailed analysis of the accounts that comprise the $2,940,000 of production costs. Suppose last year's costs were as follows:

Production Cost Report Deluxe In-Line Skates	
Production Costs	20,000 Pairs
Materials	$1,095,000
Direct labor	1,005,000
Supervisor salaries	350,000
Rent	60,000
Utilities	50,000
Depreciation	380,000
Total	$2,940,000

Using professional judgment, the accountant may decide that materials and direct labor are variable costs and all other items are fixed costs. In this case, variable and fixed costs are estimated as in Illustration 23-4. The accountant estimated total production costs as $840,000 of fixed costs per year, plus $105 of variable costs for each pair of skates produced.

An individual cost item does not need to be classified as either 100 percent fixed or 100 percent variable. For example, part of supervisor salaries and part of utilities may also be variable. In this case, the accountant can use his or her judgment to refine estimates using account analysis. Suppose the accountant believes that approximately 50 percent of supervisor salaries and utilities are variable. As indicated in Illustration 23-5, the revised estimate of total variable costs would then amount to $2,300,000, or $115.00 per pair of skates, while the revised estimate of fixed costs would amount to $640,000.

ILLUSTRATION 23-4 Estimate of Variable and Fixed Costs

Variable Cost Estimate		
Materials	$1,095,000	
Direct labor	1,005,000	
Total	$2,100,000	(a)
Production	20,000	(b)
Variable cost per unit	$105	(a) ÷ (b)

Fixed Cost Estimate	
Supervisor salaries	$350,000
Rent	60,000
Utilities	50,000
Depreciation	380,000
Total per year	$840,000

ILLUSTRATION 23-5 Revised Estimate of Variable and Fixed Costs

Variable Cost Estimate		
Materials	$1,095,000	
Direct labor	1,005,000	
Supervisor salaries (50% of $350,000)	175,000	
Utilities (50% of $50,000)	25,000	
Total	$2,300,000	(a)
Production	20,000	(b)
Variable cost per unit	$115.00	(a) ÷ (b)

Fixed Cost Estimate	
Supervisor salaries (50% of $350,000)	$175,000
Rent	60,000
Utilities (50% of $50,000)	25,000
Depreciation	380,000
Total per year	$640,000

With these estimates, how much cost would Union Skate Company expect to incur if it produced 22,000 pairs of skates? With 22,000 pairs, variable costs are estimated as $2,530,000; fixed costs as $640,000. Therefore, total cost of $3,170,000 would be expected.

Expected Annual Cost of 22,000 Pairs of Deluxe In-Line Skates	
Variable costs (22,000 × $115.00)	$2,530,000
Fixed costs per year	640,000
Total	$3,170,000

The account analysis method is somewhat subjective. That is, different accountants who view the same set of facts might reach different conclusions regarding which costs are fixed and which costs are variable. In spite of the method's limitation, most accountants view it as an important tool for estimating fixed and variable costs.

Scattergraph Approach

In some cases, an accountant may use cost information from several reporting periods to estimate how costs change in response to changes in activity. Weekly, monthly, or quarterly reports are particularly useful sources of cost information. However, annual reports are not very useful because the relationship between costs and activity generally is not consistent or stable over several years. Suppose the monthly production and cost information provided in Illustration 23-6 is available for the Union Skate Company.

ILLUSTRATION 23-6 Monthly Production Cost Information

Month	Skate Production (Pairs)	Cost
January	750	$ 170,000
February	1,000	175,000
March	1,250	205,000
April	1,750	250,000
May	2,000	265,000
June	2,250	275,000
July	3,000	400,000
August	2,750	350,000
September	2,500	300,000
October	1,250	210,000
November	1,000	190,000
December	500	150,000
Total	20,000	$2,940,000

One way to gain insight into the relationship between production cost and activity is by plotting the costs and activity levels. The plot of the data is referred to as a **scattergraph** and the scattergraph for these data is presented in Illustration 23-7. Typically, scattergraphs are prepared with cost measured on the vertical axis and activity level measured on the horizontal axis. Each point on the scattergraph represents one pair of cost and activity values.

The scattergraph in Illustration 23-7 provides a picture of what costs might be at different activity levels. For example, suppose Union Skate Company needed to estimate costs for 1,500 pairs of skates. The graph shows that costs will be approximately $225,000 when the company produces 1,500 pairs of skates.

High-Low Method

If multiple observations of cost and activity are available, **the high-low method** can estimate fixed and variable cost components. This method fits a straight line to the data points representing the highest and lowest levels of activity. The slope of the line is the estimate of variable costs and the intercept is the estimate of fixed costs. Using the data in Illustration 23-6, the highest level of production activity is 3,000 pairs in July with a corresponding cost of $400,000; the lowest level is 500 pairs in December with a corresponding cost of $150,000.

ILLUSTRATION 23-7 Scattergraph of Cost and Product Information

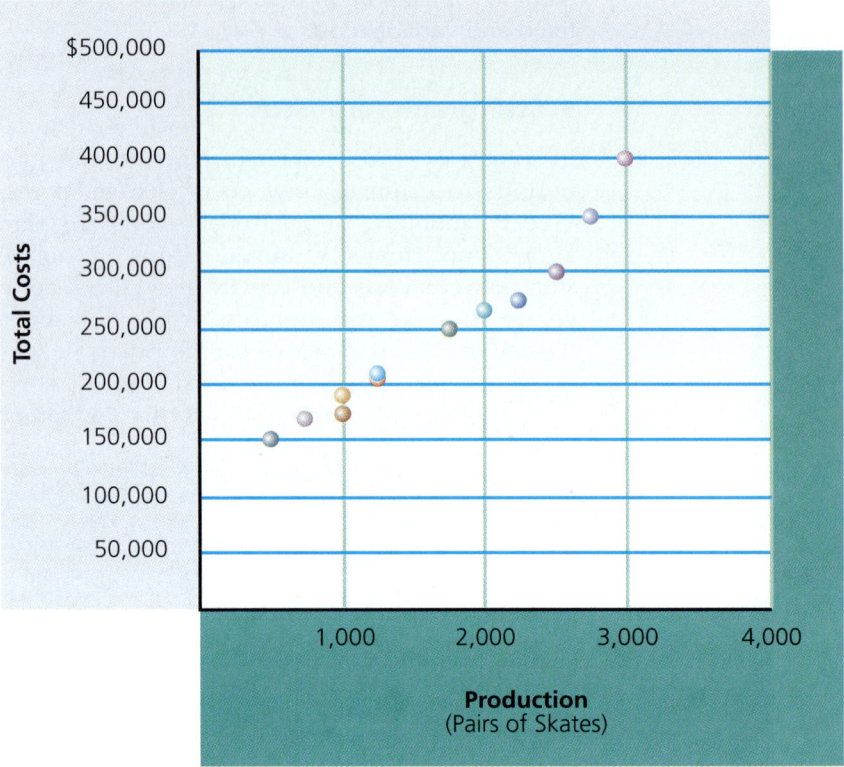

The slope is equal to the change in cost divided by the change in activity. In moving from the lowest to the highest levels of activity, cost changes by $250,000 and activity changes by 2,500 pairs. Thus, the estimate of variable costs (the slope) is $100.

$$\text{Estimate of Variable Costs} = \frac{\$400{,}000 - \$150{,}000}{3{,}000 - 500} = \$100 \text{ per pair}$$

Once obtained, an estimate of variable cost can be used to calculate an estimate of fixed costs. The amount of fixed costs is calculated as the difference between total costs and estimated variable costs. For example, at the lowest level of activity (500 pairs), total costs are $150,000. Since variable costs are $100 per pair, variable costs are $50,000 of the total costs. Thus, the remaining cost of $100,000 must be the amount of fixed costs. As indicated in the following calculation, the same estimated fixed costs amount ($100,000) works with either the lowest or the highest level of activity.

Estimate Using Lowest Activity		*Estimate Using Highest Activity*	
Total costs	$150,000	Total costs	$400,000
Less: Estimated variable costs (500 x $100)	50,000	Less: Estimated variable costs (3,000 x $100)	300,000
Estimated fixed costs per month	$100,000	Estimated fixed costs per month	$100,000

Be careful to note that since monthly data are used in this example, the fixed costs calculated are the fixed costs *per month*. If annual data were used, the fixed costs calculated would be the fixed costs *per year*.

Using the estimates from the high-low method, the straight-line cost equation is:

Total Costs = $100,000 of Fixed Costs + ($100 x Level of Activity)

Using this equation, Union Skate can predict total costs for various activity levels. For example, at an activity level of 1,500 pairs, Union Skate would expect to incur $250,000 of total cost.

$250,000 = $100,000 of Fixed Costs + ($100 x 1,500)

Illustration 23-8 presents a graph of the straight-line cost equation that is estimated using the high-low method. Notice that the cost line passes through the high-low data points but no others because only these two data points (and no others) were used to estimate the slope and intercept. The high-low estimate in Illustration 23-8 does not adequately fit the available data. Most of the data points lie below the high-low straight line. A significant weakness of the high-low method is that it uses only two data points when additional data may be available. Furthermore, the two data points may not represent the general relationship estimated between cost and activity. By definition, these two points represent unusually high and unusually low levels of activity, and costs at these levels may also be unusual. For example, at its highest level of activity, Union Skate may hire part-time workers to supplement its normal work force. These workers may not be as efficient as other workers, and Union Skate's costs may be unusually high.

ILLUSTRATION 23-8 High-Low Estimate of Production Costs

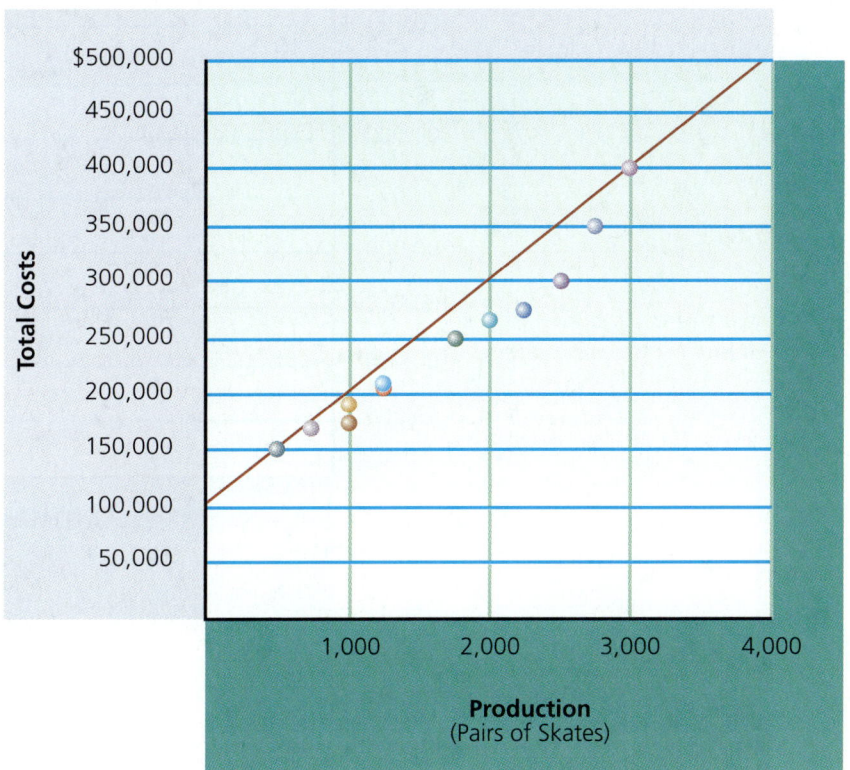

Regression Analysis

Regression analysis is a statistical technique that uses all available data points to estimate the intercept and slope of a cost equation. The line fitted to the data by regression analysis is the best straight-line fit to the data. Regression analysis programs are widely available, and many have been written for microcomputers or are built-in to some hand-held calculators. The topic of regression analysis is covered in introductory statistics classes and in cost accounting classes. For our purposes, we simply note that application of regression analysis to the data in Illustration 23-8 yields the following equation:

Total Costs = $93,619 of Fixed Costs + ($90.83 x Level of Activity)

At a production level of 1,500 units, the amount of total cost estimated is $229,864.

$229,864 = $93,619 of Fixed Costs + ($90.83 x 1,500)

This is less than the $250,000 estimated using the high-low cost equation. A graph of the regression analysis estimate of cost is presented in Illustration 23-9. Notice that the regression line better fits the data than does the line estimated with the high-low method. Because the regression line is more consistent with Union Skate's past data, it will probably provide more accurate predictions of future costs.

ILLUSTRATION 23-9 Regression Analysis Estimate of Production Cost

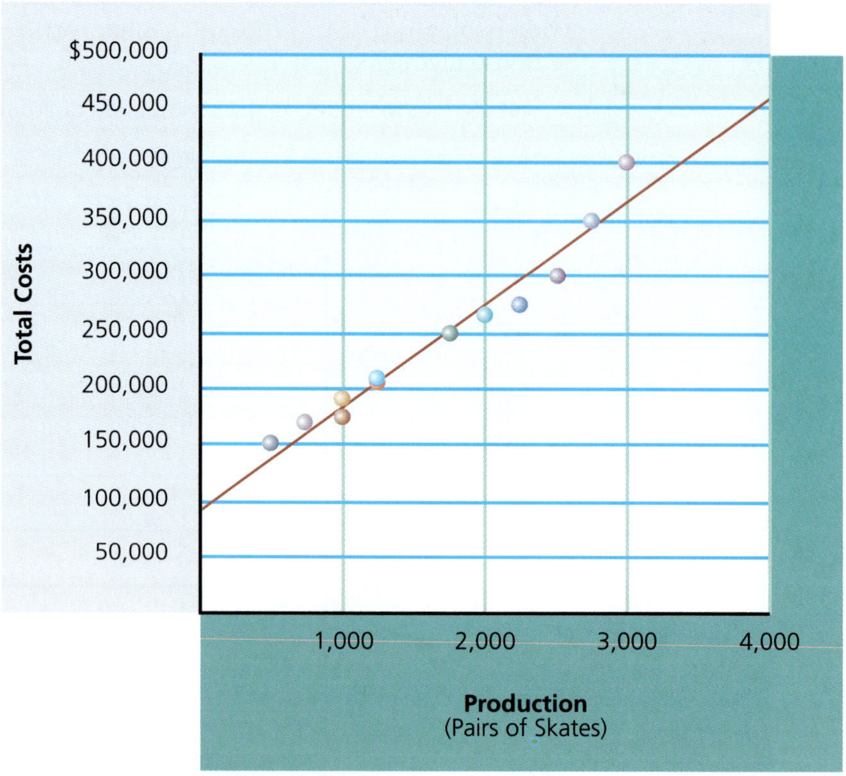

The Relevant Range

When working with estimates of fixed and variable costs, remember they are only valid for a limited range of activity. The **relevant range** is the range of activity for which estimates and predictions are likely to be accurate. Outside the relevant range, estimates of fixed and variable costs may not be very useful.

In some cases, actual costs behave differently from the common cost behavior patterns that we have discussed. All of those patterns imply linear (straight-line) relationships between cost and activity. In the real world, some costs behave as curves rather than straight lines. For example when companies produce unusually large quantities, production may not be as efficient and costs would increase more rapidly than the rate implied by a straight line. This may not be a serious limitation for a straight line approach as long as the predictions and estimates are restricted to the relevant range. Consider Illustration 23-10. Note that while the relationship between cost and activity is a curve, a straight line would closely approximate the relationship between cost and activity within the relevant range.

ILLUSTRATION 23-10 Relevant Range

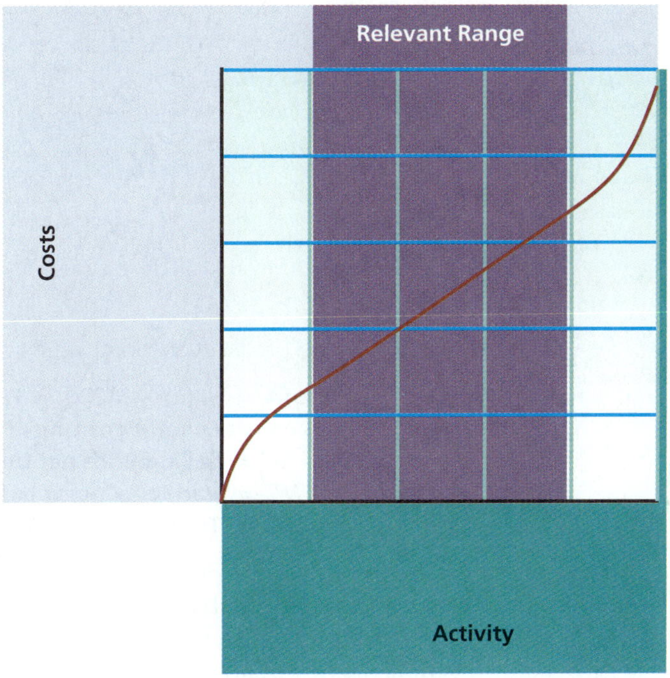

COST-VOLUME-PROFIT ANALYSIS

LO 3
Perform cost-volume-profit analysis for single products.

Once a company determines its fixed and variable costs, it can then conduct cost-volume-profit analysis (C-V-P). Basically, *C-V-P analysis* explores the relationships among costs, volume or activity levels, and profit.

Break-Even Point

One of the primary uses of C-V-P analysis is to calculate the break-even point. The **break-even point** is the number of units a company must sell to earn a zero profit (i.e., break-even). The break-even point is indicated in the profit graph presented in Illustration 23-11. At the point where sales revenue equals total costs (composed of fixed and variable cost) the company "breaks even."

ILLUSTRATION 23-11 Profit Graph and Break-Even Point

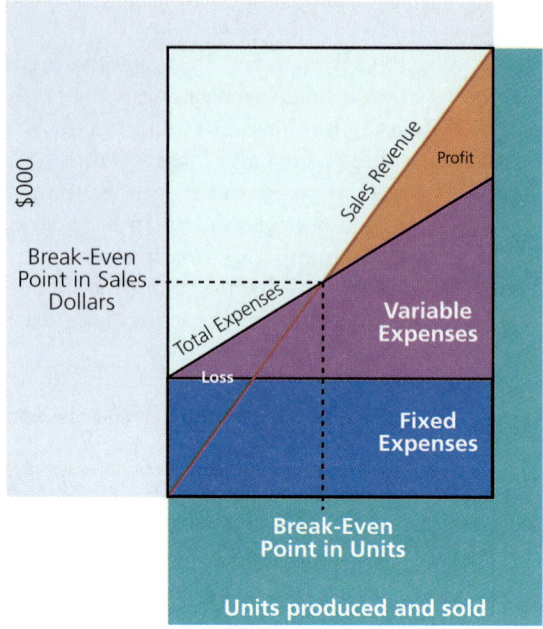

Profit Equation

The calculation of the break-even point relies on the following profit equation:

$$\text{Profit} = SP(x) - VC(x) - TFC$$

where
- x = Quantity of Units Produced and Sold
- SP = Selling Price per Unit
- VC = Variable Costs per Unit
- TFC = Total Fixed Costs

As stated in the equation, profit is equal to revenues (Selling Price per unit times Quantity) minus variable costs (Variable Costs per Unit times Quantity) minus total fixed costs. To calculate the break-even point, simply set profit to zero, insert the appropriate selling price, variable costs, and fixed costs and solve for the quantity (x).

Suppose Union Skate Company sells its deluxe in-line skates for $150 per unit (a pair of skates). Variable costs are estimated to be $100 per unit, and total fixed costs are estimated to be $100,000 per month. How many units must Union Skate sell to break even in a given month? To answer this question, solve the equation above for a particular value of x.

$$0 = \$150(x) - \$100(x) - \$100,000$$
$$0 = \$50(x) - \$100,000$$
$$\$50(x) = \$100,000$$
$$x = 2,000$$

Solving for x yields a break-even quantity of 2,000 pairs of skates. If management prefers the break-even quantity expressed in dollars of sales, rather than in units, the quantity is simply multiplied by the selling price of $150 to yield $300,000.

Margin of Safety

Obviously, managers want a level of sales greater than break-even sales. To express how close they expect to be to the break-even level, managers may calculate the **margin of safety**, which is the difference between the expected level of sales and break-even sales. For example, Union Skate Company's break-even level of sales is $300,000. If it expects to have sales of $420,000, the margin of safety is $120,000.

Contribution Margin

The profit equation can be rewritten by combining the terms with x in them.

$$\text{Profit} = (SP - VC)(x) - TFC$$

The difference between the selling price and variable costs per unit is referred to as the **contribution margin**. Each unit sold contributes this amount to cover fixed costs and increase profits. Consider what happens when sales increase by one unit. The firm benefits from revenue equal to the selling price, but it also incurs increased costs equal to the variable costs per unit. Since fixed costs are unaffected by changes in volume, they do not enter into the analysis.

If we solve the profit equation for the sales quantity in units (x), we get the following expression:

$$x = \frac{\text{Profit} + TFC}{\text{Contribution Margin}}$$

This is a handy formula for calculating the break-even point and solving for the quantity needed to earn various profit levels. Union Skate Company's amount of fixed costs is $100,000 per month. With a selling price of $150 and variable costs of $100, the contribution margin is $50. Using the formula implies that Union Skate must sell 2,000 units to break even each month.

$$2{,}000 = \frac{0 + \$100{,}000}{\$50}$$

Now Union Skate Company's management wants to know how many units the company must sell to achieve a profit of $40,000 in a given month. Using the formula implies that Union Skate must sell 2,800 units to achieve a profit of $40,000.

$$2{,}800 = \frac{\$40{,}000 + \$100{,}000}{\$50}$$

Contribution Margin Ratio

The **contribution margin ratio** is equal to the contribution margin per unit divided by the selling price.

$$\text{Contribution Margin Ratio} = \frac{SP - VC}{SP}$$

It measures the contribution of every sales dollar to covering fixed costs and generating a profit. Consider a company whose product has a selling price of $20 and requires variable costs of $15. In this case, the contribution margin ratio is 25 percent. Since its contribution margin per dollar of sales is 25 percent, the company will earn $.25 for every additional dollar of sales.

$$\text{Contribution Margin Ratio} = \frac{\$20 - \$15}{\$20} = 25\%$$

We can express the profit equation in terms of the contribution margin ratio as:

$$\text{Sales (in dollars)} = \frac{\text{Profit} + \text{TFC}}{\text{Contribution Margin Ratio}}$$

Union Skate Company can use this formula to calculate the amount of sales needed to earn a profit of $40,000 in a given month. Its contribution margin ratio is $.3333 (Contribution Margin of $50 ÷ Selling Price of $150). Thus, sales of $420,000 are needed.

$$\$420,000 = \frac{\$40,000 + \$100,000}{.3333}$$

"What If" Analysis

The profit equation can also show how profit will be affected by various options management is considering. Such analysis is sometimes referred to as **"what if" analysis** because it examines *what* will happen *if* a particular action is taken.

Change in Fixed and Variable Costs. Suppose Union Skate Company currently is selling 3,200 pairs of skates per month at a unit price of $150. Variable costs per unit are $100 and total fixed costs are $100,000 per month. Management is considering a change in the production process that will increase fixed costs per month by $50,000 but decrease variable costs to only $80 per unit. How would this change affect the company's monthly profit? Using the profit equation and assuming there will be no change in the selling price or the quantity sold, monthly profit under the alternative will be $74,000.

$$\text{Profit} = \$150(3,200) - \$80(3,200) - \$150,000 = \$74,000$$

Without the change, profit will equal only $60,000.

$$\text{Profit} = \$150(3,200) - \$100(3,200) - \$100,000 = \$60,000$$

Thus, it appears that the change in the production process is advisable. However, before making a decision, management may wish to consider how the action affects the company's break-even point. With the new production process, Union Skate will face a higher level of fixed costs and a higher break-even level. Before the change, its break-even point was 2,000 units. If Union Skate implements the new production process, its break-even point will change to 2,143 units. Since there is no significant difference in these break-even points, the change in the production process appears appropriate.

Old Break-Even Point	New Break-Even Point
$\frac{\$100,000 \text{ Fixed Costs}}{\$50 \text{ Contribution Margin}} = 2,000$ Units	$\frac{\$150,000 \text{ Fixed Costs}}{\$70 \text{ Contribution Margin}} = 2,143$ Units

Change in Selling Price. Any one of the variables in the profit equation can be considered in light of changes in the other variables. For example, suppose Union Skate's management wanted to know what the selling price would have to be to earn a profit of $80,000 if it sells 3,000 units in a given month. To answer this question, all of the relevant information is organized in terms of the profit equation and the equation then is solved for the selling price.

$$\$80,000 = SP\,(3,000) - \$100\,(3,000) - \$100,000$$
$$SP\,(3,000) = \$480,000$$
$$SP = \$160$$

MULTIPRODUCT ANALYSIS

LO 4 Perform cost-volume-profit analysis for multiple products.

The preceding examples have illustrated C-V-P analysis for a single product. C-V-P analysis can be extended to cover multiple products. In the following sections we demonstrate the use of the contribution margin and the contribution margin ratio in performing C-V-P analysis for a company with multiple products.

Contribution Margin Approach

If the products a company sells are similar (various flavors of ice cream, various types of calculators, various types of boats), the weighted average contribution margin per unit can be used in C-V-P analysis. For example, suppose the Hightech Calculator Company produces two types of calculators. Model A sells for $30 and requires $15 of variable cost per unit. Model B sells for $50 and requires $20 of variable costs per unit. Further, Hightech typically sells two Model A's for one Model B. To calculate the weighted average contribution margin, Hightech must first consider the fact that twice as many A's as B's are sold. Since two Model As are sold for each Model B, the contribution margin of A is multiplied by 2 and the contribution margin of B is multiplied by 1. The sum is then divided by 3 units to yield the weighted average contribution margin per unit of $20. (See Illustration 23-12.)

ILLUSTRATION 23-12 Calculation of Weighted Average Contribution Margin

	Contribution Margin Model A	Contribution Margin Model B
Selling price	$30	$50
Variable cost	15	20
Contribution margin	$15	$30

$$\text{Weighted Average Contribution Margin} = \frac{2\,(\$15) + 1\,(\$30)}{3} = \$20 \text{ per unit}$$

Now, suppose Hightech Company's fixed costs equal $100,000. How many calculators must it sell to break even? Working with the weighted average contribution margin, Hightech calculates its break even point as 5,000 calculators.

$$5,000 \text{ units} = \frac{0 + \$100,000}{\$20} \quad \begin{array}{l}\text{(Profit + Total Fixed Costs)}\\ \text{(Weighted Average Contribution Margin)}\end{array}$$

The 5,000 units sold to break even would be made up of the typical two-to-one mix. Thus, Hightech must sell 3,333 Model As (2/3 of 5,000) and 1,667 (1/3 of 5,000) Model Bs to break even.

Contribution Margin Ratio Approach

If a company sells very different products, it should perform C-V-P analysis using the contribution margin ratio. Consider a large department store such as

Sears. Sears sells literally thousands of different products. In this setting, it does not make sense to ask how many *units* Sears must sell to break even or how many *units* Sears must sell to generate a profit of $100,000. Because the costs and selling prices of the various items sold are considerably different, analyzing these types of questions in terms of number of units is not useful. Instead, these questions are addressed in terms of sales dollars. It is perfectly reasonable to ask how much must *sales* be to break even or how much must *sales* be to generate a profit of $100,000. To answer these questions, the contribution margin ratio, rather than the contribution margin per unit, is used.

Suppose Price-Low Drug Store is interested in using C-V-P analysis to analyze its operations. The company has three major departments—drugs, cosmetics, and household products—each of which sells a large number of different products. After performing a detailed study of fixed and variable costs in the prior year, the company prepared the analysis of departmental profitability indicated in Illustration 23-13.

ILLUSTRATION 23-13 Profitability Analysis of Departments

Price-Low Drug Store
Profitability Analysis
For the Year Ended December 31, 19X1

	Drugs	Cosmetics	Household Products	Total
Sales	$1,000,000	$700,000	$460,000	$2,160,000
Less variable costs:				
Merchandise	$ 600,000	$550,000	$260,000	$1,410,000
Wages	100,000	70,000	40,000	210,000
Total variable costs	$ 700,000	$620,000	$300,000	$1,620,000
Contribution margin	$ 300,000	$ 80,000	$160,000	$ 540,000
Contribution margin ratio	.30	.1143	.3478	.25
Less fixed costs:				
Utilities				$ 40,000
Rent				80,000
Management salaries				180,000
Total fixed costs				$300,000
Company profit				$240,000

Given the information in the report, what is Price-Low Drug Store's break-even level of sales? To answer this question, the total amount of fixed costs is divided by the contribution margin ratio for the store. The contribution margin ratio can be calculated by dividing the total contribution margin for the store by total store sales. Since the contribution margin is $540,000 and sales are $2,160,000, this yields a contribution margin ratio of .25. Thus, Price-Low's break-even sales are $1,200,000.

$$\$1,200,000 = \frac{\$300,000}{.25} \frac{\text{(Total Fixed Costs)}}{\text{(Contribution Margin Ratio)}}$$

The contribution margin ratio can also be used to analyze the effect on net income of a change in total company sales. Suppose in the coming year, Price-Low's management believes total company sales will increase by 20 percent and is interested in assessing the effect of this increase on overall company profitability. If sales increase by $432,000 (i.e., 20 percent), the contribution margin and net income will increase by $108,000 (i.e., .25 x $432,000).

Note that this approach makes one very important assumption: The increase in sales will result in increases in drugs, cosmetics, and household products in the same proportion as current sales. If this assumption is not warranted, then the contribution margin ratios of the three departments must be weighted by their share of the increase. For example, suppose the company believes sales will increase by $432,000 but expects the increase will be made up of a $200,000 increase in drug sales, a $200,000 increase in cosmetics sales, and a $32,000 increase in sales of household products. To calculate the effect on net income, Price-Low must use the contribution margin ratios of the specific departments. The expected increase in profit is $93,989.60.

Department	Increase in Sales	Contribution Margin Ratio	Increase in Profit
Drugs	$200,000	.3000	$60,000.00
Cosmetics	200,000	.1143	22,860.00
Household products	32,000	.3478	11,129.60
Total increase in profit			$93,989.60

Why did this analysis yield a smaller increase in net income than the preceding analysis? The preceding analysis assumed the increase in sales would be proportionate to the current mix of drugs, cosmetics, and household products. The current analysis assumes that of the $432,000 increase in sales only $32,000 is due to household products. Since household products is the product line with the highest contribution margin ratio, profit will be less if proportionately less of this profitable product line is sold.

ASSUMPTIONS IN C-V-P ANALYSIS

Whenever C-V-P analysis is performed, managers make a number of assumptions that affect the validity of the analysis. Perhaps the primary assumption is that costs can be accurately separated into their fixed and variable components. For some companies, this a very difficult and costly task. An additional assumption is that fixed costs remain fixed and variable costs per unit do not change over the activity levels of interest. With large changes in activity, this assumption may not be valid. In spite of these assumptions, most managers use C-V-P analysis to explore various profit targets and to perform "what if" analysis.

Union Skate Company

At the beginning of the chapter, Mary Stuart was considering whether to spend $80,000 to increase sales of the deluxe in-line skates by 1,000 units. The skates sell for $150 per pair. Suppose Mary used account analysis, and determined that variable costs per pair are $100. Using the techniques developed in the chapter and the information above, would you recommend that Mary start the advertising campaign? Hopefully, you concluded that the advertising campaign should *not* be started because profit will decrease by $30,000.

(Contribution Margin x Increase in Units) − Increase in Fixed Costs = Change in Profit
($50 x 1,000) − $80,000 = ($30,000)

INSIGHTS INTO ETHICS

Michael Sanders, president of Tuffcoat Corporation, has asked his accounting staff to prepare revised cost estimates for a metal coating referred to as X-59. He specifically instructs the staff: "Whenever there is any doubt as to whether a cost is variable or fixed, assume the cost is fixed." Sanders expects that sales of X-59 will increase by 20 percent in the coming year. The Board of Directors has asked Sanders to estimate the effect of the increase on company profit.

How will Sanders' instructions to his accounting staff affect the estimate of company profit? Are his instructions ethical?

SUMMARY

Identify the common cost behavior patterns. Several common cost behavior patterns exist: variable, fixed, and mixed. Variable costs are those that change in response to changes in volume or activity. Fixed costs remain constant across activity levels. Mixed costs contain both variable and fixed cost components.

Estimate the relationship between cost and activity using account analysis, the high-low method, and scattergraphs. Accountants use account analysis, the scattergraph approach, and the high-low method to estimate the relationship between cost and activity. Account analysis requires that the accountant use his or her judgment to classify expense accounts as either fixed or variable costs. A scattergraph is prepared by plotting cost and activity levels. It presents a picture of what costs might be at different activity levels. The high-low method fits a straight line to the costs at the highest and the lowest activity levels. Accountants also use regression analysis to estimate the relationship between cost and activity. Regression analysis is an advanced approach, however, and the chapter provided only a brief introduction to the method.

Perform cost-volume-profit analysis for single products. Once a company estimates its fixed and variable costs, it can perform cost-volume-profit analysis. C-V-P analysis makes use of the profit equation:

$$\text{Profit} = \text{Sales} - \text{Variable Cost} - \text{Fixed Cost}$$

Managers can use the profit equation to perform "what if" analysis. The effect of changing various components of the equation can be explored by solving the equation for the variable affected by the change. Specific examples include solving for the break-even point or solving the equation to determine the level of volume required to achieve a certain level of profit. Managers can determine the number of units that must be sold or the sales dollars needed to achieve a specified profit level using the following formulas:

$$\text{Number of Units} = \frac{\text{Fixed Cost} + \text{Profit}}{\text{Contribution Margin}} \qquad \text{Sales Dollars} = \frac{\text{Fixed Cost} + \text{Profit}}{\text{Contribution Margin Ratio}}$$

Perform cost-volume-profit analysis for multiple products. C-P-V analysis of multiple products is easily addressed by using the weighted average contribution margin per unit or the weighted average contribution margin ratio.

APPENDIX 23-A: VARIABLE AND FULL COSTING

Many accounting reports fail to distinguish between fixed and variable costs. For example, almost all manufacturing companies prepare income statements for external purposes using full costing (also called absorption costing). In full costing, inventory and cost of goods sold include direct material, direct labor, and all manufacturing overhead. While direct material and direct labor are generally variable costs, manufacturing overhead includes both variable and fixed cost elements. Thus, fixed and variable costs are commingled or combined, and it is very difficult to untangle the costs to perform "what if" analysis that requires separating fixed and variable costs.

LO 5
Discuss differences between variable and full costing.

VARIABLE COSTING

An alternative to full costing is variable costing. In **variable costing**, only variable production costs are included in inventory and cost of goods sold. All fixed production costs are treated as period costs and expensed in the period incurred. Variable costing is also referred to as **direct costing** although this name is not very accurate. Inventory costs under variable costing include variable overhead costs; these costs are indirect, not direct. GAAP requires that fixed production costs be included in inventory and cost of goods sold for external financial reporting purposes. However, variable costing still can be used for internal purposes. Survey data indicate that 17 percent of U.S. companies use variable costing.[1]

As shown in Illustration 23-14, the only difference between the two methods is their treatment of fixed manufacturing overhead costs. Under the full costing method, these costs are included in inventory and are entered as expense only when the inventory is sold. Under the variable costing method, fixed manufacturing costs are entered as expense in the same way as other nonmanufacturing period costs. Consider depreciation, which usually is a fixed-cost component of manufacturing overhead. Under full costing, some portion of depreciation for the period remains in ending inventory when not all of the items produced are sold. However, under the variable costing method, the total amount of depreciation is treated as an expense of the period.

VARIABLE COSTING INCOME STATEMENT

If variable costing is used, a company can prepare an income statement that classifies all expenses in terms of their cost behavior—either fixed or variable. With variable expenses separated from fixed expenses, a contribution margin can be presented. With the contribution margin information, readers of the income statement can make reasonable estimates of how much profit will change for a change in sales. Income statements prepared using variable costing

---

[1] See R.A. Howell, J.D. Brown, S.R. Soucy, and A.H. Seed, III, *Management Accounting in the New Manufacturing Environment*, (National Association of Accountants, 1987), p. 131.

ILLUSTRATION 23-14 Comparison of Full and Variable Costing

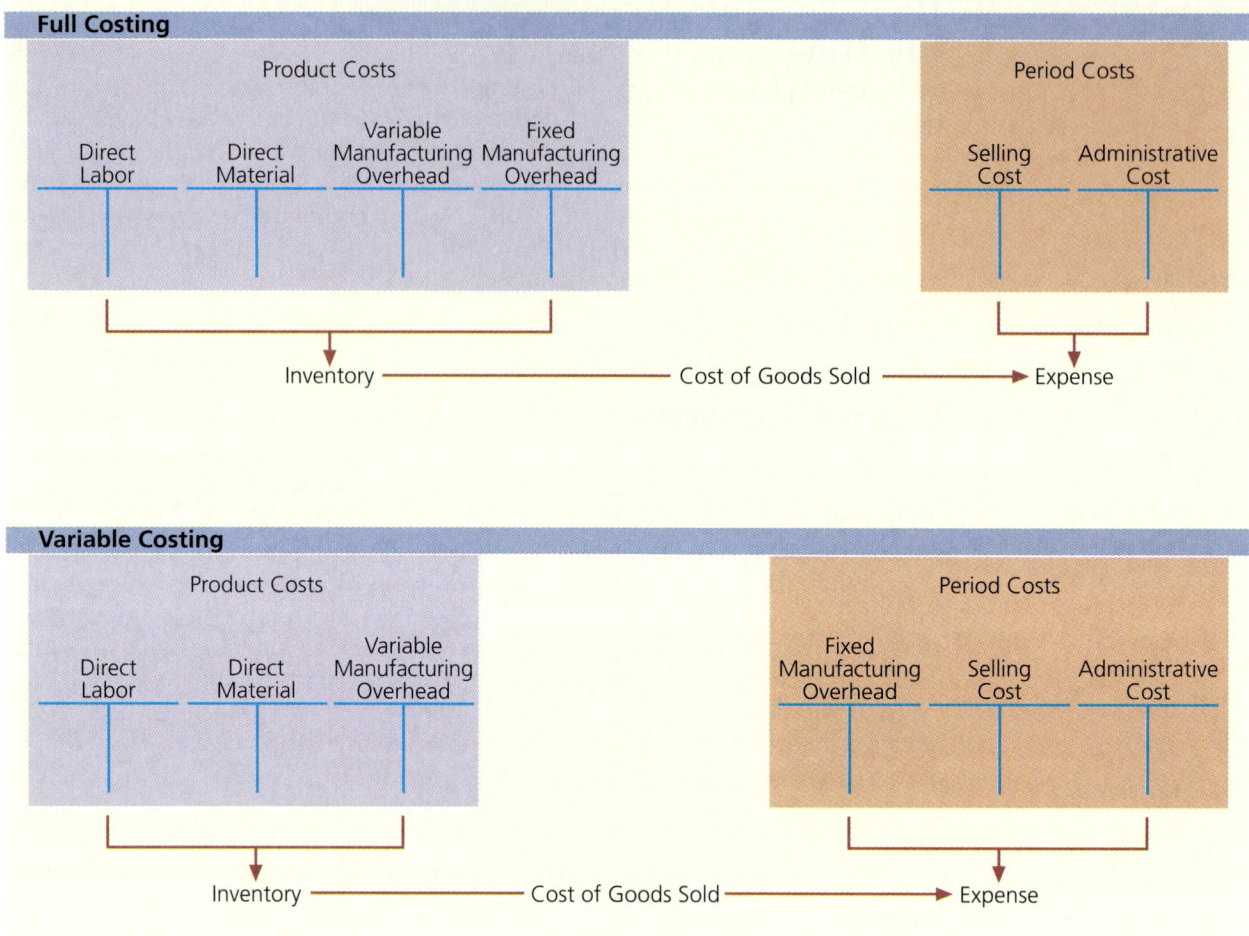

and then full costing are compared in Illustration 23-15. Suppose Federal Manufacturing Company expects its sales to increase by $10,000. What is the expected increase in profit? Using the variable costing income statement, we easily can calculate the contribution margin ratio as the contribution margin divided by sales, or 65 percent. If sales increase by $10,000, profit should increase by $6,500.

EFFECT OF FULL AND VARIABLE COSTING ON INCOME

LO 6
Discuss how income will differ between variable and full costing when the number of units produced does not equal the number of units sold.

To examine in detail the differences between full and variable costing, consider the following example. Miller Heating Company is a small manufacturer of auxiliary heaters. The units sell for $100 each. The variable production cost of each unit includes: direct material, $18; direct labor, $12; and variable manufacturing overhead, $10. In addition, Miller Heating incurs $200,000 of fixed manufactur-

ILLUSTRATION 23-15 Comparison of Income Statements Prepared Using Variable and Full Costing.

Income Statement Prepared Using Variable Costing

Federal Manufacturing Company
Income Statement
For the Period Ended December 31, 19X1

Sales		$100,000
Less variable costs:		
Variable cost of goods sold	$20,000	
Variable selling expense	10,000	
Variable administrative expense	5,000	
Total variable costs		35,000
Contribution margin		$ 65,000
Less fixed costs:		
Fixed manufacturing expense	$10,000	
Fixed selling expense	8,000	
Fixed administrative expense	7,000	
Total fixed costs		25,000
Net income		$ 40,000

Income Statement Prepared Using Full Costing

Federal Manufacturing Company
Income Statement
For the Period Ended December 31, 19X1

Sales		$100,000
Less cost of goods sold		30,000
Gross margin		$ 70,000
Less selling and administrative expense:		
Selling expense	$18,000	
Administrative expense	12,000	
Total selling and administrative expense		30,000
Net income		$ 40,000

ing overhead each period. Selling and administrative costs are fixed costs amounting to $50,000 and $100,000, respectively.

Selling price		$100
Variable production costs:		
Direct material	$18	
Direct labor	12	
Variable overhead	10	
Total variable production costs		40
Contribution margin per unit		$ 60
Fixed manufacturing overhead		$200,000
Fixed selling cost		50,000
Fixed administrative cost		100,000

Suppose that in 19X1 there is no beginning inventory of finished goods, 15,000 units are produced, and 10,000 units are sold. Illustration 23-16 provides a full costing income statement for this situation. The full cost of production is $800,000. This includes $600,000 of variable production cost ($40 per unit × 15,000 units) and $200,000 of fixed manufacturing overhead. With 15,000 units produced, Miller Heating's unit cost is $53.3333.

$$\text{Unit Cost Under Full Costing} = \frac{\text{Total Production Cost}}{\text{Number of Units Produced}}$$

$$\$53.3333 = \frac{\$800,000}{15,000}$$

Since Miller Heating sells 10,000 units, its cost of goods sold is $533,333. Net income amounts to $316,667.

ILLUSTRATION 23-16 Full Costing Income

Miller Heating Company
Income Statement
For the Year Ended December 31, 19X1

Sales		$1,000,000
Less cost of goods sold:		
Beginning inventory	$ 0	
Plus production costs:		
Variable	600,000	
Fixed	200,000	
	$800,000	
Less ending inventory:	266,667	
Cost of goods sold		533,333
Gross profit		$ 466,667
Less selling and administrative expense:		
Selling expense	$ 50,000	
Administrative expense	100,000	150,000
Net income		$ 316,667

Note: Units produced were 15,000; units sold were 10,000; ending inventory equals 5,000 units × $53.3333.

Illustration 23-17 presents Miller Heating's income statement for the same situation using variable costing. Under variable costing, each unit contains only the $40 of variable production cost. Note that the ending inventory amount in the cost of goods sold calculation is only $200,000 (5,000 units × $40 per unit), compared to $266,667 under full costing, because under variable costing, none of the $200,000 of fixed production cost was included in inventory. Under full costing, part of the $200,000 of fixed cost remains in ending inventory. Since Miller Heating produced 15,000 units, the fixed cost of each unit is $13.3333 ($200,000 ÷ 15,000). Thus the cost of the 5,000 units in ending inventory includes $66,667 of fixed cost. This accounts for the difference in income under variable and full costing.

If the quantity produced exceeds the quantity sold, full costing yields a higher income than variable costing because some of the fixed costs remain in ending inventory under full costing. If the quantity sold exceeds the quantity

ILLUSTRATION 23-17 Variable Costing Income

Miller Heating Company
Income Statement
For the Year Ended December 31, 19X1

Sales		$1,000,000
Less variable cost of goods sold:		
Beginning inventory	$ 0	
Plus variable production costs	600,000	
Less ending inventory	200,000	
Variable cost of goods sold		400,000
Contribution margin		$ 600,000
Less fixed costs:		
Fixed production costs	$200,000	
Fixed selling expense	50,000	
Fixed administrative expense	100,000	350,000
Net income		$ 250,000

Note: Units produced were 15,000; units sold were 10,000.

produced, however, the situation reverses. That is, variable costing results in the higher income because, under full costing, the units sold out of beginning inventory have a higher cost since they include fixed overhead. If the quantity sold is equal to the quantity produced, both methods result in the same level of income.

Condition	Result
Units produced exceed units sold	Full costing has the higher income
Units sold exceed units produced	Variable costing has the higher income
Units sold equal units produced	No difference in income

BENEFITS OF VARIABLE COSTING FOR INTERNAL REPORTING

Since variable costing separates fixed and variable costs, users of internal financial reports can more easily perform C-V-P analysis. Suppose a manager of Miller Heating Company is interested in forecasting profit in 19X2. Further, suppose the manager believes that sales in 19X2 will be 17,000 units. How much profit should the manager forecast? Ideally, to answer this question, the manager would multiply the 17,000 units by the contribution margin per unit and then subtract fixed cost. Unfortunately, the full costing income statement does not provide contribution margin information. Thus, the manager may be tempted to calculate net income per dollar of sales and multiply it by expected sales. This would result in an *incorrect* forecast of profit of $538,334 [i.e., ($316,667 ÷ $1,000,000) x (17,000 x $100)]. On the other hand, the manager could easily calculate the contribution margin per unit of $60 by using the variable costing income statement (i.e., $600,000 ÷ 10,000 units sold). Thus, expected profit is $670,000.

Expected Profit = (Contribution Margin x Units Sold) − Fixed Cost
$670,000 = ($60 x 17,000) − $350,000

Another reason why variable costing may be preferred for internal purposes is that it does not allow managers to inflate profit artificially by producing more than they can sell. Suppose a manager expects sales to be 1,000 units. The selling price is $100 per unit, variable costs are $50 per unit, and fixed costs are $45,000. If the manager produces 1,000 units, profit would be equal to $5,000 [i.e., 1,000 x ($100 − $50) − $45,000] under both the full costing and the variable costing methods. The manager may realize, however, that if the full costing method is used, part of the fixed costs can be assigned to ending inventory, thereby transferring the expense to a future period. Thus, if the manager produces 2,000 units, profit will be $22,500 higher because half of the fixed costs will be included in the 1,000 units remaining in ending inventory. Of course, this is a short-run strategy because eventually the inventory buildup will be noticed. However, by the time excess inventory is noted the manager may to be working for a different company and have a great "track record" as a manager at the former company. Note that the strategy of producing more than you can sell will not increase income under the variable costing method, since under that method, none of the fixed costs can be included in ending inventory.

REVIEW PROBLEM

The Dream Baking Company has a contract with a local military base to provide the base with dinner rolls. Dream receives $1.20 per dozen rolls. The costs of producing 4,000 dozen rolls for the month of January 19X3 were as follows:

Ingredients	$1,000
Labor	1,250
Depreciation of equipment	200
Rent, baking shop	400
Utilities (50% variable, 50% fixed)	300

REQUIRED:

a. Use the account analysis approach to estimate the total fixed and total variable costs of baking the 4,000 dozen rolls. Also calculate the variable costs per dozen rolls.
b. Calculate how many dozen rolls Dream must sell to the base in February to break-even. Also calculate the break-even point in dollars.
c. If Dream expects to sell 6,000 dozen rolls in February, calculate the margin of safety for February operations.
d. Calculate the contribution margin per dozen rolls.
e. Using the contribution margin, calculate how many dozen rolls must be sold in February to earn a $600 profit. Also calculate the dollar sales needed to earn a $600 profit.
f. Calculate the contribution margin ratio.
g. Using the contribution margin ratio, calculate the dollar sales in February necessary to earn a $600 profit.
h. Suppose Dream gets an order for 6,000 dozen rolls for February. Calculate the expected profit.
i. Construct a profit graph. Label the following: total revenue, total expenses, variable expenses, fixed expenses, break-even point, and margin of safety.

j. Suppose Dream has the opportunity to purchase a new oven that is more efficient. If the oven had been used in January, Dream estimates the variable utility cost would have been reduced from $150 to $40 and labor would have been reduced from $1,250 to $1,000. The monthly depreciation after the acquisition of the new oven would be $600 per month. Calculate the new break-even point. Calculate the expected profit assuming sales of 6,000 dozen rolls.

k. Should Dream purchase the new oven?

SOLUTION:

(a) *Calculate fixed and variable costs.*

The ingredients are clearly variable. The labor could be all fixed, all variable, or some combination of fixed and variable (i.e., mixed or semivariable). Direct labor is usually considered variable while indirect labor often is fixed or mixed. For our solution we will assume the labor is all variable. The depreciation and rent are assumed to be fixed, and the utilities are as given, 50% variable and 50% fixed.

The account analysis approach would provide the following results:

Variable costs:		Fixed costs:	
Ingredients	$1,000	Depreciation	$200
Labor	1,250	Rent	400
Utilities	150	Utilities	150
	$2,400		$750

The variable cost per dozen rolls is:

$$\$2,400 \div 4,000 = \$.60$$

(b) *Calculate the break-even point.*

The following profit equation yields the break-even point:

$$\text{Profit} = SP(x) - VC(x) - TFC$$

where
x = Quantity of units produced and sold
SP = Selling price per unit
VC = Variable cost per unit
TFC = Total fixed costs

To find the break-even point, let profit = 0 and solve the equation:

$$0 = \$1.20(x) - .60(x) - \$750$$
$$0 = .60(x) - \$750$$
$$.60(x) = \$750$$
$$x = 1,250 \text{ dozen}$$

The break-even point in dollar sales is 1,250 × $1.20 = $1,500

(c) *Determine the margin of safety.*

In units:	Expected sales	6,000
	Break-even point	1,250
	Margin of safety	4,750

In dollars:	Expected sales	$7,200
	Break-even point	1,500
	Margin of safety	$5,700

(d) *Determine the contribution margin.*

The difference between the selling price and the variable cost per unit is the contribution margin:

$$\$1.20 - \$.60 = \underline{\underline{\$.60}}$$

(e) *Calculate required sales using contribution margin.*

When the profit equation is solved for units (x), we get the following expression:

$$x = \frac{\text{Profit} + \text{TFC}}{\text{Contribution Margin}}$$

The contribution margin can be used with this expression to calculate how many units must be sold in February to earn a $600 profit.

$$x = \frac{\$600 + \$750}{\$.60}$$

$$x = \underline{\underline{2{,}250}} \text{ dozen rolls}$$

The dollar sales needed to earn the $600 profit are:

$$2{,}250 \times \$1.20 = \underline{\underline{\$2{,}700}}$$

(f) *Determine the contribution margin ratio.*

$$\text{Contribution margin ratio} = \frac{\text{SP} - \text{VC}}{\text{SP}}$$

$$= \frac{\$1.20 - \$.60}{\$1.20}$$

$$= .50 \text{ or } \underline{\underline{50\%}}$$

(g) *Calculate target sales using contribution margin.*

We can express the profit equation in terms of the contribution margin ratio as:

$$\text{Sales (in dollars)} = \frac{\text{Profit} + \text{TFC}}{\text{Contribution Margin Ratio}}$$

$$\text{Sales (\$)} = \frac{\$600 + \$750}{.50}$$

$$\text{Sales (\$)} = \underline{\underline{\$2{,}700}}$$

(h) *Calculate expected profit.*

$$\text{Profit} = \text{SP}(x) - \text{VC}(x) - \text{TFC}$$
$$\text{Profit} = \$1.20(6{,}000) - .60(6{,}000) - \$750$$
$$\text{Profit} = \$7{,}200 - \$3{,}600 - \$750$$
$$\text{Profit} = \underline{\underline{\$2{,}850}}$$

(i) *Create a profit graph.*

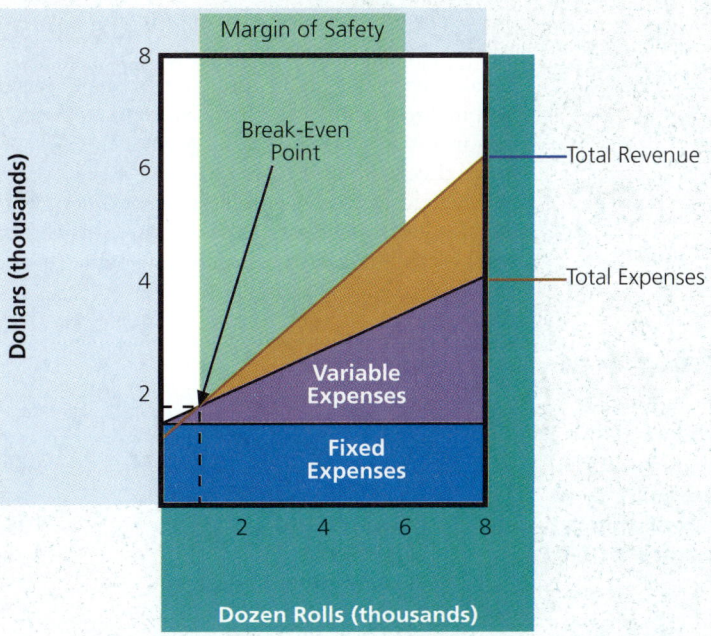

(j) *Determine the break-even point and projected profit if the new oven is purchased.*

The purchase of the oven changes Dream's cost behavior:

Variable costs:		Fixed costs:	
Ingredients	$1,000	Depreciation	$ 600
Labor	1,000	Rent	400
Utilities	40	Utilities	150
	$2,040		$1,150

The variable cost per dozen changes to:

$$\$2{,}040 \div 4{,}000 = \underline{\underline{\$.51}}$$

Solving the profit equation to find the break-even point:

$$\text{Profit} = SP(x) - VC(x) - TFC$$

To find the break-even point, let profit = 0 and solve the equation:

$$0 = \$1.20(x) - .51(x) - \$1{,}150$$
$$0 = .69(x) - \$1{,}150$$
$$.69(x) = \$1{,}150$$
$$x = \underline{\underline{1{,}667}} \text{ dozen (rounded)}$$

The break-even point in dollar sales is 1,667 × $1.20 = $\underline{\underline{\$2{,}000}}$ (rounded)

The new break-even point is higher (1,667 dozen rolls) than the old break-even point (1,250 dozen rolls). To calculate the expected profit for a sales level of 6,000 dozen rolls, use the new cost data in the profit equation:

$$\text{Profit} = SP(x) - VC(x) - TFC$$
$$\text{Profit} = \$1.20(6{,}000) - .51(6{,}000) - \$1{,}150$$
$$\text{Profit} = \$7{,}200 - \$3{,}060 - \$1{,}150$$
$$\text{Profit} = \underline{\underline{\$2{,}990}}$$

(k) *Determine if Dream should purchase the oven.*

The new oven increases Dream's fixed costs, and compensates for this by decreasing variable costs. At high production levels the savings in variable costs will at some point become greater than the increase in fixed costs. At the level of 6,000 dozen rolls the savings in variable costs (9 cents per dozen rolls x 6,000 = $540) is greater than the increase in fixed costs ($400). This results in a $140 projected increase in profit. Dream therefore will benefit from the purchase of the oven, but only at high production levels. At production levels of less than 4,444 dozen rolls (i.e., $400 ÷ .09) the increase in fixed costs will be greater than the savings in variable costs.

KEY TERMS

account analysis, *939*
break-even point, *945*
contribution margin, *947*
contribution margin ratio, *947*
cost-volume-profit (C-V-P) analysis, *936*
direct costing, *953*
fixed costs, *937*
high-low method, *941*
margin of safety, *947*
mixed costs, *937*
regression analysis, *944*
relevant range, *944*
scattergraph, *941*
variable costing, *953*
variable costs, *936*
"what if" analysis, *948*

SELF-QUIZ

LO 1 1. Variable costs:
   a. Decrease per unit of activity as activity decreases.
   b. Increase per unit of activity as activity decreases.
   c. Remain constant per unit of activity as activity decreases.
   d. None of the above.

LO 1 2. Fixed costs:
   a. Decrease per unit of activity as activity decreases.
   b. Increase per unit of activity as activity decreases.
   c. Remain constant per unit of activity as activity decreases.
   d. None of the above.

LO 1 3. Mixed costs:
   a. Are costs that are part selling and part manufacturing.
   b. Are costs that are part product and part period.
   c. Are costs that are part fixed and part variable.
   d. None of the above.

LO 3 4. One key to C-V-P analysis is determining how _____ behave when volume changes.

LO 1 5. In order to determine the effect that changes in volume have on costs, we classify costs as _____, _____, or _____.

LO 1 6. An example of a fixed cost for a company which manufactures automobiles is:
   a. Automobile tires
   b. Depreciation on the production plant
   c. Wages of production line workers
   d. None of the above

LO 1 7. Listed below are costs for a company which paints and sells custom designed T-shirts. Identify the costs as fixed (*F*) or variable (*V*). For possible mixed costs, label them *F and V*.
   ___ a. Depreciation of the air brush equipment
   ___ b. Rent on the store
   ___ c. Insurance
   ___ d. Paint
   ___ e. T-shirts
   ___ f. Advertising
   ___ g. Wages of artist employed to paint the shirts
   ___ h. Salary of cashier
   ___ i. Utilities
   ___ j. Monthly fee paid to accountant for bookkeeping
   ___ k. Solvents to clean air brush

LO 2 8. Four methods to estimate the fixed and variable components of total costs are: _____, _____, _____, and _____.

LO 3 9. The break-even point is:
   a. The activity level where total costs and total revenues are equal.
   b. The activity level where fixed costs are equal to variable costs.
   c. The activity level where revenue is equal to variable costs.
   d. None of the above.

LO 3 10. The profit equation is stated as:
   Profit = SP(*x*) − VC(*x*) − TFC.
   Identify the terms in the equation:

SP   _____
x   _____
VC   _____
TFC _____

LO 3 11. A company has the following:
Sales price per unit: $10
Variable cost per unit: $6
Total fixed cost: $1,000
The break-even point is:
a. 1,000 units.
b. 250 units.
c. 400 units.
d. None of the above.

LO 2 12. A company has the following cleaning solvent costs and activity levels for the past six months:

	Solvent Costs	Units Produced
March	$400	50
April	350	40
May	425	55
June	460	65
July	320	30
August	410	50

Using the high-low method to analyze the total cleaning solvent costs, the variable cost *per unit* and the *total* fixed costs are:
a. $4 and $200.
b. $5 and $200.
c. $3.50 and $300.
d. $3 and $500.

LO 1
LO 2
LO 3 13. Key terms and their definitions are listed below. Match the definitions with the key terms.
___ a. Account analysis
___ b. Fixed costs
___ c. Relevant range
___ d. Margin of safety
___ e. Contribution margin
___ f. High-low method
___ g. Cost-volume-profit analysis
(1) A method of estimating the fixed and variable components of total costs, based on costs at two activity levels.
(2) Explores the relationships among costs, volume or activity levels, and profit.
(3) The range of activity for which estimates of fixed and variable costs are likely to be accurate.
(4) The accountant uses his or her judgment to classify expenses as fixed or variable.
(5) The difference between selling price and variable cost per unit.
(6) Costs that do not change in response to changes in activity levels.
(7) The difference between the expected level of sales and break-even sales.

LO 3 14. A company has the following data:
Unit sales price: $20
Unit variable cost: $14
Calculate: (1) the contribution margin, and (2) the contribution margin ratio.

LO 2 15. A scattergraph:
a. Graphically illustrates total revenue, total costs, and profit or loss.
b. Plots total revenues.
c. Plots costs and activity levels to gain insight into the relationship between cost and activity.
d. None of the above.

LO 3 16. A company has the following data:
Unit sales price: $200
Unit variable cost: $150
Total fixed costs: $5,000
The contribution margin ratio is:
a. $50.
b. 3%.
c. 33.3%.
d. 25%.

LO 3 17. The break-even point on a profit graph is the point where the total revenue line intersects:
a. The fixed expense line.
b. The margin of safety.
c. The relevant range.
d. The total cost line.

LO 4 18. For a company selling more than one product:
a. C-V-P analysis cannot be used.
b. A separate C-V-P analysis must be performed for each product the company sells.
c. C-V-P is performed using the weighted average contribution margin approach or the weighted average contribution margin ratio approach.
d. None of the above.

LO 5 19. (Appendix) The difference between variable and full costing is:
a. Their treatment of variable manufacturing costs.
b. Their treatment of fixed manufacturing costs.
c. Their treatment of direct labor.
d. None of the above.

LO 6 20. (Appendix) Match the following:
___ a. Sales exceed production
___ b. Production exceeds sales
___ c. Production and sales are equal
(1) Full costing profit is greater than variable costing profit.
(2) Full costing profit is less than variable costing profit.
(3) Full costing profit and variable costing profit are equal.

SOLUTIONS TO SELF-QUIZ
1. c   2. b   3. c   4. costs   5. variable, fixed, mixed   6. b   7. a. F b. F c. F d. V e. V f. F g. F or V depending on terms of compensation h. F i. F and V (i.e., mixed) j. F k. could be F, could be V, could be mixed   8. account analysis, scattergraph, high-low, regression   9. a   10. SP = sales price per unit, x = number of units sold, i.e., activity level, VC = variable costs per unit, TFC = total fixed cost   11. b   12. a   13. a. 4 b. 6 c. 3 d. 7 e. 5 f. 1 g. 2   14. (1) contribution margin = $20 − $14 = $6 (2) contribution margin ratio = ($20 − $14)/$20 = .30 or 30%   15. c   16. d   17. d   18. c   19. b   20. a. 2 b. 1 c. 3

QUESTIONS

Q23-1 To perform C-V-P analysis, we must (1) be able to estimate revenues at different volume levels, and (2) estimate expenses at different volume levels. Which is probably easier to estimate, revenues or expenses? Why?

Q23-2 Variable costs are normally a fixed amount per unit of activity. Why then are such costs referred to as variable?

Q23-3 Fixed costs vary on a per-unit basis in relation to changes in volume. Why then are such costs referred to as fixed?

Q23-4 In many businesses, expenses may not behave in a strict fixed and variable pattern. Does this mean that C-V-P is not a practical and useful analysis? Discuss.

Q23-5 Do total fixed costs ever increase or decrease? Discuss.

Q23-6 Give two examples of variable costs.

Q23-7 What is a mixed cost?

Q23-8 Account analysis is a common approach to estimating the fixed and variable components of costs. Why do you suppose this method is so popular?

Q23-9 A widely acclaimed accounting professor once said, "For the manager of a business, C-V-P is the single most important decision-making tool there is. Period." Do you agree with this or is it an exaggeration? Discuss.

Q23-10 A hospital administrator is performing C-V-P analysis. Activity level is measured in number of patient days. Would nursing salaries be a fixed, variable, or mixed cost? Discuss.

Q23-11 This statement was made by an experienced financial executive, "A lot of variable costs are fixed in the short run." Discuss the meaning of this statement.

Q23-12 The high-low method is one technique used to estimate the fixed and variable components of a total cost. It has some problems. What are they?

Q23-13 Why is the concept of relevant range so important to C-V-P? Discuss.

Q23-14 Comment on the following statement made by a business owner. "My accountant says that total fixed costs are $500,000 per year. I am using that number in my C-V-P analysis and I like the results. My calculations show that if we triple our business volume, something I think we can do, I am going to make a heck of a lot of money."

Q23-15 (Appendix) The difference between full costing and variable costing is in the amount of fixed manufacturing costs that are expensed during an accounting period. Explain how fixed manufacturing costs become an expense under full costing. Explain how fixed manufacturing costs become an expense under variable costing.

Q23-16 (Appendix) Those who support variable costing as a method of reporting income argue that the variable costing income statement is more useful to a decision maker who is trying to use the statement to project a company's future income. Explain how the variable costing statement assists in projecting income.

CHAPTER 23 COST-VOLUME-PROFIT ANALYSIS

EXERCISES

LO 1

E23-1 Cost Behavior Information for three costs incurred in a typical manufacturing company follows:

	Period	Amount	Units produced
Depreciation:	Jan.	$500,000	3,000
	Feb.	$500,000	4,500
	Mar.	$500,000	6,000
Direct labor:	Jan.	$120,000	3,000
	Feb.	$180,000	4,500
	Mar.	$240,000	6,000
Utilities:	Jan.	$25,000	3,000
	Feb.	$32,500	4,500
	Mar.	$40,000	6,000

REQUIRED:

For each cost plot the cost on a two dimensional graph, making the vertical axis dollars and the horizontal axis activity, and label it fixed, variable, or mixed.

LO 2

E23-2 High-Low Method The Rough River Rafting Company wants to identify the behavior of their raft repair expense so that they will be able to project the expense at different levels of activity. The following data has been gathered:

Period	Repair Expense	Number of Customers
May	$ 8,000	2,000
June	$12,000	4,000
July	$20,000	8,000
Aug.	$16,000	6,000
Sept.	$10,000	3,000

REQUIRED:

Determine the fixed and variable components of raft repair expense using the high-low method.

LO 2

E23-3 Scattergraph Ocean Rentals is interested in learning about the behavior of their utility costs in relation to the rental activity of one of their typical Ocean side condominiums. The climate is similar year-round and seasons do not materially influence utility cost. Activity level is measured in rental days per month. Use the following information to prepare a scattergraph of the utility costs. Based on the scattergraph, are the utility costs fixed, variable or mixed?

Period	Utility Expense	Rental Days
May	$150	10
June	$165	12
July	$120	4
August	$190	20

LO 2

E23-4 Account Analysis Sunshine Tee Shirt Company has the following information available regarding the costs of operating their business, which consists of purchasing plain shirts, painting them with various designs and logos, and selling them to tourists.

Cost Information for May
2,000 shirts sold

Rent	$ 400
Insurance	100
Utilities	200
Artist salary	1,500
Cashier salary	800
Paint	500
Cost of plain shirts sold	10,000
Depreciation	900

REQUIRED:

Use the account analysis method to determine:
a. total fixed costs.
b. total variable costs.
c. variable costs per shirt.

For expenses which could be either fixed or variable, assume they are fixed.

E23-5 C-V-P Analysis, Profit Equation A single-product company has the following information for a particular accounting period.

Unit sales price	$500
Unit variable costs	$200
Fixed costs	$75,000

REQUIRED:

Calculate the break-even point in units using the profit equation.

E23-6 C-V-P Analysis, Contribution Margin A single-product company has the following information for its current accounting period.

Unit sales price	$500
Unit variable costs	$200
Fixed costs	$75,000

REQUIRED:

a. Calculate the contribution margin.
b. Use the contribution margin to calculate the break-even point in units.

E23-7 C-V-P Analysis, Contribution Margin Ratio A single-product company has the following information for a particular accounting period.

Unit sales price	$500
Unit variable costs	$200
Fixed costs	$75,000

REQUIRED:

a. Calculate the contribution margin ratio.
b. Use the contribution margin ratio to calculate the break-even point in sales dollars.

E23-8 C-V-P Analysis, Margin of Safety A single-product company has the following information for a particular accounting period. They expect to sell 5,000 units.

Unit sales price	$100
Unit variable costs	$70
Fixed costs	$100,000

CHAPTER 23 COST-VOLUME-PROFIT ANALYSIS

REQUIRED:

a. Calculate the break-even point in units using the contribution margin method.
b. Calculate the margin of safety in units.
c. Calculate the projected profit in dollars.

LO 3

E23-9 C-V-P Analysis A single-product company has the following information for a particular accounting period.

Unit sales price	$100
Unit variable costs	$70
Fixed costs	$100,000

REQUIRED:

a. Use the contribution margin method to calculate the unit sales needed to produce a $25,000 profit.
b. Use the contribution margin method to calculate the dollar sales needed to produce a $25,000 profit.

LO 3

E23-10 C-V-P Analysis, "What If" Analysis A single-product company has the following information for its current accounting period.

Unit sales price	$25
Unit variable costs	$15
Fixed costs	$50,000

The company expects to sell 7,000 units. They are considering increasing advertising by $10,000 and feel the additional promotion would sell an additional 500 units.

REQUIRED:

a. Calculate the expected profit from the sale of 7,000 units.
b. Calculate the expected profit if they increase advertising.

LO 3

E23-11 C-V-P Analysis, "What If" Analysis A single- product company has the following information for its current accounting period.

Unit sales price	$25
Unit variable costs	$15
Fixed costs	$50,000

The company expects to sell 7,000 units. They are considering purchasing more modern and efficient production equipment. The new equipment would increase their fixed costs by $15,000, but the increased efficiency would reduce variable labor costs by $3 per unit.

REQUIRED:

a. Calculate the expected profit without the new equipment
b. Calculate the expected profit with the new equipment.

LO 4

E23-12 C-V-P Analysis, Multiproduct, Contribution Margin Approach The Head Gear Helmet Company produces two helmets, Model A for kayaking and rockclimbing, and model B for motorcycling. Model A sells for $35 and has a variable cost of $20; Model B sells for $150 and has a variable cost of $75. Head Gear typically sells three Model Bs for every one Model A. Their annual fixed costs are $250,000.

REQUIRED:

a. Calculate the weighted average contribution margin.
b. Use the weighted average contribution margin to calculate the break-even point in total helmets.
c. Break the total helmet sales into Model A and Model B helmets.

LO 4

E23-13 C-V-P Analysis, Multiproduct, Contribution Margin Ratio Approach Assume the same set of facts as in E23-12. That is, the Head Gear Helmet Company produces two helmets, Model A for kayaking and rockclimbing, and Model B for motorcycling. Model A sells for $35 and has a variable cost of $20; Model B sells for $150 and has a variable cost of $75. Head Gear typically sells three Model Bs for every one Model A. Their annual fixed costs are $250,000.

REQUIRED:

a. Calculate the weighted average contribution margin ratio.
b. Use the weighted average contribution margin ratio to calculate the break-even point in dollar sales.

LO 5,6

E23-14 Variable and Full Costing (Appendix) A manufacturing company began operations on January 1, 19X3. Information for their first year of operations is as follows:

Units produced	100,000
Units sold	80,000
Units in ending inventory	20,000
Fixed manufacturing costs	$500,000

REQUIRED:

a. Calculate the amount of fixed manufacturing costs that would be expensed for 19X3, assuming an income statement based on full costing.
b. Calculate the amount of fixed manufacturing costs that would be expensed for 19X3 assuming an income statement based on variable costing.
c. Calculate the difference in profit reported by the two methods.

PROBLEM SET A

LO 1,2

P23-1A Cost Behavior Patterns, Account Analysis The Beach Party Tanning Salon is interested in investigating the behavior patterns of their operating costs so that they can make better projections of their costs and profits. Beach Party caters to an exclusive clientele and provides the following services which are included in the basic tanning fee: tanning oil, towels, hot tub, sauna, shower facilities, soap, shampoo, body lotion, and the morning newspaper. Coffee, tea, and exotic non-alcoholic tropical drinks are provided as are hors d'oeuvres.

REQUIRED:

Selected Beach Party costs follow. Label each cost as fixed (F), variable (V), or mixed (M).

___ a. Building rental (rent is $400 per month plus 5% of gross tanning fees)
___ b. City occupational tax (2% of gross tanning fees)
___ c. Chlorine, PH +, PH –, other miscellaneous chemicals for operation of the hot tub
___ d. Depreciation of computer
___ e. Depreciation of typewriter
___ f. Depreciation of cash register
___ g. Salaries of two attendants
___ h. Salary of one janitorial worker

___ i. Water
___ j. Electricity
___ k. Repairs and maintenance—tanning beds
___ l. Insurance
___ m. Professional fees (accountant is paid a monthly fee to keep books, prepare monthly financial statements and all required tax returns)
___ n. Towel service (a company provides clean towels and laundry service, monthly fee is $100 plus $.025 for each towel provided)
___ o. Newspapers (A subscription to 12 copies of the local newspaper, 6 copies of the *New York Times*, and 6 copies of the *Wall Street Journal*)
___ p. Soap, shampoo, body lotion
___ q. Beverages and hors d'oeuvres (provided by a local caterer, fee $150 per month plus a charge for food and beverages provided).
___ r. Radio commercials
___ s. Office supplies
___ t. Depreciation of tanning beds

LO 1,2   **P23-2A**   **Estimating Costs**   The Wildwood Country Club operates a swimming pool for its members. Records are kept of the number of people who enter the pool area. Wildwood is interested in learning about the behavior of their pool operating costs in relation to pool usage. Operating costs and usage data for last season are as follows:

	June	*July*	*August*
Admissions	2,600	4,000	2,000
Depreciation	$1,000	$1,000	$1,000
Life guard wages	1,600	2,000	1,500
Water	200	300	200
Chemicals	1,000	1,500	800
Total costs	$3,800	$4,800	$3,500

REQUIRED:

a. Use the high-low method to determine the fixed and variable components of the total pool operating costs.
b. Estimate the total monthly costs of operating the pool if the admissions are 5,000.
c. Draw a scattergraph plotting admissions on the horizontal axis and total costs in dollars on the vertical axis.

LO 1,2,3   **P23-3A**   **Cost Behavior Patterns, Estimating Costs, C-V-P, Margin of Safety, "What If" Analysis**   Nancy Adams has the opportunity to operate a refreshment stand at the state fair. The fair operates from August 1 through August 12. Nancy plans to sell a single item, a 16-ounce cola. It is served with six ounces of finely ground ice, similar to the consistency of a snow cone. She has named the drink "Cola Cooler." She has obtained the following information about the costs of operating the refreshment stand for the 12-day period.

License fee from the state fair board	$250
Rental of a 20 ft x 20 ft space	$500
Sales price of the Cola Cooler	$1.50
Cost of 16-ounce cola	$0.21
Cost of cup with special Cola Cooler label	$0.02
Cost of 6 ounces of ice	$0.01
Wages, (2 employees will be on hand for 8 of the days, 3 employees on hand for 4 of the days; hours 11 a.m. to 12 midnight, rate $4.25 per hour); 364 hrs. x $4.25	$1547
Employer's social security	$121

Rental of concession stand, coolers, cash registers, ice making machine	$ 600
Promotional signs	$ 300

REQUIRED:

a. Use the account analysis approach to calculate: (1) the total fixed costs, and (2) the variable costs per drink.
b. Calculate: (1) the contribution margin per Cola Cooler, and (2) the contribution margin ratio per Cola Cooler.
c. Calculate the break-even point three ways: (1) using the profit equation, (2) using the contribution margin, and (3) using the contribution margin ratio. Express the break-even point in both the number of drinks sold and in dollars.
d. Suppose Nancy is expecting to sell 5,000 Cola Coolers, assuming normal weather, and 7,000 if it is abnormally hot. Calculate the expected profit under: (1) normal weather, and (2) abnormally hot weather.
e. Calculate the margin of safety in units assuming normal weather.
f. Assuming normal weather, Nancy feels that she could sell 40% more Coolers if she drops the price to $1.00. Should she drop the price?

LO 3

P23-4A C-V-P, Profit Graph The Redline Oil Company was organized to produce and distribute a single product, a high-grade blended synthetic racing oil that is used in high-performance sport bikes and racing bikes. The oil is expensive and is targeted to a narrow market. Redline purchases the petroleum and chemical agents, blends them, packages the oil, and distributes the product to retail outlets (motorcycle dealers and parts shops). Information about Redline's expected costs of operations is as follows:

Wholesale price of quart of Redline	$9
Variable production costs:	
Chemical and petroleum ingredients	$3
Labor in mixing process	$0.40
Fixed production costs:	
Depreciation of production facilities (plant and equipment)	$50,000
Other fixed production costs	$50,000
Selling and administrative costs (fixed)	$100,000

REQUIRED:

a. Calculate: (1) the total fixed costs, and (2) the variable costs per quart of oil.
b. Calculate: (1) the contribution margin, and (2) the contribution margin ratio.
c. Calculate the break-even point three ways: (1) using the profit equation, (2) using the contribution margin, and (3) using the contribution margin ratio. Express the break-even point in both dollars and units.
d. Calculate the number of quarts Redline must sell to earn a $50,000 profit.
e. Draw a profit graph. Label sales revenue, total expenses, variable expenses, fixed expenses, the profit area, the loss area, and the break-even point.

LO 4

P23-5A C-V-P, Multiproducts The Redline Oil Company was organized to produce and distribute a single product, a high-grade blended synthetic racing oil that is used in high-performance sport bikes and racing bikes. Last year they added a second product, a high-performance chain lubricant. The oil is expensive and is targeted to a narrow market; the chain lubricant is more competitively priced and is targeted to a broader market. Redline purchases the petroleum and chemical agents for both products, blends, packages, and distributes them to retail outlets (motorcycle dealers and parts shops). Information about Redline's expected costs of operations is as follows:

	Wholesale price of quart of Redline synthetic racing oil		$9
	Wholesale price for 12-ounce tube of Redline chain lubricant		$3

	Racing Oil	Chain Lubricant
Variable production costs:		
Chemical and petroleum ingredients	$3.00	$1.50
Labor in mixing process	$0.40	$0.40
Fixed production costs:		
Depreciation of production facilities (plant and equipment)		$60,000
Other fixed production costs		$60,000
Selling and administrative costs (fixed)		$120,000

Redline expects to sell three tubes of chain lubricant for every one quart of racing oil.

REQUIRED:

a. Calculate the weighted average contribution margin ratio.
b. Use the weighted average contribution margin ratio to calculate the dollar sales necessary to earn a $50,000 profit.
c. Suppose Redline's actual product mix is four tubes of chain lubricant to every one quart of racing oil. Calculate: (1) the weighted average contribution margin ratio for this mix, and (2) the dollar sales needed to earn a $50,000 profit. Comment on how the changed product mix affects Redline's operations.

LO 5,6 **P23-6A** **Full Costing and Variable Costing (Appendix)** The following information relates to BingoBird Seed Company for the past three years. Ignore selling and administrative costs.

	19X3	19X4	19X5
Pounds produced	100,000	100,000	100,000
Pounds sold	100,000	90,000	110,000
Fixed overhead	$50,000	$50,000	$50,000
Variable production cost per pound	$1.50	$1.50	$1.50
Selling price per pound	$3.00	$3.00	$3.00

REQUIRED:

a. Prepare an income statement each year under variable costing.
b. Prepare an income statement each year under full costing.
c. Calculate the amount of fixed overhead expensed each year under: (1) variable costing, and (2) full costing.
d. What relationship do you see between variable and full costing profits when: (1) production and sales are equal, (2) production is greater than sales, and (3) production is less than sales?

PROBLEM SET B

LO 1,2 **P23-1B** **Cost Behavior Patterns, Account Analysis** The Tri-City Manufacturing Company is interested in investigating the behavior pattern of their operating costs so that they can make better profit projections. Tri-City manufactures condensers for large industrial grade heat pumps.

REQUIRED:

Selected Tri-City costs follow. Label each cost as fixed (*F*), variable (*V*), or mixed (*M*).

___ a. Depreciation of factory building and warehouses
___ b. Raw materials
___ c. Cleaning supplies for factory
___ d. Lubricants for factory machinery
___ e. Depreciation of computer
___ f. Depreciation of factory machinery (depreciation is based on machine hours, because the wear and tear of machine usage is the primary cause of decline in asset utility)
___ g. Wages of production line workers
___ h. Wages of machine operators
___ i. Wages of factory machine mechanics
___ j. Salaries of factory security officers
___ k. Salaries of factory production supervisors
___ l. Wages of factory maintenance workers
___ m. Salaries of accounting and bookkeeping department
___ n. Salaries of sales department (salespersons are paid a monthly salary plus commissions)
___ o. Electricity (about 75% to 90% of the electricity bill relates to the factory. The machinery used in the production process uses a large amount of electricity.)
___ p. Administrative salaries
___ q. Advertising in trade journals
___ r. Office supplies
___ s. Excess of cafeteria costs over revenues (the company provides meals to all employees for $1 per meal as a company benefit)

LO 1,2

P23-2B **Estimating Costs** The Slick Wheels Go-Cart Track provides go-cart rides on a highly banked quarter-mile course which simulates a NASCAR race track. Slick is interested in learning about the behavior of their track operation costs in relation to track usage. Operating costs and usage data for last season are as follows:

	June	*July*	*August*
Rides	30,000	35,000	46,000
Depreciation of carts	$ 1,500	$ 1,500	$ 1,500
Depreciation of track	1,200	1,200	1,200
Depreciation of building	250	250	250
Pit crew wages	9,600	12,000	14,400
Cashier wages	2,400	2,400	2,400
Gas and oil	9,400	10,900	12,500
Cart repairs and maintenance	1,300	1,350	1,400
Total costs	$25,650	$29,600	$33,650

REQUIRED:

a. Use the high-low method to determine the fixed and variable components of the total track operating costs.
b. Estimate the total monthly costs of operating the track assuming 37,000 rides.
c. Draw a scattergraph plotting rides on the horizontal axis and total costs in dollars on the vertical axis.

LO 1,2,3 P23-3B **Cost Behavior Patterns, Estimating Costs, C-V-P, Margin of Safety, "What If" Analysis** Richard Glass has made arrangements to operate a parking service at the Kentucky Derby. The business will operate two days, Friday for the Kentucky Oaks and Saturday for the Derby. Richard plans to attract additional customers by providing a mint julep glass to each driver. He has obtained the following information about the costs of operating the parking service for the two days.

Rental of nine vacant lots for two days: $1,800 plus $2 for each car parked
Parking fee: $10
Total wages of parking attendants: $720 plus $1 for each car
Cost of mint julep glass: $1
Employer's social security: 7% of wages
Parking receipts: 3 cents per receipt
Promotional signs: $500
City business license: $100 plus 5% of gross

REQUIRED:

a. Use the account analysis approach to calculate: (1) the total fixed costs, and (2) the variable costs per car.
b. Calculate: (1) the contribution margin, and (2) the contribution margin ratio per car.
c. Calculate the break-even point three ways: (1) using the profit equation, (2) using the contribution margin, and (3) using the contribution margin ratio. Express the break-even point in both the number of cars parked and in dollars.
d. Suppose Richard is expecting to fill all lots to capacity. Each lot holds 100 cars, providing a total capacity of 900 cars. Calculate the expected profit.
e. Calculate the margin of safety in units.
f. Richard estimates he could charge $12 and park 25% less cars. Should he increase the price?

LO 3 P23-4B **C-V-P, Profit Graph** The Matrix Chemical Company was organized to produce and distribute a single product, a highly toxic compound used in home and industrial pest control treatments. The Matrix compound is used by about a dozen manufacturers of pest treatment products, and goes by the name Matrix Seven. Information about Matrix's expected costs of operations is presented below.

Wholesale price of quart of Matrix Seven	$90
Variable production costs:	
Ingredients	$28
Labor in mixing process	$5
Disposal of hazardous waste material	$2
Fixed production costs:	
Depreciation of production facilities (plant and equipment)	$800,000
Other fixed production costs	$200,000
Selling and administrative costs (fixed)	$100,000

REQUIRED:

a. Calculate: (1) the total fixed costs, and (2) the variable costs per quart of Matrix Seven.
b. Calculate: (1) the contribution margin, and (2) the contribution margin ratio.
c. Calculate the break-even point three ways: (1) using the profit equation, (2) using the contribution margin, and (3) using the contribution margin ratio. Express the break-even point in both dollars and units.
d. Calculate the number of quarts Matrix must sell to earn a $100,000 profit.
e. Draw a profit graph. Label sales revenue, total expenses, variable expenses, fixed expenses, the profit area, the loss area, and the break-even point.

LO 4

P23-5B C-V-P, Multiproducts The First Environment Chemical Company produces and markets three products; FEC 1, a chemical used in producing household pest control products; FEC 1 Plus, a chemical used in producing industrial pest control products; and FEC 2, a chemical used in producing agricultural pest control products. Information about First's operations is as follows:

Wholesale price of quart of FEC 1	$15
Wholesale price of quart of FEC 1 Plus	$20
Wholesale price of quart of FEC 2	$12

	FEC 1	FEC 1 Plus	FEC 2
Variable production costs:			
Ingredients	$4	$6	$5
Labor in mixing process	$1	$2	$2
Hazardous waste disposal costs	$1	$1	$1

Fixed production costs:	
Depreciation of production facilities (plant and equipment)	$1,000,000
Other fixed production costs	$300,000
Selling and administrative costs (fixed)	$400,000

First expects sales to reflect the following product mix: FEC 1, one quart; FEC 1 Plus, five quarts; FEC 2, four quarts.

REQUIRED:

a. Calculate the weighted average contribution margin.
b. Use the weighted average contribution margin to calculate the total units that must be sold to earn a $100,000 profit. Break the total units into quarts of FEC 1, FEC 1 Plus, and FEC 2.
c. Calculate the weighted average contribution margin ratio.
d. Use the weighted average contribution margin ratio to calculate the dollar sales necessary to earn a $100,000 profit.
e. Suppose First's actual product mix for FEC 1, FEC 1 Plus, and FEC 2 is 2:5:3. Calculate: (1) the weighted average contribution margin ratio for this mix, and (2) the dollar sales needed to earn a $100,000 profit. Comment on how the changed product mix affects First's operations.

LO 5,6

P23-6B Full Costing and Variable Costing (Appendix) The following information relates to the New River Coal Company for the past three years. Ignore selling and administrative costs.

	19X1	19X2	19X3
Tons produced	250,000	250,000	250,000
Tons sold	250,000	230,000	270,000
Fixed overhead	$5,000,000	$5,000,000	$5,000,000
Variable production cost per ton	$8	$8	$8
Selling price per ton	$30	$30	$30

REQUIRED:

a. Prepare an income statement each year under variable costing.
b. Prepare an income statement each year under full costing.
c. Calculate the amount of fixed overhead expensed each year under: (1) variable costing, and (2) full costing.
d. What relationship do you see between variable and full costing profits when: (1) production and sales are equal, (2) production is greater than sales, and (3) production is less than sales?

CRITICAL THINKING AND COMMUNICATING

C23-1 You are considering investing in a newly started business, called Freedom Freeze, which produces and sells a recently developed frozen dessert that is low in cholesterol and fat and is sugar free. The desserts are sold in five company-operated outlets, similar in their concept to several national franchises. The founder of the company tells you that they expect to open new stores at a rapidly increasing pace, doubling their sales and the number of stores each year for the next three years. The company has 100,000 shares of common stock outstanding and does not plan to issue additional stock during the three-year expansion period, planning instead to obtain expansion funds through internally generated capital.

Naturally, you are very interested in projecting the company's earnings for the next three years, assuming the owner's growth projections are realistic. An income statement for Freedom Freeze's first year of operations, prepared under Generally Accepted Accounting Principles, is as follows:

Freedom Freeze
Income Statement
For the Year Ended December 31, 19X5

Sales	$5,000,000
Cost of goods sold	3,000,000
Gross profit	$2,000,000
Selling and administrative expenses	1,500,000
Income before taxes	$ 500,000
Income taxes	200,000
Net income	$ 300,000
Earnings per share	$3

REQUIRED:

a. The above income statement, in accordance with Generally Accepted Accounting Principles, is prepared under full costing. What problems are you going to encounter as you attempt to project income at sales of $10,000,000, $20,000,000, and $40,000,000?

b. Suppose you are able to obtain an income statement prepared under variable costing. Explain how this format would assist you in projecting income for the next three years.

c. What problems are you going to have in projecting income, even with the availability of a variable costing statement?

C23-2 **Krog's Metalfab** John Krog is President, Chairman of the Board, Production Supervisor, and majority shareholder of Krog's Metalfab, Inc. He formed the company in 1978 to manufacture custom-built aluminum storm windows for sale to contractors in the greater Chicago area. Since that time the company has experienced tremendous growth and currently operates two plants: one in Chicago, the main production facility and a smaller plant in Moline, Illinois. The company now produces a wide variety of metal windows, framing materials, ladders, and other products related to the construction industry. Recently, the company developed a new line of bronz-finished storm windows and initial buyer reaction has been quite favorable. The company's future seemed bright but on January 3, 1994, a light fixture overheated causing a fire which virtually destroyed the entire Chicago plant. Three days later, Krog had moved 50% of his Chicago work force to the Moline plant. Workers were housed in hotels, paid overtime wages and provided with bus transportation home on weekends. Still, the company could not meet delivery schedules due to reduced operating capacity and total business began to decline. At the end of 1994, Krog felt that the worst was over. A new plant had been leased in Chicago and the company was about back to normal.

Finally, Krog could turn his attention to a matter of considerable importance: settlement with the insurance company. The company's policy stipulated that the building and equipment loss be calculated at replacement cost. This settlement had been fairly straight forward and the proceeds had aided the rapid rebuilding of the company. A valued feature of the insurance policy was "lost profit" coverage. This coverage was to "compensate the company for profits lost due to reduced operating capacity related to fire or flood damage." The period of "lost profit" was limited to twelve months. Interpreting the exact nature of this coverage proved to be difficult. The insurance company agreed to reimburse Krog for the overtime premium, transportation and housing costs related to emergency operations in the Moline plant. These expenses obviously minimized the damages related to the 12 months of lost or reduced profits. But, was the company entitled to any additional compensation?

Krog got out the latest edition of *Construction Today*. According to this respected trade journal, sales of products similar to products produced by Krog's Metalfab had increased by 7% during 1994. Krog felt that were it not for the fire, his company could also have increased sales by this percentage.

Income statement information is avaliable for 1993 (the year prior to the fire) and 1994 (the year during which the company sustained "lost profit"). The expenses in 1994 include excess operating costs of $240,000, which include overtime costs, hotel costs, meals, etc. related to emergency operations in Moline.

The chief accountant at Krog, Peter Newell, has estimated lost profit to be only $34,961. Thus, he does not feel that it's worthwhile spending a lot of company resources trying to collect more than the $240,000. Peter arrived at his calculation as follows.

	Sales in 1993	$5,079,094
	Predicted sales in 1994 with 7% increase	5,434,630
	Actual sales in 1994	3,845,499
(A)	Lost sales	$1,589,131
(B)	Profit in 1993 as a percent of 1993 sales ($111,928 ÷ $5,079,094)	.0220
	Lost profit (A x B)	$ 34,961

REQUIRED:

Mr. Krog is not convinced by Peter's analysis and has turned to you, an outside consultant, to provide a preliminary estimate of lost profit over and above the $240,000 amount. Using the limited information contained in the financial statements for 1993 and 1994, estimate lost profit. What is the fundamental flaw in Peter Newell's analysis? (Hint: Consider using account analysis or the high-low method to estimate fixed and variable costs.)

CHAPTER 23 COST-VOLUME-PROFIT ANALYSIS

Krog's Metalfab
Income from Operations
1993–1994

1993	1st Quarter	2nd Quarter	3rd Quarter	4th Quarter	Total
Sales	$1,208,770	$1,247,985	$1,583,045	$1,039,294	$5,079,094
Less:					
Cost of goods sold	$1,164,665	$1,095,630	$1,230,701	$1,016,502	$4,507,498
Selling expense	52,370	53,076	66,283	44,939	216,668
Administrative expense	60,750	60,750	60,750	60,750	243,000
Total expense	$1,277,785	$1,209,456	$1,357,734	$1,122,191	$4,967,166
Income from operations	$ (69,015)	$ 38,529	$225,311	$ (82,897)	$ 111,928

1994	1st Quarter	2nd Quarter	3rd Quarter	4th Quarter	Total
Sales	$971,984	$ 807,871	$1,171,679	$ 893,965	$3,845,499
Less:					
Cost of goods sold	$1,034,623	$ 968,950	$1,112,708	$1,001,738	$4,118,019
Selling expense	43,229	36,666	51,217	40,108	171,220
Administrative expense	69,575	73,035	70,787	68,340	281,737
Total expense	$1,147,427	$1,078,651	$1,234,712	$1,110,186	$4,570,976
Income from operations	$ (175,443)	$ (270,780)	$ (63,033)	$ (216,221)	$ (725,477)

CHAPTER 24

Cost Allocation and Activity-Based Costing

Gardenrite Manufacturing Company produces garden tools and lawn maintenance products that are sold through a national chain of hardware stores. More than 60 products are manufactured, and approximately 80 percent of revenue comes from selling small home garden tools such as rakes, pruners, and spades. The company also manufactures high-quality lawn mowers, edgers, and blowers that are popular with professional lawn service companies. However, sales of these products have been relatively small. In recent months, Ben Jakes, the CFO at Gardenrite, has become concerned about the apparent profitability of several products. In particular, some high-volume products such as the Model 250 spade are barely breaking even. On the other hand, low-volume products such as the new Model 900 mower are selling for much more than the cost of production. The high profit that the Model 900 mower generates is particularly surprising since the company only recently began manufacturing mowers. Ben expected production inefficiencies, associated with any new product line, to keep profit margins low for at least three years. Ben knows that manufacturing overhead is allocated to products based on labor cost. The approach is simple, but he suspects it may be causing allocations of cost that are too high for spades and too low for mowers.

Firms that produce more than one product or provide more than one type of service invariably have substantial indirect costs. Because indirect costs cannot be directly traced to products or services, firms must develop some means of assigning these costs. The process of assigning indirect costs is referred to as **cost allocation**. Unfortunately, cost allocation frequently results in problems similar to the one Ben Jakes faces. To prepare yourself to deal with them, you need a good understanding of why and how costs are allocated. Providing you with that understanding is the purpose of this chapter. One of the key points of the chapter is that costs are allocated for a variety of purposes. Also, allocations that are adequate for one purpose may not be adequate for another purpose. Thus, it is important to remember the maxim "Different costs for different purposes."

Many managers have expressed concern that the way overhead is typically allocated may seriously distort product cost for manufacturing firms. The problem arises because most product costing systems allocate overhead using measures related to production volume. This is the case at Gardenrite where manufacturing overhead is allocated based on labor cost. However, many overhead costs are not proportional to volume. Activity-based costing (ABC) is an approach to allocating overhead costs that addresses this problem. We briefly discussed ABC in the chapter on job order costing. Here, you will gain a better understanding of the general process of cost allocation, which allows for a more detailed treatment of ABC.

LEARNING OBJECTIVES

1. Explain why indirect costs are allocated.
2. Describe the cost allocation process.
3. Discuss allocation of service department costs.
4. Discuss allocation of joint costs.
5. Identify potential problems with cost allocation.
6. Discuss activity-based costing and cost drivers.

Explain why indirect costs are allocated.

PURPOSES OF COST ALLOCATION

Reasons to allocate cost include:

1. To provide information for important decisions.
2. To calculate the "full cost" of products for financial reporting purposes and for determining cost-based prices.
3. To reduce the frivolous use of common resources.
4. To encourage managers to evaluate the efficiency of internally provided services.

We discuss each of these purposes below.

To Provide Information for Decision Making

As we have seen in previous chapters, information on variable costs is crucial for making appropriate business decisions. Because some indirect costs are variable costs, allocating them may provide useful information. Consider a company that manufactures several different wood stoves, including the Yukon model. The Yukon requires $600 of direct material and $400 of direct labor per unit. In addition, the company incurs a variety of indirect costs to produce the stove. Suppose the company receives an offer from a customer to purchase 2,000 Yukons for $1,500 each. This is $500 more than the direct costs of producing the stove. Should management accept the offer? Acceptance of the offer depends in part on whether the *variable* indirect costs of the stove exceed $500. Examples of indirect variable costs include indirect material, the variable portion of indirect labor, and the variable portion of maintenance cost.

If indirect costs are allocated to the Yukon model, management will have the information required to evaluate the customer's order. Suppose the indirect variable costs allocated to the stove amount to $200. In this case, the total variable costs of the Yukon are $1,200 per unit, which is less than the $1,500 revenue generated from selling each unit. Therefore, management would be inclined to accept the customer's offer.

To Provide "Full Cost" Information

Since GAAP requires full costing, firms must allocate indirect production costs to goods produced for external financial reporting. In addition to the GAAP requirement, full cost information is required when companies have agreements whereby the amount of revenue received depends on the amount of cost incurred. For example, defense contractors with the federal government often have contracts that specify they will be paid the cost of production plus some fixed amount or percentage of cost. Such contracts are commonly called "cost-plus" contracts. An interesting feature of these contracts is that the cost of production specified in the contract often includes not only manufacturing costs but also a share of general and administrative costs. Thus, a substantial amount of cost allocation is required to assign indirect manufacturing costs and indirect general and administrative costs to the contract work.

Cost-plus contracts have a major problem. They create an incentive for firms to allocate as much cost as possible to goods produced on a cost-plus basis but little cost to those goods not produced on a cost-plus basis. The more cost companies allocate to cost-plus contracts, the larger the total amount they receive. In spite of this limitation, cost-plus contracts serve a useful purpose. Without assurances that they will be reimbursed for their costs and that they will earn some profit, many manufacturers would not be willing to bear the financial risks associated with producing state-of-the-art products for the government. For example, since such products often require use of untried technologies, only a few companies would be willing to produce a new fighter aircraft without assurance of reimbursement for all production costs incurred.

To Reduce Frivolous Use of Common Resources

Allocated costs also serve as a charge or fee for using internal resources or services. Consider a company that purchases a computer that each of its three divisions will use. Further, assume that almost all of the costs associated with running the computer are fixed and amount to $100,000 per year. Some accountants argue that if costs are fixed, no cost should be allocated to the user divisions because their use causes no incremental costs. However, if the three divisions are not charged for using the computer, they may use the computer for frivolous or nonessential purposes (e.g., playing computer games or requesting unnecessary computer-prepared reports).

This situation may not seem that detrimental to the company's welfare. After all, the costs associated with the computer are primarily fixed. If frivolous use does not cause additional costs, why discourage it? The reason is that frivolous use may have some hidden costs. The primary hidden cost in the example would be slower service to departments that need to use the computer when another department is using it. For example, reports that usually take minutes to prepare may take hours to produce when the computer is being used to prepare unnecessary reports.

One common way to eliminate frivolous use of centrally provided services is to allocate their costs. For example, suppose Division 1 planned to use the computer for 1,000 hours, Division 2 for 1,000 hours, and Division 3 for 2,000 hours. In this case, a charge of $25 per hour ($100,000 ÷ 4,000 hours) could be assessed. Note that this rate would allocate the entire cost of the computer ($100,000) among the three users, assuming their plans worked out as expected. Divisions 1 and 2 would each be charged $25,000; Division 3 would be charged $50,000. If this method of cost allocation is used, then each division would reduce its frivolous use of the computer because such use would reduce its reported profit.

To Encourage Evaluation of Services

Cost allocation also encourages managers to evaluate carefully the services for which they are being charged. If no costs are charged for use of centrally administered services such as computer or janitorial services, then users have no incentive to evaluate these services carefully. After all, the services are free. However, if users are charged for the services (i.e., they receive an allocation of the cost), then they have a strong incentive to evaluate them and to consider lower-cost alternatives. If lower-cost alternatives exist, and if users bring them to the company's attention, then the company can evaluate whether the services are provided in an efficient manner.

For example, suppose the manager of Division 3 determines that similar computer services can be purchased outside the company for less than the $50,000 currently being allocated to Division 3. After the manager brings this matter to management's attention, management can consider alternatives. In this case, it could encourage the manager of the computer system to lower that operation's costs. If the costs cannot be lowered, then management might consider replacing the computer system with separate computers for the divisions or buying computer services outside the company.

Describe the cost allocation process.

PROCESS OF COST ALLOCATION

The cost allocation process consists of three steps:

1. Identify the cost objectives.
2. Form cost pools.
3. Select an allocation base and allocate the cost pools to the cost objectives.

Once in place, the allocation process operates as shown in Illustration 24-1.

ILLUSTRATION 24-1 The Cost Allocation Process

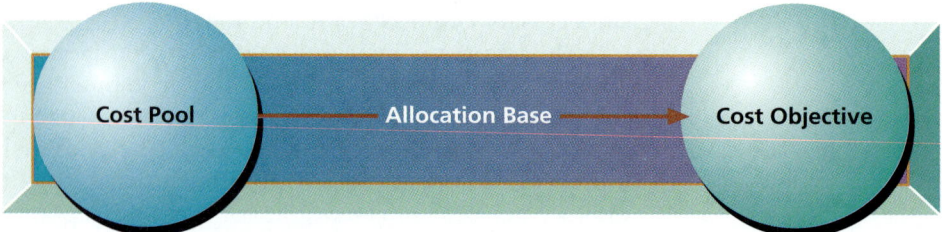

Determining the Cost Objectives

In designing the cost allocation process, the first step is determining the product, service, or department to receive the allocation. The object of the allocation is referred to as the **cost objective**. For example, if a company allocates depreciation of a drilling press to products such as flanges and brackets, the products are the cost objectives. If computer processing costs are allocated to the contracts a computer-aided design group works on, then contracts are the cost objectives (See Illustration 24-2.)

ILLUSTRATION 24-2 Cost Objectives

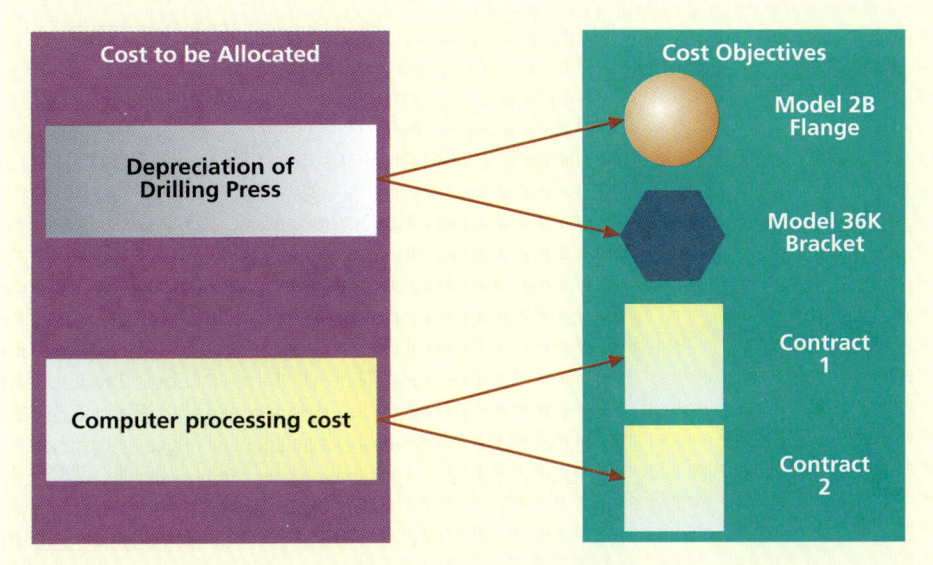

Forming Cost Pools

The second step in designing the cost allocation process is to form cost pools. A **cost pool** is a grouping of individual costs whose total is allocated using one allocation base. For example, all maintenance department costs could be treated as a cost pool. In this case, the cost pool would include the wages of workers in the maintenance department, supplies, small tools, and a variety of additional cost items. Cost pools are commonly formed along departmental lines (e.g., maintenance department costs in one cost pool and personnel department costs in another) or by major activities (costs related to equipment setups—a major activity in most manufacturing firms—in one cost pool and costs related to inspecting products for defects—another major activity—in another cost pool). However, they may also be formed in terms of cost behavior (e.g., fixed costs in one cost pool and variable costs in another).

In forming a cost pool, the overriding concern is to ensure that the costs in the pool are homogeneous or similar. One way to determine this is to compare the allocations with those that result from breaking the pool into smaller pools and using a variety of allocation bases. If there is no substantial difference in the allocations, then, for practical purposes, the costs in the pool are considered homogeneous.

Some manufacturing companies include all manufacturing overhead (including power costs, computing costs, material handling costs, etc.) in a single cost pool. Allocations from a large pool containing costs related to very different activities will not be accurate. While use of a single cost pool for overhead seems too broad, the exact number of appropriate cost pools is not clear. Managers must make a cost/benefit decision. More pools involve more record keeping, which is costly. However, more pools ensure more accurate information.

Selecting an Allocation Base and Allocating Costs

In designing the allocation process, the third step is selecting an allocation base that relates the cost pool to the cost objectives. The allocation base must be some characteristic that all of the cost objectives share. If the cost objectives are manufactured products, then direct labor hours, direct labor cost, and machine hours are characteristics that a company could use as allocation bases. If the cost objectives are the divisions of a multi-divisional firm, then sales dollars, total assets, and divisional profit could be used as allocation bases.

Deciding which of the possible allocation bases to use is not easy. Ideally, a department should select an allocation base that results in costs being allocated to cost objectives that *caused* the costs to be incurred. This is referred to as an allocation based on a **cause-and-effect** relationship. For example, if additional activity in a production department causes an increase in the costs the maintenance department incurs, then an allocation base that will result in the additional costs being allocated to the production department when there is additional activity should be selected. Direct labor hours, direct labor cost, or machine hours in the production department would be likely choices for the allocation base because they represent the increase in activity that leads to the increase in the maintenance cost. However, it would be difficult to argue that one of these allocation bases is better than another on cause-and-effect grounds. As we will see below, this is one of the problems of cost allocation. A number of allocation bases may appear to be equally valid, but they may also result in substantially different costs being assigned to the cost objectives.

Suppose Pratt Equipment company has two producing departments, Assembly and Finishing, that receive allocations of indirect costs from the maintenance department. In the coming year, the maintenance department expects to incur $200,000 of variable costs. These costs are related to both labor and machine hours incurred in the producing departments. The quantity of labor and machine hours are indicated below. With labor hours as the allocation base, the allocation rate is $4 per labor hour, and the assembly department receives an $80,000 allocation of cost from the maintenance department. However, with machine hours as the allocation base, the allocation rate is $10, and the assembly department receives a $110,000 allocation of cost from the maintenance department. The $30,000 difference in the allocations occurs in spite of the fact that both labor and machine hours are reasonable allocation bases to use.

	Labor Hours	Allocations	Machine Hours	Allocations
Assembly	20,000	$ 80,000	11,000	$110,000
Finishing	30,000	120,000	9,000	90,000
Total	50,000	$200,000	20,000	$200,000
Allocation Rate	$4 per labor hour		$10 per machine hour	

In many cases, establishing a cause-and-effect relationship between costs and cost objectives is not feasible. In these cases, accountants use other criteria such as relative benefits, ability to bear costs, and equity. Unfortunately, these terms are rather vague and difficult to implement. The **relative benefits** notion suggests that the allocation base should result in more costs being allocated to the cost objectives that benefit most from incurring the cost. This might suggest that computer costs should be allocated to departments based on time each spends using the computer. More use implies greater benefit. However, this could result in fixed computer costs being allocated to departments that did not exist (and could not have caused the cost of the computer to be incurred) when the computer was acquired. The **ability to bear costs** notion suggests that the allocation base should result in more costs being allocated to products, services, or departments that are more profitable. Because they are more profitable, they can *bear* the increased costs from the higher allocations. The **equity** notion suggests that the allocation base should result in allocations that are perceived to be fair or equitable. Obviously, this is a difficult criterion to apply because different individuals have different perceptions of what is equitable.

ALLOCATING SERVICE DEPARTMENT COSTS

LO 3 Discuss allocation of service department costs.

The organizational units in most manufacturing firms can be classified as either production departments or service departments. Production departments engage in direct manufacturing activity, while service departments provide indirect support. For example, in a furniture manufacturing company the assembly and finishing departments are production departments, while maintenance, janitorial, personnel, cafeteria, cost accounting, and power are service departments.

Service department costs are allocated to production departments that, in turn, allocate the costs to specific products. Two approaches are commonly used to allocate service department costs to production departments: the direct method and the sequential method. Both approaches are discussed below.

Direct Method of Allocating Service Department Costs

In the **direct method of allocating costs**, a company allocates service department costs to production departments but not to other service departments. Thus, even though the janitorial department provides a service to the personnel department, the company would not allocate janitorial costs to the personnel department. Instead, it would allocate these to the production departments. The process is presented in Illustration 24-3. Note the absence of an arrow between janitorial costs and personnel costs; there is no allocation of costs between the janitorial and the personnel departments.

Suppose janitorial costs at Bradley Furniture Company are $100,000. The company decides to allocate these costs to Assembly and Finishing based on the number of square feet in each of the production departments. Since Assembly has 20,000 square feet and Finishing has 30,000 square feet, the allocation rate is $2 per square foot ($100,000 ÷ 50,000 square feet). Assembly receives an allocation of $40,000 (20,000 square feet x $2) and Finishing receives an allocation of $60,000 (30,000 square feet x $2).

Suppose Bradley's personnel costs are $200,000. Bradley allocates these costs based on the number of employees in each production department. The assembly department has 60 employees and the finishing department has 40 employees. Thus, the allocation rate for personnel costs is $2,000 per employee

ILLUSTRATION 24-3 Allocating Service Department Costs to Production Departments and then to Products with the Direct Method

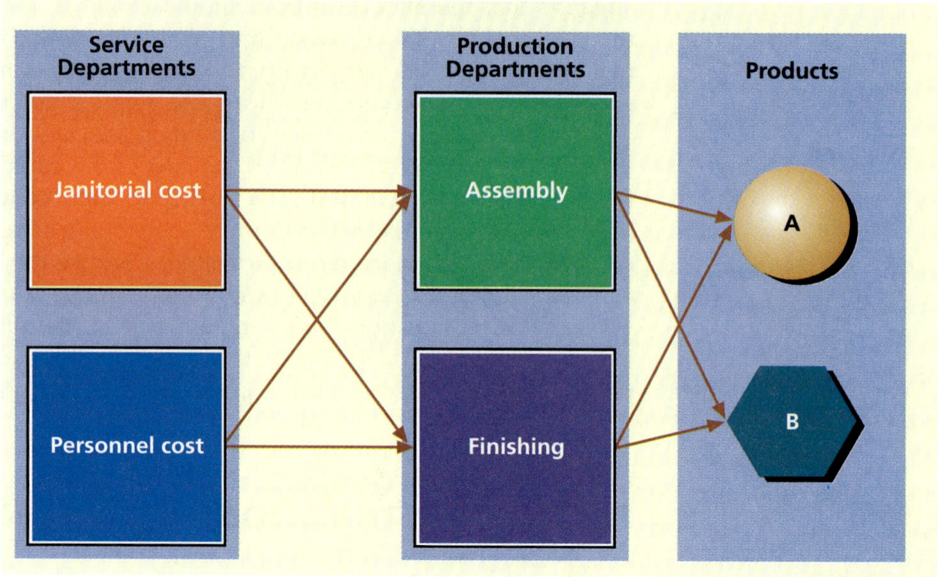

ILLUSTRATION 24-4 Direct Allocations of Service Department Costs for Bradley Furniture

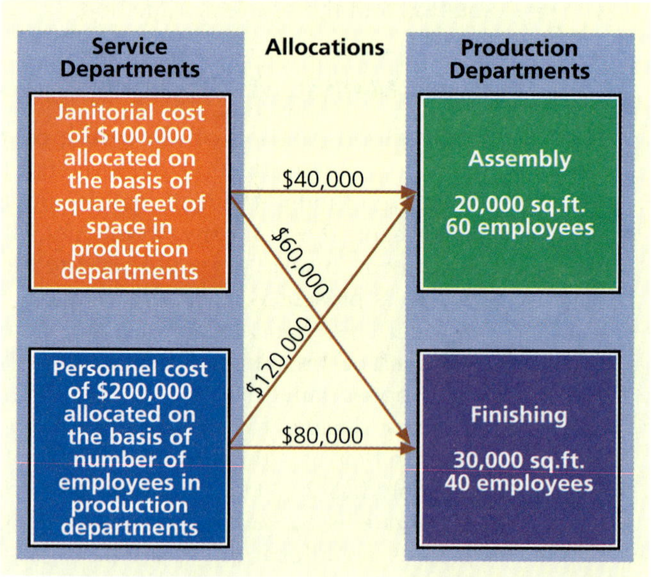

($200,000 ÷ 100 employees). The assembly department receives an allocation of $120,000 (60 employees x $2,000) and the finishing department receives an allocation of $80,000 (40 employees x $2,000). The allocations are presented in Illustration 24-4.

Sequential Method of Allocating Service Department Costs

Typically, service departments as well as producing departments consume the services a service department provides. For example, the personnel department may use the services of the janitorial department. The **sequential method of allocating costs** takes into account the fact that service departments make use of each other's services. However, to implement the method, the company must establish a hierarchy or order of services. At the top of the hierarchy is the service department that provides the greatest amount of service to the other service departments. At the bottom of the hierarchy is the service department that provides the least amount of service to the other service departments. Service departments that are lower in the order do not allocate costs to service departments that are higher in the order. For this reason, the method is sometimes referred to as the *step-down method*.

Suppose Bradley Furniture's janitorial department provides more service to the personnel department than the personnel department provides to the janitorial department. This is consistent with the hierarchy in Illustration 24-5.

ILLUSTRATION 24-5 Sequential Method of Cost Allocation

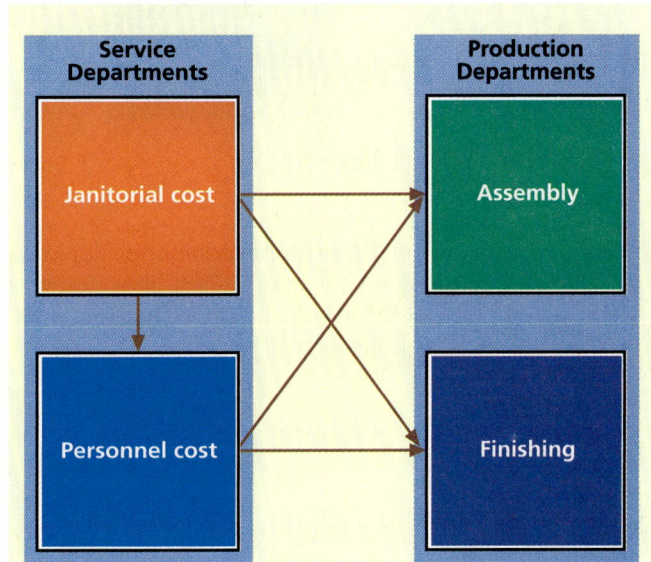

At Bradley Furniture, the personnel department occupies 1,282 square feet of space. In this case, the allocation of janitorial department cost will be at a rate of $1.95 per square foot.

Janitorial department cost		$100,000	
Divided by square feet of space:			
Personnel	1,282		
Assembly	20,000		
Finishing	30,000		÷ 51,282
Cost per square foot			$1.95

With a rate of $1.95 per square foot, the personnel department will receive an allocation of $2,500 (1,282 square feet x $1.95); the assembly department, $39,000 (20,000 square feet x $1.95); and the finishing department, $58,500 (30,000 square feet x $1.95). (See Illustration 24-6).

ILLUSTRATION 24-6 Allocation of Janitorial Department Costs to Personnel, Assembly, and Finishing

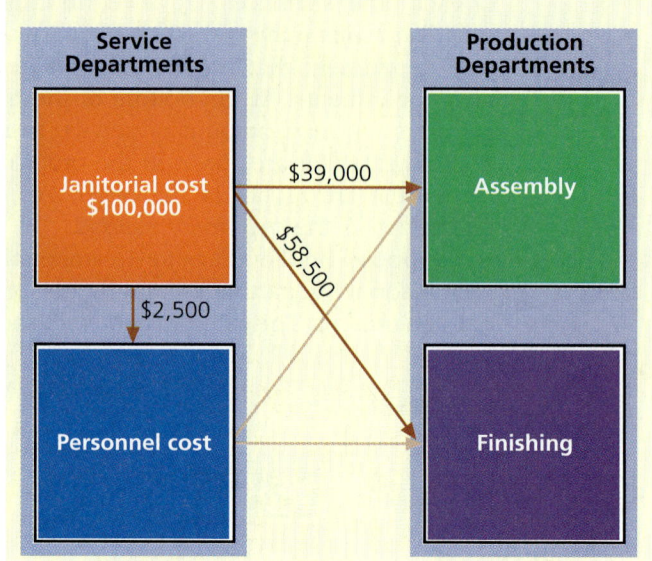

At this point, the personnel department has costs of $202,500, or $200,000 of its own cost and $2,500 allocated from the janitorial department. Its allocation rate will be $2,025 per employee.

Personnel department cost:		
Own cost	$200,000	
From Janitorial	2,500	$202,500
Divided by number of employees:		
Assembly	60	
Finishing	40	÷ 100
Cost per employee		$2,025

Thus, $121,500 of personnel department cost will be allocated to Assembly (60 employees x $2,025) and $81,000 of personnel department cost will be allocated to Finishing (40 employees x $2,025). (See Illustration 24-7).

In applying the sequential method, a company exercises considerable judgment in determining an appropriate order of service departments. Thus, the results of the method are somewhat arbitrary. However, the method often yields similar allocations to producing departments irrespective of the order chosen. Thus, the choice of the order may not present an important practical problem.

As a logical extension of the sequential method, a company could use a reciprocal allocation method to allow for allocations back and forth among its service departments. Such an approach requires solving simultaneous equations and is not presented here. It is covered in more advanced treatments of cost accounting topics.

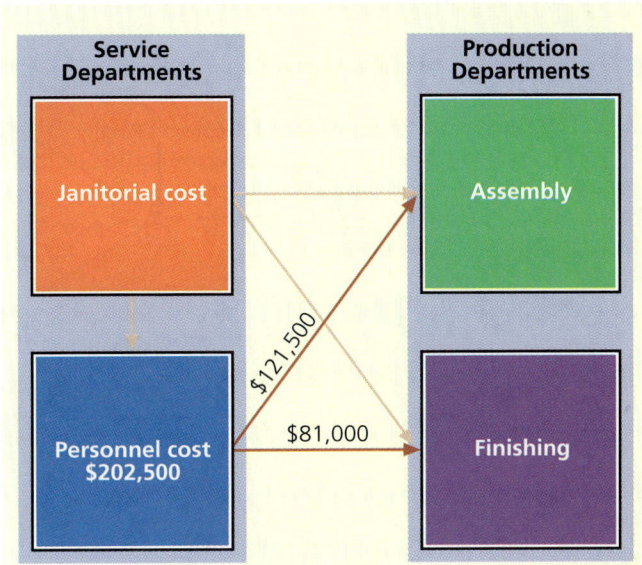

ILLUSTRATION 24-7 Allocation of Personnel Department Costs to Assembly and Finishing

ALLOCATING JOINT COSTS

LO 4 Discuss allocation of joint costs.

Joint products, which arise when two or more products always result from common inputs, present an interesting cost allocation problem. The costs of the common inputs are referred to as **joint costs**, and these costs are common in the food processing, extractive, and chemical industries. For example, in the dairy processing business the common input of raw milk is converted into cream, skim milk, and whole milk. For lumber companies, the common input of a log is converted into various grades of lumber. For fuel companies, the common input of crude oil is converted into a variety of fuels and lubricants.

A graphic treatment of the joint costing problem is presented in Illustration 24-8. The incurred joint costs lead to two joint products. The stage of production when individual products are identified is referred to as the **split-off point**. Beyond this point, each product may undergo further separate processing, and the company incurs additional costs. However, these further processing costs do not present a cost allocation problem because they are directly attributable to individual products.

For financial reporting purposes, the company must allocate the cost of the common inputs to the joint products. However, managers must review carefully the resulting information about the profitability of the joint products. For example, suppose a lumber company spends $600 for an oak log and $20 to saw it into two grades of lumber. The process results in 500 board feet of Grade A lumber that sells for $1.00 per board foot and 500 board feet of Grade B lumber that sells for $.50 per board foot. How should the $620 joint cost be allocated to the joint products? The lumber company could use one approach to allocate the cost based on the physical quantity of output. Since the production process results in equal quantities of physical output, the company would allocate an equal share of the joint cost to each of the grades of lumber. In this case, both Grades A and B lumber would show a cost of $310. With this allocation, man-

ILLUSTRATION 24-8 Joint Costs and Joint Products

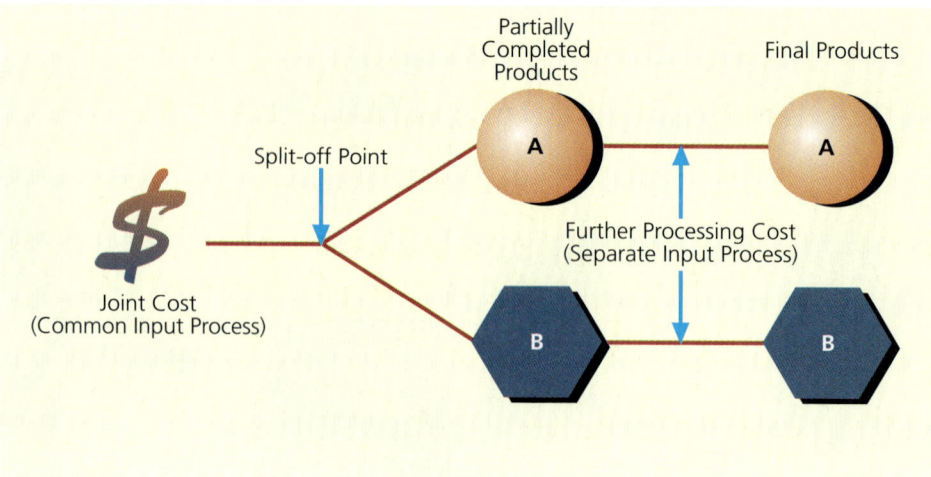

agers might think that Grade B lumber is not profitable and should be scrapped. After all, its cost is $310, while revenue from its sale is only $250. However this logic is not correct. If the Grade B lumber was scrapped, the company would loose $250 that helped cover the joint cost of $620. Remember: The company will incur total joint cost, regardless of what it does with the joint products beyond the split-off point. Therefore, the joint cost is largely irrelevant to any decision regarding a single joint product. However, the joint cost is relevant to decisions involving all of the joint products. If the total revenue from the sale of the joint products is less than the joint cost, then the company should cease production of all of the joint products.

A company can better allocate joint cost by using the **relative sales value method**. With this method, the amount of joint cost the company allocates to products depends on the relative sales values of the products at the split-off point. In the example below, the relative sales values are .333 for A and .667 for B.

Sales value of A at split-off	$500	Relative sales value of A ($500 ÷ $750)	.667
Sales value of B at split-off	250	Relative sales value of B ($250 ÷ $750)	.333
Total	$750	Total	1.000

Thus the company would assign an allocation of $413.33 (i.e., $620 x .667) to the Grade A lumber and an allocation of $206.67 (i.e., $620 x .333) to the Grade B lumber. One of the good features of this method is that the amount of joint cost a company allocates to a product cannot exceed its sales value at the split-off point. Thus, products that make a positive contribution to covering joint cost will not look unprofitable.

The costs allocated to the two grades of lumber using the physical quantity and the relative sales value approaches are compared in Illustration 24-9. In particular, note that for Grade B lumber, the physical quantity approach yields a negative gross margin of $60, while the relative sales value approach yields a positive gross margin of $43.33.

ILLUSTRATION 24-9 Comparison of Physical Quantity and Relative Sales Value Approaches to Allocation of Joint Costs

Joint cost:
Cost of log	$600.00
Cost of sawing	20.00
Total	$620.00

Joint process yields:
500 board feet of Grade A lumber selling for $1.00 per board foot
500 board feet of Grade B lumber selling for $.50 per board foot

Results using physical quantities to allocate joint costs:

	Grade A	Grade B
Sales revenue:		
500 bf × $1.00	$500.00	
500 bf × $.50		$250.00
Cost:		
$620 × (500 bf ÷ 1,000 bf)	310.00	
$620 × (500 bf ÷ 1,000 bf)		310.00
Gross margin	$190.00	$ (60.00)

Results using relative sales values to allocate joint costs:

	Grade A	Grade B
Sales revenue:		
500 bf × $1.00	$500.00	
500 bf × $.50		$250.00
Cost:		
$620 × .667	413.33	
$620 × .333		206.67
Gross margin	$ 86.67	$43.33

PROBLEMS WITH COST ALLOCATION

LO 5 Identify potential problems with cost allocation.

There are a number of problems associated with the way costs are allocated in practice. In this section, we discuss four problems brought about by:

1. Allocations of costs that are not controllable.
2. Arbitrary allocations.
3. Allocations of fixed costs that make the fixed costs appear to be variable costs.
4. Allocations of manufacturing overhead to products using too few overhead cost pools.

Responsibility Accounting and Controllable Costs

Previous chapters have stressed that a primary use of managerial accounting is to evaluate the performance of managers and the operations under their control. Performance evaluation is facilitated by a system of accounting that traces revenues and costs to organizational units (e.g., departments and divisions) and individuals (e.g., plant manager, supervisor of assembly workers, vice president of operations) with related responsibility for generating revenue and controlling costs. Such a system is referred to as a **responsibility accounting system**.

Consider a company that produces tennis rackets and tennis clothes in two separate plants. The company could prepare monthly production cost reports that list the total amount of material, labor, and overhead costs for the two plants combined. However, this would *not* be consistent with responsibility accounting because the reports would not trace the production costs to the plants responsible for controlling them. A responsibility accounting system would require not only that the costs of producing the tennis rackets and tennis clothes be traced to their respective plants, but also that the costs in each plant be traced to the departments or other units responsible for those costs. For example, within the plant producing the tennis rackets, labor costs should be traced to each supervisor responsible for an identifiable group or team of workers (e.g., assembly workers and finishing workers).

Cost allocation is generally required in a responsibility accounting system because one organizational unit is often responsible for the costs another organizational unit incurs. For example, activity in a production department increases the costs the machine repair department incurs. Therefore, the production department's performance reports should reflect some share of the machine repair department cost. This can be achieved by allocating machine repair department costs to the production department.

However, some allocations of costs are not consistent with a responsibility accounting system. Most accountants believe that managers should be held responsible only for costs they can control. These costs, called **controllable costs**, are those that are affected by the manager's decisions. Allocating the cost of a building to the performance report of a supervisor responsible for controlling labor costs is not appropriate because the supervisor cannot control building costs. If allocated costs beyond their control appear on their performance reports, managers may experience considerable frustration. Managers want their performance evaluations to reflect their own strengths and weaknesses. However, in some cases, managers are allocated costs beyond their control simply to make them aware that the costs exist and that the firm's revenue must cover them. In such situations, the costs clearly should be labeled noncontrollable. This way managers know that company officials are aware the items are not the managers' responsibility. In labeling the costs as uncontrollable, the company will minimize possible resentment from their managers.

Arbitrary Allocations

In practice, cost allocations are the topic of numerous and often heated discussions. Managers may believe their departments receive unnecessarily large allocations of indirect costs, causing their departments to appear less profitable. Government agencies that have cost-plus contracts may believe products produced by contractors on a cost-plus basis receive unfairly high allocations of indirect costs. Unfortunately, such discussions will continue. The reason is that allocations of costs are inherently arbitrary. In almost all cost allocation situations, determining the one "true," "correct," or "valid" allocation is not possible. As noted earlier in the chapter, various allocation bases (e.g., labor hours, labor cost, and machine hours) may be equally justifiable but will result in substantially different allocations. Managers will naturally support allocations that make

INSIGHTS INTO ACCOUNTING

THE $7 ASPIRIN

In a recent Ann Landers column, a former patient complained about being charged $7 for a single aspirin tablet received during his hospitalization. How can a hospital justify such a charge? Look to the allocated costs. The product cost of that aspirin likely included allocations for: (1) the prescribing physician's time, (2) the dispensing pharmacist's time, (3) the administering nurse's time, (4) costs of the medical records department, and (5) a new cost category referred to as "shifted costs." This last classification includes such factors as unreimbursed Medicare costs, the cost to provide care to indigent and impoverished patients, and the cost of malpractice insurance. On top of these costs hospitals add a charge for other overhead costs not included in previous allocations.

After various costs have been added to the aspirin through cost-shifting and straightforward cost allocation, the aspirin has a cost basis of about $3.50. Add profit, and presto—the $7 aspirin. (See photo.)

Source: David W. McFadden, "The Legacy of the $7 Aspirin," published in *Management Accounting* (April 1990), pp. 38–41, copyright by the Institute of Management Accountants, Montvale, NJ.

County Community Hospital
Production Cost Sheet

	Unit	Unit Cost	Total Units	Total Cost
Raw material				
Aspirin	ea.	$0.006	2	$0.012
Direct labor				
Physician	hr.	60.000	0.0083	0.500
Pharmacist	hr.	30.000	0.0200	0.603
Nurse	hr.	20.000	0.0056	0.111
Indirect labor				
Orderly	hr.	12.000	0.0167	0.200
Recordkeeping	hr.	12.000	0.0167	0.200
Supplies				
Cup	ea.	0.020	1	0.020
Shared & shifted costs				
Unreimbursed Medicare		0.200	1	0.200
Indigent care		0.223	1	0.223
Uncollectible receivables		0.084	1	0.084
Malpractice insurance		0.034	2	0.068
Excess bed capacity		0.169	1	0.169
Other operating costs		0.056	1	0.056
Other administrative costs		0.112	1	0.112
Excess time elements		0.074	1	0.074
Product cost				$2.632
Hospital overhead costs @32.98%				.868
Full cost (including overhead)				$3.500
Profit				3.500
Price (per dose)				$7.000

their performance look best and reject those that cast an unfavorable light on their performance.

Unitized Fixed Costs and Lump-Sum Allocations

One significant problem with cost allocation is the fact that the allocation process may make fixed costs appear to be variable costs. This happens when fixed costs are **unitized**, that is, stated on a per-unit basis. To illustrate the problem, suppose the Jones Tool Co. has several divisions. One of the divisions, referred to as the carpenter division, produces a variety of carpenter tools (e.g., hammers, saws, and drills). At the start of each year, Jones Tool Co. estimates the amount of general and administrative costs that are incurred centrally on behalf of the operations of the divisions. Such costs include administrative salaries, clerical costs, central accounting costs, and a variety of other costs, all of which are essentially fixed in the short run. In the current year, Jones expects these costs to be $2,000,000. Jones decides to let the divisions know these costs are being incurred on their behalf and, therefore, allocates them among the divisions based on their relative sales. In the current year, divisional sales are expected to be $50,000,000. Thus, Jones decides to allocate general and administrative costs to the divisions at a rate of $.04 per dollar of sales (i.e., $2,000,000 ÷ $50,000,000). Here general and administrative costs are unitized by sales dollar.

While the general and administrative costs are fixed, how will the manager of the carpenter division perceive them? This manager observes that as divisional revenue increases, the allocated costs increase. Thus, the manager perceives the costs as variable and may make decisions to maximize divisional profitability at the expense of the company's best interest. For example, suppose the carpenter division considers producing a new hammer that will sell for $20. At this price, the division expects to sell 100,000 units. Production of the hammer will require $12 of direct material cost, $6 of direct labor cost, and an increase in fixed manufacturing costs of $130,000. An analysis of the effect on the carpenter division's profit is presented in Illustration 24-10.

As indicated, sale of the hammer will result in an increase of $2,000,000 in sales. There will also be a $1,800,000 increase in variable costs (direct material and direct labor) and a $130,000 increase in fixed manufacturing cost. Thus, production and sale of the hammer will result in a $70,000 increase in profit. From this information, production of the hammer appears to be a profitable addition to the division's product line. However, will the manager be motivated to produce the hammer? Probably not. The reason is that, with the increase in sales, the division will receive a larger allocation of central general and administrative costs. With an allocation rate of $.04 per dollar of sales and an expected increase in sales of $2,000,000, the manager expects allocated costs to increase by $80,000. Since the manager perceives the additional allocated costs as variable when, in fact, they are fixed (that is, central administrative salaries, clerical costs, and accounting costs will not increase if the hammer is produced), the manager concludes that production of the hammer will result in the division losing $10,000 (i.e., $70,000 − $80,000).

To remedy the problem described above, firms need to allocate *fixed costs* in such a way that they *appear fixed* to the managers whose departments receive the allocation. This is achieved by **lump-sum allocations** of fixed costs, which allocate predetermined amounts not affected by changes in the activity levels of the organizational units receiving the allocation. Firms acquire resources based on the long-run needs of users. Thus, firms should also base

ILLUSTRATION 24-10 Problems of Unitized Fixed Costs

Sales of hammers (100,000 x $20)		$2,000,000
Less additional costs:		
Direct material (100,000 x $12)	$1,200,000	
Direct labor (100,000 x $6)	600,000	
Additional fixed manufacturing cost	130,000	
		1,930,000
Real increase in profit		$ 70,000
Less allocated fixed costs ($2,000,000 increase in sales x $.04)		80,000
Perceived loss on sale of hammers		$ (10,000)

allocations of fixed costs on the projected long-run needs that lead managers to incur the costs. For example, suppose Dyer Company purchases a computer to serve each of its two divisions. Purchase of the computer results in annual fixed costs of $40,000. In deciding what type of computer to purchase, management estimates that Division A would use the computer for 2,000 hours per year and Division B for 3,000 hours per year. Thus, allocating $16,000 to Division A (i.e., $40,000 x 2/5) and $24,000 to Division B ($40,000 x 3/5) is appropriate.

Although the activity of the two departments may deviate from expectations, lump-sum allocations should generally remain the same year after year. Suppose that Division A expanded and required 3,000 hours per year while Division B lost business and required only 2,000 hours. Should Dyer reverse the lump-sum allocations of the two divisions? Probably not. If Dyer reversed the allocations, the managers of the two divisions would perceive their allocations as based on their activity levels. In other words, they would view the fixed costs as variable. Thus, if lump-sum allocations of *fixed* costs are to *appear fixed*, the amount of the allocation must not depend on changes in activity.

Suppose the activity of Division A stayed at 2,000 hours, but Division B's activity level decreased from 3,000 hours to 2,000 hours. If the cost of the computer is allocated based upon current activity levels, the amount allocated to Division A would increase from $16,000 to $20,000, in spite of the fact that its use of the computer did not change. Obviously, the manager of Division A would be dissatisfied. Also, planning would be more difficult because the costs of the division would depend on the activity of the other division. This is not the case with a lump-sum allocation because, once the amount of the lump sum is determined, it does not vary in response to changes in activity.

How can lump-sum allocations improve a manager's decisions? Consider the Jones Tool Co. example presented earlier. Suppose Jones allocated the general and administrative costs on a lump-sum basis and assigned the carpenter division an allocation of $80,000. Note that this is the same amount allocated on the basis of revenue. However, when allocated as a lump-sum basis, the amount does not adversely affect the manager's decisions. The manager of the carpenter division now perceives the lump-sum allocation as a fixed cost. Thus, in the interest of maximizing divisional profit, the manager decides to produce the hammer because it contributes $70,000 toward covering the allocated costs that would be incurred whether or not the hammer is produced.

The Problem of Too Few Cost Pools

As you know from previous chapters, product costs consist of direct labor, direct material, and manufacturing overhead. Direct material and direct labor

INSIGHTS INTO ETHICS

Balsom Corporation has an informal policy of paying divisional managers a bonus that historically has amounted to 2% of the growth in divisional profit. Last year, the consumer products division had profit of $15,000,000. This year, preliminary figures show a profit of $20,000,000. This profit figure implies a bonus of $100,000, which the president of Balsom believes is excessive. (The manager of the consumer products division, no doubt, believes the bonus is well-deserved.) Accordingly, the president instructs the controller of Balsom to revise the allocation of centrally administered cost (e.g., administrative salaries, interest, and advertising) in such a way that the consumer products division will receive higher charges and have reduced profit. "After all," the president argues, "that division can stand to absorb more of these costs than our less profitable operations."

Would a change in the allocation system be fair to the manager of the consumer products division? Would a change violate GAAP?

---

are traced directly to the products produced, and overhead is assigned to products using an overhead allocation rate. Many companies assign overhead to products using only one or two overhead cost pools. While this approach is simple and easy to use, product costs may be seriously distorted when a company uses only a small number of cost pools. Consider the problem in the context of the Electra Manufacturing Company, which manufactures products in two departments: Assembly and Finishing. Electra has total manufacturing overhead of $1,000,000 and each year the company incurs 50,000 labor hours. Thus, if the company includes all overhead in one cost pool and allocates overhead using labor hours, the overhead rate will be $20 per labor hour. Now, suppose that of the $1,000,000 of overhead, $600,000 is due to Assembly and $400,000 is due to Finishing. Further, Assembly has 40,000 labor hours; Finishing, only 10,000 labor hours. You can see that overhead per labor hour is much more expensive in the Finishing Department: overhead is $15 per labor hour in Assembly and $40 per labor hour in Finishing. (See Illustration 24-11.)

ILLUSTRATION 24-11 Overhead Rates Using One Versus Two Cost Pools

One Cost Pool

$$\frac{\text{Total Overhead}}{\text{Total Labor Hours}} = \frac{\$1,000,000}{50,000} = \$20 \text{ per labor hour}$$

Two Cost Pools (one for Assembly and one for Finishing)

$$\frac{\text{Assembly Overhead}}{\text{Assembly Labor Hours}} = \frac{\$600,000}{40,000} = \$15 \text{ per assembly labor hour}$$

$$\frac{\text{Finishing Overhead}}{\text{Finishing Labor Hours}} = \frac{\$400,000}{10,000} = \$40 \text{ per finishing labor hour}$$

Now, assume that Electra has two products (A and B) that both require 10 labor hours. Product A requires 2 hours of assembly time and 8 hours of finishing, while Product B requires 8 hours of assembly time and 2 hours of finishing.

How much overhead will Electra allocate to each product if all overhead is included in a single cost pool and allocated on the basis of labor hours? The answer is that both products will receive the same allocation. They both require 10 hours of total labor, and use of a single cost pool allocates the average cost per labor hour. Both will receive $200 of overhead ($20 x 10 labor hours).

Which product is being under-costed and which product is being over-costed? Product A is under-costed because it requires relatively more production time in Finishing, which is a high-cost department in terms of overhead cost. Product B is over-costed because it requires relatively more production time in Assembly, which is a low-cost department in terms of overhead. Still, Product B receives the same charge per labor hour as Product A when only a single cost pool is used. Electra can easily solve this problem by setting up separate cost pools for overhead in each department. In general, product costs will be more accurate when a company uses more overhead cost pools. Also, decisions such as product pricing decisions that rely on product cost information will be improved. However, the more pools a company forms, the more costly will be its record keeping. The company must make a cost-benefit trade-off. Is the cost of forming more cost pools worth the benefit of improved information? This is a question a company must always address when considering improvements in accounting information.

LO 6
Discuss activity-based costing and cost drivers.

ACTIVITY-BASED COSTING

In the previous section, we discussed four potential problems with allocations of costs. Manufacturing companies face another problem when they use only measures of production volume as allocation bases to assign overhead to products. The problem and its solution, *activity-based costing* (ABC), are presented here.[1] A relatively recent development in managerial accounting, ABC has received a tremendous amount of attention from both academics and practitioners interested in improving managerial accounting information.[2] We briefly discussed ABC in Chapter 21; the discussion here is more detailed.

The Problem of Using Only Measures of Production Volume to Allocate Overhead

Manufacturing companies commonly use direct labor hours, direct labor cost, and machine hours as allocation bases when assigning overhead to products. Each of these items is a measure of production volume. Because most companies continue to allocate overhead using only measures of production volume as allocation bases, we refer to this as the "traditional approach." The problem with the traditional approach is that it assumes all overhead costs are proportional to production volume. (By "proportional," we mean that when volume

---

[1]Our discussion of activity-based costing is in a manufacturing context. However, banks, hospitals, insurance companies, and other service companies also have adopted an activity-based costing approach. See Yee-Ching Lilian Chan, "Improving Hospital Cost Accounting with Activity-Based-Costing," *Health Care Management Review*, Vol. 18 (Winter, 1993), pp. 71–77, for an example of activity-based costing in a service company context.

[2]Credit for developing activity-based costing is usually given to Robin Cooper and Robert Kaplan. See R. Cooper, "The Rise of Activity-Based Costing—Part One: What is an Activity-Based Cost System?" *Journal of Cost Management* (Summer, 1988), pp. 45–54, and R. Cooper, and R. Kaplan, "How Cost Accounting Distorts Product Costs," *Management Accounting* (April, 1988), pp. 20–27.

increases by 20 percent, overhead increases by 20 percent; when volume increases by 50 percent, overhead increases by 50 percent, etc.) However, many overhead costs (such as the cost of setting up equipment for a production run, the cost of inspecting raw materials, and the cost of handling materials) are not proportional to volume. Thus high-volume products often are over-costed, while low volume products are under-costed.

Consider the overhead costs a company incurs when starting a production line. Both a high-volume product (which is associated with a large amount of labor and machine time) and a low-volume product (which is associated with a small amount of labor and machine time) may require the same amount of setup time and setup cost. However, since the company allocates setup costs (along with all other overhead) only on the basis of production volume, the high-volume product will receive a larger *allocation* of setup cost. Thus, the high-volume product is over-costed. Let's see how the ABC approach avoids this problem.

The ABC Approach

In the ABC approach, companies identify the major activities that cause overhead costs to be incurred. Some of these activities are related to production volume, while others are not. Companies group the costs of the resources consumed performing these activities into cost pools. Finally, companies assign the costs to products using a measure of activity referred to as a *cost driver*. The steps involved in the ABC approach are:

1. Identify major activities.
2. Group costs of activities into cost pools.
3. Identify measures of major activities (called cost drivers).
4. Relate cost pools to products using cost drivers.

Some common activities and associated cost drivers are listed in Illustration 24-12. Note that some of the cost drivers are volume related (such as machine hours and assembly labor hours). Other cost drivers such as number of inspections and number of setups are not related to production volume. Some low-volume products that involve complex or fragile parts may need a large number of inspections, while some high-volume products that involve simple or rugged parts may need relatively few inspections. Also, both low-volume and high-volume products may require the same number of setups.

Each firm must decide how many separate activities (and related cost pools and cost drivers) to identify. If a company identifies too many activities, its system will be unnecessarily costly and confusing. For example, consider a company that produces 200 products and identifies 100 key activities. In this case, there are 20,000 (200 x 100) product-activity relationships. On the other hand, if a company uses too few activities the ABC system will not produce accurate data. Most companies that design ABC systems use 25 to 100 distinct activities.[3]

Relating Cost Pools to Products Using Cost Drivers

Before pursuing a comprehensive example, we will examine the last step in the ABC approach relating cost pools to products using cost drivers. Lacet

---

[3]See R. Cooper, R. Kaplan, L. Maisel, E. Morrissey and R. Oehm, *Implementing Activity-Based Cost Management Moving From Analysis to Action*, (Institute of Management Accountants, 1992), p. 13.

ILLUSTRATION 24-12 Common Activities and Associated Cost Drivers

Major Activities	Associated Costs	Cost Drivers
Processing purchase orders for materials and parts	Labor cost for workers determining order quantities, contacting vendors, and preparing purchase orders	Number of purchase orders processed
Handling material and parts	Labor cost for workers handling material and parts, depreciation of equipment used to move material and parts (e.g, depreciation of fork-lift trucks), etc.	Number of material requisitions
Inspecting incoming material and parts	Labor cost for workers performing inspections, depreciation of equipment used to test strength of materials, tolerances, etc.	Number of orders received
Setting up equipment	Labor cost for workers involved in setups, depreciation of equipment used to adjust equipment	Number of setups
Producing goods using manufacturing equipment	Depreciation on manufacturing equipment	Number of machine hours
Supervising assembly workers	Salary of assembly supervisors	Number of assembly labor hours
Inspecting finished goods	Labor cost for finished goods inspectors, depreciation of equipment used to test whether finished goods meet customer specifications, etc.	Number of inspections
Packing customer orders	Labor cost for packing workers, cost of packing materials, etc.	Number of boxes shipped

Electronics produces a variety of electronic products ranging from simple hand-held calculators to hard disk drives. Inspection to ensure that products are of high quality is a major activity at Lacet. In the coming year, the company expects to incur inspection costs of $2,500,000. Forty workers are employed in the inspection process, and they are expected to perform 1,000,000 product inspections in the coming year. Using inspection cost as a cost pool and number of inspections as a cost driver, the company determines a rate of $2.50 per inspection for purposes of allocating inspection costs to products.

Lacet produces 20,000 Model ZX disk drives. Each drive is inspected three times during the production process, and workers test various functions for conformance with rigorous standards set by the company. How much of the total $2,000,000 inspection cost will Lacet allocate to the Model ZX? With 20,000 disk drives and three inspections per drive, a total of 60,000 inspections will be performed. A rate of $2.50 per inspection implies that $7.50 of inspection cost will be allocated to each disk drive ($2.50 rate x 3 inspections) for a total of $150,000 ($7.50 x 20,000). Lacet would take a similar approach to determine the amount of inspection cost to allocate to the other products it produces.

Comprehensive Example of the ABC Approach

In this section, we pursue a comprehensive example of the ABC approach using the situation Gardenrite Manufacturing Company faced at the start of the chapter. As you read the example, make sure you can explain why Gardenrite's

INSIGHTS INTO ACCOUNTING

ACTIVITY-BASED COSTING AT CAL ELECTRONIC CIRCUITS

Cal Electronic Circuits, Inc. (CECI) manufactures printed circuit boards (PCBs), which are sold to microcomputer manufacturers. Manufacturing involves a capital-intensive process that is partially automated. Historically, direct labor represented only 8% of total manufacturing costs while overhead accounted for 79%. Overhead allocations had been made on the basis of direct labor hours.

With direct labor contributing less than 10% of total production costs, CECI accountants felt they could not justify the allocation of overhead on the basis of direct labor hours. The solution was to implement an activity-based costing (ABC) system. The new system, like the old, was a full cost absorption approach to costing. Implementation of the new ABC system involved identification of multiple manufacturing and support processes. These were grouped into cost centers and a cost driver was assigned to each cost center (see below).

The accountants believe their new ABC system will assist in identifying the costs of various processes, incorporate the complexities of PCB production into their cost accounting system, and identify cost-volume-profit relationships more clearly for different products.

Cost Center	Driver
Engineering	Engineering hours
Prototype/tooling	Piece/panel volume
Site services and administration	Number of workers
Quality assurance	Number of setups
Waste treatment	Chemical dollar volume
Procurement	Piece/panel volume
Tab plate option	Number of sides
Soldermask	Number of sides
Component legend	Number of sides
Maintenance	Work hours

Source: John Y. Lee, "Activity-Based Costing at Cal Electronic Circuits," published in *Management Accounting* (October 1990), pp. 36–38, copyright by the Institute of Management Accountants, Montvale, NJ.

use of the ABC approach reduced the cost of the high-volume product (the Model 250 spade) and increased the cost of the low-volume product (the Model 900 Mower).

For product costing purposes, Gardenrite traces labor and material costs directly to products produced. The company allocates manufacturing overhead to products based on labor cost. At the start of 19X1, the company estimated manufacturing overhead at $40,000,000 and labor cost at $8,000,000. Thus, the overhead application rate was $5 per dollar of labor.

For 19X1, Gardenrite expected certain costs and revenues from sale of the Model 250 spade and the Model 900 mower (shown on the next page). Note that the overhead allocated to the Model 250 spade of $459,000 is equal to the overhead rate of $5 per dollar of labor times the $91,800 of direct labor incurred in production of the spade.

The production process for spades is fairly simple. The company uses one supplier for the metal handle and blade. The company produces shafts on an

	Model 250 Spade	Model 900 Mower
Number of units	85,000	800
Sales revenue	$765,000	$240,000
Direct labor	$ 91,800	$ 12,000
Direct material	153,000	48,000
Overhead	459,000	60,000
Total cost	$703,800	$120,000
Gross profit	$ 61,200	$120,000
Cost per unit	$8.28	$150.00
Gross profit per unit	$ .72	$150.00
Profit as a % of sales	8.00%	50.00%

automatic lathe and the workers assemble the handles, blades, and shafts by hand at a single workstation.

Two years ago, the company began manufacturing lawn mowers. The production process for lawn mowers is more complicated than the process used in spade production. The company uses 20 suppliers to provide the 50 components involved in production of the Model 900 mower. Further, assembly of mowers uses 15 separate assembly workstations.

Recall that Ben Jakes, the CFO at Gardenrite, suspects the low profit margin (less than 10% of sales) for spades may be due to problems with the current costing system. Further, he is somewhat surprised that the company is able to earn such a high margin on mowers (50%). Since the company only recently began manufacturing mowers, he expected production inefficiencies to keep profit margins low for at least three years.

Ben should be concerned about the product costing system at Gardenrite. The approach to allocating overhead assumes that all overhead is proportional to a single measure of production volume—labor cost. However, overhead is caused by several key activities. Suppose Ben authorizes a study of how the costs of the Model 250 spade and the Model 900 mower will change if Gardenrite takes an ABC approach. The study determines that the $40,000,000 of overhead cost is related to the four cost drivers identified in Illustration 24-13. As indicated, setup costs are related to the number of setups; material handling costs, to the number of material requisitions; and depreciation of equipment, to the number of machine hours required to produce products. All other overhead is categorized in a cost pool simply referred to as "Other."

ILLUSTRATION 24-13 Overhead Cost Items and Cost Drivers

Overhead Cost Items	Annual Cost	Cost Driver	Estimated Annual Value	Cost per Unit
Setup costs	$ 4,000,000	Number of setups	1,000 setups	$4,000 per setup
Material handling requisitions	$ 2,000,000	Number of material requisitions	$2,000 requisitions for all products produced	$1,000 per requisition
Depreciation of equipment	$10,000,000	Machine hours	20,000 machine hours	$500 per machine hour
Other	$24,000,000	Number of workstations used in production of a product	3,000 workstations used for all products	$8,000 per workstation

Gardenrite has decided that "manufacturing complexity" is a major factor contributing to the incurrence of other overhead costs. The cost driver for complexity is the number of workstations required to produce a product. Products that require many workstations to produce are more complex products and cause more overhead.

Manufacturing spades requires two setups and three material requisitions. Forty machine hours are used to produce the 85,000 Model 250 spades. Assembly of spades requires one workstation. Production of the 800 Model 900 mowers requires 5 setups and 50 material requisitions. One hundred machine hours are used to produce the 800 mowers. Assembly of mowers requires 15 workstations. This information is summarized in Illustration 24-14.

ILLUSTRATION 24-14 Production Information for 85,000 Spades and 800 Mowers

	Model 250 Spade	Model 900 Mower
Number of setups	2	5
Number of material requisitions	3	50
Number of machine hours	40	100
Number of workstations	1	15

Using the information above, Ben can calculate the costs per unit of Model 250 spades and Model 900 mowers, assuming the company changes to an ABC system. The calculations are presented in Illustration 24-15. With the ABC approach, the cost of the Model 250 Spade drops from $8.28 to $3.34 per unit, while the cost of the Model 900 mower increases from $150.00 to $375.00 per unit.

	Model 250 Spade	Model 900 Mower
Cost per unit using traditional approach to allocating overhead	$8.28	$150.00
Cost per unit using ABC approach to allocating overhead	$3.34	$375.00

Recall that the Model 250 spades sold for $9.00 per unit; thus, the ABC approach reveals that this high-volume product is very profitable. However, the Model 900 mower sells for only $300 per unit. The ABC approach reveals that the selling price is not even covering the full cost of this low-volume product.[4] The CFO's intuition that the traditional product costing system at Gardenrite might be providing misleading information was correct. Because the traditional system only allocated costs using a volume-related allocation base, the high-volume product (spades) was over-costed and did not appear to be particularly profitable. The low-volume product (mowers) was under-costed and appeared to be highly profitable when, in fact, it was not covering its costs. This example has a clear message. Namely, companies should consider taking an ABC approach to product costing and use a variety of cost drivers in addition to dri-

---

[4] The fact that costs exceed revenue for the Model 900 mower does not *necessarily* imply that the product should be immediately dropped. Some of the costs included in the cost of the mower (such as depreciation) will exist whether or not the mower is produced. See the discussion in the chapter dealing with cost information and management decisions.

vers that measure only production volume. Otherwise, they run the risk of making poor product pricing decisions and continuing to produce products that are not profitable in the long run.

ILLUSTRATION 24-15 Costs of Model 250 Spade and Model 900 Mower Using an ABC Approach

Model 250 Spade			Model 900 Mower		
Number of units		85,000	Number of units		800
Direct labor		$ 91,800	Direct labor		$ 12,000
Direct material		153,000	Direct material		48,000
Overhead:			Overhead:		
Setup cost ($4,000 x 2)	$ 8,000		Setup cost ($4,000 x 5)	$ 20,000	
Material handling cost			Material handling cost		
($1,000 x 3)	3,000		($1,000 x 50)	50,000	
Depreciation of equipment			Depreciation of equipment		
($500 x 40)	20,000		($500 x 100)	50,000	
Other ($8,000 x 1)	8,000		Other ($8,000 x 15)	120,000	
Total overhead		39,000	Total overhead		240,000
Total cost		$283,800	Total cost		$300,000
Cost per unit		$3.34	Cost per unit		$375.00
Selling price per unit		$9.00	Selling price per unit		$300.00
Gross profit per unit		$5.66	Gross profit (loss) per unit		$(75.00)
Gross profit as a % of sales		63%	Gross profit (loss) as a % of sales		(25%)

Different Costs for Different Purposes

Allocations of costs that are quite suitable for one purpose may be inappropriate for another purpose. In particular, allocations that are satisfactory from a product costing standpoint may not provide useful information for decision making. For example, using a single overhead rate may result in product costs that are quite acceptable from a financial reporting standpoint. However, for decision-making purposes, an ABC approach may be more appropriate. Thus, when making an allocation, companies must carefully consider the purpose of the allocation and decide whether the allocated cost serves the particular purpose.

SUMMARY

Explain why indirect costs are allocated. Indirect costs are allocated to provide information for decision making, to calculate the full cost of products, to reduce the frivolous use of common resources, and to encourage managers to evaluate the efficiency of internally provided services.

Describe the cost allocation process. The cost allocation process has three steps: (1) identify the cost objectives, (2) form cost pools, and (3) select an allocation base and allocate the cost pools to the cost objectives.

Discuss allocation of service department costs. Service department costs are allocated to production departments that, in turn, allocate these costs to products. The direct method allocates service department costs to production departments but not to other service departments. The sequential method considers the fact that service departments make use of each other's services.

Discuss allocation of joint costs. The costs of common inputs that result in multiple products are referred to as joint costs. Companies may allocate these costs by using a physical measure of output. However, such an approach may make one or more of the joint products appear to be unprofitable when, in fact, they contribute to covering common costs. Allocating joint costs using the relative sales value of the joint products is a better approach. With this method, products that make a positive contribution to covering joint cost will not look unprofitable.

Identify potential problems with cost allocation. Generally, managers should not receive allocations of costs they cannot control. This is a central idea of responsibility accounting, which is a system of accounting that traces revenues and costs to organizational units with related responsibility.

Companies must exercise care when they allocate fixed costs on a per unit basis (i.e., the fixed costs are unitized). Unitized fixed costs appear to be variable to the manager who receives the allocation. In many cases, it is better to allocate fixed costs with lump-sum allocations. Managers need to be aware that problems arise because allocations are often arbitrary. Also, accurate costs are seldom obtained when companies allocate costs using only one or two cost pools.

Discuss activity-based costing and cost drivers. Activity-based costing is a product costing method that recognizes that costs are caused by activities. Measures of the key activities that cause costs to be incurred are referred to as cost drivers. The cost drivers are used as the allocation bases to relate indirect costs to products. Unlike traditional systems, ABC does not focus solely on volume-related cost drivers.

REVIEW PROBLEM

The Expeditions Food Company has three service departments (maintenance, personnel and security) and three production departments (cooking, freezing, and vacuum packing). Costs for the service departments are collected in cost pools and are allocated to the producing departments. The costs are then re-allocated to the company's products as part of the overhead of the production departments. Maintenance and security department costs are allocated on the basis of square footage, and personnel department costs allocated on the basis of the number of employees.

Selected data for Expeditions are as follows:

	Costs	Square Footage	Number of Employees
Service departments:			
Maintenance	$600,000	5,000	30
Personnel	$300,000	3,000	10
Security	$200,000	2,000	10
Production departments:			
Cooking		25,000	100
Freezing		10,000	50
Vacuum packing		5,000	50

REQUIRED:

a. Allocate the costs for each service department to the production departments using the direct method.

b. Allocate the costs for the service departments to the production departments using the sequential method. Assume maintenance is allocated first, then personnel, then security.
c. Using the information from a and b above, tabulate the total service department costs allocated to each production department under: (1) the direct method and (2) the sequential method. Comment on which method seems appropriate.
d. Expeditions is unsure of what allocation base to select for the allocation of security costs. The controller wants to use square footage and the chief cost accountant wants to use the number of employees. They settled on square footage after a full discussion of the merits of each allocation base. Do you think they made a good choice? Discuss.

SOLUTION:

(a) *Allocation of service department costs to production departments, direct method.*

$600,000 maintenance department costs:

To cooking: $600,000 \times \dfrac{25,000}{40,000} = \$375,000$ (See note)

To freezing: $600,000 \times \dfrac{10,000}{40,000} = \$150,000$

To vacuum packing: $600,000 \times \dfrac{5,000}{40,000} = \$75,000$

$300,000 personnel department costs:

To cooking: $300,000 \times \dfrac{100}{200} = \$150,000$

To freezing: $300,000 \times \dfrac{50}{200} = \$75,000$

To vacuum packing: $300,000 \times \dfrac{50}{200} = \$75,000$

$200,000 security department costs:

To cooking: $200,000 \times \dfrac{25,000}{40,000} = \$125,000$

To freezing: $200,000 \times \dfrac{10,000}{40,000} = \$50,000$

To vacuum packing: $200,000 \times \dfrac{5,000}{40,000} = \$25,000$

Note: The calculation could be performed as follows:

(1) Determine cost per unit of activity:

$\dfrac{\$600,000}{40,000} = \$15$ per square ft.

(2) Multiply cost per unit of activity by the activity level for the department:

$15 \times 25,000$ square ft. $= \$375,000$

(b) *Allocation of service department costs, to production departments, sequential method (rounded to nearest dollar).*

$600,000 maintenance department costs:

To personnel: $600,000 \times \dfrac{3,000}{45,000} = $40,000

To security: $600,000 \times \dfrac{2,000}{45,000} = $26,667

To cooking: $600,000 \times \dfrac{25,000}{45,000} = $333,333

To freezing: $600,000 \times \dfrac{10,000}{45,000} = $133,333

To vacuum packing: $600,000 \times \dfrac{5,000}{45,000} = $66,667

$340,000 personnel department costs ($300,000 + $40,000 from maintenance):

To security: $340,000 \times \dfrac{10}{210} = $16,190

To cooking: $340,000 \times \dfrac{100}{210} = $161,905

To freezing: $340,000 \times \dfrac{50}{210} = $80,952

To vacuum packing: $340,000 \times \dfrac{50}{210} = $80,952

$242,857 security department costs ($200,000 + $26,667 from maintenance + $16,190 from personnel):

To cooking: $242,857 \times \dfrac{25,000}{40,000} = $151,786

To freezing: $242,857 \times \dfrac{10,000}{40,000} = $60,714

To vacuum packing: $242,857 \times \dfrac{5,000}{40,000} = $30,357

(c) *(1) Service department costs allocated under the direct method.*

	Costs Allocated	Cooking	Freezing	Vacuum Packing
Maintenance	$ 600,000	$375,000	$150,000	$ 75,000
Personnel	300,000	150,000	75,000	75,000
Security	200,000	125,000	50,000	25,000
Total	$1,100,000	$650,000	$275,000	$175,000

(2) Service department costs allocated under the sequential method.

	Costs Allocated	Personnel	Security	Cooking	Freezing	Vacuum Packing
Maintenance	$ 600,000	$ 40,000	$ 26,667	$333,333	$133,333	$ 66,667
Personnel	340,000		16,190	161,905	80,952	80,953
Security	242,857			151,786	60,714	30,357
Total	$1,182,857	$(40,000)	$(42,857)	$647,024	$274,999	$177,977

Comment: Although conceptually the sequential method reflects a more logical allocation of costs than the direct method, the sequential method is more complex, and in Expeditions' case does not result in a substantially different allocation of costs to the producing departments. Therefore, the direct method seems preferable.

(d) *Discuss the accountants' choice of allocation base.*

Ideally, an allocation base should result in costs being allocated to cost objectives (the three production departments in this instance) on a cause-and-effect basis. For example, in evaluating square footage as a basis of allocating security costs, cause-and-effect is present if a department with twice the square footage generates twice the costs in the security department. In other words, security cost should be a function of square footage. The relationship between the number of employees and security can be studied in the same manner, to determine if security costs are in some way a function of the number of employees. Many times a strong cause-and-effect relation to an allocation base cannot be found, and the selection of the base is determined by other criteria. Without being familiar with Expeditions' security operations, it is difficult to determine which allocation base, square footage or number of employees, represents the best cause and effect characteristics.

KEY TERMS

ability to bear costs, *985*
cause-and-effect, *984*
controllable costs, *992*
cost allocation, *979*
cost objective, *983*
cost pool, *983*
direct method of allocating costs, *985*
equity, *985*

joint costs, *989*
joint products, *989*
lump-sum allocations, *994*
relative benefits, *985*
relative sales value method, *990*
responsibility accounting system, *992*
split-off point, *989*

sequential method of allocating costs, *987*
unitized fixed cost, *994*

SELF QUIZ

LO 1 1. Costs are allocated:
   a. To provide information for important decisions.
   b. To calculate the "full cost" of products for financial reporting purposes.
   c. To reduce the frivolous use of common resources.
   d. To encourage managers to evaluate the efficiency of internally provided services.
   e. All of the above

LO 2 2. In the cost allocation process, the cost objective is:
   a. The allocation base used to allocate costs.
   b. A grouping of individual costs whose total is allocated using one allocation base.
   c. The product, service, or department that is to receive the allocation.
   d. None of the above.

LO 2 3. There are, in order, three steps in the cost allocation process. List them: (1) _____, (2) _____, and (3) _____.

LO 2 4. The overriding concern in forming a cost pool is to:
   a. Avoid placing similar costs in a pool.
   b. Limit the number of costs which make up the pool.
   c. Insure that the costs in the pool are homogeneous or similar.
   d. None of the above.

LO 2 5. The third step in the allocation process is to select an allocation base to allocate cost pools to the cost objectives. An allocation base:
   a. Must have some characteristic that is common to all cost objectives.
   b. Ideally, should result in costs being allocated based on a cause-and-effect relationship.
   c. Both a and b.
   d. None of the above.

LO 3 6. The direct method of allocating costs:
   a. Allocates service department costs to other service departments.

b. Allocates only direct costs.
c. Allocates service department costs to producing departments only.
d. Both b and c.

LO 3 7. X Company has three service departments and three production departments. They use the sequential method of allocating costs.
a. Each service department will allocate its costs to the other two service departments.
b. The production departments receive a smaller allocation of service department costs because some service department costs are allocated to other service departments.
c. All service department costs are allocated directly to production departments.
d. None of the above.

LO 4 8. The Southern Meat Packing Company pays $160 for a hog. The hog is slaughtered and processed into: hams, tenderloins, sausage, pork chops, and pigs feet. The cost of the hog is referred to as a _____ cost. The products are referred to as _____ products.

LO 4 9. The Southern Lumber Company pays $1,000 for a walnut log. They saw the log into boards totaling 500 board feet. There are two grades of boards. Grade A sells for $3 per board foot and grade B sells for $2 per board foot. The best method to allocate the cost of the log to the grade A and B lumber is the _____ _____ _____ _____ .

LO 4 10. The joint costs incurred in a joint product situation:
a. Are incurred before the split-off point.
b. Are incurred after the split-off point.
c. Should never be allocated.
d. None of the above.

LO 4 11. A joint product has a cost of $18, which includes $6 of allocated joint costs, and a sales price of $16.
a. Profit would improve if the company discontinued production of the product.
b. The company should sell as few of the products as possible to minimize the loss on product sales.
c. The data is misleading because the $6 allocated joint cost will have to be incurred even if the product is eliminated.
d. Both a and b.

LO 5 12. When fixed costs are stated on a per unit basis:
a. Fixed costs are said to be "unitized."
b. Fixed costs appear to be variable to managers receiving allocations.
c. Decision making is improved.
d. Both a and b.

LO 5 13. A way to avoid the problems of unitized fixed costs is to:
a. Not allocate fixed costs.
b. Use a lump-sum method of allocating fixed costs.
c. Combine fixed and variable costs in a single cost pool.
d. None of the above.

LO 5 14. Allocation of indirect costs:
a. Can be done with great accuracy and precision, if one applies the proper techniques.
b. Is an inherently arbitrary process, a characteristic that can lead to problems.
c. Can often be justified a variety of ways, leading to substantially different costs being allocated.
d. Both b and c.

LO 5 15. In allocating costs to products, more accurate
LO 6 costing is obtained by:
a. Having only one cost pool.
b. Having more than one cost pool.
c. Always using allocation bases that are based on production volume.
d. None of the above.

LO 5 16. Controllable costs for the manager of department A are:
a. Costs of the controller's department which are allocated to department A.
b. Costs of supplies used in department A.
c. All costs related to the final product.
d. All the above.

LO 6 17. Cost drivers in activity-based costing are:
a. Always related to production volume.
b. Often assign more costs to low-volume production than traditional allocation methods.
c. Often assign less costs to low-volume production than traditional allocation methods.
d. None of the above.

LO 2 18. Terms and their definitions are listed below.
LO 3 Match the definitions with the terms.
LO 4 ___ a. Ability to bear costs
LO 5 ___ b. Joint products
LO 6 ___ c. Cause-and-effect
___ d. Controllable costs
___ e. Cost allocation
___ f. Cost objective
___ g. Cost pool
___ h. Direct method of allocating costs
___ i. Equity
___ j. Activity-based costing
(1) A grouping of individual costs whose total is allocated using one allocation base.

CHAPTER 24 COST ALLOCATION AND ACTIVITY-BASED COSTING   1009

(2) Two or more products arising from common inputs.
(3) A concept of cost allocation which suggests that the allocations should be fair.
(4) The concept of an allocation base resulting in allocations to cost objectives that caused the costs to be incurred.
(5) The object of the cost allocation: usually a product, service, or department.
(6) An approach in managerial accounting that uses cost pools related to activities and cost drivers to assign costs to products.
(7) Costs which a manager can control.
(8) A cost allocation concept which suggests that the allocation base should result in more costs being allocated to products, services, or departments that are more profitable.
(9) The process of assigning indirect costs.
(10) Allocating costs from service departments directly to producing departments without any intermediate allocations among the service departments.

LO 2
LO 3
LO 4
LO 5
LO 6

19. Key terms and their definitions are listed below. Match the definitions with the key terms.
___ a. Cost pool
___ b. Cost drivers
___ c. Lump-sum allocations
___ d. Relative benefits
___ e. Relative sales value method
___ f. Responsibility accounting system
___ g. Split-off point
___ h. Sequential method of allocating costs
___ i. Unitized fixed costs
___ j. Joint products

(1) The stage of production when individual joint products are identified.
(2) Two or more products result from common inputs.
(3) A system of accounting which traces costs and revenues to organizational units and individuals responsible for the revenues and costs.
(4) Stating fixed costs on a per unit basis.
(5) A concept of cost allocation which allocates costs based on the amount of benefit the cost objective receives from the incurrance of the cost.
(6) Measures of activity used to allocate cost pools in activity-based costing.
(7) A grouping of individual costs whose total is allocated using one allocation base.
(8) Allocations of fixed costs in such a way that the costs appear to be fixed to the managers whose departments receive the allocations.
(9) A method of allocating service department costs which takes into account service departments using each other's services.
(10) A way of allocating joint costs based on the sales price of the joint products at the split-off point.

SOLUTIONS TO SELF-QUIZ
1. e   2. c   3. (1) Identify the cost objectives, (2) form cost pools, and (3) select an allocation base and allocate the cost pools to the cost objectives   4. c   5. c   6. c   7. d   8. joint cost, joint products   9. relative sales value method
10. a   11. c   12. d   13. b   14. d   15. b   16. b   17. b   18. a. 8   b. 2   c. 4   d. 7   e. 9   f. 5   g. 1   h. 10   i. 3   j. 6   19. a. 7   b. 6   c. 8   d. 5   e. 10   f. 3   g. 1   h. 9   i. 4   j. 2

QUESTIONS

Q24-1 List four reasons why indirect costs are allocated.

Q24-2 "All variable costs are direct, and all fixed costs are indirect." Is this a true statement? Discuss.

Q24-3 A defense contractor has been awarded a contract to produce a submarine that includes a lot of high-cost electronic surveillance equipment. The contract is on a "cost plus" basis. The contractor is entitled to allocate indirect administrative costs to the submarine. Accordingly, the administrative costs are allocated to the submarine and to other jobs the contractor is working on using direct material costs as the allocation base. Is direct material a good allocation base? Discuss.

Q24-4 Allocated costs can serve as the basis for charging for the use of internal resources or services. What are the possible advantages obtained from charging for internal resources and services?

Q24-5 Explain what a cost objective is and give two examples.

Q24-6 Explain one possible advantage of having two cost pools for each service department, one for variable costs and one for fixed costs.

Q24-7 If a company is allocating the cafeteria costs to all departments within the company, what allocation base might result in a good cause-and-effect relationship?

Q24-8 If direct cause-and-effect relationships cannot be established when choosing an allocation base, accountants use other criteria. Name three such criteria.

Q24-9 How do controllable costs relate to a responsibility accounting system?

Q24-10 Should noncontrollable costs ever be allocated to a department?

Q24-11 "Unitizing" fixed costs might cause a manager to elect not to produce a product on the grounds that it is unprofitable, when, in fact, production of the product would be profitable. How can a company avoid this problem?

Q24-12 Explain the difference in the direct method of allocating service department costs and the sequential method of allocating service department costs.

Q24-13 A company has a joint product with allocated joint costs of $10 using a physical quantity method of allocation. They are only able to sell the product for $8. Should they discontinue the product? Discuss.

Q24-14 Why is the relative sales value a more logical way to allocate joint costs than is physical quantity? Discuss.

Q24-15 What is a cost driver?

Q24-16 Briefly explain how traditional methods of allocating overhead to products might under-allocate costs to low-production-volume products.

EXERCISES

LO 1

E24-1 Reasons for Allocating Indirect Costs The Quest Production Company operates a security department that provides protection to all departments within the company. Departmental managers are responsible for working with the head of security to ensure that their departments are protected. Briefly explain why Quest might want to allocate the security department costs to departments.

LO 2

E24-2 Basic Allocation Process Quick Company's copy department, which does all of the bulk photocopying for the company, budgets the following costs for the year, based on expected activity of 5,000,000 copies.

Salaries (fixed)	$60,000
Depreciation of copy machines (fixed)	15,000
Employee benefits (fixed)	15,000
Utilities (fixed)	2,000
Paper (variable, 1 cent per copy)	50,000
Toner (variable, 1 cent per copy)	50,000

The costs are assigned to two cost pools, one for fixed costs and one for variable costs. The copy costs are then assigned to the sales department and the administrative department. Fixed costs are assigned on a lump-sum basis, 30 percent to sales and 70 percent to administration. The variable costs are assigned at a rate of 2 cents per copy.

REQUIRED:

Assuming 4,000,000 copies were made during the year, 1,500,000 by sales and 2,500,000 by administration, calculate the copy department costs allocated to Sales and Administration.

LO 2

E24-3 Basic Allocation Process, Selecting Allocation Bases Following is a list of cost pools which must be allocated to two cost objectives: (1) general and administrative and (2) sales.

Cost Pools	Allocation Base
a. Maintenance	_____
b. Cafeteria	_____
c. Security	_____
d. Copying	_____
e. Child care	_____
f. Car fleet	_____
g. Nursing Station	_____
h. Career Counseling	_____
i. Utilities	_____

REQUIRED:

For each cost pool identify a cost allocation base.

LO 2,3

E24-4 Basic Allocation Process, Problems with Allocations The maintenance department for the Wells Distribution Company budgets annual costs of $3,000,000 based on the expected operating level for the next year. The costs are assigned to two production departments using the direct method of allocation and a single cost pool. Wells is considering two allocation bases for the departmental assignments of cost: (1) square footage and (2) direct labor hours. The following data relate to the bases.

	Production Dept. 1	Production Dept. 2
Square footage	20,000	30,000
Direct labor hours	30,000	20,000

REQUIRED:

Calculate the costs allocated to the production departments using each allocation base. Comment on: (1) the problem that the significantly different allocation bases present, and (2) which base might be preferable.

LO 3

E24-5 Allocation of Service Department Costs, Direct Method Ryan Company has three service departments (S1, S2, S3) and two production departments (P1, P2). The following data relate to Ryan's cost allocations.

	Budgeted Costs	Number of Employees
S1	$3,000,000	75
S2	$2,000,000	50
S3	$1,000,000	25
P1		150
P2		225

The service department costs are allocated by the direct method. The number of employees is used as the allocation base for service department costs.

REQUIRED:

a. Allocate service department costs to production departments.
b. Calculate the total service department costs allocated to each production department.

LO 3

E24-6 Allocation of Service Department Costs, Sequential Method Ryan Company has three service departments (S1, S2, S3) and two production departments (P1, P2). The following data relate to Ryan's cost allocations.

	Budgeted Costs	Number of Employees
S1	$3,000,000	75
S2	$2,000,000	50
S3	$1,000,000	25
P1		150
P2		225

The service department costs are allocated by the sequential method, S1 first, S2 second, S3 third. The number of employees are used as the allocation base for service department costs.

REQUIRED:

a. Allocate service department costs to production departments.
b. Calculate the total service department costs allocated to each production department.

LO 4

E24-7 Allocating Joint Costs The Western Produce company purchased a truckload of watermelons for $600. The load weighed 6,000 pounds. Western separated the melons into two grades: superior and economy. The superior grade melons had a total weight of 4,000 pounds and the economy grade melons totaled 2,000 pounds. Western sells the superior grade at 25 cents per pound and the economy grade at 10 cents per pound.

REQUIRED:

Calculate the allocation of the $600 cost of the truckload to the superior grade and economy grade melons, assuming (1) the physical quantity method of allocation, and (2) the relative sales value method of allocation.

LO 5

E24-8 Problems Associated with Cost Allocation Qualla Company's outdoor wear division receives an offer from a motorcycle company to purchase 1,000 rainproof riding suits for $175 each. Qualla's accountants determine that the following costs apply to the production of the rain suit.

Direct material	$80
Direct labor	40
Variable overhead	10
Allocation of fixed Production department overhead	10
Allocation of fixed Service department costs	40

Although the manager, Cindy Brown, of the outdoor wear division questions the allocation of fixed service department costs to the rainwear, she is told that the fixed service department costs are allocated using an allocation base of direct labor dollars and that the $1 overhead rate must be applied to the $40 of direct labor in the rainsuit. The manager's performance is evaluated based on division profits.

REQUIRED:

a. Explain how "unitized" fixed costs may be creating a problem for Qualla.
b. Suggest a way to correct the problem.
c. Calculate the change in income from accepting the motorcycle company's offer.

LO 5

E24-9 Responsibility Accounting, Controllable Costs David Mott, the manager of the service department at the Dirt Bike Sales and Service Company, is evaluated based on the profit performance of his department. The profit of the service department is down this year because the service department's share of the allocated cost of the accounting and bookkeeping department is much higher than last year. Discuss how this situation relates to a responsibility accounting system and controllable costs.

LO 6   **E24-10**   **Activity-Based Costing**   The following are six cost pools established for a company using activity-based costing. The pools are related to the company's products using cost drivers.

Cost Pools:
(1) Raw materials quality control
(2) Production equipment repairs and maintenance
(3) Raw materials storage
(4) Plant heat, light, water, and power
(5) Finished product quality control
(6) Production line setups

REQUIRED:

For each cost pool, identify a possible cost driver.

PROBLEM SET A

LO 1,2,5   **P24-1A**   **Reasons Indirect Costs are Allocated; Basic Allocation Process; Problems with Cost Allocation**   Railroads have been a regulated industry in the past with the rates set to transport coal based on the railroad's cost per mile of hauling a carload of coal. The president of a large coal company was reported to have said, "God in heaven, in all of His wisdom, cannot calculate a railroad's cost of hauling a carload of coal from Eastern Kentucky to Hampton Roads."

REQUIRED:

a. In reference to the situation above, why does the railroad allocate indirect costs?
b. Identify several indirect costs that the railroad would have to allocate.
c. In reference to the above situation, identify the cost objective.
d. Suggest some possible allocation bases that might be used by a railroad.
e. What do you think the president of the coal company is implying in his statement?

LO 2,3   **P24-2A**   **Allocating Service Department Costs, Direct Method**   New-World Airlines has three service departments: (1) tickets/booking, (2) baggage and handling, and (3) maintenance. The service department costs are collected in separate cost pools for each department and are allocated to the two revenue-producing departments—(1) domestic flights and (2) international flights. New-World does not differentiate between fixed and variable costs in making allocations. The following data relate to the allocations.

	Budgeted Costs	*Budgeted Air Miles*
Tickets/booking	$4,000,000	
Baggage/handling	$2,000,000	
Maintenance	$6,000,000	
Domestic flights		5,000,000
International flights		20,000,000

REQUIRED:

a. Allocate the service department costs to the revenue producing departments using air miles as the allocation base and the direct allocation method.
b. Evaluate the cause-and-effect relationship resulting from the use of air miles as the allocation base. In which of the cost pools do you think the cause and effect is the strongest? In which pool is it probably the weakest? Suggest an alternative allocation base for the cost pool with the weakest cause-and-effect relationship.

LO 2,5

P24-3A **Choice of Allocation Base, Problems with Cost Allocation** Smith Manufacturing has two production departments, molding and finishing, which are served by one service department, maintenance. Smith's accountants are trying to select an allocation base to allocate the service department costs to the production departments. Possible allocation bases identified are: (1) square footage of space occupied, (2) direct labor hours, (3) machine hours, and (4) cost of equipment. The following data relate to the allocation.

Budgeted maintenance department costs $500,000

	Molding	Finishing
Square footage of space occupied	20,000	30,000
Budgeted direct labor hours	200,000	400,000
Budgeted machine hours	50,000	50,000
Cost of equipment	3,000,000	2,000,000

REQUIRED:

a. Prepare a schedule showing the maintenance costs allocated to the production departments under each of the four possible allocation bases.
b. Do all of the allocation bases appear to have a good cause-and-effect relationship with maintenance department costs? What type of information is needed to answer this question?
c. Why are allocations sometimes considered arbitrary?
d. Suppose that the large majority of maintenance costs results from upkeep and repair of the equipment. Which allocation base appears to have the best cause-and-effect relationship with maintenance costs?
e. Discuss why it might be advantageous to separate the maintenance department costs into fixed and variable and allocate the fixed costs using a lump-sum allocation.

LO 3

P24-4A **Allocating Service Department Costs, Direct and Sequential Methods** Blair Industries produces electronic equipment for the aviation industry. Blair has two service departments, maintenance and computing, and two production departments, assembly and testing. Maintenance costs are allocated on the basis of square footage occupied and computing costs are allocated on the basis of the number of computer terminals. The following data relate to the cost allocations of the service departments.

	Maintenance	Computing	Assembly	Testing
Service department costs	$400,000	$600,000		
Square footage		20,000	70,000	30,000
Terminals			5	10

REQUIRED:

a. Allocate the service department costs using the direct method.
b. Allocate the service department costs using the sequential method. Start with the maintenance department.
c. When using the sequential method, what should have been the basis for selecting maintenance as the first service department allocated?

LO 4

P24-5A **Allocation of Joint Costs** The Cannon Petroleum Company purchases raw crude oil and refines the crude into petroleum products. The refining process produces three petroleum products that require no further processing and are sold at the split-off point to other petroleum refiners in bulk quantities. The products are labeled Product A, Product B, and Product C. The following information relates to Cannon's operations.

Crude oil and refining costs	$10,000,000
Petroleum products produced:	
Product A	2,000,000 gallons
Product B	3,000,000 gallons
Product C	5,000,000 gallons
Sales price per gallon:	
Product A	$4.00
Product B	3.00
Product C	0.50

REQUIRED:

a. What is meant by the term "split-off point?"
b. Allocate the joint costs to Products A, B, and C using physical quantity as the basis of allocation. Calculate the cost per gallon and the profit or loss on the sale of a gallon of each product.
c. Based on your calculations in b, is Cannon loosing money on the sale of Product C? Would they be better off to eliminate product C? Discuss.
d. Allocate the joint costs to Products A, B, and C using the preferable method, which is the relative sales value method. Calculate the cost per gallon and the gross margin on the sale of a gallon of each product.
e. Compare the costs allocated under the two methods and discuss why the relative sales value method seems to be a more logical way to allocate joint costs.

LO 6

P24-6A **Activity-Based Costing** The Western Edge Manufacturing company produces two products. One is a recreational whitewater kayak molded from a cross link plastic and designed to perform as a durable whitewater playboat. The other product is a high-performance competition kayak molded with high-tech, fiberglass-like materials which are very light. The recreational boat is uniform in its dimensions and style. However the competition boat is custom designed to fit the paddler and his or her taste in certain features, such as rocker and cockpit size.

Most of the sales come from the recreational boat, but recently sales of the competition boat have been increasing. The following information relates to the products for the most recent accounting year.

	Recreational Kayak	*Competition Kayak*
Sales and production (boats)	900	100
Sales price	$600	$650
Unit costs:		
Direct materials	$150	$200
Direct labor	100	100
Overhead	135	135
Total unit costs	$385	$435

Overhead costs:		
Building depreciation and maintenance	$ 25,000	
Equipment depreciation and maintenance	25,000	
Materials ordering	15,000	
Quality control	10,000	
Maintenance and security	10,000	
Setup and drafting	20,000	
Supervision	30,000	
Total	$ 135,000	
Overhead rate based on direct labor dollars:		
Total overhead	$ 135,000	$1.35 overhead per
Total direct labor	$ 100,000*	dollar of direct labor

*(900 x $100) + (100 x $100)

Victor Mason, the president, is concerned that the traditional cost accounting system used by Western may not be providing accurate costing information and that the sales price of the competition boat might not be enough to recover its true costs.

REQUIRED:

a. The traditional system that Western is using assigns 90% of the $135,000 total overhead to the recreational boat because 90% of the direct labor dollars were spent on the recreational boat. Discuss why this might not be an accurate way to assign overhead to the boats.
b. Discuss how Western might be able to improve their cost allocations by adapting more than one cost pool.
c. Assume Western retains a consultant to create an activity-based costing system, and the consultant develops the following data. Determine the overhead allocated to each model of boat using the activity-based costing information and compute the total unit costs for each boat.

Cost Pool	Amount	Cost Driver	Driver Activity Rec. Boat	Driver Activity Comp. Boat
Building	$25,000	square footage	6,000	1,000
Equipment	25,000	machine hours	3,400	600
Materials ordering	15,000	number of orders	200	100
Quality control	10,000	number of inspections	300	150
Maintenance and security	10,000	square footage	6,000	1,000
Set up and drafting	20,000	number of setups	20	40
Supervision	30,000	direct labor $	$90,000	$10,000

d. Discuss why the activity-based allocations are different than the traditional allocation method used by Western.

PROBLEM SET B

LO 1,2,5

P24-1B Reasons Indirect Costs are Allocated; Basic Allocation Process; Problems with Cost Allocation   The president of a bank comes to the chief accountant and states, "I need some information for the board of directors meeting next week. A couple of the directors are on our case. They think everything we do is old-fashioned and inefficient. Now they are questioning the efficiency of our preparation and mailing of monthly bank statements. What I need from you is a report showing what it costs us to prepare and mail a bank statement each month. Let's show them we are not throwing money away around here."

REQUIRED:

a. Briefly discuss the concept of different costs for different purposes and how it relates to this problem.
b. Identify several direct costs of preparing a bank statement.
c. Identify several indirect costs that possibly could be allocated as part of the cost of preparing the statements.
d. For each indirect cost you identify, suggest an allocation base.
e. For each cost and its allocation base identified in d, rate the cause and effect relationship as: (1) good, (2) acceptable, or (3) poor.
f. Does the chief accountant face something of an ethical dilemma in this situation? Explain how the arbitrary nature of cost allocations exacerbates the accountant's

problems. If you were the chief accountant, what approach would you take to preparing the report?

P24-2B **Allocating Service Department Costs, Sequential Method** The Water Wonder Park has three service departments: (1) maintenance, (2) security, and (3) parking. Wonder has two revenue-producing departments: (1) olympic pool and (2) water slides. The following data relate to the cost allocations.

Cost Pool	Budgeted Costs	Square Footage	Ticket Sales
Maintenance	$500,000		
Security	100,000	5,000	
Parking	50,000	100,000	
Olympic pool	600,000	50,000	180,000
Water slides	900,000	75,000	300,000

REQUIRED:

a. Allocate the service department costs using the sequential method and square footage as the allocation base. The order of allocation is maintenance, security, and parking.
b. Assuming the budgeted costs for the revenue-producing departments represent their projected operating costs, compute a projected cost per ticket which includes all allocated costs.
c. What is the basis for selecting the order of service departments for sequential allocation?

P24-3B **Allocating Service Department Costs, Separate Allocations of Fixed and Variable Costs, Direct Method** The American Washing Machine Company has two service departments, equipment maintenance and grounds keeping, and two production departments, assembly and packing. Fixed and variable service department costs are collected in separate cost pools and are allocated using different allocation bases. Fixed costs are allocated based on the percentages given, which represent the expected long term usage by each service department. Variable costs are allocated using labor hours. The following relates to the allocations.

	Equipment Maintenance	Grounds Keeping	Assembly	Packing
Costs:				
Fixed	$190,000	$150,000		
Variable	60,000	78,000		
Allocation bases:				
Equipment maintenance—fixed			60%	40%
Grounds keeping—fixed			70%	30%
Labor hours			40,000	40,000

REQUIRED:

a. Allocate the service department costs using the direct method of allocation.
b. What advantage might result from allocating fixed and variable service costs separately?

P24-4B **Allocating Service Department Costs, Sequential Method** Quick Stop makes brake pads for heavy trucks. They have two producing departments, cutting and finishing, and three service departments, maintenance, cafeteria, and environmental monitoring. The service department allocations are square footage for Maintenance, and number of employees for Cafeteria and Monitoring. The following data relate to the cost allocations.

	Maint.	Cafeteria	Monitoring	Cutting	Finishing
Budgeted costs	$80,000	$125,000	$130,000		
Square footage	3,000	2,000	1,000	35,000	25,000
Employees	5	6	4	35	25

The budgeted costs represent all direct operating costs for the service departments.

REQUIRED:

a. Allocate the service department costs to production departments using the sequential method. Use the order: maintenance, cafeteria, and monitoring.
b. What criteria should Quick Stop consider in selecting the order of allocation? Discuss.

LO 4

P24-5B Joint Cost Allocations Coal Products uses a common process to make coal into fireplace logs which are used in residential homes, and coal pellets, which are used in industry to fuel boilers. As raw material, Coal Tech purchases coal fines from several large industrial users of coal. Coal fines are essentially coal dust left in the coal storage areas of the industrial users. Coal Products then combines the coal fines with a special bonding agent in a patented process which yields small bonded chunks that are compressed into the fireplace logs and the pellets in a single process. In May 1993, 100,000 tons of coal fines were purchased at $3 per ton. The fines were processed with the bonding agent and compressed for an additional cost of $450,000. The yield was 100,000 tons of pellets and 50,000 tons of fire place logs. The pellets are sold for $7 per ton and the logs are sold for $20 per ton.

REQUIRED:

a. Allocate the joint costs to the pellets and logs using tons as the allocation base and calculate the cost per ton of each product.
b. Allocate the joint costs to the pellets and logs using the relative sales value method and calculate the cost per ton of each product.
c. Calculate the profit margins per ton on the pellets and logs based on (1) allocations of joint costs using tons as the allocation base, and (2) allocations of joint costs using the relative sales value as the allocation base.

LO 6

P24-6B Activity-Based Costing The Electronic Rodent Company manufactures mouse devices for computers. They make 12 different models of mouse devices, as well as several other types of computer components. They have recently adopted an activity-based costing system to assign manufacturing overhead to their products. The following data relates to one of their products, the wireless Field Mouse, and the ABC system cost pools.

Field Mouse:
    Annual production   20,000 units
    Direct material per unit $31
    Direct labor per unit $6

Manufacturing overhead cost pools:

Pool	Costs in Pool	Cost Driver
Materials ordering	$ 800,000	number of purchase orders
Materials inspection	400,000	number of receiving reports for fragile materials
Equipment setup	2,000,000	number of setups
Quality control	900,000	number of inspections
Other	15,000,000	Direct labor dollars
Total annual manufacturing overhead	$19,100,000	

Activity information related to cost drivers:

Pool	Annual Activity All Products	Annual Activity Field Mouse
Materials ordering	100,000 (orders)	1,000
Materials inspection	2,000 (receiving reports)	300
Equipment setup	100 (setups)	0*
Quality control	4,000 (inspections)	400
Other	$10,000,000 (direct labor $)	$120,000

*Field mouse production utilizes machinery which does not require significant setup activity.

REQUIRED:

a. Calculate the overhead rate per unit of activity for each of the five cost pools.
b. Calculate the *total* overhead assigned to the production of the Field Mouse.
c. Calculate the *overhead costs per unit* for the Field Mouse.
d. Calculate the *total unit cost* for the Field Mouse.
e. Assume Rodent allocates overhead by a traditional production volume based method using direct labor dollars as the allocation base and one cost pool. Determine: (1) the overhead rate per direct labor dollar, (2) the per unit overhead assigned to the field mouse, and (3) discuss the differences in cost allocations between the traditional method and activity-based costing.

CRITICAL THINKING AND COMMNICATING

C24-1 A group of students toured the production facilities of a large well-known steel manufacturer located in the eastern United States. The production process involved manufacturing steel ingots and then rolling the ingots into rolls of steel of different widths, lengths, and thicknesses.

After the tour, the plant controller discussed with the group the problems the company was having in determining the costs of the different rolls of steel manufactured at the plant. In fact, it was learned that although the company had operated the plant for many years, they did not have a satisfactory way of allocating common costs to different rolls of steel. A study was currently under way to identify a way of allocating common costs that would be based on a strong cause-and-effect relationship. The controller stated that the preliminary results of the study indicate "that in fact, we have miscalculated the costs of the different types of steel under the old methods of allocation, and we have been establishing sales prices that have not reflected the true costs of producing the steel. I must tell you that management is disappointed that it has taken the company this long to get the bookkeeping to the point that we know what our product costs us to produce." Further discussion with the controller revealed that the old way of allocating common costs was based on the quantity of steel in each roll.

REQUIRED:

a. Discuss what problems, if any might result from the steel company's lack of information about the true cost of each type of steel.
b. Identify several common costs that would need to be allocated to the different types of steel.
c. Can you identify a major problem with using the quantity of steel as an allocation base?
d. Suggest an allocation base that would have a better cause-and-effect relationship.

C24-2 Buy-Mart is a small chain of discount department stores similar to several national chains, although Buy-Mart is a regional operation. They have a policy of preparing departmental income statements for all revenue-producing departments within each store. The departmental statements use the following format.

Department _____
Operating Statement for Month Ended _____

Direct departmental sales	$XXXXXX
Less cost of goods sold	XXXXXX
Departmental gross margin	$XXXXXX
Less other direct departmental expenses	XXXXXX
Departmental contribution to indirect expenses and profits	$XXXXXX
Less allocation of indirect costs	XXXXXX
Departmental income before taxes	$XXXXXX

A typical Buy-Mart store assigns all local store indirect costs to one of three local cost pools: (1) general and administrative, (2) maintenance and security, and (3) advertising and promotion. All home office common costs are also assigned to similar cost pools and are in turn allocated to local store cost pools. All local store cost pools, including the pool's share of home office costs, are allocated to the eight revenue-producing departments within the local store.

A Buy-Mart store normally has the following revenue-producing departments: (1) housewares, (2) sporting goods, (3) automotive, (4) hardware, (5) appliances, (6) adult apparel, (7) children's apparel, and (8) lawn and garden shop.

REQUIRED:

a. If Buy-Mart uses the departmental statements as part of a responsibility accounting system, which part of the departmental statement should be used for the purpose of evaluating managers of the revenue-producing departments?
b. Suggest a possible allocation base to allocate local store maintenance and security costs to the eight revenue-producing departments.
c. Suggest a possible allocation base to allocate the home office general and administrative expenses to each local store.
d. Suppose, in reality, Buy-Mart allocates all cost pools based on sales, i.e., the home office costs are allocated to stores based on total store sales, and the local cost pools are allocated to departments based on departmental sales. Is this a good method of allocation? Discuss.
e. Suggest a reason why Buy-Mart might allocate all indirect costs to stores and finally to each revenue department.

CHAPTER 25

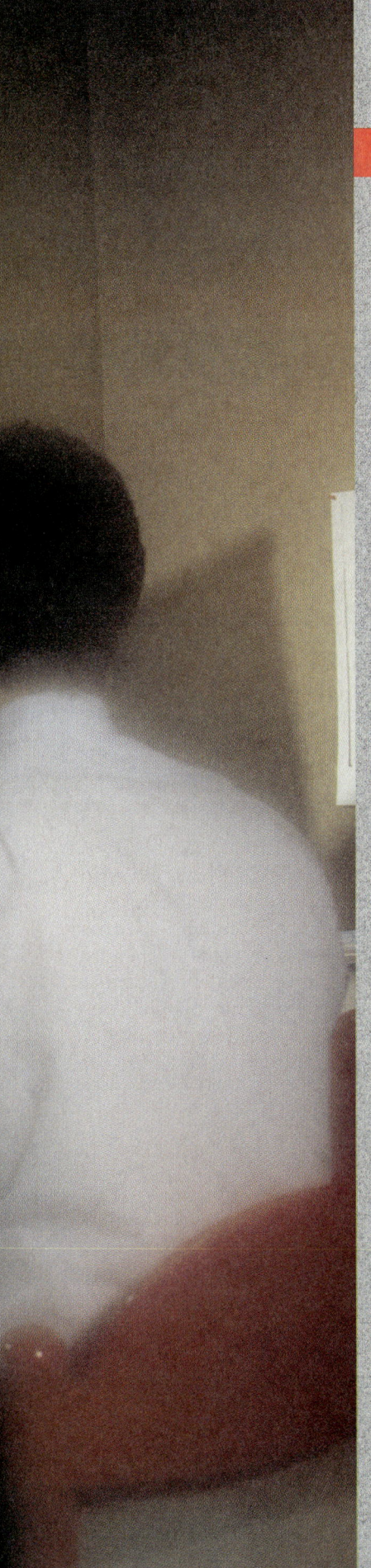

Budgetary Planning and Control

Preston Manufacturing Company produces metal containers that are designed to protect sensitive electronic equipment in shipment. At a meeting of key managers, Alan Renton, president of Preston Manufacturing, reviewed the past successes and failures of his firm. "As you know," he concluded, "we've begun a new marketing campaign, and I am confident that next year sales will increase by at least 15 percent." Jack North, the production manager, seemed caught off guard by this good news. "Look, Alan," he said, "If you really think sales are going to take off, we've got to plan for the increase. I'll have to hire additional workers, and the people in Purchasing will need to make larger purchases of materials so we don't run out." Pam Smith, vice president of Finance, chimed in, "Also, more sales means more inventory, and more inventory means we'll have to borrow additional funds to finance the expansion. I'll need some lead time to arrange the loan."

The meeting ended with everyone agreeing that more attention needed to be devoted to planning company activities. Alan returned to his office convinced that without a plan to guide and coordinate company activities, the coming year would be a series of "near disasters." He concluded, "The marketing, production, and financing groups must know what is anticipated so we can produce the right quantities of the right stuff."

In business, **budgets** are the formal documents that quantify a company's plans for achieving its goals. The entire planning and control process of many companies is built around budgets. This chapter illustrates the preparation of several different budgets that are in common use. The role of budgets in the performance evaluation process is presented, and a number of issues associated with budgets are discussed.

> **LEARNING OBJECTIVES**
>
> 1. Discuss how budgets are used in planning and control.
> 2. Prepare the individual budgets that make up the master budget.
> 3. Describe why flexible budgets are needed for performance evaluation.
> 4. Discuss the conflict between the planning and control uses of budgets.

LO 1
Discuss how budgets are used in planning and control.

USE OF BUDGETS IN PLANNING AND CONTROL

Budgets are used by many companies to both plan and control operations.

Planning

Budgets are useful in the planning process because they enhance *communication* and *coordination*. The process of developing a formal plan (i.e., a budget) forces managers to consider carefully their goals and objectives and to specify means of achieving them. Budgets are the vehicle for communicating information about where the company is heading. They also aid coordination of managers' activities. For example, the marketing department may prepare a budget that includes estimates of sales for each month of a future year. The production department may use the information contained in this budget to schedule workers and material deliveries. Thus, the necessary coordination of product sales and product production is achieved.

Control

In the control process, budgets are useful because they provide a basis for *evaluating performance*. To control a company, and to ensure it is heading in the proper direction and operating efficiently, assessing the performance of managers and the operations for which they are responsible is essential. Generally, performance evaluation is best carried out by comparing actual performance to planned or budgeted performance. Significant deviations from planned performance indicate a need to consider corrective action. A graphic presentation of the role of budgets in the evaluation of performance is presented in Illustration 25-1.

DEVELOPING THE BUDGET

The group responsible for preparing budgets is often referred to as the **budget committee**. Members of the committee do not simply impose a budget on a particular department. Rather, they work with each department to develop realistic plans that are consistent with overall company goals. A distinction is often made between top-down and bottom-up approaches to the development of a budget. In a top-down approach, budgets are developed at higher organizational levels without substantial input from lower-level managers. In a bottom-up approach, lower-level managers are the primary source of information used in setting the budget. Most managers believe a successful budgeting process requires a bottom-up approach. After all, lower-level managers often have the

ILLUSTRATION 25-1 Role of Budgets in Performance Evaluation

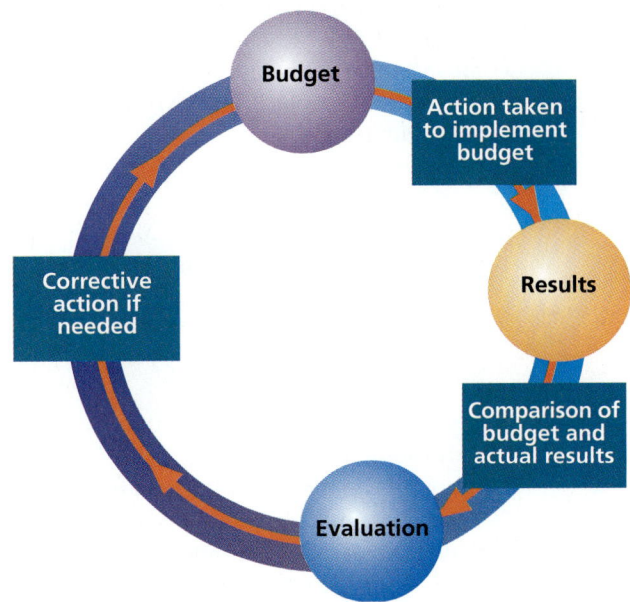

best information regarding business conditions affecting their departments. If this is the case, their input is critical in developing realistic financial plans.

Budget Time Period

Before preparing budgets, managers must decide on an appropriate budget period. Budgets are prepared for a variety of time periods, depending on a company's needs. In some cases, long-run budgets are prepared for a five- or even a ten-year period. Short-run budgets may cover a month, a quarter, or a year. Generally, the longer the time period, the less detailed the budget.

Zero Base Budgeting

A common starting point in developing a budget is the costs and revenues of the previous period. These amounts are adjusted up or down based on current information and assumptions or estimates of what will happen in the future. However, this approach may *not* lead to a fresh consideration of activities. So-called **zero base budgeting**, a method of budget preparation, requires each department to justify budgeted amounts at the start of each budget period, even if the amounts were supported in prior budget periods. That is, managers must start from zero in developing their budgets. This results in a fresh consideration of the budget's validity. However, the technique is time-consuming and expensive. While zero base budgeting has gained considerable support in governmental budgeting, business enterprises do not widely practice it.

THE MASTER BUDGET

The **master budget**, a comprehensive planning document, incorporates a number of individual budgets. Typically, it includes budgets for sales, production, direct materials, direct labor, manufacturing overhead, selling and administrative expenses, capital acquisitions, and cash receipts and disbursements, as well as a budgeted income statement and a budgeted balance sheet. In this section we present examples of each of these components of a master budget. For purposes of the example, budgetary information is prepared by quarter for the Preston Manufacturing Company. We assume that the company produces only a single product (metal shipping containers) and does not have a material amount of work in process inventory. Thus, any complications work in process inventory introduces can be ignored. Monthly budgets for a multiproduct firm with work in process inventory require more computations, but these budgets are not conceptually more difficult.

Sales Budget

In the budget process, the first step involves preparation of sales forecasts and development of a sales budget. This budget comes first because other budgets cannot be prepared without an estimate of sales. For example, the production budget requires an estimate of future sales before production necessary to meet demand can be determined. A company can use numerous methods to estimate sales. Very large companies may hire economists to prepare sales forecasts using sophisticated mathematical models that consider the rate of inflation, national capital expenditures, and other economic data. Smaller companies may develop forecasts based on an analysis of the trend in their own sales data.

Trade journals or magazines exist for almost every industry and may provide useful information for developing sales forecasts. Typically, these journals contain information on past industry sales and make predictions about the industry's growth. Sales personnel may be another good source of information for forecasting sales. Some companies periodically ask all of their salespeople to estimate sales in their territories for the coming year. These estimates may be highly accurate if the salespeople base their estimates on thorough knowledge of their customers' needs. In general, forecasts of sales are part science and part art. The forecasts of even the most sophisticated mathematical models are often adjusted based on the professional judgment of experienced managers.

Based on the trend of sales and consideration of a planned marketing campaign, Alan Renton, president of Preston Manufacturing, predicts unit sales of its product, metal shipping containers, will increase by 15% in the coming year. Sales personnel generally agree that this level of increase is realistic, provided the company maintains a price per unit of $45. Accordingly, the company budgets sales for each quarter simply by increasing prior year sales in units by 15%. The result is the sales budget presented in Illustration 25-2.

Production Budget

Once the sales budget has been prepared, the company can develop a production budget. In deciding how much to produce, managers must consider how much they expect to sell, how much is in beginning inventory, and how much they want in ending inventory. The quantity that must be produced can be calculated from the following formula:

$$\text{Finished Units to be Produced} = \text{Expected Sales in Units} + \text{Desired Ending Inventory of Finished Units} - \text{Beginning Inventory of Finished Units}$$

ILLUSTRATION 25-2 Sales Budget

Preston Manufacturing Company
Sales Budget
For the Year Ended December 31, 19X2

	First Quarter	Second Quarter	Third Quarter	Fourth Quarter	Year
Prior year sales in units	18,261	21,739	20,000	19,130	79,130
Projected at 115% of prior year (units)	21,000	25,000	23,000	22,000	91,000
Sales price per unit	x $45	x $45	x $45	x $45	x $45
Budgeted sales revenue	$945,000	$1,125,000	$1,035,000	$990,000	$4,095,000

Preston Manufacturing Company would like the ending inventory of finished goods to be equal to 10% of next quarter's sales. In the first quarter, Preston estimates that 21,000 units will be sold. Two thousand five hundred units are needed in ending inventory (i.e., 10% of 25,000 units expected to be sold in the second quarter). Thus, a total of 23,500 units are required. However, the company has 2,100 units in beginning inventory; thus, only 21,400 units must be produced. The production budget for Preston Manufacturing Company is presented in Illustration 25-3.

ILLUSTRATION 25-3 Production Budget

Preston Manufacturing Company
Production Budget
For the Year Ended December 31, 19X2

	First Quarter	Second Quarter	Third Quarter	Fourth Quarter	Year
Unit sales[1]	21,000	25,000	23,000	22,000	91,000
Plus: Desired ending inventory of finished units[2]	2,500	2,300	2,200	2,400[3]	2,400
Total units needed	23,500	27,300	25,200	24,400	93,400
Less: Beginning inventory of finished units	2,100	2,500	2,300	2,200	2,100
Units to be produced	21,400	24,800	22,900	22,200	91,300

[1] Information from sales budget, Illustration 25-2.
[2] Equals 10% of next quarter's sales.
[3] Based on estimate of sales in the first quarter of the following year.

Direct Material Purchases Budget

The quantity of direct materials that must be purchased depends on the amounts needed for production and ending inventory. Obviously, a company needs some direct materials on hand at the end of the period for use in production at the start of the subsequent period. The quantity that must be purchased can be calculated from the following formula:

$$\text{Required Purchases of Direct Materials} = \text{Quantity Required for Production} + \text{Desired Ending Quantity of Direct Materials} - \text{Beginning Quantity of Direct Materials}$$

Preston Manufacturing Company has established a policy of maintaining direct materials inventory equal to 10% of the amount required for production in the subsequent quarter. In the first quarter, the company plans on producing 21,400 units. Each unit requires 2 pounds of direct material. Thus, 42,800 pounds of direct material are required for production. In addition, 4,960 pounds must be on hand at the end of the quarter (i.e., 10% of the quantity required for next quarter's production), but 4,280 pounds are on hand at the start of the quarter. Thus, 43,480 pounds must be purchased. The cost per pound is $3. Therefore, the cost of purchases of direct material in the first quarter is budgeted to be $130,440. This information is presented in the purchases budget, Illustration 25-4.

ILLUSTRATION 25-4 Purchases Budget

Preston Manufacturing Company Direct Material Purchases Budget For the Year Ended December 31, 19X2					
	First Quarter	Second Quarter	Third Quarter	Fourth Quarter	Year
Units to be produced[1]	21,400	24,800	22,900	22,200	91,300
Pounds of direct material per unit of finished product	x 2	x 2	x 2	x 2	x 2
Number of pounds required for production	42,800	49,600	45,800	44,400	182,600
Plus: Desired ending quantity of direct material[2]	4,960	4,580	4,440	4,900[3]	4,900
Total pounds needed	47,760	54,180	50,240	49,300	187,500
Less: Beginning quantity of direct material	4,280	4,960	4,580	4,440	4,280
Number of pounds to be purchased	43,480	49,220	45,660	44,860	183,220
Cost per pound	x $3	x $3	x $3	x $3	x $3
Cost of purchases	$130,440	$147,660	$136,980	$134,580	$549,660

[1]Information from production budget, Illustration 25-3.
[2]Equals 10% of quantity required for next quarter's production.
[3]Based on estimate of quantity required for production in the first quarter of next year.

Direct Labor Budget

The direct labor budget for Preston Manufacturing Company (Illustration 25-5) presents direct labor cost by quarter. Direct labor cost is easily calculated by multiplying the number of units produced each quarter by the labor hours per unit and the rate per hour. In the first quarter, the company expects to produce 21,400 units and 1.5 labor hours per unit are required. In total, 32,100 labor hours are needed. At a rate of $10 per labor hour, this amounts to $321,000. Preston estimates that, on average, each employee works 520 hours per quarter. Preston can use this information to estimate the approximate number of employees needed each quarter. In the first quarter, 32,100 labor hours are required. Since an average employee works 520 hours per quarter, approximately 62 employees will be needed for production. Note that the direct labor budget indicates that 72 employees are needed in the second quarter, while only 62 are needed in the first quarter. With this information, the company may decide to adjust its production plans to keep employment stable. The new employees hired in the second quarter may not be efficient. Also, if several of these employees are fired in the third quarter when only 66 employees are needed, morale may suffer.

ILLUSTRATION 25-5 Direct Labor Budget

Preston Manufacturing Company
Direct Labor Budget
For the Year Ended December 31, 19X2

	First Quarter	Second Quarter	Third Quarter	Fourth Quarter	Year
Units to be produced[1]	21,400	24,800	22,900	22,200	91,300
Direct labor hours per unit	x 1.5	x 1.5	x 1.5	x 1.5	x 1.5
Total hours	32,100	37,200	34,350	33,300	136,950
Labor rate per hour	x $10	x $10	x $10	x $10	x $10
Direct labor cost	$321,000	$372,000	$343,500	$333,000	$1,369,500
Total hours	32,100	37,200	34,350	33,300	
Average hours per quarter per employee	÷ 520	÷ 520	÷ 520	÷ 520	
Approximate number of employees needed	62	72	66	64	

[1]Information from production budget, Illustration 25-3.

Manufacturing Overhead Budget

Preston Manufacturing Company separates variable and fixed costs in the budget for manufacturing overhead. The cost per unit of production of each variable cost item is multiplied by the quantity produced each quarter. The fixed costs are identical each quarter, except for the amount of depreciation. This cost increases in the third and fourth quarters due to planned acquisitions of equipment that increase the level of depreciation. The manufacturing overhead budget is presented in Illustration 25-6.

Selling and Administrative Expense Budget

To this point, we have presented only production-related budgets. However, budget information is also necessary for selling and administrative expenses. Preston Manufacturing Company estimates that these expenses are all fixed. The 19X2 selling and administrative expense budget is presented in Illustration 25-7.

Budgeted Income Statement

The company uses much of the information contained in the previous budgets to prepare a **budgeted income statement**. Preston Manufacturing Company prepares its budgeted income statement using the *variable costing* method. With this method, only variable manufacturing costs are included in inventory. Fixed manufacturing costs are treated as period costs and deducted from the contribution margin to derive net income.

ILLUSTRATION 25-6 Manufacturing Overhead Budget

Preston Manufacturing Company
Manufacturing Overhead Budget
For the Year Ended December 31, 19X2

	First Quarter	Second Quarter	Third Quarter	Fourth Quarter	Year
Units to be produced[1]	21,400	24,800	22,900	22,200	91,300
Variable costs:					
Indirect material ($2/unit)	$ 42,800	$ 49,600	$ 45,800	$ 44,400	$182,600
Indirect labor ($1.50/unit)	32,100	37,200	34,350	33,300	136,950
Power and light ($1/unit)	21,400	24,800	22,900	22,200	91,300
Total variable costs	$ 96,300	$111,600	$103,050	$ 99,900	$410,850
Fixed costs:					
Supervisory salaries	$ 90,000	$ 90,000	$ 90,000	$ 90,000	$360,000
Depreciation of plant and equipment[2]	20,000	20,000	26,000	28,000	94,000
Other	5,000	5,000	5,000	5,000	20,000
Total fixed costs	$115,000	$115,000	$121,000	$123,000	$474,000
Total overhead	$211,300	$226,600	$224,050	$222,900	$884,850

[1]Information from production budget, Illustration 25-3.
[2]Increase in third and fourth quarters due to acquisition of additional equipment. See capital acquisition budget, Illustration 25-9.

ILLUSTRATION 25-7 Selling and Administrative Expense Budget

Preston Manufacturing Company
Selling and Administrative Expense Budget
For the Year Ended December 31, 19X2

	First Quarter	Second Quarter	Third Quarter	Fourth Quarter	Year
Salaries	$160,000	$160,000	$160,000	$160,000	$ 640,000
Advertising	70,000	70,000	70,000	70,000	280,000
Depreciation of office equipment	5,000	5,000	5,000	5,000	20,000
Other	15,000	15,000	15,000	15,000	60,000
Total	$250,000	$250,000	$250,000	$250,000	$1,000,000

The variable costs per unit are $25.50. This amount is derived as follows:

Direct materials	$ 6.00	(2 units at $3.00. See the direct material purchases budget, Illustration 25-4.)
Direct labor	15.00	(1.5 hours at $10. See the direct labor budget, Illustration 25-5.)
Variable overhead	4.50	($2.00 indirect material; $1.50 indirect labor; and $1.00 power and light. See the manufacturing overhead budget, Illustration 25-6.)
Total	$25.50	per unit

The budgeted income statement is presented in Illustration 25-8. As you know, the contribution margin is equal to sales minus variable expenses (including variable cost of goods sold, variable selling, and variable administrative expenses). However, to simplify presentation, the only variable expense for Preston Manufacturing Company is variable cost of goods sold. Therefore, the contribution margin is equal to sales minus variable cost of goods sold. Fixed production overhead and fixed selling and administrative expenses are deducted from the contribution margin to derive at net income.

ILLUSTRATION 25-8 Budgeted Income Statement

Preston Manufacturing Company
Budgeted Income Statement (Variable Costing Method)
For the Year Ended December 31, 19X2

	First Quarter	Second Quarter	Third Quarter	Fourth Quarter	Year
Sales[1]	$945,000	$1,125,000	$1,035,000	$990,000	$4,095,000
Less: Variable cost of goods sold	535,500[2]	637,500	586,500	561,000	2,320,500
Contribution margin	$409,500	$ 487,500	$ 448,500	$429,000	$1,774,500
Less: Fixed production overhead[3]	(115,000)	(115,000)	(121,000)	(123,000)	(474,000)
Fixed selling and administrative expense[4]	(250,000)	(250,000)	(250,000)	(250,000)	(1,000,000)
Net income	$ 44,500	$ 122,500	$ 77,500	$ 56,000	$ 300,500

[1]Information from sales budget, Illustration 25-2.
[2]First quarter calculation is: 21,000 units sold x $25.50 = $535,500.
[3]Information from manufacturing overhead budget, Illustration 25-6.
[4]Information from selling and administrative expense budget, Illustration 25-7.

Management should evaluate the budgeted income statement to ensure that anticipated profit is consistent with company goals. If budgeted profit is less than the amount management considers satisfactory, then the company can take steps to increase sales and reduce costs. For example, the company may undertake an expanded advertising campaign to increase sales, or it can reduce overhead costs through more efficient use of part-time labor. If management decides to take steps to increase profit, then it must adjust the previous budgets to reflect the anticipated changes.

Capital Acquisitions Budget

The company must carefully plan acquisitions of capital assets (i.e., property, plant, and equipment) since they may substantially reduce cash reserves in the period of acquisition. The budget for capital assets is referred to as the capital acquisitions budget. Preston Manufacturing Company anticipates purchases of office equipment and machinery during the coming year, and this is reflected in the capital acquisitions budget presented in Illustration 25-9.

Cash Receipts and Disbursements Budget

In the cash receipts and disbursements budget, managers plan the amount and timing of cash flows. The information in this budget is a necessary supplement to the information presented in the budgeted income statement. It is quite possible for a company to project a substantial amount of net income and still face financial distress because its entire set of plans implies more cash outflows than

ILLUSTRATION 25-9 Capital Acquisitions Budget

Preston Manufacturing Company
Capital Acquisitions Budget
For the Year Ended December 31, 19X2

	First Quarter	Second Quarter	Third Quarter	Fourth Quarter	Year
Office equipment (5-year life)	$10,000	$ 0	$ 0	$ 0	$ 10,000
Machinery (5-year life)	0	0	120,000[1]	40,000[2]	160,000
Total	$10,000	$ 0	$120,000	$40,000	$170,000

[1] Increases depreciation by $6,000 in third quarter [i.e., ($120,000 ÷ 5 year life) x 1/4 for third quarter]. See manufacturing overhead budget, Illustration 25-6.
[2] Increases depreciation by $2,000 in fourth quarter [i.e., ($40,000 ÷ 5 year life) x 1/4 for fourth quarter]. See manufacturing overhead budget, Illustration 25-6.

cash inflows. For example, the company may recognize a substantial amount of income when it makes a major sale. However, the cash received in payment for the sale may not arrive for many months. Or, consider a company that makes a substantial purchase of equipment. While cash reserves may be reduced immediately by the *total* cost of the equipment, current period income will only be reduced by a *fraction* of the cost of the equipment (i.e., by the amount of depreciation). By carefully planning cash receipts and disbursements, a company can anticipate cash shortages and arrange to borrow funds to enhance its cash positions. Or, if cash surpluses are anticipated, a company can seek additional investment opportunities or consider paying higher dividends to shareholders.

To prepare an estimate of cash collections, management must determine the percent of credit sales revenue that is collected in the period of sale and the percent collected in the subsequent period. The percentages can usually be estimated based on past collection experience. Preston Manufacturing Company has only credit sales, with 50% of the sales revenue collected in the quarter of sale and the other 50% collected in the next quarter.

To prepare an estimate of cash disbursements, management must determine the percent of material purchases paid in the period of purchase and the percent paid in the subsequent period. Preston Manufacturing Company determines that 70% is paid in the quarter of purchase and 30% is paid in the subsequent quarter. The company has determined that, for practical purposes, all other disbursements are made in the quarter the related cost is incurred.

In preparing a cash receipts and disbursements budget, it is important to remember that some expenses do not require cash outlays. For example, depreciation is part of manufacturing overhead, but it does not require a current outlay of cash. Cash is disbursed when an asset is purchased, not when depreciation is recorded. Another example of a noncash expense is the amortization of prepaid insurance. Cash is disbursed when the insurance is purchased, not when the expense is recognized through amortization of prepaid insurance.

In the cash receipts and disbursements budget for Preston Manufacturing Company, Illustration 25-10, note that cash disbursed for manufacturing overhead in the first quarter is only $191,300. This is $20,000 less than the $211,300 of overhead cost planned for the first quarter in the manufacturing overhead budget, Illustration 25-6. The $20,000 is the amount of depreciation in the first quarter.

CHAPTER 25 BUDGETARY PLANNING AND CONTROL

ILLUSTRATION 25-10 Cash Receipts and Disbursements Budget

Preston Manufacturing Company
Cash Receipts and Disbursements Budget
For the Year Ended December 31, 19X2

	First Quarter	Second Quarter	Third Quarter	Fourth Quarter	Year
Cash receipts:					
Collection of credit sales:					
4th quarter prior year ($860,870)	$430,435				$ 430,435
1st quarter ($945,000)[1]	472,500	$ 472,500			945,000
2nd quarter ($1,125,000)		562,500	$ 562,500		1,125,000
3rd quarter ($1,035,000)			517,500	$ 517,500	1,035,000
4th quarter ($990,000)				495,000	495,000
Total cash receipts	$902,935	$1,035,000	$1,080,000	$1,012,500	$4,030,435
Cash disbursements:					
Purchase of materials:					
4th quarter prior year ($120,600)	$ 36,180				$ 36,180
1st quarter ($130,440)[2]	91,308	$ 39,132			130,440
2nd quarter ($147,660)		103,362	$ 44,298		147,660
3rd quarter ($136,980)			95,886	$ 41,094	136,980
4th quarter ($134,580)				94,206	94,206
Total payments for purchases	$127,488	$ 142,494	$ 140,184	$ 135,300	$ 545,466
Direct labor[3]	321,000	372,000	343,500	333,000	1,369,500
Manufacturing overhead[4]	191,300	206,600	198,050	194,900	790,850
Selling and administrative expense[5]	245,000	245,000	245,000	245,000	980,000
Capital acquisitions[6]	10,000	0	120,000	40,000	170,000
Total cash disbursements	$894,788	$ 966,094	$1,046,734	$ 948,200	$3,855,816
Excess of receipts over disbursements	$ 8,147	$ 68,906	$ 33,266	$ 64,300	$ 174,619
Plus beginning cash balance	20,000	28,147	97,053	130,319	20,000
Ending cash balance	$ 28,147	$ 97,053	$ 130,319	$ 194,619	$ 194,619

---

[1]See Illustration 25-2 for sales information. Fifty percent collected in quarter of sale and 50% collected in subsequent quarter.
[2]See Illustration 25-4 for purchase information. Seventy percent paid in quarter of purchase and 30% paid in subsequent quarter.
[3]See Illustration 25-5 for labor cost information.
[4]Does not include depreciation indicated in manufacturing overhead budget, Illustration 25-6, since depreciation does not require a cash outlay.
[5]Does not include depreciation indicated in selling and administrative expense budget, Illustration 25-7, since depreciation does not require a cash outlay.
[6]See capital acquisitions budget, Illustration 25-9.

As indicated in the cash budget, the anticipated cash flows fluctuate significantly from quarter to quarter. The result is that at the end of the first quarter, Preston expects the cash balance to be only $28,147, but it expects the cash balance at the end of the fourth quarter to be $194,619. Obviously, a low cash balance is dangerous because the company may not have enough funds to pay employees and suppliers. Thus, Preston Manufacturing company may wish to consider borrowing money to improve the cash position in the first quarter. The cash budget is useful because it alerts management to a potential problem well in advance. This gives management sufficient time to arrange a loan on favorable terms. As the budget indicates, the loan can easily be repaid in the fourth quarter when cash reserves are high.

Excessively large cash balances should generally be avoided since they earn little, if any, interest. If a company is building up financial reserves for expansion (purchasing a major piece of equipment or even another company), then it should invest excess cash in low-risk, highly marketable securities. The return on these securities will most likely exceed interest earned from a bank on the cash balance. If the company is not building up reserves to expand, then it should distribute the excess cash to shareholders as dividends.

Budgeted Balance Sheet

The last component of the master budget we consider is the **budgeted balance sheet**, which is simply a planned balance sheet (sometimes called a *pro-forma balance sheet*). Managers can use this budget to assess the effect of their planned decisions on the firm's future financial position. The budgeted balance sheet for Preston Manufacturing Company is presented in Illustration 25-11.

ILLUSTRATION 25-11 Budgeted Balance Sheet

Preston Manufacturing Company
Budgeted Balance Sheet (Partial)
December 31, 19X2

Current assets:	
Cash[1]	$ 194,619
Accounts receivable[2]	495,000
Raw materials inventory[3]	14,700
Finished goods inventory[4]	61,200
Property, plant, and equipment (net)	620,000
Total assets	$1,385,519
Current liabilities:	
Accounts payable[5]	$ 40,374
Stockholders' equity:	
Common stock	894,000
Retained earnings	451,145
Total liabilities and stockholders' equity	$1,385,519

[1] Ending balance from cash receipts and disbursements budget, Illustration 25-10.

[2] From cash receipts and disbursements budget, Illustration 25-10, 50% of 4th quarter sales not yet collected.

[3] 4,900 units at $3.00 = $14,700. See direct material purchases budget, Illustration 25-4.

[4] From production budget, Illustration 25-3, 2,400 units of finished goods are required. Variable cost per unit equals $25.50. Only variable costs are included in inventory since the company uses the variable costing method.

[5] From the cash receipts and disbursements budget, Illustration 25-10, 30% of 4th quarter purchases of materials not yet paid.

USE OF COMPUTERS IN THE BUDGET PLANNING PROCESS

As pointed out previously, during the budget process, management may review a budget and decide it is inconsistent with company goals. This may lead management to explore a variety of actions that affect future costs and revenues. If changes are anticipated, the budgets must be revised. Since the budgets are highly interdependent, a change in one budget can affect several other budgets. Computers are very useful in this regard. Many companies define the budget relationships in a computer model using spreadsheet programs such as Lotus 1-2-3™ and Excel,™ or custom programs specifically designed for them. With computerized budget information, an item in a budget can be changed; the computer can then recalculate that budget and any other budget affected by the change. Obviously, this results in a substantial savings in time and managerial effort.

"What if" analysis is also facilitated when budgets are prepared using a spreadsheet program. Suppose the management of Preston Manufacturing Company wants to know *what* the cash balance will be in the fourth quarter *if* sales in the first quarter are 22,000 units instead of the 21,000 units budgeted. If all budgetary relationships have been properly specified in a spreadsheet, the answer can be found by simply changing the sales figure in the first quarter sales budget from 21,000 to 22,000 and letting the computer recalculate the cash balance in the fourth quarter cash receipts and disbursements budget.

BUDGETARY CONTROL

The examples above indicate how budgets are used in the planning process to communicate company goals and coordinate diverse activities. Budgets also facilitate *control* of operations because they provide a standard for evaluating performance. Differences between budgeted and actual amounts are referred to as **budget variances**, and reports that indicate budget variances are referred to as **performance reports**. If budgeted and actual costs are approximately equal, management needs to take no action because results are consistent with its expectations. However, if actual costs differ from budgeted costs by a material amount, management should launch an investigation to determine the cause of the difference.

How would a company evaluate performance if budgets were not prepared? Most likely, actual performance in the current period would be compared to actual performance in the prior period. This is obviously an inferior approach since conditions may change significantly from one period to the next, making a comparison of the two periods meaningless. For example, suppose Preston Manufacturing Company evaluates the performance of the marketing department by comparing sales in the current year to sales in the past year. Further, suppose sales in the prior year are 79,130 units and actual sales in the current year are 85,000 units. An evaluation of performance based on a comparison with the prior year would lead to a favorable evaluation of the marketing department since sales increased by approximately 7%. However, suppose the overall market for Preston's product had grown by 15%. If this increase was forecasted at the start of the period, the company would have budgeted sales of 91,000 units (i.e., 79,130 x 1.15). A comparison of actual sales to budgeted sales indicates that, rather than receiving a favorable evaluation, the marketing department should be asked to explain why actual sales are only 85,000 units instead of the 91,000 units forecasted.

Static and Flexible Budgets

LO 3
Describe why flexible budgets are needed for performance evaluation.

In evaluating performance using budgets, a company must take care to ensure that the level of activity used in developing the budget is equal to the *actual* level of activity. Suppose the manager responsible for manufacturing overhead at Preston Manufacturing Company was evaluated at the end of the first quarter by comparing the actual level of overhead cost to the overhead costs budgeted at the start of the year. This comparison is presented in Illustration 25-12.

ILLUSTRATION 25-12 Performance Evaluation with a Static Budget

Preston Manufacturing Company
Performance Report, Manufacturing Overhead
Static Budget Comparison
First Quarter, 19X2

	Static Budget	Actual	Variance
Units produced	21,400	25,000	3,600
Variable costs:			
Indirect materials (budgeted at $2 per unit)	$ 42,800	$ 49,000	$ (6,200)
Indirect labor (budgeted at $1.50 per unit)	32,100	38,000	(5,900)
Power and light (budgeted at $1 per unit)	21,400	24,600	(3,200)
Total variable costs	$ 96,300	$111,600	$(15,300)
Fixed costs:			
Supervisory salaries	$ 90,000	$ 90,200	$ (200)
Depreciation on plant and equipment	20,000	20,300	(300)
Other	5,000	5,000	0
Total fixed cost	$115,000	$115,500	$ (500)
Total overhead	$211,300	$227,100	$(15,800)

( ) denotes unfavorable variance

The analysis implies that the manager responsible for overhead costs has not done a good job of cost control. After all, total variable overhead costs are $15,300 higher than planned, and total fixed overhead costs are $500 higher than planned. However, careful consideration of the comparison reveals that actual production was 25,000 units, while planned production was only 21,400 units. The extra production may be due to an unexpected increase in sales necessitating increased production. With the increase in production, an increase in variable costs is expected. Fixed costs, however, would be expected to remain the same. Since changes in cost are expected when actual production is different from planned production, the analysis presented is not very useful for evaluating performance.

The budget presented in Illustration 25-12 is referred to as a **static budget** because it is not adjusted for the actual level of production. A more appropriate analysis of performance would make use of a **flexible budget**, which is a budget adjusted for the actual level of production. Flexible budgets take into account the fact that when production increases or decreases, variable costs change. Fixed costs, however, stay the same. Consider a company that anticipates variable production costs of $10 per unit and fixed production costs of $500,000. With this cost structure, flexible budgets for production levels of 20,000 units, 30,000 units and, 40,000 units can be prepared as in Illustration 25-13.

CHAPTER 25 BUDGETARY PLANNING AND CONTROL

ILLUSTRATION 25-13 Flexible Budgets for Various Production Levels

	\multicolumn{3}{c}{Flexible Budgets for Production Levels of 20,000, 30,000, and 40,000 Units}		
Units produced	20,000	30,000	40,000
Variable costs ($10 per unit)	$200,000	$300,000	$400,000
Fixed costs	500,000	500,000	500,000
Total	$700,000	$800,000	$900,000

In Illustration 25-14, a flexible budget evaluates the performance of the manager responsible for manufacturing overhead at Preston Manufacturing Company. Note that the variable costs are adjusted to the actual level of units produced. Since they are not expected to change when production increases or decreases, the fixed costs are at the same level as in the static budget. Comparison of actual overhead costs to the overhead costs in a flexible budget reveals more about the manager's ability to control costs. Actual variable costs are $900 less than the *flexible* budget amount. This contrasts sharply with the $15,300 amount by which actual costs were greater than the *static* budget amount for variable costs. The variance with respect to fixed costs is still $500 more than budgeted—the same as in the static budget comparison.

ILLUSTRATION 25-14 Performance Evaluation with a Flexible Budget

Preston Manufacturing Company
Performance Report, Manufacturing Overhead
Flexible Budget Comparison
First Quarter, 19X2

	Flexible Budget	Actual	Variance
Units produced	25,000	25,000	0
Variable costs:			
Indirect materials (budgeted at $2 per unit)	$ 50,000	$ 49,000	$1,000
Indirect labor (budgeted at $1.50 per unit)	37,500	38,000	(500)
Power and light (budgeted at $1 per unit)	25,000	24,600	400
Total variable costs	$112,500	$111,600	$ 900
Fixed costs:			
Supervisory salaries	$ 90,000	$ 90,200	$ (200)
Depreciation on plant and equipment	20,000	20,300	(300)
Other	5,000	5,000	0
Total fixed cost	$115,000	$115,500	$ (500)
Total overhead	$227,500	$227,100	$ 400

( ) denotes unfavorable variances.

INVESTIGATING BUDGET VARIANCES

A budget variance may exist for several reasons. Budget variances are sometimes due to inefficiencies resulting from poor management techniques or decisions. In this case, top management may adjust the compensation of the manager responsible for attaining the budget (e.g., reduce or eliminate his or her bonus compensation) and suggest ways the manager can improve the performance of his or her operation. In some cases the company may even have to fire the manager if he or she is incapable of improving. On the other hand, if the budget is not carefully developed with reasonable estimates of cost, the company should not be surprised if actual costs are not equal to the budgeted amounts. In this case, management cannot blame budget variances on the manager responsible for attaining the budget. Even if the budget is carefully developed, the company may nonetheless experience unforeseen price increases that result in actual costs being different from budgeted costs.

While they may indicate inefficiencies, in some cases budget variances indicate only that the budget needs to be adjusted. The cause of the variance cannot be determined without an investigation. However, because of the cost of investigation, a company cannot investigate all budget variances. Rather, **a management by exception** approach is more economical. That is, only the exceptional variances are investigated. Generally, variances that are large in absolute dollars or relative to budgeted amounts are considered exceptional. It is important to point out that both exceptional "unfavorable" *and* exceptional "favorable" variances should be investigated. For example, in the performance report (Illustration 25-14), there is a $1,000 favorable variance for indirect materials, indicating that actual costs are less than budgeted costs. This seems to indicate a favorable state of affairs. However, it may be that cheap, low-quality materials are being used. This could result in substandard products that damage the company's reputation.

CONFLICT IN PLANNING AND CONTROL USES OF BUDGETS

LO 4
Discuss the conflict between the planning and control uses of budgets.

Conflict is inherent in the planning and control uses of budgets. On the one hand, top management would like the managers responsible for carrying out plans to participate in the development of budgets. After all, these managers have the best knowledge of the technology and costs of their operations. However, since their performance is evaluated in comparison to the budget, they have an incentive to make sure that the budget contains some **slack**. That is, managers want budgeted costs that they can easily achieve. To have slack, managers may suggest budgeted costs that are too high; thus, their actual costs will be lower than the budgeted amounts. Or they may suggest revenue levels that are too low; thus, their actual revenues will be higher than the budgeted amounts. If this happens, the company's budgets will not be plans for achieving maximum firm profit. There is no ready solution to this problem. Perhaps the best that can be done is to assure managers that their performance in comparison to the budget will be fairly evaluated. Managers should be confident that they will be allowed to comment on the real causes of budget variances and tell their side of the story. The problem is minimized, we believe, in organizations that foster open communication among all levels of employees.

EVALUATION, MEASUREMENT, AND MANAGEMENT BEHAVIOR

Managers pay great attention to those aspects of their jobs that are measured and evaluated. Thus, it is important to quantify in budgets key "success factors"

INSIGHTS INTO ETHICS

As manager of the waste treatment facility for Chemtron Industries, Ann Paxton is in the process of preparing an annual expense budget. "Next year, my department will probably be asked to process some 80,000 gallons of waste. Our variable costs are about $10 per gallon, and our fixed costs are about $1,000,000. So, the total cost should be somewhere around $1,800,000. I better submit a budget of around $2,300,000. Top management will probably reduce my budget. After all, when was the last time they ever approved a higher budget than the one submitted? And, what if I end up incurring higher expenses than anticipated? A new labor contract, for instance, could increase costs by more than $100,000. The last thing I want is to incur more costs than budgeted. My annual bonus would likely be reduced, and I could kiss any chance for promotion next year good-bye."

Is it ethical to submit a budget for an amount higher than the cost expected to be incurred? Explain.

for the company. Historically, budgets have primarily included dollar amounts. However, including some nonmonetary measures of performance in the budget may be advantageous. For example, if a key aspect of a company's success is high-quality, defect-free products, budgeting the number of defects and the number of customer complaints at levels consistent with high quality is useful. This way, the company can compare the actual number of defects and complaints with the budgeted quantities to evaluate performance. Or, if a company is experiencing problems with employee absenteeism, it may budget an acceptable number of days missed and compare actual days missed to the target.

THE PRESTON MANUFACTURING COMPANY CASE

At the start of the chapter, Alan Renton, President of Preston Manufacturing, noted that "The marketing, production, and financing groups must know what is anticipated so we can produce the right quantities of the right stuff." How can Alan plan and coordinate the activities of his company? As you know from reading the material above, the answer lies in developing budgets. Once a sales budget is produced, the production group can develop budgets for labor, material, and overhead that are consistent with the production level needed to meet expected sales. Once these budgets are produced, the finance group can prepare budgets that take into account the cash inflows and outflows anticipated in the sales and production budgets.

SUMMARY

Discuss how budgets are used in planning and control. Budgets are useful in the planning process because they enhance communication and coordination. Budgets are also useful in the control process because they provide a standard for evaluating performance.

Prepare the individual budgets that make up the master budget. The master budget is a comprehensive planning document and usually includes budgets for sales, production, direct materials, direct labor, manufacturing overhead, selling and administrative expenses, capital acquisitions, and cash receipts and disbursements, as well as a budgeted income statement and a budgeted balance sheet. These budgets are highly interrelated in that the amounts presented in one budget may be dependent on the amounts in one or more other budgets.

Describe why flexible budgets are needed for performance evaluation. In evaluating performance, companies should use flexible budgets because they present amounts adjusted to the actual level of production. Comparing actual performance to a static budget is not very useful because variable costs are expected to differ from the budget if actual production is different from the production level indicated in the static budget.

Discuss the conflict between the planning and control uses of budgets. The fact that budgets are used for both planning and performance evaluation presents a difficulty. Managers who participate in the development of their own budgets may tend to understate budgeted revenues and overstate budgeted expenses. The result is budgets that are easy to achieve and contain budget slack. However, this problem is minimized in companies that foster open communication among all levels of employees. In such organizations, managers are less likely to feel the need to build slack into budgets because they know their performance will be evaluated fairly.

REVIEW PROBLEM

Jimbo Manufacturing Company reported the following net income for the fourth quarter of 19X0:

Sales		$860,000
Less: Variable cost of goods sold		516,000
Contribution margin		$344,000
Less: Fixed production costs	$ 82,000	
Fixed selling and administrative expense	130,000	212,000
Income before taxes		$132,000
Less income taxes		52,800
Net income		$ 79,200

Note: Jimbo Manufacturing Company uses the variable costing method. Thus, only variable production costs are included in inventory and cost of goods sold. Fixed production costs are charged to expense in the period incurred.

Additional Information:
1. Sales and variable cost of sales are expected to increase by 10% in the next quarter.
2. Jimbo expects that 20% of all sales will be for cash. Of the remaining credit sales, 40% will be collected in the quarter of sale and 60% will be collected in the quarter following sale.
3. Variable cost of sales consists of 50% materials, 30% direct labor, and 20% variable overhead. Materials are purchased on credit and 70% are paid for in the quarter of purchase and the remaining amount is paid for in the quarter after purchase. Direct labor and variable overhead are paid for in the quarter incurred.
4. Fixed production costs are expected to increase by 5% in the next quarter. The fixed production costs consist of 75% depreciation and 25% other fixed costs. Fixed production costs requiring payment are paid in the quarter they are incurred.

5. Fixed selling and administrative expenses are expected to increase by 8%. Ten percent of selling and administrative costs consists of depreciation of the administrative building and equipment. Remaining costs are paid in the quarter they are incurred.
6. The tax rate is expected to be 40%. All taxes are paid in the quarter they are incurred.
7. The cash balance on January 1, 19X1, is $107,670.

REQUIRED:

a. Prepare a budgeted income statement for the first quarter of 19X1.
b. Prepare a cash receipts and disbursements budget for the first quarter of 19X1.

SOLUTION:

(a) *Prepare a budgeted income statement.*

Jimbo Manufacturing Company
Budgeted Income Statement (Variable Costing Method)
For the Quarter Ending March 31, 19X1

Sales[1]		$946,000
Less: Variable cost of goods sold[2]		567,600
Contribution margin		$378,400
Less: Fixed production costs[3]	$ 86,100	
Fixed selling and administrative expense[4]	140,400	226,500
Income before taxes		$151,900
Less income taxes[5]		60,760
Net income		$ 91,140

[1] 110% x $860,000.   [3] 105% x $82,000.   [5] 40% x $151,900.
[2] 110% x $516,000.   [4] 108% x $130,000.

(b) *Prepare a Cash receipts and disbursements budget.*

Jimbo Manufacturing Company
Cash Receipts and Disbursement Budget
For the Quarter Ending March 31, 19X1

Cash receipts:		
Collection of cash sales (20% x $946,000)		$189,200
Collection of credit sales:		
4th quarter prior year (80% x $860,000 x 60%)	$412,800	
1st quarter (80% x $946,000 x 40%)	302,720	715,520
Total cash receipts		$904,720
Cash disbursements:		
Purchase of material:		
4th quarter prior year ($516,000 x 50% x 30%)	$ 77,400	
1st quarter ($567,600 x 50% x 70%)	198,660	$276,060
Direct labor ($567,600 x 30%)		170,280
Variable overhead ($567,600 x 20%)		113,520
Fixed production costs ($86,100 x 25%)		21,525
Selling and administrative expense ($140,400 x 90%)		126,360
Income taxes		60,760
Total cash disbursements		$768,505
Excess of receipts over disbursements		$136,215
Plus beginning cash balance		107,670
Ending cash balance		$243,885

KEY TERMS

budget committee, *1024*
budgeted balance sheet, *1034*
budgeted income statement, *1029*
budgets, *1023*
budget variances, *1035*
flexible budget, *1036*
management by exception, *1038*
master budget, *1025*
performance reports, *1035*
slack, *1038*
static budget, *1036*
zero base budgeting, *1025*

SELF QUIZ

LO 1 1. Which of the following is not a true statement about budgets?
   a. They are formal documents that quantify a company's plans.
   b. They enhance communication and coordination.
   c. They should be prepared infrequently.
   d. They provide a basis for evaluating performance.

LO 1 2. Budgets are useful in the planning process because they enhance _____ and _____.

LO 1 3. The group within the company that is responsible for preparing budgets is usually called the _____ _____.

LO 2 4. Which of the following is *not* a true statement about the sales budget?
   a. Input from the sales force may be useful in predicting sales.
   b. Very large companies may hire economists to help prepare sales budget.
   c. The first step in the budget process is to develop this budget.
   d. The production budget is developed before this budget.

LO 2 5. Which of the following is the correct formula to determine required purchases of direct materials?
   a. Quantity required for production + Desired ending quantity − Beginning quantity.
   b. Quantity required for production − Desired ending quantity + Beginning quantity.
   c. Quantity required for production + Desired ending quantity + Beginning quantity.
   d. Beginning quantity + Purchases − Desired ending quantity.

LO 2 6. True or False? A primary purpose of the budgeted income statement is to insure that anticipated profit is consistent with company goals.

LO 2 7. Which of the following items do *not* require a cash outflow?
   a. Wage expense.
   b. Purchase of raw materials.
   c. Selling expense.
   d. Depreciation expense.

LO 2 8. Differences between budgeted and actual amounts are referred to as _____ _____.

LO 3 9. The _____ budget is not adjusted for the actual level of production whereas a _____ budget is adjusted for the actual level of production.

LO 3 10. Which of the following is true about management by exception?
   a. Only large favorable variances are investigated.
   b. Management by exception is an economical approach to cost control.
   c. Management by exception can only be used with computers.
   d. Large unfavorable variances should not be investigated.

LO 4 11. True or False? Management should encourage subordinates to include a lot of slack in their budgets.

LO 4 12. True or False? The number of defects in a process is an example of a nonmonetary measure of employee performance.

SOLUTIONS TO SELF-QUIZ
1. c   2. communication, coordination   3. budget committee   4. d   5. a   6. true   7. d   8. budget variances   9. static, flexible   10. b   11. false   12. true

QUESTIONS

Q25-1 Why are budgets useful in the planning process?

Q25-2 Why are budgets useful in the control process?

Q25-3 What is the difference between the top-down and bottom-up approach to developing a budget?

Q25-4 What is meant by a *zero base budget*?

Q25-5 What are the typical components of a master budget?

Q25-6 What are the main purposes of preparing a cash receipts and disbursements budget?

Q25-7 How do computers assist in the budget planning process?

Q25-8 What are some possible causes for an unfavorable budget variance?

Q25-9 What are some nonmonetary performance measures that could be included in a budget?

Q25-10 Why is there an inherent conflict between the planning and control uses of budgets?

EXERCISES

LO 2

E25-1 Order of Budgets Determine the order in which each of the following budgets are generally prepared.
a. Materials purchase budget
b. Sales budget
c. Budgeted income statement
d. Production budget
e. Budgeted balance sheet

LO 2

E25-2 Sales Budget The Locktight Company manufactures burglar-resistant commercial door locks. Due to a recent increase in burglaries, Locktight expects sales to dramatically increase compared to the prior year. Prepare a sales budget for Locktight Company using the following information. Locktight Company had sales of locks for 19X0 as follows:

First quarter	21,000
Second quarter	26,000
Third quarter	25,000
Fourth quarter	30,000

Assume that sales for each quarter in 19X1 are expected to be 10% higher than they were in 19X0 and the selling price per lock is $20.

LO 2

E25-3 Production Budget Prepare the production budget for Powerhouse Computer Company for the months of January, February, and March using the following information:
Powerhouse expects sales to be 15,600 computer workstations in January, 16,500 computer workstations in February, 16,000 computer workstations in March, and 18,500 workstations in April. There are 9,200 computer workstations on hand on January 1. Powerhouse desires to maintain monthly ending inventory at 40% of next month's expected sales.

LO 2   **E25-4**   **Direct Materials Purchases Budget**   Prepare quarterly direct materials purchases budgets for Ajax Chemical Company for 19X2 using the following information. Expected unit production for each quarter is as follows:

First quarter	47,000
Second quarter	42,000
Third quarter	50,000
Fourth quarter	39,000
First quarter (19X3)	48,000

Finished units of production require three pounds of raw material per unit. The raw material cost is $4 per pound. There are 45,000 pounds of raw material on hand at the beginning of the first quarter. Ajax desires to keep 40% of next quarter's material requirements on hand at the end of each quarter.

LO 2   **E25-5**   **Direct Labor Budget**   Prepare quarterly direct labor budgets for Ajax Chemical Company for 19X2 using the production information from E25-4. It takes 2.5 hours of direct labor to produce each finished unit of product. Direct labor costs are $7 per hour. Each employee can work 500 hours per quarter.

LO 2   **E25-6**   **Manufacturing Overhead Budget**   Prepare quarterly manufacturing overhead budgets for Ajax Chemical Company for 19X2 using the production information from E25-4. Ajax has overhead costs as follows:

Variable Costs		*Fixed Costs Per Quarter*	
Indirect material	$2.25/unit	Supervisory salaries	$80,000
Indirect labor	1.50/unit	Factory depreciation	30,000
Utilities	1.00/unit	Other	4,100

LO 2   **E25-7**   **Cash Receipts Budget**   Prepare cash receipts budgets for Duncan Company for the months of April, May, and June using the following expected sales information:

	April	*May*	*June*
Budgeted sales	$85,000	$70,000	$98,000

Prior experience has indicated that 40% of a month's sales are collected in the month of sale, 50% in the month following sale, and the remaining 10% in the second month following sale. February and March sales were $80,000 and $90,000 respectively.

LO 2   **E25-8**   **Cash Disbursements Budget for Purchases**   Prepare cash disbursements budgets for the Mayper Company for the months of April, May, and June using the following expected sales information:

	April	*May*	*June*
Budgeted purchases	$65,000	$70,000	$58,000

Prior experience has indicated that 30% of a month's purchases are paid in the month of purchase, 45% in the month following purchase, and the remaining 25% in the second month following purchase. February and March purchases were $60,000 and $55,000 respectively.

LO 3   **E25-9**   **Flexible Budget**   Determine Bedding Unlimited Company's expected total cost for production of 8,000 mattresses, 10,000 mattresses, and 12,000 mattresses given the following information:

Variable Costs		*Fixed Costs*	
Direct material	$5.50/unit	Supervisory salaries	$14,000
Direct labor	2.50/unit	Factory depreciation	8,500
Variable overhead	1.20/unit	Other factory costs	1,100

CHAPTER 25 BUDGETARY PLANNING AND CONTROL

LO 3

E25-10 **Performance Report** Prepare a performance report from the following information for Bookbinder Manufacturing Company. During the period, Bookbinder produced 12,000 units and incurred the following costs:

Variable Costs		Fixed Costs	
Direct material	$71,900	Supervisory salaries	$13,750
Direct labor	28,250	Factory depreciation	8,500
Utilities	15,300	Other factory costs	1,260

Bookbinder budgeted the following costs:

Variable Costs		Fixed Costs	
Direct material	$5.30/unit	Supervisory salaries	$12,900
Direct labor	2.60/unit	Factory depreciation	8,500
Utilities	1.40/unit	Other factory costs	1,390

PROBLEM SET A

LO 2

P25-1A **Combined Production and Purchases Budget** BugAway, Inc. produces and sells exterminating products in liquid form. Information about the budget for the second quarter, 19X1, is as follows:

(1) The company expects to sell 60,000 bottles of BugAway in the second quarter, 93,000 in the third quarter, and 42,000 in the fourth quarter.
(2) A bottle of BugAway requires 6 oz. of Chemical A and 10 oz. of Chemical B.
(3) The desired ending inventory of finished goods is 35% of next quarter's sales whereas the desired ending inventory for material is 25% of next quarter's production requirements.
(4) There are 21,000 bottles of BugAway, 117,000 oz. of Chemical A, and 197,000 oz. of Chemical B on hand at the beginning of the second quarter.
(5) The cost of Chemical A is 12 cents per oz., the cost of Chemical B is 9 cents per oz., and the selling price of BugAway is $9.95 per bottle.
(6) The cost of direct labor is 60 cents per bottle and the cost of variable overhead is 90 cents per bottle. Fixed manufacturing overhead is $28,000 per quarter.
(7) Variable selling and administrative expense is 4% of sales and fixed selling and administrative expenses are $39,000 per quarter.

REQUIRED:

a. Prepare a production budget for the second and third quarter, 19X1.
b. Prepare a material purchases budget for the second quarter, 19X1.
c. Prepare a budgeted income statement (variable costing method) for the second quarter, 19X1.

LO 2

P25-2A **Integrating Budgets** CycleEase Corporation has a policy of keeping 30% of next quarter's sales in ending finished goods inventory and 25% of raw materials needed for next quarter's production in ending raw materials inventory. It takes 2 units of raw materials to make one unit of finished goods. The cost of raw material is $2.50 per unit. Unit information for the budget of CycleEase Corporation is as follows:

	1st Quarter	2nd Quarter	3rd Quarter	4th Quarter
Sales	26,000	?	?	36,000
Production	?	35,000	?	?
Beginning finished goods	7,000	?	?	?
Ending finished goods	12,000	?	?	?
Beginning raw materials	13,600	?	?	12,600
Ending raw materials	?	?	?	13,800
Material purchases	?	76,280	?	67,200

REQUIRED:

a. Fill in the missing information for 19X2.
b. Prepare a production budget for 19X2.
c. Prepare a material purchases budget for 19X2.

LO 2

P25-3A **Cash Budget** Estimated data for Casey Corporation for 19X1 is as follows:

	1st Quarter	2nd Quarter	3rd Quarter	4th Quarter
Sales	$84,100	$80,800	$108,600	$96,200
Purchases	21,600	19,800	23,400	22,900
Direct labor	14,400	13,300	17,300	16,500
Manuf. overhead	39,400	35,600	37,800	36,200
Selling and administrative expense	21,800	23,400	24,300	23,500
Income taxes	11,200	9,800	10,100	8,800

(1) Prior experience has indicated that 60% of a quarter's sales are collected in the quarter of sale, 30% in the quarter following sale, and the remaining 10% in the second quarter following sale.

(2) Prior experience has indicated that 60% of a quarter's purchases are paid in the quarter of purchase, 25% in the quarter following purchase, and the remaining 15% in the second quarter following purchase.

(3) Casey pays 90% of its direct labor in the quarter incurred and 10% in the following quarter.

(4) Manufacturing overhead includes $30,000 depreciation per quarter. The remainder is paid in the quarter incurred.

(5) Selling and administrative expense includes $20,000 depreciation per quarter. The remainder is paid in the quarter incurred.

(6) A capital expenditure for $62,000 is planned for the fourth quarter.

(7) There is an expected beginning balance of cash of $49,330 at the beginning of the third quarter.

REQUIRED:

a. Prepare a cash receipts and disbursements budget for the 3rd quarter of 19X1.
b. Prepare a cash receipts and disbursements budget for the 4th quarter of 19X1.

LO 2

P25-4A **Master Budget** The results of operations for the Washington Manufacturing Company, a sole proprietorship, for the fourth quarter of 19X5 are as follows:

Sales		$688,000
Less: Variable cost of goods sold		412,800
Contribution margin		$275,200
Less: Fixed production expense	$ 65,600	
Fixed selling and administrative expense	104,000	169,600
Income before taxes		$105,600
Less income taxes		42,200
Net income		$ 63,400

Note: Washington Company uses the variable costing method. Thus, only variable production costs are included in inventory and cost of goods sold. Fixed production costs are charged to expense in the period incurred.

Additional Information:

1. Sales and variable cost of sales are expected to increase by 10% in the next quarter.
2. It is expected that 30% of all sales will be for cash. Of the remaining credit sales, 65% will be collected in the quarter of sale and 35% will be collected in the quarter following sale.

3. Variable cost of sales consists of 50% materials, 30% direct labor, and 20% variable overhead. Materials are purchased on credit and 60% are paid for in the quarter of purchase and the remaining amount is paid for in the quarter after purchase. Direct labor and variable overhead are paid for in the quarter incurred. Ending raw materials inventory is expected to equal $56,000 at the end of the first quarter. Finished goods inventory is expected to equal $136,000 at the end of the first quarter. Raw materials purchases equal materials used in production. Finished goods produced equal units sold.
4. Fixed production costs are expected to increase by 5% in the next quarter. The fixed production costs consist of 70% depreciation and 30% other fixed costs. Fixed production costs requiring payment are paid in the quarter they are incurred.
5. Fixed selling and administrative expenses are expected to increase by 6%. Ten percent of these costs consist of depreciation of administrative buildings and equipment. Fixed selling and administrative expenses (excluding depreciation) are paid in the quarter that they are incurred.
6. The tax rate is expected to be 40%. All taxes are paid in the quarter they are incurred.
7. The cash balance on January 1, 19X6, is $107,670.
8. Property, plant, and equipment has a cost of $1,900,000 on January 1, 19X6. Accumulated depreciation of $385,000 is expected at the end of the first quarter. No purchases or retirements of property, plant, and equipment are expected.
9. There is an expected noncurrent note payable of $180,000 at the end of the first quarter, 19X6.
10. Land held for investment has a cost of $375,000 at the end of the first quarter, 19X6.
11. Common stock is $1,250,000 on January 1, 19X6. No issue or purchase of stock and no stock dividends are expected for the first quarter.

REQUIRED:

a. Prepare a budgeted income statement for the first quarter of 19X6.
b. Prepare a cash receipts and disbursements budget for the first quarter of 19X6.
c. Prepare a budgeted balance sheet for the end of the first quarter of 19X6.

LO 3

P25-5A **Performance Report** The Toast-R Manufacturing Corporation has expected production costs as follows:

Variable Costs		*Fixed Costs*	
Direct material	$4.50/unit	Supervisory salaries	$15,600
Direct labor	1.50/unit	Factory depreciation	7,500
Indirect material	0.80/unit	Factory insurance	3,900
Indirect labor	1.20/unit	Other factory costs	2,100
Power and light	1.25/unit		

Actual costs for 18,000 units of production for the first quarter of 19X7 are as follows:

Variable Costs		*Fixed Costs*	
Direct material	$81,540	Supervisory salaries	$15,750
Direct labor	26,640	Factory depreciation	7,500
Indirect material	13,500	Factory insurance	4,500
Indirect labor	21,960	Other factory costs	2,260
Power and light	24,300		

REQUIRED:

a. Prepare a flexible budget for 18,000, 20,000 and 22,000 units of production.
b. Prepare a performance report for the first quarter of 19X7.

PROBLEM SET B

LO 2

P25-1B **Combined Production and Purchases Budget** Grow-Up, Inc. produces and sells plant growth products in liquid form. Information about the budget for the third quarter, 19X2, is as follows:

(1) The company expects to sell 90,000 bottles of Grow-Up in the third quarter and 139,500 in the fourth quarter of 19X2, and 63,000 in the first quarter of 19X3.
(2) Each bottle of Grow-Up requires 4 oz. of Chemical A and 9 oz. of Chemical B.
(3) The desired ending inventory of finished goods is 40% of next quarter's sales whereas the desired ending inventory for material is 30% of next quarter's production requirements.
(4) There are 31,500 bottles of Grow-Up, 175,500 oz. of Chemical A and 295,500 oz. of Chemical B on hand at the beginning of the third quarter.
(5) The cost of Chemical A is 14 cents per oz., the cost of Chemical B is 7 cents per oz., and the selling price of Grow-Up is $9.95 per bottle.
(6) The cost of direct labor is 50 cents per bottle and the cost of variable overhead is $1.00 per bottle. Fixed manufacturing overhead is $37,000 per quarter.
(7) Variable selling and administrative expense is 5% of sales and fixed selling and administrative expenses are $36,000 per quarter.

REQUIRED:

a. Prepare a production budget for the third and fourth quarter, 19X2.
b. Prepare a material purchases budget for the third quarter, 19X2.
c. Prepare a budgeted income statement (variable costing method) for the third quarter, 19X2.

LO 2

P25-2B **Integrating Budgets** Nonex Corporation has a policy of keeping 30% of next quarter's sales in ending finished goods inventory and 25% of raw materials needed for next quarter's production in ending raw materials inventory. It takes 2 units of raw materials to make one unit of finished goods. The cost of raw material is $2.50 per unit. Unit information for the budget of Nonex Corporation is as follows:

	1st Quarter	2nd Quarter	3rd Quarter	4th Quarter
Sales	65,000	100,000	?	90,000
Production	?	87,500	?	?
Beginning finished goods	17,500	?	?	?
Ending finished goods	?	?	?	?
Beginning raw materials	34,000	?	?	31,500
Ending raw materials	?	?	?	34,500
Material purchases	?	190,700	?	168,000

REQUIRED:

a. Fill in the missing information for 19X1.
b. Prepare a production budget for 19X1.
c. Prepare a material purchases budget for 19X1.

LO 2

P25-3B **Cash Budget** Estimated data for the Drexin Corporation for 19X4 follows:

	January	February	March	April
Sales	$67,280	$64,640	$86,880	$76,960
Purchases	17,280	15,840	18,720	18,320
Direct labor	11,520	10,640	13,840	13,200
Manuf. overhead	31,520	28,480	30,240	28,960
Selling and admin. exp.	17,440	18,720	19,440	18,800
Income taxes	8,960	7,840	8,080	7,040

(1) Prior experience has indicated that 50% of a month's sales are collected in the month of sale, 40% in the month following sale, and the remaining 10% in the second month following sale.
(2) Prior experience has indicated that 55% of a month's purchases are paid in the month of purchase, 30% in the month following purchase, and the remaining 15% in the second month following purchase.
(3) Drexin pays 90% of its direct labor in the month incurred and 10% in the following month.
(4) Manufacturing overhead includes $24,000 depreciation per month. The remainder is paid in the quarter incurred.
(5) Selling and administrative expenses include $12,000 depreciation per month. The remainder is paid in the quarter incurred.
(6) A capital expenditure for $49,600 is planned for April.
(7) There is an expected beginning balance of cash of $102,400 at the beginning of March.

REQUIRED:

a. Prepare a cash receipts and disbursements budget for March of 19X4.
b. Prepare a cash receipts and disbursements budget for April of 19X4.

P25-4B Master Budget The results of operations for the Suhm Manufacturing Company, a sole proprietorship, for the fourth quarter of 19X8 are as follows:

Sales		$1,204,000
Less: Variable cost of goods sold		722,400
Contribution margin		$ 481,600
Less: Fixed production expense	$114,800	
Fixed selling and administrative expense	182,000	296,800
Income before taxes		$ 184,800
Less income taxes		73,850
Net income		$ 110,950

Note: Suhm Manufacturing Company uses the variable costing method. Thus, only variable production costs are included in inventory and cost of goods sold. Fixed production costs are charged to expense in the period incurred.

Additional Information:
1. Sales and variable cost of sales are expected to increase by 15% in the next quarter.
2. It is expected that 40% of all sales will be for cash. Of the remaining credit sales, 75% will be collected in the quarter of sale and 25% will be collected in the quarter following sale.
3. Variable cost of sales consists of 60% materials, 25% direct labor, and 15% variable overhead. Materials are purchased on credit and 70% are paid for in the quarter of purchase and the remaining amount is paid for in the quarter after purchase. Direct labor and variable overhead are paid for in the quarter incurred. Ending raw materials inventory is expected to equal $112,000 at the end of the first quarter. Finished goods inventory is expected to equal $272,000 at the end of the first quarter. Raw materials purchases equal materials used in production. Finished goods produced equal units sold.
4. Fixed production costs are expected to increase by 2% in the next quarter. The fixed production costs consist of 80% depreciation and 20% other fixed costs. Fixed production costs requiring payment are paid in the quarter they are incurred.
5. Fixed selling and administrative expenses are expected to increase by 5%. Fifteen percent of these costs consist of allocated depreciation of administrative buildings and equipment. Fixed selling and administrative expenses (excluding depreciation) are paid in the quarter that they are incurred.

6. The tax rate is expected to be 40%. All taxes are paid in the quarter they are incurred.
7. The cash balance on January 1, 19X9, is $269,200.
8. Property, plant, and equipment has a cost of $5,230,000 on January 1, 19X9. Accumulated depreciation of $962,500 is expected at the end of the first quarter. No purchases or retirements of property, plant, and equipment are expected.
9. There is a noncurrent note payable of $280,000 at the end of the first quarter, 19X9.
10. Land held for investment has a cost of $575,000 at the end of the first quarter, 19X9.
11. Common stock is $2,500,000 on January 1, 19X9. No issue or purchase of stock and no stock dividends are expected for the first quarter.

REQUIRED:

a. Prepare a budgeted income statement for the first quarter of 19X9.
b. Prepare a cash receipts and disbursements budget for the first quarter of 19X9.
c. Prepare a budgeted balance sheet for the first quarter of 19X9.

LO 3

P25-5B **Performance Report** The Cantrell Manufacturing Company has expected production costs as follows:

Variable Costs		Fixed Costs	
Direct material	$2.25/unit	Supervisory salaries	$23,400
Direct labor	0.75/unit	Factory depreciation	11,250
Indirect material	0.40/unit	Factory insurance	5,850
Indirect labor	0.60/unit	Other factory costs	3,150
Power and light	1.10/unit		

Actual costs for 18,000 units of production for the first quarter of 19X4 are as follows:

Variable Costs		Fixed Costs	
Direct material	$40,770	Supervisory salaries	$25,750
Direct labor	13,320	Factory depreciation	11,200
Indirect material	6,750	Factory insurance	5,500
Indirect labor	10,980	Other factory costs	3,260
Power and light	20,700		

REQUIRED:

a. Prepare a flexible budget for 14,000, 16,000 and 18,000 units of production.
b. Prepare a performance report for the first quarter of 19X4.

CRITICAL THINKING AND COMMUNICATING

C25-1 Amy Schwartz is the divisional manager of the candy bar division of Universal Food. Every year, Amy has to submit an annual budget to Barney Strange, the chief financial officer of Universal Food. Amy's bonus, salary, and promotion opportunities are based on how her performance compares to budgeted net income. Barney and Amy negotiate the budget each year. Barney always insists that Amy is underestimating revenues and overestimating expenses, whereas Amy tells Barney that he is expecting too much from her department.

During 19X0, the candy bar division had a record year. Barney insisted that the budget for 19X1 be at least at last year's level of performance. Amy stated that last year was an exception and could not be repeated. After getting into a rather heated argument, they scheduled a meeting with the president of Universal Food to resolve their conflict.

REQUIRED:

a. Explain why Barney and Amy had conflicting opinions.
b. If you were the president of Universal Food, how would you resolve the argument between Barney and Amy?
c. How would you modify Universal's budget system to reduce future conflict between Barney and Amy?

C25-2 The Athletic Equipment Division of Physique International had a very poor year in 19X2. Sales were down and there were quality problems with the manufactured products. Also, manufacturing output was 30% below the amount forecasted. A performance report based on a static budget comparison for the athletic equipment division was sent to the John Martinez, the president of Physique International. John was puzzled by the number of highly favorable variances because he heard that the division was having difficulty with its manufacturing operations.

REQUIRED:

Write a memo to John Martinez explaining why the variances were positive. Suggest how the performance report may be modified and some additional performance measures to improve the performance report.

CHAPTER 26

Standard Costs and Variance Analysis

At the start of the year, Frosty Ice Cream Company budgeted material costs at $2 per gallon. During the year, the company produced 1,000,000 gallons; the material cost was $2,200,408. After receiving year-end information, Linda Evert, director of operations, immediately called a meeting with the plant manager and the production supervisor.

Linda's opening statement grabbed their undivided attention. "What's going on? Our actual costs are 10 percent higher than budgeted."

Both managers assured her that the increased costs were not due to waste in the use of materials. The plant manager was confident that the increased costs were due to a sudden jump in sugar and milk prices. "And", he added, "Price changes are beyond our control. Talk to Purchasing; they'll back me up on the price increase."

Linda returned to her office and continued thinking about the situation. "What would really be useful," she concluded, "is a report that broke down the material cost increase into two parts: the part due to using more material than planned and the part due to paying a higher price than planned. I wonder if Jane in the accounting department can help with these calculations."

Fortunately, Linda is on the right track. A trained accountant can help her with the needed calculations. Frosty Ice Cream Company needs a standard costing system. In such systems, a company does not record manufactured goods at their actual product cost but rather at the cost that *should have been incurred* to produce the items. This cost is referred to as the *standard cost*. A primary benefit of a standard costing system is that it allows a company to compare differences between standard and actual costs. Such differences are referred to as *standard cost variances*.

For material costs, the standard cost variances distinguish between variances due to the actual price and the actual quantity of raw material being different from standard. Standard costing systems also generate variances for direct labor and manufacturing overhead. Management can then investigate large or unusual variances to determine if production is inefficient. If problems exist, management can take corrective action. Thus, standard costs play an important role in *controlling operations* as well as in determining *product costs*. This chapter illustrates both of these uses of standard costs.

LEARNING OBJECTIVES

1. Explain how standard costs are developed.
2. Calculate and interpret variances for direct material.
3. Calculate and interpret variances for direct labor.
4. Calculate and interpret variances for manufacturing overhead.
5. Discuss how the management by exception approach is applied to investigate standard cost variances.
6. Record standard costs in a manufacturing firm's accounts.

STANDARD COSTS AND BUDGETS

The term **standard cost** refers to the cost management believes *should be incurred* to produce a good or service under anticipated conditions. A tool manufacturing company may set a standard cost for the production of a hammer, while a bank may set a standard cost for processing a check. In the following examples, we concentrate on standard costing in a manufacturing setting. However, much of the discussion also applies to service companies that use standard costs.

Some accountants use the terms "budgeted cost" and "standard cost" interchangeably. However, standard cost often refers to the cost of a single unit, while budgeted cost often refers to the cost, at standard, of the total number of budgeted units. The cost information contained in budgets must be consistent with standard costs. For example, suppose the standard cost of a unit of production is:

Standard cost per unit:	
Direct material (2 pounds x $5 per pound)	$10.00
Direct labor (3 hours x $10 per hour)	30.00
Manufacturing overhead ($5 per labor hour)	15.00
Standard cost per unit	$55.00

If the direct material purchases budget calls for 5,000 pounds of raw material, it would show an expected cost of $25,000 (i.e., 5,000 pounds x $5 per pound). Likewise, if the direct labor budget is prepared for an expected production level of 1,000 units, it would indicate 3,000 hours of labor costing $30,000.

LO 1
Explain how standard costs are developed.

DEVELOPMENT OF STANDARD COSTS

Standard costs for material, labor, and overhead are developed in a variety of ways. The standard quantity of material may be specified in engineering plans that provide detailed lists of raw materials needed in production. For some companies, the standard quantity of raw material is actually specified in recipes. This would be the case in large commercial bakeries and other companies that produce food products. The standard price of the materials is often determined from price lists that suppliers provide.

Industrial engineers can perform time and motion studies to determine the standard quantity of direct labor. In time and motion studies, engineers observe workers under simulated or actual working conditions to determine standard labor hours. A company also can estimate standard labor hours from an analysis of past data. For example, suppose a company developed the following information on production and labor hours:

	Production in Units	Labor Hours
First quarter, 19X1	2,025	6,500
Second quarter, 19X1	2,500	7,400
Third quarter, 19X1	2,100	6,800
Fourth quarter, 19X1	2,600	7,900
Total	9,225	28,600

Based on these data, the average time to produce one unit is approximately 3.10 hours (28,600 hours ÷ 9,225 units). If the company does not anticipate any major changes in the production process, it could use this average as the standard quantity of labor. However, if the company had operated inefficiently in the past, and now bases its standards on past performance, its standards will not reflect efficient production practices. The standard labor wage rates are usually set at the rates management expects to pay the various categories of workers. In many cases, the wage rates are set equal to the rates specified in labor contracts.

Developing standard costs for overhead involves procedures similar to those used to develop the predetermined overhead rates discussed earlier in the text. Dividing the amount of anticipated overhead by the standard quantity of the allocation base results in a standard cost of overhead. For example, suppose a company anticipates it will incur $60,000 of overhead if workers perform 5,000 standard labor hours. In this case, the standard overhead rate would be $12 per standard labor hour. Companies that use activity-based costing develop standard costs for a number of overhead cost drivers such as the numbers of setups, purchase orders, and shipments received.

IDEAL AND ATTAINABLE STANDARDS

In developing standard costs, some managers emphasize **ideal standards**, while others emphasize **attainable standards**. Ideal standards are developed under the assumption that no obstacles to the production process will be encountered. Thus, they do not allow for equipment breakdown that would increase the quantity of labor hours or for defects in raw material that would increase the quantity of material required for production. Ideal standards are sometimes referred to as *perfection standards* because they emphasize production in a "perfect" environment. However, if a company expects occasional equipment failure, occasional substitution of inexperienced for experienced workers, and some raw material defects, then it should set standards at a level that allows for the cost of these events. Currently attainable standards are standard costs that take into account the possibility that a variety of circumstances may lead to costs that are greater than "ideal."

Managers who support ideal standards believe these standards motivate employees to strive for the best possible control over production costs. Such managers argue that if the cost of defects and breakdowns are built into the standards, the result will be an acceptance of defects and breakdowns rather than an effort to eliminate them. However, because they do not allow for *expected* deviations, ideal standards may not be useful for planning. If equipment breakdowns and defects are a "fact of life," then it makes sense to plan for their associated costs. Most managers support the use of attainable standards.

GENERAL APPROACH TO VARIANCE ANALYSIS

Companies that have standard costing systems can analyze the difference between a standard and an actual cost, referred to as a **standard cost variance**, to determine if operations are being performed efficiently. The analysis—referred to as *variance analysis*—involves dividing the total variance between standard and actual cost for material, labor, and overhead into two components. By breaking down the total variance, managers gain insight into the specific areas that need attention. For example, suppose the standard cost of materials per unit of production is 2 pounds at $5 per pound. During the year, the company produces 1,000 units and uses 2,010 pounds of material costing $6 per pound. In this case, the standard cost of materials is $10,000, and the actual cost is $12,060. Thus, the total variance is $2,060, which is labeled "unfavorable" since the actual cost is greater than standard.

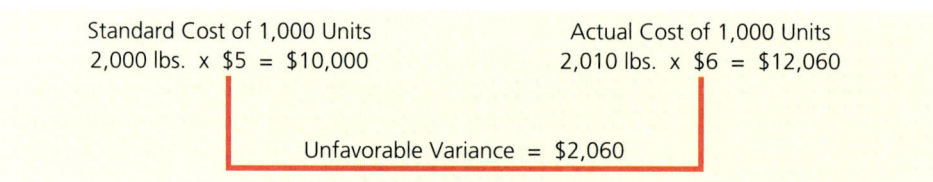

This total variance provides information that material costs may be out of control and in need of management attention, but it does not suggest the nature of the problem. The actual cost may be greater than standard because too much material was used or because the price paid for material was greater than standard. A close look at the facts reveals that the actual quantity of material used is very close to the standard quantity of material—2,010 pounds were used, and the standard quantity is 2,000 pounds. However, the actual price per pound is $6, while the standard price per pound is only $5. We demonstrate in the next section how to divide the total material variance into the part due to the price paid for material and the part due to the use of material. Similar procedures for labor and overhead are presented later in the chapter.

MATERIAL VARIANCES

LO 2 Calculate and interpret variances for direct material.

The total material variance can be divided into a material price variance and a material quantity variance.

Material Price Variance

The **material price variance** equals the difference between the standard and actual prices per unit of material times the actual quantity of material used.[1]

$$\text{Material Price Variance} = \left(\begin{array}{c} \text{Standard Price per} \\ \text{Unit of Material} \end{array} - \begin{array}{c} \text{Actual Price per} \\ \text{Unit of Material} \end{array} \right) \times \begin{array}{c} \text{Actual Quantity of} \\ \text{Material Used} \end{array}$$

Suppose Acme Manufacturing Company actually paid $9.50 per pound, rather than the standard price of $10, for 6,500 pounds of material it used in July. In this case, there would be a favorable $3,250 material price variance.

$$\$3{,}250 \text{ Favorable} = (\$10.00 - \$9.50) \times 6{,}500$$

Note that the material price variance is labeled favorable because the actual price per pound is less than the standard price.[2]

Material Quantity Variance

The **material quantity variance** equals the difference between the standard quantity of material allowed for the number of units produced and the actual quantity of material used times the standard price of material.

$$\begin{array}{c} \text{Material Quantity} \\ \text{Variance} \end{array} = \left(\begin{array}{c} \text{Standard Quantity of Material Allowed} \\ \text{for the Number of Units Produced} \end{array} - \begin{array}{c} \text{Actual Quantity of} \\ \text{Material Used} \end{array} \right) \times \begin{array}{c} \text{Standard} \\ \text{Price} \end{array}$$

Suppose Acme Manufacturing Company produces 3,000 units during July. The standard quantity of material is 2 pounds per unit with a standard price of $10 per pound. The standard quantity of material for 3,000 units is 6,000 pounds (3,000 units × 2 pounds per unit). During the month, Acme actually uses 6,500 pounds of material. Thus, the material quantity variance is $5,000 unfavorable.

$$\$5{,}000 \text{ Unfavorable} = (6{,}000 - 6{,}500) \times \$10$$

Note that the material quantity variance is labeled unfavorable. Acme actually used more material than required by its standards. This is considered an unfavorable outcome since it has a negative effect on company profit.

Reconciling the Material Price and Quantity Variances to the Total Material Variance

The total variance for materials is the difference between the standard and actual costs of materials. You can check the accuracy of your material price and quantity variance calculations by making sure they equal the total material variance. This check is performed for Acme Manufacturing Company in Illustration 26-1.

---

[1] An alternative approach calculates the material price variance with the actual quantity of material *purchased* rather than *used*.

[2] Using the variance formulas presented in this chapter, positive variances will be favorable and negative variances will be unfavorable. However, rather than concentrating on the sign of the variance, you should understand that prices or quantities greater than standard are labeled unfavorable and actual prices or quantities less than standard are labeled favorable.

ILLUSTRATION 26-1 Reconciliation of the Material Price and Quantity Variances to the Total Material Variance

Total Variance	
Standard cost for 3,000 units (6,000 pounds × $10)	$60,000
Actual cost (6,500 pounds × $9.50)	61,750
Excess of actual over standard cost	$(1,750) Unfavorable

Material Price Variance	
Paid $.50 less per pound on all 6,500 pounds used	$3,250 Favorable

Material Quantity Variance	
Used an extra 500 pounds at standard price of $10	(5,000) Unfavorable
Total of material price and quantity variances	$(1,750) Unfavorable

DIRECT LABOR VARIANCES

LO 3 Calculate and interpret variances for direct labor.

The difference between the standard and actual costs of direct labor can be separated into labor rate and labor efficiency variances using formulas similar to those used to calculate material variances.

Labor Rate Variance

The **labor rate variance** equals the difference between the standard and actual wage rates times the actual number of labor hours worked. This variance is very similar to the material price variance.

Labor Rate Variance = (Standard Wage Rate − Actual Wage Rate) × Actual Number of Labor Hours Worked

Suppose Acme Manufacturing Company's standards call for a standard wage rate of $8.00 per hour. During July, the actual wage rate was $8.25 and 9,400 actual hours were worked. In this case, the labor rate variance is an unfavorable $2,350.

$2,350 Unfavorable = ($8.00 − $8.25) × 9,400

Labor Efficiency Variance

The **labor efficiency variance** equals the difference between the standard labor hours allowed for the number of units produced and the actual number of labor hours worked times the standard labor wage rate. This variance is very similar to the material quantity variance.

Labor Efficiency Variance = (Standard Labor Hours Allowed for the Number of Units Produced − Actual Number of Labor Hours Worked) × Standard Wage Rate

Acme Manufacturing Company uses 9,400 hours to produce 3,000 units. Standards call for 3 hours per unit at a standard wage rate of $8 per hour. The standard number of hours for 3,000 units is 9,000 (3,000 units × 3 hours per unit). In this case, the labor efficiency variance is $3,200 unfavorable.

$3,200 Unfavorable = (9,000 − 9,400) × $8

CHAPTER 26 STANDARD COSTS AND VARIANCE ANALYSIS

Reconciling the Labor Efficiency and Labor Rate Variances to the Total Labor Variance

The total labor variance equals the difference between the standard and actual costs of labor. As with the material variance, it is a good practice to reconcile the labor rate and efficiency variances to the total labor variance. The reconciliation for Acme Manufacturing Company is presented in Illustration 26-2.

ILLUSTRATION 26-2 Reconciliation of the Labor Rate and Efficiency Variances to the Total Labor Variance

Total Variance	
Standard cost for 3,000 units (9,000 hours x $8)	$72,000
Actual cost (9,400 hours x $8.25)	77,550
Excess of actual over standard cost	$ (5,550) Unfavorable

Labor Rate Variance	
Paid $.25 more per hour on all 9,400 actual hours	$(2,350) Unfavorable

Labor Efficiency Variance	
Used an extra 400 hours at standard rate of $8	(3,200) Unfavorable
Total of labor efficiency and rate variances	$(5,550) Unfavorable

Calculate and interpret variances for manufacturing overhead.

OVERHEAD VARIANCES

The total variance for manufacturing overhead is the difference between standard and actual overhead costs. The total overhead variance can be separated into overhead volume and controllable overhead variances.

Overhead Volume Variance

The **overhead volume variance** equals the difference between the amount of overhead applied to production at standard and the amount of overhead included in the flexible budget.

$$\text{Overhead Volume Variance} = \text{Overhead Applied to Production at Standard} - \text{Flexible Budget Amount of Overhead}$$

Suppose Acme Manufacturing Company budgets $40,000 of fixed overhead and $5 per unit of variable overhead cost. Recall that a flexible budget is a budget restated for the actual level of production. For Acme Manufacturing, the flexible budget for overhead would be:

$40,000 + ($5 x Number of Units Produced)

Acme expects to produce 2,500 units. In this case, the standard overhead rate would be $21 per unit, which is calculated as follows:

Expected amount of overhead [$40,000 + ($5 x 2,500 units)]	$52,500
Expected production	÷2,500 units
Standard overhead rate	$ 21 per unit

Note that the standard overhead rate in this example is expressed on a per unit basis. This is because Acme only produces a single product. When multiple products are produced, a company must base the overhead rate on labor hours, machine hours, or some other measure of activity that is common to the various products.

If Acme actually produces 3,000 units, it would apply $63,000 of standard overhead to production (i.e., 3,000 x $21). However, the flexible budget amount for 3,000 units of production is $55,000. Thus, the overhead volume variance is $8,000 favorable.

$$\text{Overhead Volume Variance} = \text{Overhead Applied to Production at Standard} - \text{Flexible Budget Amount of Overhead}$$

$$\$8,000 \text{ favorable} = \$21 \times 3,000 \text{ units} - \$40,000 + (\$5 \times 3,000)$$

Interpreting the Overhead Volume Variance. Volume variances do not signal that overhead costs are in or out of control. The controllable overhead variance, discussed in the next section, provides this signal. An overhead volume variance simply signals that the quantity of production was greater or less than anticipated when the standard overhead rate was developed. When a company produces more units than anticipated, the amount of overhead it applies to inventory exceeds the flexible budget because the amount of fixed cost per unit is being applied to more units than anticipated. Consider the standard overhead rate for Acme Manufacturing Company. The rate of $21 per unit is composed of $5 per unit of variable costs and $16 of fixed costs. The $16 of fixed costs per unit results from dividing the expected amount of fixed costs ($40,000) by the anticipated production of 2,500 units.

Standard overhead rate:	
Variable costs per unit	$ 5.00
Fixed costs per unit ($40,000 ÷ 2,500 expected units)	16.00
Total	$21.00

When this rate is applied to 3,000 units, Acme applies fixed costs of $48,000 to inventory. This exceeds the $40,000 of fixed costs in the flexible budget (which is not affected by the level of activity) by $8,000.

	Standard Cost Applied to 3,000 Units	Flexible Budget for 3,000 Units	Difference
Variable costs	$15,000 ($5 x 3,000)	$15,000 ($5 x 3,000)	0
Fixed costs	48,000 ($16 x 3,000)	40,000	$8,000
Total	$63,000	$55,000	$8,000

If Acme had anticipated 3,000 units would be produced, the fixed costs per unit would have been $13.3333 and the standard overhead rate would have been set at $18.3333.

Standard overhead rate:	
Variable costs per unit	$ 5.0000
Fixed costs per unit ($40,000 ÷ 3,000 expected units)	13.3333
Total	$18.3333

With a rate of $18.3333 per unit, Acme would have applied $55,000 of overhead to the 3,000 units produced, and the volume variance would be zero. The usefulness of the volume variance is limited. It only signals that more or less units have been produced than planned when the company set its standard overhead rate. If more units are produced than were originally planned, the company has a favorable variance; if less units are produced, the company has an unfavorable variance.

Controllable Overhead Variance

The **controllable overhead variance** is the difference between the amount of overhead that would be included in a flexible budget for the actual level of production and the actual amount of overhead. The variance is referred to as "controllable" because managers should be able to control costs to keep them in line with the amount included in the flexible budget.

Controllable Overhead Variance = Flexible Budget Amount of Overhead − Actual Overhead Cost

Suppose Acme Manufacturing Company has the flexible budget noted above ($40,000 of fixed overhead and $5 per unit of variable overhead). During the month of July, Acme produces 3,000 units and incurs $52,000 of overhead. Thus, it has a $3,000 favorable controllable overhead variance.

Controllable Overhead Variance = Flexible Budget Amount of Overhead − Actual Overhead Cost

$3,000 Favorable   = $ 40,000 + ($5 x 3,000)   − $52,000

The variance is labeled favorable because the actual cost is less than the amount indicated in the flexible budget.

Reconciling the Overhead Volume Variance and the Controllable Overhead Variance to the Total Overhead Variance

In a standard costing system, the amount of overhead applied to production is based on standard costs rather than on actual costs. The total overhead variance equals the difference between the amount of overhead applied to production at standard and the actual amount of overhead. The reconciliation of the overhead volume variance and the controllable overhead variance to the total overhead variance for Acme Manufacturing Company is presented in Illustration 26-3.

COMPREHENSIVE EXAMPLE

In this section, a comprehensive example of standard cost variances is presented for Frosty Ice Cream Company. Recall from the scenario at the start of the chapter that Linda Evert, director of operations for Frosty, was concerned about a 10 percent increase in material cost. The plant manager assured her that the increase was not due to waste in the use of raw materials. The material variances we will calculate provide insight into the validity of the plant manager's statement.

At the start of the year, Frosty Ice Cream Company planned to produce 900,000 gallons of ice cream. Production of ice cream requires various raw materials (e.g., milk, cream, sugar, and flavorings), and Frosty would most likely develop separate standards for each. However, to simplify the setting, we assume Frosty uses only one raw material. Each gallon of ice cream requires .8

ILLUSTRATION 26-3 Reconciliation of the Overhead Volume Variance and the Controllable Overhead Variance to the Total Overhead Variance

Total Variance

Standard overhead applied (3,000 units × $21)		$63,000
Actual overhead cost		52,000
Excess of standard over actual cost		$11,000 Favorable

Overhead Volume Variance

Applied overhead (3,000 × $21)	$63,000	
Flexible budget overhead ($40,000 + $5 × 3,000 units))	55,000	$ 8,000 Favorable

Controllable Overhead Variance

Flexible budget overhead ($40,000 + $5 × 3,000 units)	$55,000	
Actual overhead	52,000	3,000 Favorable
Total of overhead volume and controllable overhead variance		$11,000 Favorable

gallons of raw material costing $2.50 per gallon. (A gallon of ice cream does not require a gallon of raw material since air is incorporated in the production process.) Each gallon of ice cream also requires .125 hours of direct labor costing $12.00 per hour.

The company estimates that fixed production costs will equal $450,000 per year and variable production costs will equal $.25 per gallon. Thus, Frosty sets its standard overhead rate at $.75 per gallon.

Standard Overhead Rate = Expected Amount of Overhead at Standard ÷ Expected Production

$.75 per gallon = [$450,000 + ($.25 × 900,000 gallons)] ÷ 900,000 gallons

In summary, the standard cost per unit is:

	Standard Cost Per Unit
Direct material (.8 gallons × $2.50)	$2.00
Direct labor (.125 hours × $12)	1.50
Manufacturing overhead	.75
Total	$4.25

Actual demand during the year is somewhat greater than anticipated, necessitating production of 1,000,000 gallons. Frosty uses 809,000 gallons of material, costing $2.72 per gallon, to produce the 1,000,000 gallons of ice cream. Frosty incurs actual direct labor costs of $1,573,000 for 130,000 actual hours. Thus, the actual wage rate is $12.10 per hour ($1,573,000 ÷ 130,000). Finally, Frosty incurs actual overhead costs of $680,000.

At this point, you should attempt to calculate the standard cost variances for the Frosty Ice Cream Company data. For your convenience in working through the example and in solving problems at the end of the chapter, a summary of the variance formulas is presented in Illustration 26-4. Some key figures needed in the calculation of the variances for Frosty Ice Cream Company are summarized in Illustration 26-5.

CHAPTER 26 STANDARD COSTS AND VARIANCE ANALYSIS

ILLUSTRATION 26-4 Standard Cost Variance Formulas

$$\text{Material Price Variance} = \left(\text{Standard Price per Unit of Material} - \text{Actual Price per Unit of Material}\right) \times \text{Actual Quantity of Material Used}$$

$$\text{Material Quantity Variance} = \left(\text{Standard Quantity of Material Allowed for the Number of Units Produced} - \text{Actual Quantity of Material Used}\right) \times \text{Standard Price}$$

$$\text{Labor Rate Variance} = (\text{Standard Wage Rate} - \text{Actual Wage Rate}) \times \text{Actual Number of Labor Hours Worked}$$

$$\text{Labor Efficiency Variance} = \left(\text{Standard Labor Hours Allowed for the Number of Units Produced} - \text{Actual Number of Labor Hours Worked}\right) \times \text{Standard Wage Rate}$$

$$\text{Overhead Volume Variance} = \text{Overhead Applied to Production at Standard} - \text{Flexible Budget Amount of Overhead}$$

$$\text{Controllable Overhead Variance} = \text{Flexible Budget Amount of Overhead} - \text{Actual Overhead Cost}$$

ILLUSTRATION 26-5 Summary of Data for Production of 1,000,000 Gallons of Ice Cream

	Standard Cost Information	Actual Cost Information
Direct material	800,000 gallons x $2.50 per gallon	809,000 gallons x $2.72 per gallon
Direct labor	125,000 hours x $12 per hour	130,000 hours x $12.10 per hour
Overhead:		
Applied at standard	$.75 x 1,000,000 gallons	
Flexible budget	$450,000 + ($.25 x 1,000,000 gallons)	
Actual		$680,000

Material Variances

The standard price of material is $2.50 per gallon, and the actual price is $2.72 per gallon. The actual quantity of material used is 809,000 gallons. Thus, the material price variance is:

$$\$177{,}980 \text{ Unfavorable} = (\$2.50 - \$2.72) \times 809{,}000$$

Since 1,000,000 gallons of ice cream were produced and the standard quantity of material per gallon is .8 gallons, the standard quantity of material for the total units produced is 800,000 gallons. The actual quantity used is 809,000 gallons, and the standard price is $2.50 per gallon. Thus, the material quantity variance is:

$$\$22{,}500 \text{ Unfavorable} = (800{,}000 - 809{,}000) \times \$2.50$$

Reconciliation of Material Variances

Total Variance

Standard cost for 1,000,000 units (800,000 gallons x $2.50 per gallon)	$2,000,000
Actual cost (809,000 gallons x $2.72 per gallon)	2,200,480
Excess of actual over standard cost	$ (200,480) Unfavorable

Material Price Variance

Paid $.22 more per gallon on all 809,000 gallons used	$(177,980) Unfavorable

Material Quantity Variance

Used an extra 9,000 gallons at standard price of $2.50 per gallon	(22,500) Unfavorable
Total of material price and quantity variances	$(200,480) Unfavorable

Note that the material variances support the plant manager's contention that the large material variance was not due to wasting materials. Of the total $200,480 unfavorable variance, only $22,500 is due to using more material than planned. Most of the variance is due to paying more per gallon for raw material than planned.

Labor Variances

The standard wage rate is $12.00 per hour, and the actual wage rate is $12.10 per hour. Since 130,000 actual hours are worked, the labor rate variance is:

$$\$13,000 \text{ Unfavorable} = (\$12.00 - \$12.10) \times 130,000$$

The standard quantity of labor for the 1,000,000 gallons produced is 125,000 hours (1,000,000 gallons x .125 hours per gallon). The actual quantity of labor is 130,000 hours, and the standard wage rate is $12.00 per hour. Thus, the labor efficiency variance is:

$$\$60,000 \text{ Unfavorable} = (125,000 - 130,000) \times \$12.00$$

Reconciliation of Labor Variances

Total Variance

Standard cost for 1,000,000 gallons (125,000 hours x $12)	$1,500,000
Actual cost (130,000 hours x $12.10 per hour)	1,573,000
Excess of actual over standard cost	$ (73,000) Unfavorable

Labor Rate Variance

Paid $.10 more per hour on all 130,000 actual hours	$(13,000) Unfavorable

Labor Efficiency Variance

Used an extra 5,000 hours at standard rate of $12 per hour	(60,000) Unfavorable
Total of labor efficiency and rate variances	$(73,000) Unfavorable

Overhead Variances

The amount of overhead applied to production equals the standard overhead rate of $.75 per gallon times the 1,000,000 gallons produced. This amounts to $750,000. The flexible budget amount of overhead is $700,000 (i.e, $450,000 + $.25 x 1,000,000 gallons). The difference between the amount of overhead applied and the flexible budget amount of overhead is the overhead volume variance.

$$\$50,000 \text{ Favorable} = \$750,000 - \$700,000$$

The flexible budget amount of overhead for 1,000,000 gallons is $700,000, while the actual amount of overhead is $680,000. Thus, the controllable overhead variance is:

$$\$20,000 \text{ Favorable} = \$700,000 - \$680,000$$

Reconciliation of Overhead Variances

Total Variance

Standard overhead applied (1,000,000 gallons x $.75 per gallon)	$750,000	
Actual overhead cost	680,000	
Excess of standard over actual cost	$ 70,000	Favorable

Overhead Volume Variance

Applied overhead (1,000,000 gallons x $.75 per gallon)	$750,000	
Flexible budget overhead ($450,000 + $.25 per gallon x 1,000,000 gallons)	700,000	$50,000 Favorable

Controllable Overhead Variance

Flexible budget overhead ($450,000 + $.25 per gallon x 1,000,000 gallons)	$700,000	
Actual overhead	680,000	20,000 Favorable
Total of overhead volume and controllable overhead variances		$70,000 Favorable

INVESTIGATION OF STANDARD COST VARIANCES

All of the standard cost variances computed in the preceding comprehensive example are presented in Illustration 26-6.

ILLUSTRATION 26-6 Variance Summary

Frosty Ice Cream Company
Variance Summary
For the Period Ended December 31, 19X1

Material price variance	$(177,980)	Unfavorable
Material quantity variance	(22,500)	Unfavorable
Labor rate variance	(13,000)	Unfavorable
Labor efficiency variance	(60,000)	Unfavorable
Overhead volume variance	50,000	Favorable
Controllable overhead variance	20,000	Favorable
Total	$(203,480)	Unfavorable

Standard cost variances do not provide definitive evidence that costs are "in or out of control" or that managers are performing effectively or ineffectively. Rather, they should be viewed as indicators of *potential* problem areas. Whether costs are being effectively controlled can only be determined by investigating the facts behind the variances. For example, as indicated in Illustration 26-6, there is a $177,980 unfavorable material price variance. Does this imply that the purchasing department is not doing a good job of searching for the lowest cost material consistent with desired quality levels? Not necessarily. Subsequent investigation may reveal that unavoidable price increases have taken place. Obviously, there is not much the purchasing department can do if all suppliers increase their prices.

As another example, consider the $60,000 unfavorable labor efficiency variance indicated in Illustration 26-6. What factors might account for this unfavorable variance? The first logical explanation may be that the manager responsible for supervising the production work force has not done a competent job. However, this is just one possibility. Perhaps workers went on strike and Frosty had to hire inexperienced substitutes. These substitutes would have a difficult time meeting standard allowable production times even if they were properly supervised. Another possibility is that Frosty may have placed a new piece of equipment into production during the period. Workers may simply require additional time to become familiar with the new equipment. Which of these, or other possible explanations, is correct can only be determined by an investigation to determine the real cause of the variance.

Management by Exception

LO 5 Discuss how the management by exception approach is applied to investigate standard cost variances.

Since investigation of standard cost variances is itself a costly activity, management must decide which variances to investigate. Most managers take a **management by exception** approach and investigate only those variances they deem are exceptional. Of course, this implies that managers must develop some criteria for determining what is meant by "exceptional." The absolute dollar value of the variance or the variance as a percent of actual or standard is often used as a criterion. Suppose Frosty Ice Cream Company decides to investigate any variance in excess of $40,000. This implies that Frosty should investigate the material price, labor efficiency, and overhead volume variances. However, the cause of the overhead volume variance is quite obvious—more units were produced than anticipated when Frosty developed its standard overhead rate. Thus, management need only investigate the material price and labor efficiency variances.

"Favorable" Variances May Be Unfavorable

The fact that a variance is "favorable" does not mean it should not be investigated. Indeed, a favorable variance may be indicative of poor management decisions. For example, suppose the price of raw materials increases. To avoid an unfavorable material price variance, a manager could order the purchase of cheap, inferior materials. This could generate a favorable material price variance if the price of the inferior goods is less than the standard price of materials. However, the inferior materials may result in undetected product defects and cause the company to lose its reputation as a high-quality producer. If the defects are detected, items would be scrapped or "reworked." This would lead to an unfavorable material quantity variance since the company would use additional materials to replace or rework defective items.

INSIGHTS INTO ETHICS

Bill Clayton is the CEO of Textile Products, Inc. At the end of last quarter, he received a performance report that listed the material, labor, and overhead variances of each of the company's ten production facilities. Bill wrote congratulatory memos to the seven plant managers whose reports indicated large favorable variances. He wrote negative memos to the three plant managers whose reports indicated large unfavorable variances, and he plans to reduce their annual bonuses. Bill doesn't believe in letting managers comment on their variances. As he explained to his assistant, Steve Olson, "If I ask them to explain the variances, the plant managers always find an excuse as to why their costs are so high. I don't want excuses. I want good cost control."

Does Bill have an ethical responsibility to allow the plant managers to explain why variances are unfavorable? Is Bill's policy a good business practice?

RESPONSIBILITY ACCOUNTING AND VARIANCES

As noted previously, the central idea of responsibility accounting is that managers should only be held responsible for costs they can control. The implication for variances is that managers and workers should only be held responsible for variances they can control. Thus, a supervisor who can control material usage but has no control over the price paid for materials should be held responsible for the material quantity variance but not for the material price variance. The purchasing agent responsible for buying material at the lowest price consistent with quality considerations should be held responsible for the price variance.

RECORDING STANDARD COSTS IN ACCOUNTS

LO 6
Record standard costs in a manufacturing firm's accounts.

Manufacturing companies use standard costing systems to control their operations and to determine product costs. We have previously illustrated the calculation of standard cost variances and discussed how managers can use them to evaluate operations. In this section, we illustrate how a manufacturing company records product costs at standard in its accounts. In a standard costing system, the costs a company adds to the work in process inventory, finished goods inventory, and cost of goods sold accounts are all recorded at standard rather than actual cost. In the process of recording inventory at standard cost, variances also are calculated and recorded for management's use in performance evaluation. As a concrete example, we will present the entries for recording material, labor, and manufacturing overhead using the information presented for Frosty Ice Cream Company. (See Illustration 26-5.)

Recording Material Costs

Frosty Ice Cream Company used 809,000 gallons of material in production. The material cost $2.72 per gallon, or $2,200,480 in total. The standard quantity of material was 800,000 gallons. At the standard price of $2.50 per gallon, the standard material cost is $2,000,000. Frosty records the standard amount as a debit in Work in Process Inventory; the actual amount is recorded as a credit in Raw Materials Inventory. The difference between the debit and the credit is due to the material quantity variance and the material price variance. Variance accounts are temporary cost accounts and are always closed before a company prepares its financial statements. We demonstrate the closing process below. Note that in this example, both the material price and material quantity variances are unfavorable and are recorded as debits. Unfavorable variances are associated with increases in a company's expenses and have debit balances like expense accounts. Favorable variances are associated with reductions in a company's expenses and have credit balances.

(Date)	Work in Process Inventory	2,000,000	
	Material Price Variance	177,980	
	Material Quantity Variance	22,500	
	Raw Materials Inventory		2,200,480
	To record material cost.		

Recording Labor Cost

During the year, 130,000 actual labor hours are worked at a rate of $12.10 per hour or a total cost of $1,573,000. The standard number of hours is 125,000 and the standard wage rate is $12 per hour. Thus, the total standard cost of labor Frosty must add to Work in Process Inventory is $1,500,000. The difference between the total actual labor cost payable and the total standard labor cost assigned to Work in Process Inventory equals the labor rate and labor efficiency variances.

(Date)	Work in Process Inventory	1,500,000	
	Labor Rate Variance	13,000	
	Labor Efficiency Variance	60,000	
	Wages and Salaries Payable		1,573,000
	To record labor cost.		

Recording Manufacturing Overhead

Recording manufacturing overhead in a standard costing system is a three-step process. First, a company records actual overhead in the Manufacturing Overhead account. Second, it applies overhead to Work in Process Inventory at the standard cost. Third, the company closes the difference between actual overhead and overhead applied at standard and identifies overhead variances. These three steps are illustrated below.

Frosty incurs actual overhead during the year of $680,000. Frosty would credit various accounts (e.g., Wages and Salaries Payable, Utilities Payable, and Accumulated Depreciation) to record this amount, and it would debit the actual cost of overhead in the manufacturing overhead account.

(Date)	Manufacturing Overhead	680,000	
	Various Accounts		680,000
	To record actual overhead cost.		

Frosty assigns to Work in Process Inventory the standard cost of overhead, which is equal to the standard overhead rate times the number of units produced. In the example, this amounts to $750,000 (i.e., 1,000,000 gallons x $.75 per gallon). When Frosty applies this amount to Work in Process Inventory, it reduces Manufacturing Overhead by the same amount.

(Date)	Work in Process Inventory	750,000	
	Manufacturing Overhead		750,000
	To apply overhead cost to inventory at standard.		

At this point, Frosty has debited Manufacturing Overhead for the actual amount of overhead and has credited it for the amount of overhead applied to Work in Process Inventory at the standard overhead rate. The difference between the actual overhead cost and the standard overhead applied to inventory ($70,000) equals the sum of the overhead volume and controllable overhead variances. These two variances are identified when Frosty records the journal entry to close Manufacturing Overhead.

(Date)	Manufacturing Overhead	70,000	
	Overhead Volume Variance		50,000
	Controllable Overhead Variance		20,000
	To close Manufacturing Overhead and record overhead variances.		

Recording Finished Goods

At this point, Work in Process Inventory contains the following costs:

Raw material	$2,000,000
Direct labor	1,500,000
Overhead	750,000
Total	$4,250,000

The total of $4,250,000 equals the 1,000,000 gallons produced at a standard cost per gallon of $4.25. When the units are completed, Frosty transfers the cost from Work in Process Inventory to Finished Goods Inventory.

(Date)	Finished Goods Inventory	4,250,000	
	Work in Process Inventory		4,250,000
	To record completed units in Finished Goods Inventory.		

Recording Cost of Goods Sold

When it sells units, Frosty reduces the Finished Goods Inventory and increases Cost of Goods Sold by the standard cost of the units sold. Assume Frosty sells all 1,000,000 gallons of ice cream produced. The standard cost is $4.25 per gallon. Therefore, Frosty's entry to record the cost of goods sold is:

(Date)	Cost of Goods Sold	4,250,000	
	Finished Goods Inventory		4,250,000
	To record cost of goods sold.		

CLOSING VARIANCE ACCOUNTS

At the end of the accounting period, a company must close its temporary variance accounts. As a practical matter, this is usually accomplished by debiting or crediting the variances to Cost of Goods Sold. Before closing the variance accounts, a company records Cost of Goods Sold at standard cost. Thus, closing the variances results in the account being adjusted to approximately actual cost. It would be more accurate to adjust Work in Process Inventory and Finished Goods Inventory (as well as Cost of Goods Sold) to actual cost by allocating part of the total variance to these accounts. However, unless the variances are material and the balances in Work in Process Inventory and Finished Goods Inventory are large relative to Cost of Goods Sold, closing the total variance to Cost of Goods Sold is convenient and not misleading. For Frosty Ice Cream, there is no Work in Process or Finished Goods Inventory at the end of the year. (It sold all of the ice cream produced.) Therefore, it closes the variances to Cost of Goods Sold.

Frosty's journal entry to close the variance accounts is as follows. Note that a favorable variance reduces the amount of Cost of Goods Sold, while an unfavorable variance increases the account.

(Date)	Cost of Goods Sold	203,480	
	Overhead Volume Variance	50,000	
	Controllable Overhead Variance	20,000	
	Material Price Variance		177,980
	Material Quantity Variance		22,500
	Labor Rate Variance		13,000
	Labor Efficiency Variance		60,000
	To close variance accounts to Cost of Goods Sold.		

SUMMARY

Explain how standard costs are developed. Standard costs are developed in a variety of ways. Engineering studies may determine standard material quantities. Companies may use supplier price lists to determine standard prices of materials and time and motion studies to determine standard labor hours.

Calculate and interpret variances for direct material. The total material variance can be divided into material price and material quantity variances.

Calculate and interpret variances for direct labor. The total labor variance can be divided into labor rate and labor efficiency variances.

Calculate and interpret variances for manufacturing overhead. The total overhead variance can be divided into overhead volume and controllable overhead variances.

Discuss how the management by exception approach is applied to investigate standard cost variances. Since investigation of variances is costly, managers only investigate exceptional variances. Variances that are large in absolute dollar value or as a percent of actual or standard cost are generally considered exceptional.

Record standard costs in a manufacturing firm's accounts. Journal entries are required to record material, labor, and overhead at standard cost. At the end of the accounting period, a firm must record a journal entry to close the variance accounts to Cost of Goods Sold.

REVIEW PROBLEM

The Long Company uses a standard cost system. The standard cost for producing one unit of finished goods is:

Materials (2 lbs. @ $2.25)	$ 4.50
Direct labor (0.5 hours @ $8.00)	4.00
Standard overhead	10.00
Total standard cost per unit	$18.50

The flexible budget amount of variable overhead is $5.50 per unit and the fixed overhead per year is $90,000. Expected production is 20,000 units. During 19X1, Long Company produced 21,000 units. The costs incurred for production in 19X1 are:

Materials (43,000 lbs @ $2.20)	$ 94,600
Direct labor (10,300 hours @ $8.05)	82,915
Actual overhead	208,000
Total cost	$385,515

REQUIRED:

a. Calculate the material variances.
b. Calculate the labor variances.
c. Calculate the overhead variances.
d. Prepare a variance summary.
e. Prepare the journal entries for 19X1.

SOLUTION:

Planning and Organizing Your Work

1. Insert the actual and standard cost information into the formulas for variances given in Illustration 26-4.
2. List each of the variances in a variance summary.
3. Record journal entries using a standard cost system.

(a) *Calculate the material variances.*

Material price variance = ($2.25 − $2.20) x 43,000 = $2,150 Favorable
Material quantity variance = (42,000[1] − 43,000) x $2.25 = $2,250 Unfavorable

[1] 21,000 units x 2 lbs. per unit

(b) *Calculate the labor variances.*

Labor rate variance = ($8.00 − $8.05) x 10,300 = $ 515 Unfavorable
Labor efficiency variance = (10,500[2] − 10,300) x $8.00 = $1,600 Favorable

[2] 21,000 units x 0.5 hours per unit

(c) *Calculate the overhead variances.*

Controllable overhead variance = $205,500[3] − $208,000 = $2,500 Unfavorable
Overhead volume variance = $210,000[4] − $205,500 = $4,500 Favorable

[3] $90,000 + ($5.50 x 21,000)
[4] $10 x 21,000

(d) *Prepare a variance summary.*

Long Company
Variance Summary
For the Year Ended December 31, 19X1

Material price variance	$2,150	Favorable
Material quantity variance	(2,250)	Unfavorable
Labor rate variance	(515)	Unfavorable
Labor efficiency variance	1,600	Favorable
Controllable overhead variance	(2,500)	Unfavorable
Overhead volume variance	4,500	Favorable
Total	$2,985	Favorable

(e) *Prepare the journal entries.*

Work in Process (42,000 x $2.25)	94,500	
Material Quantity Variance	2,250	
Material Price Variance		2,150
Raw Materials		94,600
To record material variances and the use of materials in production.		
Work in Process (10,500 x $8.00)	84,000	
Labor Rate Variance	515	
Labor Efficiency Variance		1,600
Wages and Salaries Payable		82,915
To record labor variances and the use of labor in production.		

Manufacturing Overhead	208,000	
Various Accounts		208,000
To record actual overhead cost.		
Work in Process Inventory	210,000	
Manufacturing Overhead		210,000
To apply overhead cost to inventory at standard.		
Manufacturing Overhead	2,000	
Controllable Overhead Variance	2,500	
Overhead Volume Variance		4,500
To close manufacturing overhead and record overhead variance.		
Material Price Variance	2,150	
Labor Efficiency Variance	1,600	
Overhead Volume Variance	4,500	
Material Quantity Variance		2,250
Labor Rate Variance		515
Controllable Overhead Variance		2,500
Cost of Goods Sold		2,985
To close the variance accounts.		

KEY TERMS

attainable standards, *1055*
controllable overhead variance, *1061*
ideal standards, *1055*
labor efficiency variance, *1058*
labor rate variance, *1058*
management by exception, *1066*
material price variance, *1057*
material quantity variance, *1057*
overhead volume variance, *1059*
standard cost, *1054*
standard cost variance, *1056*

SELF-QUIZ

LO 1 1. What is the primary benefit of a standard costing system?
    a. It records costs at what should have been incurred.
    b. It allows the comparison of differences between actual and standard costs.
    c. It is easy to implement.
    d. It is inexpensive and easy to use.

LO 1 2. Which of the following is *not* a way to develop a standard cost?
    a. By using a fixed rate that is higher every period.
    b. By performing time and motion studies.
    c. By analyzing past data.
    d. By using what is specified in engineering plans.

LO 2 3. The total material variance can be divided into a material _____ variance and a material _____ variance.

LO 2 4. Which statement below correctly describes an unfavorable material price variance?

a. Too much material was purchased.
b. Too much was paid for material used in production compared to the standard cost.
c. More material was used than called for by the standard.
d. Less material was used than called for by the standard.

LO 3 5. True or False? The labor rate variance is equal to the difference between the standard wage rate and the actual wage rate times the standard number of labor hours worked.

LO 3 6. What does a favorable labor efficiency variance mean?
a. Labor rates were higher than called for by the standard.
b. Inexperience labor was used causing the rate to be lower than standard.
c. More labor was used than called for by the standard.
d. Less labor was used than called for by the standard.

LO 4 7. What does an unfavorable overhead volume variance mean?
a. Overhead costs are out of control.
b. Overhead costs are in control.
c. Production was greater than anticipated.
d. Production was less than anticipated.

LO 4 8. State the formula for calculating the controllable overhead variance.

LO 5 9. True or False? Standard cost variances provide definitive evidence that costs are "out of control" and managers are not performing effectively.

LO 5 10. True or False? A favorable variance may be indicative of poor management decisions.

LO 6 11. For a standard cost accounting system, a journal entry must be made at the end of the accounting period to close the variance accounts to _____ __ _____ _____.

SOLUTIONS TO SELF-QUIZ
1. b   2. a   3. price, quantity   4. b   5. false   6. d   7. d   8. Flexible budget amount of overhead − Actual overhead cost   9. false   10. true   11. Cost of Goods Sold

---

QUESTIONS

Q26-1 What role do standard costs play in a business?

Q26-2 What is the difference between a budgeted cost and a standard cost?

Q26-3 How could the standard quantity of material be developed?

Q26-4 What is the difference between an ideal standard and an attainable standard?

Q26-5 What is the meaning of an unfavorable material quantity variance?

Q26-6 What action should management take if there is a large unfavorable variance?

Q26-7 What factors should be considered when investigating variances?

Q26-8 What is management by exception?

Q26-9 What is the central idea of responsibility accounting as it relates to variances?

Q26-10 What are the alternative methods to close variance accounts?

EXERCISES

LO 2

E26-1 Calculating Material Variances Crown Company produced 1300 rings during March 19X1. The standard cost of each ounce of gold used in the rings is $400 per ounce. The standard quantity of material for each ring is one-half ounce of gold per ring. The cost incurred for March production was $266,625 at $395 per ounce. Determine the material price variance and the material quantity variance for March 19X1. Indicate whether each variance is favorable or unfavorable.

LO 3

E26-2 Calculating Labor Variances Texas Electronics produced 1,428,000 calculators during August 19X2. The standard cost of each direct labor hour is $7.00 and the standard output is 80 calculators per labor hour. The cost incurred for August production was $137,088 for 19,040 actual direct labor hours. Determine the labor rate variance and the labor efficiency variance for August 19X2. Indicate whether each variance is favorable or unfavorable.

LO 2,3

E26-3 Calculating Material and Labor Variances J. A. Bootery uses a standard costing system. The standard cost for producing each pair of boots is as follows:

Materials (1.5 yards @ $9.00) $13.50
Direct labor (0.5 hours @ $7.00)   3.50

During May 19X3, Bootery company produced 7,000 pairs of boots. The material and labor costs incurred during May are $96,250 and $26,790, respectively. The actual cost of material was $8.75 per yard. During May there were 3,800 direct labor hours worked. Calculate all material and labor variances.

LO 4

E26-4 Calculating Overhead Variances Aquapit Company produced 15,200 aquariums during 19X4. The flexible budget amount of variable overhead is $8.50 per unit and the fixed overhead per year is $59,200. Expected production is 16,000 aquariums. Actual overhead incurred is $186,200. Determine the overhead volume variance and the controllable overhead variance.

LO 3,4

E26-5 Calculating Labor and Overhead Variances At the start of 19X1, U.S.A. Threads determined its standard labor cost to be $5.50 per hour. The budget for variable overhead was $6.00 per unit and budgeted fixed overhead was $135,000 for the year. Expected production was 30,000 units. During 19X1, the actual cost of labor was $5.75. U.S.A. Threads produced 32,500 units requiring 52,000 direct labor hours. Actual overhead for the year was $326,800. Determine labor and overhead variances.

LO 2,6

E26-6 Calculating Material Variances and Recording Material Costs Leahnka Company produced 2,200 cabinets during May 19X6. Leahnka uses a standard costing system. The standard cost of wood used in the cabinets is $25 per linear foot. The standard quantity of material for each cabinet is 30 linear feet. The cost incurred for March production was $1,601,600 at $26 per foot. Determine the material price variance, the material quantity variance, and record all necessary journal entries for May 19X6.

LO 6

E26-7 Recording Labor Variances LapTop Company uses a standard costing system. During 19X7, 93,280 actual labor hours were worked at a rate of $11.75 per hour. The standard number of hours is 94,000 and the standard wage rate is $11.90 per hour. Prepare the journal entry to record labor cost during 19X7.

LO 6

E26-8 Recording Manufacturing Overhead Krell Cosmetics uses a standard costing system. During 19X8, Krell incurred actual overhead of $381,000. The standard overhead rate is $2.25 per unit and 180,000 units were produced in 19X8. One-third of the total overhead variance is attributed to the volume variance and the remainder is attributed to the controllable overhead variance. Prepare the journal entries to record overhead.

LO 6

E26-9 Closing Variance Accounts The variance summary for Reasonable Facsimile is as follows:

Reasonable Facsimile
Variance Summary
For the Year Ended December 31, 19X9

Material price variance	$ 4,150	Favorable
Material quantity variance	(3,250)	Unfavorable
Labor rate variance	115	Favorable
Labor efficiency variance	(2,600)	Unfavorable
Controllable overhead variance	(2,500)	Unfavorable
Overhead volume variance	(4,500)	Unfavorable
Total	$(8,585)	Unfavorable

Close the variance accounts presented for Reasonable Facsimile.

PROBLEM SET A

LO 1,2,3,4

P26-1A Calculating Material, Labor, and Overhead Variances The Short Company uses a standard costing system. The standards per unit produced for material and labor are 0.5 gallons and 1.5 hours, respectively. The standard cost per gallon of material is $6.50. The standard cost per hour for labor is $9.00. Overhead is applied at the rate of $10.50 per unit. Expected production is 15,000 units with fixed overhead per year of $30,000 and variable overhead of $8.50 per unit. Total overhead at expected production is $157,500. During 19X1, 17,500 units of finished goods were produced. The cost of 9,100 gallons of material used was $59,605. The cost of direct labor incurred in 19X1 was $229,643.75 based on an average wage rate of $9.05 per hour. Actual overhead for 19X1 was $169,750.

REQUIRED:

a. Determine the standard cost per unit.
b. Calculate and reconcile material variances.
c. Calculate and reconcile labor variances.
d. Calculate and reconcile overhead variances.

LO 2,3

P26-2A Calculating Material and Labor Variances With Missing Information Barnes Corporation produces bottles of liquid fertilizer. Partial information for June 19X2 is as follows:

Standard material per bottle	3 liters
Standard cost of material per liter	$0.40
Standard labor hours per bottle	0.2 hours
Actual production for June	10,000 bottles
Total material cost for June	$12,390
Total liters used in production	29,500
Material price variance	$590 Unfavorable
Total labor cost for June	$12,980
Actual cost per labor hour	$5.90
Labor rate variance	$220 Favorable

REQUIRED:

Determine the following:

a. Actual cost of material per liter.
b. Total standard liters of material for actual production.
c. Material quantity variance.

d. Total standard material cost for actual production.
e. Labor hours worked.
f. Standard cost per labor hour.
g. Labor efficiency variance.
h. Total standard labor cost for actual production.

LO 1

P26-3A **Determining Standard Costs** Computochair manufactures special chairs for use by data input personnel. They have decided to initiate a standard cost system to help improve planning and control. The president of the company assigned the task of developing standards to the company controller and the plant engineer. They came up with the following estimates:

Amount per Chair	Average Amount	Best Amount
Steel	1.5 lbs. @ $6.30	1.2 lbs. @ $5.95
Fabric	2.5 yds. @ $9.50	2.1 yds. @ $9.20
Direct labor	1.2 hrs. @ $7.50	1.0 hrs. @ $7.45
Variable overhead	$11.52	$9.40

In addition, the controller and engineer determined that fixed overhead has averaged $49,680 per year in the past and the lowest amount of fixed overhead incurred was $40,500. Expected production is 18,000 chairs per year. The company controller believes that the standard should be set using the average amounts whereas the plant engineer believes that they should be set at the best amounts. In a meeting with the controller and the plant engineer, the president decided to set the standard at the midpoint between the average and the best amount.

REQUIRED:

a. Determine the controller's standard cost per unit.
b. Determine the plant engineer's standard cost per unit.
c. Determine the president's standard cost per unit.

LO 3,4

P26-4A **Calculating Labor Variances With Missing Information** Noble Corporation produces dental crowns. Partial information for 19X4 is as follows:

	Labor
Actual cost	$208,950
Actual cost per hour	$10.50
Standard cost per hour	?
Total standard hours	?
Total actual hours	?
Labor rate variance	$9,950 Favorable
Labor efficiency variance	$9,900 Unfavorable
Standard hours per crown	?

REQUIRED:

Determine the unknown amounts listed as "?" in the information provided.

LO 2,3,4,5

P26-5A **Comprehensive Variance Problem** The VanPro Company uses a standard costing system. The standards per unit produced for material and labor are 3.5 pounds and 0.5 hours, respectively. The standard cost per pound of material is $3.50. The standard cost per hour of labor is $7.50. Standard overhead is $3.15 per unit. For 19X5, expected production is 104,000 units wih fixed overhead of $91,000 per year and variable overhead of $2.275 per unit. During 19X5, 99,000 units of finished goods were produced. The total cost of material used was $1,222,650 with each pound costing $3.25. The cost of direct labor incurred in 19X5 was $403,072 based on an average wage rate of $7.52 per hour. Actual overhead for 19X5 was $299,750.

REQUIRED:

a. Determine the standard cost per unit.
b. Calculate the material, labor, and overhead variances.
c. Prepare a variance summary.
d. Prepare journal entries for 19X5 including the closing entry.

PROBLEM SET B

LO 1,2,3,4

P26-1B Calculating Material, Labor, and Overhead Variances The Lopez Company uses a standard costing system. The standards per unit produced for material and labor are 0.25 gallons and 0.75 hours, respectively. The standard cost per gallon of material is $11.60. The standard cost per hour for labor is $7.40. Overhead is applied at a rate of $13.20 per unit. Expected production is 20,000 units with fixed overhead per year of $70,000 and variable overhead of $3.10 per unit. The total overhead at expected production is $132,000. During 19X6, 21,500 units of finished goods were produced. The cost of 5,600 gallons of material used was $65,520. The cost of direct labor incurred in 19X6 was $116,070 based on an average wage rate of $7.30 per hour. Actual overhead for 19X6 was $139,750.

REQUIRED:

a. Determine the standard cost per unit.
b. Calculate and reconcile material variances.
c. Calculate and reconcile labor variances.
d. Calculate and reconcile overhead variances.

LO 2,3

P26-2B Calculating Material and Labor Variances With Missing Information Loren Corporation produces economy size bottles of bath oil. Partial information for June 19X6 is as follows:

Standard material per bottle	3 liters
Standard cost of material per liter	$0.80
Standard labor hours per bottle	0.2 hours
Actual production for June	10,000 bottles
Total actual material cost for June	$24,780
Total liters of material used in production	29,500
Material price variance	$1,180 Unfavorable
Total labor cost for June	$6,490
Actual labor cost per labor hour	$2.95
Labor rate variance	$110 Favorable

REQUIRED:

Determine the following:

a. Actual cost of material per liter.
b. Total standard liters for actual production.
c. Material quantity variance.
d. Total standard material cost for actual production.
e. Labor hours worked.
f. Standard cost per labor hour.
g. Labor efficiency variance.
h. Total standard labor cost for actual production.

LO 1

P26-3B Determining Standard Costs Quiver International manufactures archery bows. They have decided to initiate a standard costing system to help improve planning and control.

The president of the company assigned the task of developing standards to the company controller and the plant engineer. They came up with the following estimates:

Amount per Bow	Average Amount	Best Amount
Wood	1.4 ft. @ $9.25	1.1 ft. @ $8.90
Aluminum	0.6 lbs. @ $7.50	0.5 lbs. @ $7.40
Direct Labor	2.4 hrs. @ $9.50	2.1 hrs. @ $9.45
Variable Overhead	$21.12	$17.85

In addition, the controller and engineer determined that fixed overhead has averaged $74,880 per year in the past and the lowest amount of fixed overhead incurred was $63,882. Expected production is 7,800 bows per year. The company controller believes that the standard should be set using the average amounts whereas the plant engineer believes that they should be set at the best amounts. In a meeting with the controller and the plant engineer, the president decided to set the standard at the midpoint of the average and the best amount.

REQUIRED:

a. Determine the controller's standard cost per unit.
b. Determine the plant engineer's standard cost per unit.
c. Determine the president's standard cost per unit.

LO 3,4

P26-4B **Calculating Labor Variances With Missing Information** Wheelie Corporation produces bicycles. Partial information for 19X8 is as follows:

	Labor
Actual cost	$313,425
Actual cost per hour	?
Standard cost per hour	?
Total standard hours	?
Total actual hours	29,850
Labor rate variance	$14,925 Favorable
Labor efficiency variance	$14,850 Unfavorable
Standard hours per bicycle	?

REQUIRED:

Determine the unknown amounts listed as "?" in the information provided.

LO 1,2,3,4,6

P26-5B **Comprehensive Variance Problem** The Manahawkin Company uses a standard costing system. The standards per unit produced for material and labor are 10.5 pounds and 1.5 hours, respectively. The standard cost per pound of material is $2.50. The standard cost per hour for labor is $7.60. Standard overhead is $9.00 per unit. For 19X9, expected production is 312,000 units with fixed overhead per year of $624,000 and variable overhead of $7.00 per unit. The total overhead at expected production is $2,808,000. During 19X9, 297,000 units of finished goods were produced. The total cost of material used was $8,030,880 with each pound costing $2.60. The cost of direct labor incurred in 19X9 was $3,704,778 based on an average wage rate of $7.56 per hour. Actual overhead for 19X9 was $2,799,250.

REQUIRED:

a. Determine the standard cost per unit.
b. Calculate the material, labor, and overhead variances.
c. Prepare a variance summary.
d. Prepare journal entries for 19X9 including the closing entry.

CRITICAL THINKING AND COMMUNICATING

C26-1 The Griffin Company manufactures bumper stickers. During the past four months they have found that, on average, they have been able to manufacture the following number of bumper stickers per hour:

Month	Output
January	240
February	260
March	300
April	240
Average	260

Brenda Griffin, the plant engineer, said that if everyone did what they were supposed to do, 320 bumper stickers per hour could be produced and therefore the standard should be set at 320 per hour. John Lewis, the controller, said that the standard should be set at 295 units, whereas Michael Levy, the plant supervisor, suggested that the standard should be set at 260.

REQUIRED:

a. Determine the advantages of each position.
b. Select a standard that would best accomplish the purpose of motivation, control, and planning.

C26-2 Will Simmons, the chemical division controller for Gulf and Eastern Corporation, was reviewing the variance summary for the Southside Chemical Plant. The variance summary revealed a large favorable material price variance and large unfavorable material quantity and labor efficiency variances. All other variances were immaterial. Will Simmon's initial instinct was to request a large bonus for Al Putnam, the purchasing manager and to give no bonus to Patty Smith, the plant supervisor.

REQUIRED:

a. Determine if Will Simmons should act in accordance with his initial instincts.
b. What other procedures should Will Simmons perform before requesting bonuses?
c. Explain a scenario other than "good performance in purchasing and poor performance in manufacturing" that would lead to the same variances.

CHAPTER 27

Cost Information and Management Decisions

At the start of the year, the president of General Refrigeration Company asked his three plant managers to examine their operations and search for ways to cut costs and improve profitability. The president also promised substantial bonuses to managers who achieved cost savings in excess of $1,000,000.

Wendy Grant, manager of the plant in Tennessee, thought she had a sure-fire way to save money. Her plant manufactures refrigeration units used by food processors and retail food stores. One main component of the refrigeration units is a compressor. Wendy anticipates producing 50,000 compressors in the coming year at a cost per unit of $345. Concerned that General's production of compressors is not efficient, Wendy asked Dillard Compressor Corporation to bid on supplying the 50,000 units. After studying the specifications of the compressor, Dillard indicated it is willing to supply the compressors at $310 per unit.

"Look," Wendy explained to Ed Anderson, the plant accountant, "if we close the compressor operation and buy compressors from Dillard, we'll save about $1,750,000 a year! That kind of cost saving should really grab the president's attention."

Ed seemed skeptical. "Wendy, let's look at the costs of producing the compressors. More than $1,000,000 of the cost is depreciation on plant and equipment purchased years ago. Another $500,000 represents the salaries of production supervisors. I don't think all of those costs will go away just because we shut down the compressor operation and turn to an outside supplier. I think you better let me analyze the cost information in some detail before you make a recommendation."

Ed's point is well taken. Before making a decision, managers must gain a thorough understanding of relevant cost information.

Cost information is necessary for planning, evaluation, and for making *nonroutine decisions*. The primary emphasis in previous chapters has been on how manufacturing companies record cost information in their accounts (using job and process costing systems) and on how they use cost information to plan and evaluate operations (using budgets and standard costing systems). While several examples of using cost information for decision making have already been presented, this chapter presents a more complete analysis of how management uses cost information in making decisions. The decision situations covered are referred to as nonroutine decisions because they are *not* the type of decisions that managers face daily. Decisions involving making or buying a component or discontinuing a product are critical to a company's success, but they are not everyday occurrences. Careful consideration of the decision examples presented here should help you gain insight into the cost information needed to solve a number of important problems that managers confront.

LEARNING OBJECTIVES

1. Explain the role of differential costs and revenues in management decisions.
2. Define sunk cost, avoidable cost, and opportunity cost.
3. Explain why the contribution margin per unit of a constrained resource is more important than the contribution margin per unit produced when there are production constraints.
4. Discuss how managers use cost information for product pricing decisions.
5. Discuss the important role of qualitative considerations in management decisions.

DIFFERENTIAL COSTS AND REVENUES

LO 1 Explain the role of differential costs and revenues in management decisions.

All decisions involve a choice between two or more alternatives. Managers must identify which of the alternatives is best for their company. Many business decisions can be approached by comparing the alternatives in terms of their differential costs and revenues. As the name implies, **differential costs and revenues** are cost and revenue items that differ among alternatives. Differential costs are sometimes referred to as **relevant costs** because they are the only relevant cost items managers need to consider when analyzing decision alternatives. In evaluating differential costs and revenues, managers decide which alternative will have the most positive impact on company profitability. This approach, referred to as differential analysis, is demonstrated here for a variety of decision settings.

Additional Processing Decision

Occasionally, manufacturers must decide whether to sell a product in a partially completed stage or to incur additional processing costs required to complete the product. Dandy Electronics has decided to discontinue manufacturing its Model 250 computer. Currently, it has 5,000 partially completed units on hand. To date, the company has spent $800 per unit or $4,000,000 to bring the computers to their current stage of completion. The company estimates it will incur additional costs of $400 per unit to complete the computers.

Dandy Electronics
Costs of Model 250 Computer

	Costs Per Unit Incurred to Date	Costs Per Unit to Complete
Material	$300	$200
Labor	200	100
Variable overhead	100	100
Fixed overhead	200	
	$800	$400

Because the company has announced that the Model 250 will be discontinued, the price of the computer has fallen. If the units are completed, they can be sold for only $1,000 per unit, which is less than the $1,200 per unit ($800 cost to date plus $400 of additional cost) total cost of producing the computers. On the other hand, a rival computer company is willing to buy the partially completed units for $500 per unit.

Which action should Dandy take? Should it sell computers in their current state of completion or should it incur the additional processing costs? Without a thorough understanding of accounting information and differential analysis, a manager at Dandy Electronics might conclude that further processing is not appropriate. After all, with further processing, total costs will amount to $1,200 per unit, which is more than the selling price of $1,000 per unit. The error of this analysis is revealed by analyzing the problem in terms of differential costs and revenues. The differential analysis is presented in Illustration 27-1. Compared to selling the units in their current state, revenue from selling completed units will be $500 more per unit. Since the costs of completing the units is only $400 more per unit, the company is better off by $100 per unit if it completes the computers. The differential analysis indicates that the $800 per unit costs incurred to date are not relevant to the further processing decision. Whether Dandy sells the units "as is" or processes them further, the costs incurred to date will not change.

Sunk Costs. Costs incurred in the past are irrelevant to present and future decisions and are referred to as **sunk costs**. Sunk costs are not differential costs because they do not differ among decision alternatives. Because Dandy incurred the expenditures in the past to bring the Model 250 computers to their current state of completion, these costs cannot be reversed. Thus, they have no economic relevance to decisions affecting future periods.

Make or Buy Decisions

Most manufactured goods have numerous components. In some cases, a company may purchase one or more of the components from another company. This may lead to considerable savings if the outside supplier is particularly efficient at manufacturing the component and can offer it at a reasonable price. Two decision alternatives are presented in this situation: either make or buy the component. No differential revenues are involved. Therefore, to analyze this decision, managers concentrate solely on differential costs.

ILLUSTRATION 27-1 Differential Analysis of Further Processing Decision

Dandy Electronics
Differential Analysis of Further Processing

	Sell in Current State of Completion	Complete Processing	Differential Revenues and Costs
Revenue	$500	$1,000	$500
Less prior production costs:			
Material	$300	$300	$0
Labor	200	200	0
Variable overhead	100	100	0
Fixed overhead	200	200	0
Total	$800	$800	$0
	$(300)	$200	$500
Less additional processing costs:			
Material	$0	$200	$200
Labor	0	100	100
Variable overhead	0	100	100
Total	$0	$400	$400
Gain (loss) per unit	$(300)	$(200)	$100

Recall that Wendy Grant, manager of the Tennessee plant of General Refrigeration Company, is considering Dillard Compressor Corporation's offer to supply 50,000 compressors at $310 per unit. Last year, when her plant produced 50,000 compressors, the company incurred the following costs:

General Refrigeration Company
Cost of Manufacturing 50,000 Compressors

Variable costs:	
Direct material ($100 per unit)	$ 5,000,000
Direct labor ($120 per unit)	6,000,000
Variable overhead ($80 per unit)	4,000,000
Total variable costs	$15,000,000
Fixed costs:	
Depreciation of building	$ 600,000
Depreciation of equipment	800,000
Supervisory salaries	500,000
Other	350,000
Total fixed costs	$ 2,250,000
Total costs	$17,250,000

Additional analysis reveals the following: (1) The market value of the machinery used to produce the compressors is approximately zero. (2) Five of the seven production supervisors will be fired if General discontinues production of compressors. However, two of the supervisors, who each has more than ten years of service, are protected by a clause in their union contract. They will be reassigned to other duties although their services will not really be needed. Their salaries total $110,000.

At first, you might assume that General should buy the compressors rather than manufacture the units internally. After all, the company can buy the units for $310 each while the cost of manufacturing them is $345 each (i.e., $17,250,000 ÷ 50,000 units). However, careful consideration of the differential costs reveals that it is cheaper to manufacture the compressors internally.

As indicated in Illustration 27-2, General will incur none of the $15,000,000 of variable manufacturing costs if it purchases the compressors outside the company. Thus, this is a differential cost between the two alternatives. However, the fixed costs associated with depreciation on the building and equipment do not represent a cost savings. General incurred the costs of purchasing the building and the pieces of equipment in prior periods. Remember: The approach to analyzing decisions requires consideration of only the differential revenues and costs of decision alternatives. The sunk costs related to purchasing the building and the pieces of equipment are not differential costs because General has already incurred them and they will not change, no matter what decision alternative General selects. The example assumes that fixed costs classified as "other" are also irrelevant sunk costs.

Avoidable Costs. Not all fixed costs are irrelevant sunk costs. Some fixed costs are **avoidable costs** or costs that can be avoided if a company takes a particular action. If General purchases the compressors outside the company, it will save the salaries of five production supervisors. This totals $390,000 (total supervisory salaries of $500,000 less the $110,00 that must still be paid to supervisors with seniority). Supervisory salaries of $390,000 is an avoidable cost. That is, General will no longer incur this cost if it purchases the compressors outside the company. Avoidable costs are also differential costs.

While General can eliminate $15,000,000 of variable costs and $390,000 of fixed costs if it purchases the compressors from Dillard Compressor Corporation, this cost savings of $15,390,000 is exceeded by the $15,500,000 cost of purchasing the compressors from Dillard (50,000 units x $310). In total, General would be $110,000 worse off if it decided to buy rather than to make the compressors.

ILLUSTRATION 27-2 Differential Analysis of Make or Buy Decision

General Refrigeration Company
Differential Cost Analysis

	Cost of Manufacturing 50,000 Compressors	Cost of Buying 50,000 Compressors	Differential Costs
Variable costs:			
Direct material	$ 5,000,000	$ 0	$ 5,000,000
Direct labor	6,000,000	0	6,000,000
Variable overhead	4,000,000	0	4,000,000
Total variable cost	$15,000,000	$ 0	$15,000,000
Fixed costs:			
Depreciation of building	$ 600,000	$ 600,000	$ 0
Depreciation of equipment	800,000	800,000	0
Supervisory salaries	500,000	110,000	390,000
Other	350,000	350,000	0
Total fixed costs	$ 2,250,000	$ 1,860,000	$ 390,000
Cost of buying compressors	0	15,500,000	(15,500,000)
Total costs	$17,250,000	$17,360,000	$ (110,000)

In Illustration 27-2, we present a three-column approach to differential analysis. The first two columns present the costs of the two alternatives, while the third column presents the differential costs. However, once the concept of differential analysis is understood, it is easier to present the analysis in a single-column format that concentrates only on the differential costs. A single-column analysis of the make or buy decision that General Refrigeration Company faces is presented in Illustration 27-3.

As indicated, it will cost General $15,500,000 to buy the units outside. However, the company will only save $15,390,000 of internal manufacturing costs if it purchases the compressors. General will not incur the $15,000,000 of variable manufacturing costs if it purchases the compressors; thus, this item represents a major cost saving. However, the only fixed cost savings is the $390,000 of supervisory salary, which is avoidable if General purchases the compressors. Because the cost of buying the compressors exceeds the cost savings by $110,000, it appears the company should continue manufacturing the compressors. Before reaching a final decision, General should also consider qualitative factors, which we discuss later.

ILLUSTRATION 27-3 Single-Column Format for Differential Analysis

General Refrigeration Company Differential Cost Analysis		
Cost of buying compressors outside (50,000 units x $310)		$15,500,000
Cost savings (avoidable if purchase compressors outside):		
Variable costs	$15,000,000	
Supervisory salaries (salaries of 5 of 7 supervisors)	390,000	15,390,000
Excess cost of buying compressors outside		$ 110,000

Opportunity Costs. **Opportunity costs** are the values of benefits foregone by selecting one decision alternative over another. For example, if you choose to purchase a $1,000 stereo system rather than investing in a certificate of deposit (CD), the potential interest that you could have earned on the CD is an opportunity cost associated with buying the stereo. Since opportunity costs differ,

INSIGHTS INTO ACCOUNTING

"MAKE VERSUS BUY" DECISIONS FACING BANKS

To gain cost savings, many manufacturing companies buy components from outside suppliers rather than making them internally. Smart car companies don't make steel, glass, or radios anymore. And, smart bankers are following the lead of auto and other manufacturers. They critically evaluate whether they can outsource processing operations. For bankers, it's not a "make or buy" decision—it's a "purchase outside or process internally" decision. Some services that banks may decide to purchase outside include building management, security, check processing, data processing, and printing.

Source: Charles H. Nobs, "Tracking the True Costs of Outsourcing." *The American Banker* (September 2, 1992), p. 4.

depending on which decision alternative is selected, they are also differential costs and are relevant in evaluating decision alternatives.

The opportunity cost concept can also be illustrated using the General Refrigeration example. Suppose the Tennessee plant is currently spending $500,000 per year to rent space for manufacturing metal shelving units that are used in the refrigeration units. If it discontinues production of compressors, the company will move the shelving operation to space currently occupied by the compressor operation. Thus, an opportunity cost of continuing to produce the compressors is the $500,000 in rent savings that is foregone. If General considers this opportunity cost, then the analysis presented in Illustration 27-4 indicates that purchasing the compressors outside is the best alternative because it results in a net $390,000 annual cost savings to the firm.

ILLUSTRATION 27-4 Make or Buy Analysis With Opportunity Costs Considered

General Refrigeration Company Differential Cost Analysis		
Cost of buying compressors outside (50,000 units x $310)		$15,500,000
Cost savings (avoidable if purchase compressors outside):		
Variable costs	$15,000,000	
Supervisory salaries (salaries of 5 of 7 supervisors)	390,000	
Opportunity cost of using the plant to produce compressors (foregone rent savings)	500,000	$15,890,000
Net savings resulting from buying the compressors outside		$ 390,000

Dropping a Product Line

Dropping a product line is a very significant decision and one that receives a great deal of attention. The proper approach to analyzing the problem is to calculate the change in income that will result if the company drops the product line. If income will increase, the company should drop the product line. If income will decrease, the company should keep the product line. This amounts to comparing the differential costs and revenues that result from dropping the product line.

Magnolia Hardware has three product lines: Tools, Hardware Supplies, and Garden Supplies. Illustration 27-5 presents a product line income statement for the prior year. To arrive at net income for each product line, both direct and allocated fixed costs are deducted from each product line's contribution margin. Direct fixed costs are fixed costs that are directly traceable to a product line. For example, the salary of a worker who spends 100% of his or her time working in the tool section of the hardware store would be a direct fixed cost to the Tools product line. Allocated fixed costs are those fixed costs that are not directly traceable to an individual product line. These costs are also referred to as **common costs** because a company incurs them for the common benefit of all product lines. An example of an allocated fixed cost would be the salary of the owner/manager of the hardware store. Magnolia Hardware allocates common fixed costs to product lines based on their relative sales revenues. Thus, of the

$80,000 of common costs, 43.373% (i.e., $180,000 tool sales ÷ $415,000 total sales) or $34,699 is allocated to Tools.

ILLUSTRATION 27-5 Product Line Income Statement for Magnolia Hardware

	Magnolia Hardware			
	Product Line Income Statement			
	For the Year Ended December 31, 19X1			
	Tools	Hardware Supplies	Garden Supplies	Total
Sales	$180,000	$160,000	$75,000	$415,000
Cost of goods sold	108,000	90,000	60,000	258,000
Gross margin	$ 72,000	$ 70,000	$15,000	$157,000
Other variable costs	2,000	4,000	1,000	7,000
Contribution margin	$ 70,000	$ 66,000	$14,000	$150,000
Direct fixed costs	$ 8,000	$ 5,000	$ 3,500	$ 16,500
Allocated fixed costs	34,699	30,843	14,458	80,000
Total fixed costs	$ 42,699	$ 35,843	$17,958	$ 96,500
Net income	$ 27,301	$ 30,157	$(3,958)	$ 53,500

The owner of Magnolia Hardware observes that the Garden Supplies line is currently showing a loss of $3,958. Would dropping this product line increase the profitability of the hardware store? To answer this question, we turn again to differential analysis. As indicated in Illustration 27-6, sales revenue will decline by $75,000 if Magnolia drops Garden Supplies. However, some costs will decrease or be eliminated altogether. Cost of goods sold will decrease by

ILLUSTRATION 27-6 Analysis of Dropping a Product Line

	Income With Garden Supplies				Income Without Garden Supplies			Difference[3]
	Tools	Hardware Supplies	Garden Supplies	Total	Tools	Hardware Supplies	Total	
Sales	$180,000	$160,000	$75,000	$415,000	$180,000	$160,000	$340,000	$(75,000)
Cost of goods sold	108,000	90,000	60,000	258,000	108,000	90,000	198,000	60,000
Gross margin	$ 72,000	$ 70,000	$15,000	$157,000	$ 72,000	$ 70,000	$142,000	$(15,000)
Other variable costs	2,000	4,000	1,000	7,000	2,000	4,000	6,000	1,000
Contribution margin	$ 70,000	$ 66,000	$14,000	$150,000	$ 70,000	$ 66,000	$136,000	$(14,000)
Direct fixed costs	$ 8,000	$ 5,000	$ 3,500	$ 16,500	$ 8,000	$ 5,000	$ 13,000	$ 3,500
Allocated fixed costs	34,699	30,843[1]	14,458[1]	80,000	42,353[2]	37,647[2]	80,000	0
Total fixed costs	$ 42,699	$ 35,843	$17,958	$ 96,500	$ 50,353	$ 42,647	$ 93,000	$ 3,500
Net income	$ 27,301	$ 30,157	$ (3,958)	$ 53,500	$ 19,647	$ 23,353	$ 43,000	$(10,500)

[1]Allocation of common costs based on percentage of total sales with Garden Supplies
($180,000 ÷ $415,000) x $80,000 = $34,699
($160,000 ÷ $415,000) x $80,000 = $30,843
($75,000 ÷ $415,000) x $80,000 = $14,458
[2]Allocation of common costs ased on percentage of total sales without Garden Supplies
($180,000 ÷ $340,000) x $80,000 = $42,353
($160,000 ÷ $340,000) x $80,000 = $37,647
[3]Differences with a favorable effect are reported as positive numbers. Differences with an unfavorable effect are shown in parentheses.

$60,000, and other variable costs will decrease by $1,000. These variable costs can be avoided by dropping the Garden Supplies product line. Whether the direct fixed costs will decrease depends on the nature of these costs.

For purposes of this example, assume that the direct fixed costs of $3,500 for Garden Supplies represents the salary paid a part-time employee. If Magnolia drops the Garden Supplies product line, this employee will not be retained. In this case, the direct fixed costs of $3,500 are avoidable and represent a cost savings achieved by dropping Garden Supplies. Allocated fixed costs are generally not avoidable and, thus, Magnolia achieves no cost savings with respect to the $14,458 of fixed costs allocated to Garden Supplies. For example, one component of the allocated fixed costs is rent of the hardware store. The rent will not decrease simply because one product line is eliminated. Another allocated fixed cost is electricity. This cost is also not likely to decrease if Magnolia drops Garden Supplies since the store still needs approximately the same amount of heat and light. Rather than being eliminated, the share of fixed costs allocated to Tools and Hardware Supplies will simply increase if the company drops Garden Supplies.

To summarize, the analysis of differential costs and revenues indicates that Magnolia will lose income of $10,500 if it drops Garden Supplies.

Differential Analysis Dropping Garden Supplies	
Lost revenue	$(75,000)
Cost savings:	
Cost of goods sold	$ 60,000
Other variable costs	1,000
Direct fixed costs	3,500
Total cost savings	$ 64,500
Net loss from dropping	$(10,500)

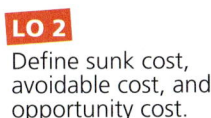

LO 2
Define sunk cost, avoidable cost, and opportunity cost.

SUMMARY OF DIFFERENTIAL, AVOIDABLE, SUNK, AND OPPORTUNITY COSTS

We have used a number of costs terms in this chapter; in this section, we briefly summarize them. Recall that the basic approach to decision making is to analyze the costs and revenues that differ among decision alternatives. These items are referred to as *differential* or *relevant* costs and revenues. Costs that can be *avoided* by taking a particular course of action are always differential costs and, therefore, relevant to the analysis of a decision. Costs that are *sunk*, (i.e., already incurred and not reversible) are never differential costs since they do not differ among the decision alternatives. Therefore, they are not relevant in making a decision.

Students of managerial accounting often assume that fixed costs are equivalent to sunk costs and irrelevant (i.e., they are not differential costs). This is not always the case. Fixed costs may be sunk and, therefore, irrelevant; or they may not be sunk but still be irrelevant. Finally, fixed costs may not be sunk but relevant. Examples of these three possibilities are presented in Illustration 27-6.

ILLUSTRATION 27-6 Fixed Costs and Decision Relevance

Fixed Costs	Classification
Depreciation on equipment already purchased	Sunk and irrelevant (not differential)
President's salary, which will not change for both Action A and Action B	Not sunk but still irrelevant (not differential)
Salary of supervisor who will be retained if Action A is taken and fired if Action B is taken	Not sunk and relevant (differential)

When making a decision, managers must consider *opportunity costs*. Opportunity costs represent the benefit foregone by selecting a particular decision alternative. To illustrate opportunity costs, consider the Magnolia Hardware example. In this example, the company considers dropping its Garden Supplies product line. Suppose that if Magnolia drops Garden Supplies, it can devote more space to selling tools. Sales of tools will increase, and the contribution margin associated with Tools will increase by $15,000. In this case, Magnolia has a $15,000 opportunity cost associated with its decision to keep the Garden Supplies product line. Considering this opportunity cost would make dropping the product line desirable rather than undesirable. Recall that our previous analysis indicated a $10,500 decrease in income from dropping the product line. However, considering the $15,000 opportunity cost representing forfeiture of tools sales, it appears that Magnolia will be better off by $4,500 (i.e., $15,000 − $10,500) if it drops Garden Supplies.

DECISIONS INVOLVING PRODUCTION CONSTRAINTS

LO 3 Explain why the contribution margin per unit of a constrained resource is more important than the contribution margin per unit produced when there are production constraints.

For products with a positive contribution margin (i.e., the selling price is greater than the variable cost of the product), a company would like to produce and sell as many units as possible. The reason is that company income increases with the sale of each unit. However, in most cases, there are limits or constraints on the number of items a company can produce. The number of hours of machine time available to produce an item may be limited by the number of machines a company has. Or, a company may have a limited number of skilled workers—at least in the short run. If a company faces production constraints, then how many units should it produce? If only one product is involved, the

INSIGHTS INTO ETHICS

Pat Smith, president of Regal Apparel, is considering closing a plant in Michigan that manufactures cotton uniforms (one of Regal's major product lines). Regal can purchase the uniforms from a firm in Korea at a cost savings of $2,000,000 per year. However, closing the plant will put 200 employees out of work in an area that already has substantial unemployment.

Does Smith have an ethical responsibility to consider the hardship imposed on employees from a plant closure? What is Smith's ethical responsibility to shareholders who will lose $2,000,000 per year if the plant is not closed?

answer is to produce as many units as allowed by the constraint. However, if more than one product is involved, the analysis becomes more complicated.

Consider a company that produces two products (Products A and B) that have the following selling prices and production costs per unit:

	Product A	Product B
Selling price	$100	$80
Variable costs	50	60
Contribution margin	$ 50	$20

Suppose 10 machine hours are needed to produce each unit of Product A, 2 machine hours are needed to produce each unit of Product B, and 1,000 machine hours are available. Which product should the company concentrate on producing? At first, it may appear that Product A should be produced because it has the higher contribution margin per unit. However, since production of Product A requires much more machine time than does Product B, fewer units of A can be produced. In fact, if just Product A is produced, the company can produce only 100 units in total (1,000 hours ÷ 10 hours per unit). The company's contribution margin will be $5,000 (i.e., $50 per unit x 100 units). On the other hand, with 1,000 available machine hours, the company can produce 500 units of Product B. Product B's contribution margin is $20 per unit, and if just Product B is produced, the company's contribution margin will be $10,000. Thus, the company is much better off producing the product with the smaller contribution margin per unit because it uses much less of the constrained resource (machine hours).

To decide which product to produce, one can perform a differential total contribution margin analysis. However, the same result is obtained by calculating the *contribution margin per unit of the constrained resource*. Product A's contribution margin is $50 per unit. However, each unit requires 10 hours of machine time (the constrained resource). Therefore, the contribution margin per unit of the constrained resource is $5. On the other hand, Product B's contribution margin is $20 per unit. However, since each unit only requires 2 hours of machine time, the contribution margin per unit of the constrained resource is $10. Multiplying the contribution margin per unit of the constrained resource by the amount of the resource available yields the available contribution margin. Thus, producing the product with the largest contribution per unit of the constrained resource ensures that the company will maximize total contribution margin and income.

	Product A	Product B
Selling price	$ 100	$ 80
Variable costs	50	60
Contribution margin	$ 50	$ 20
Machine hours per unit	÷ 10	÷ 2
Contribution margin per machine hour	$ 5	$ 10
Available machine hours	x 1,000	x 1,000
Feasible contribution margin	$ 5,000	$10,000

LO 4
Discuss how managers use cost information for product pricing decisions.

PRICING DECISIONS

Pricing decisions play a very important role in a company's success. If products are priced either too low or too high, the company may not maximize income or may sustain significant losses. While setting appropriate prices is a crucial business activity, the process of price setting is quite complex; most managers consider it to be more of an art than a science. Economic theory suggests an approach to pricing that requires knowledge of the relationship between price and the quantity demanded (the so-called "demand function"). However, estimating demand functions with reasonable accuracy can be very difficult.

Full Cost Pricing

Recognizing the difficulty of estimating demand functions, many companies have turned to so-called cost-based pricing approaches. With a cost-based approach, companies mark up an estimate of cost to a price that allows a reasonable level of profit. When the cost marked up is the full cost of an item (including fixed and variable cost), the approach is referred to as **full cost pricing**. To illustrate full cost pricing, suppose Ajax Pump Company produces three different models of fuel pumps: Model A, Model B, and Model C. The company's approach to pricing is to mark up the standard full cost of each pump by 30%. As indicated in Illustration 27-7, the full cost of the Model A pump is $100. With a 30% markup, the selling price is $130.

ILLUSTRATION 27-7 The Full Cost Pricing Approach

	Model A	Model B	Model C
Standard variable costs:			
Direct labor	$ 10.00	$ 20.00	$ 35.00
Direct material	20.00	25.00	40.00
Variable overhead ($2 per $1 of direct labor)	20.00	40.00	70.00
Total variable costs	$ 50.00	$ 85.00	$145.00
Standard fixed costs ($5 per $1 of direct labor)	50.00	100.00	175.00
Total production cost	$100.00	$185.00	$320.00
Profit markup (30% of total cost)	30.00	55.50	96.00
Selling price	$130.00	$240.50	$416.00

The obvious advantage of a full cost pricing approach is that it is simple to apply. Also, if a sufficient quantity can be sold at the specified price, the company will earn a reasonable profit. However, the approach has an obvious limitation. What markup percent should a company use? Is 30% an appropriate markup, or should a company use 10%, 20%, or 40%? Determination of an appropriate markup requires considerable judgment and experimentation with different markups before a company can make a final decision.

Contribution Approach to Pricing

A further problem with the full cost approach to pricing is that it focuses managers' attention on the full cost of production. Companies that use full cost pricing generally believe that no product should be sold for a price less than full cost. However, in some circumstances, the companies may benefit from charging a price that is less than full cost. This is often the case when companies face special orders from customers. If the products under consideration are somewhat unique or the customers' markets are different from the companies' normal markets, then companies need not charge the "normal" prices of the products.

Quality Lens Company manufacturers camera lenses. Their lenses are sold through camera shops with a variety of mounting adapters to fit most popular 35 millimeter cameras. Recently, Kanic Camera Company has asked them to produce 20,000 lenses for their compact 35 millimeter camera. The lens is identical to the Model A lens that Quality currently sells for $85. However, the model to be produced for Kanic will substitute the Kanic name for the Quality name stamped on the lens.

In the past year, Quality sold 280,000 units of the Model A. However, the company has been operating at only 75% of normal productive capacity and can easily accommodate production of the 20,000 additional units. The standard cost of producing Model A is $75.

Model A Standard Unit Cost	
Direct material	$30.00
Direct labor	15.00
Variable overhead	10.00
Fixed overhead	20.00
Total	$75.00

Kanic Camera Company has offered to buy the 20,000 lenses for $73 each. Since the total standard cost is $75, it appears that Quality should turn down the special order. However, the differential analysis presented in Illustration 27-8 indicates that the special order will make a substantial contribution to company income.

ILLUSTRATION 27-8 Analysis of Special Order

Differential Revenues and Costs of Special Order		
Differential revenue (20,000 × $73)		$1,460,000
Less differential costs:		
Direct material (20,000 × $30)	$600,000	
Direct labor (20,000 × $15)	300,000	
Variable overhead (20,000 × $10)	200,000	
		1,100,000
Net benefit of special order		$ 360,000

The special order decision presents two alternatives: either accept or reject the special order. Since the income from the main business is the same under both alternatives, it is not *differential*, and Quality need not consider this in the decision. The most obvious differential item is the revenue associated with the special order. If Quality accepts the order, its revenue will increase by $1,460,000. In addition, direct material, direct labor, and variable overhead will increase by $1,100,000 if Quality accepts the special order. These costs are differential. They will be incurred if Quality accepts the special order, and not incurred if Quality rejects it. Since the differential revenues exceed the differential costs by $360,000, it appears to be quite beneficial to accept the special order.

Note that in the calculation of the net benefit of accepting the special order, none of the fixed costs of production are considered as differential costs. This is because these costs will be incurred whether or not Quality accepts the special order. This assumption seems reasonable given that Quality Lens Company has excess capacity. However, suppose the management of Quality anticipates some increase in fixed costs if it accepts the special order. By how much could fixed costs increase before acceptance of the special order would not be advisable? As long as fixed costs increase by less than $360,000, the excess of differential revenues over differential costs, acceptance of the special order will increase company income.

The **contribution approach** to pricing basically suggests that a company should accept any order as long as it has a positive contribution margin. Acceptance of the special order would be consistent with the contribution approach. Kanic Camera Company offered $73 for each lens, while the variable cost is only $55. Thus, at a price of $73, each lens has an $18 contribution margin. Opponents of this approach argue that no company can stay in business unless it sells its products at a price greater than the full cost of production, including some share of fixed overhead. The contribution approach, they suggest, will lead to prices that are too low to sustain the business.

As you probably suspect, some validity exists for both full cost and contribution margin approaches to pricing. Obviously, companies need to charge prices that in the *long run* are greater than their total costs, including fixed costs. However, it is equally true that in some cases a company will be better off selling a product in the *short run* for less than its full cost as long as the price yields a positive contribution toward covering fixed costs. Probably the best approach is to make sure that a company does not implement any full cost pricing formula too rigidly. If sales are lagging or if special orders are received and a company has excess capacity, then management must consider the contribution margin that will be achieved with various prices. Also, it is important to remember that cost is just half of the product pricing equation. Demand is the other half. Thus a company should not set prices based only on a consideration of cost. Managers also need to consider the prices that competitors charge and the quantities consumers will demand at various prices.

QUALITATIVE CONSIDERATION IN DECISION ANALYSIS

LO 5
Discuss the important role of qualitative considerations in management decisions.

The solutions to the problems presented have concentrated on the *quantitative* features of the decision situations. In particular, we have concentrated on quantitative differences in costs and revenues among decision alternatives. However, most important problems have one or more features that are very difficult, if not impossible, to quantify. These *qualitative* aspects must receive the same careful attention as do the quantitative components.

The importance of qualitative considerations can be illustrated in the context of the make or buy decision discussed earlier. Recall that General Refrigeration Company was considering whether to continue producing compressors or to purchase them from another firm. Our analysis in Illustration 27-3 indicated that it would cost General $110,000 more to buy the compressors from an outside supplier. However, our analysis only considered the easily quantifiable differences in costs between the two decision alternatives. In addition, qualitative benefits and costs are associated with using an outside supplier.

Perhaps the primary benefit of using an outside supplier is that the adverse effect of a downturn in business is less severe. Suppose there is a temporary downturn in the demand for refrigeration units. In this case, General can simply order fewer compressors from its outside supplier, thus avoiding a major cost. On the other hand, if General continues to manufacture the compressors and a temporary downturn in business is experienced, it will have more difficulty eliminating some of the fixed costs associated with manufacturing the compressors. For example, the company probably could not eliminate the fixed costs of the supervisor's salary if the downturn was thought to be only temporary. Experienced supervisors are difficult to find, and they cannot be hired and fired based on temporary fluctuations in business.

Using an outside supplier also leads to a loss of control over the production process. Purchased items may not be of sufficiently high quality and delivery schedules may not be honored. The outside supplier may also believe it has the company "over a barrel" (i.e., it would be too costly to restart an internal operation), and may raise prices significantly in the future. Also, if a company decides to purchase a component outside, employee morale may suffer if the reduction in productive activity results in employees being fired or transferred. The cost to the firm of reduced morale is difficult to quantify, but it may have a significant effect on the quantity and quality of the products the remaining employees produce.

SUMMARY

Explain the role of differential costs and revenues in management decisions. Decisions involve a choice between two or more alternatives. Management can make the best decision by comparing alternatives in terms of the cost and revenue items that differ among them. These costs and revenues are referred to as differential costs and revenues.

Define sunk cost, avoidable cost, and opportunity cost. Costs that companies have incurred in the past are irrelevant to present and future decisions. These costs are referred to as sunk costs. Avoidable costs are those that companies can avoid by taking a particular action. The term opportunity costs refers to the benefits companies forfeit by selecting a particular decision alternative.

Explain why the contribution margin per unit of a constrained resource is more important than the contribution margin per unit produced when there are production constraints. When a production constraint exists, a company can earn the largest contribution margin by producing the product with the highest contribution margin per unit of the constrained resource.

Discuss how managers use cost information for product pricing decisions. Pricing products is one of the most important and challenging decisions businesses face. In practice, companies often use full cost pricing. With this approach, companies mark up the full cost of an item by a fixed profit percentage. This approach is simple to apply, but it is difficult to determine the appropriate profit percentage. The contribution approach to pricing recognizes that, in the short run, prices that are greater than variable cost will lead to increases in income. However, in the long run and if companies are to survive, they must sell products for amounts greater than their total costs (including fixed costs).

Discuss the important role of qualitative considerations in management decisions. When making decisions, management must consider a variety of qualitative factors (e.g., quality of goods, employee morale, and customer service). Qualitative factors are often even more important than costs and benefits which are easy to quantify.

REVIEW PROBLEM A

Clear Sounds manufactures compact disc players. During 19X0, Clear Sounds manufactured 5,000 players. In the past, Clear Sounds has manufactured the lasers that are an integral part of the players. In order to determine if it is efficient to manufacture their own lasers, they found out it would cost $61.50 to purchase each laser from an outside supplier. From past information, the following costs are associated with producing 5,000 units.

Clear Sounds
Cost of Manufacturing 5,000 Lasers

Variable costs:	
Direct material ($18.75 per unit)	$ 93,750
Direct labor ($8.30 per unit)	41,500
Variable overhead ($24.60 per unit)	123,000
Total variable costs	$258,250
Fixed costs:	
Insurance (lasers only)	$ 17,900
Depreciation of equipment (lasers only)	21,700
Engineer's salary (lasers only)	36,000
Miscellaneous administrative costs	8,700
Total fixed costs	$ 84,300
Total costs	$342,550

REQUIRED:

Prepare a differential cost analysis to determine if the lasers should be manufactured or purchased in 19X1.

SOLUTION:

Planning and Organizing Your Work
1. Determine the cost of buying lasers.
2. Determine the cost savings from buying the lasers for variable and fixed costs.
3. Subtract the cost savings from buying the lasers from the cost of buying the lasers.
4. If the result of step 3 is positive, purchase the lasers; if it is negative, produce the lasers.

Clear Sounds Differential Cost Analysis

Cost of buying lasers (5,000 x $61.50)		$307,500
Cost savings:		
Variable costs [5,000 x ($18.75 + $8.30 + $24.60)]	$258,250	
Engineers salary	36,000	
Insurance	17,900	312,150
Excess cost of producing lasers internally		$ 4,650

Therefore, Clear Sounds would be better off to buy the lasers from the outside. This ignores qualitative factors that may favor buying the lasers.

REVIEW PROBLEM B

Seaside Incorporated manufactures sailboards. Pricelow, a large discount chain, has offered to purchase 1,000 sailboards at a cost of $365 each as a one-time special purchase. The discount chain was willing to have their own logo on the sailboards. The standard cost of producing a sailboard is as follows:

Sailboard Standard Cost

Direct material	$168.00
Direct labor	57.50
Variable overhead	82.50
Fixed overhead	72.75
Total	$380.75

The cost of putting the Pricelow logo on the sailboard is estimated to be $13.00 per unit. Seaside Incorporated's current production is near capacity, making it necessary to rent additional equipment for $10,950. Also, overtime premiums of $121,460 will have to be paid in order to complete the special order.

REQUIRED:

Determine if Seaside Incorporated should accept the special order from Pricelow.

SOLUTION:

Planning and Organizing Your Work
1. Determine the differential revenue from the special order.
2. Determine the differential variable costs and fixed costs from the special order.
3. Subtract the differential costs from the differential revenue.
4. If the result of step 3 is positive, accept the special order; if it is negative, reject the special order.

Differential Revenue and Costs of Special Order

Differential revenue (5,000 x $365)		$1,825,000
Less differential costs:		
Direct material (5,000 x $168)	$840,000	
Direct labor (5,000 x $57.50)	287,500	
Variable overhead (5,000 x 72.75)	363,750	
Rental equipment	10,950	
Overtime premiums	121,460	1,623,660
Net benefit of special order		$ 201,340

Therefore, Seaside Incorporated should accept the special order from Pricelow unless there are qualitative factors that would change the decision.

KEY TERMS

avoidable costs, *1085*
common costs, *1087*
contribution approach, *1094*
differential costs and revenues, *1082*
full cost pricing, *1092*
opportunity costs, *1086*
relevant costs, *1082*
sunk costs, *1083*

SELF-QUIZ

LO 1 1. Differential costs are sometimes referred to as _____ costs.

LO 1
LO 2 2. Which of the following costs should not be taken into consideration when making a decision?
   a. Opportunity costs.
   b. Sunk costs.
   c. Relevant costs.
   d. Differential costs.

LO 1 3. Which of the following is often not a differential cost?
   a. Material.
   b. Labor.
   c. Variable overhead.
   d. Fixed overhead.

LO 4 4. True or False? For products with a positive contribution margin a company would like to produce and sell as many units as possible.

LO 4 5. When the cost marked up for pricing is the full cost of an item (including fixed and variable cost) the approach is referred to as _____ _____.

LO 4 6. True or False? Fixed costs of production may not be differential costs when accepting a special order.

LO 4 7. An approach to pricing known as the _____ approach basically suggests that any order should be accepted as long as it has a positive contribution margin.

LO 4 8. Which of the following should not be considered when accepting a special order?
   a. The contribution margin.
   b. The impact on the price regular customers are willing to pay.
   c. Available manufacturing capacity.
   d. Allocated common costs.

LO 5 9. Which of the following is not a qualitative benefit of using an outside supplier?
   a. The supplier lessens the impact of business downturns.
   b. A working relationship is established with the supplier that may prove useful in the future.
   c. There is more control over the production process and availability of components.
   d. There is greater flexibility to order the number of components needed.

LO 5 10. True or False? Qualitative aspects of a decision should receive the same careful attention as the quantitative components.

SOLUTIONS TO SELF-QUIZ
1. relevant 2. b 3. d 4. true 5. full cost pricing 6. true 7. contribution 8. d 9. c 10. true

QUESTIONS

Q27-1 What are differential costs and revenues?

Q27-2 Why are sunk costs irrelevant to present and future decisions?

Q27-3 What are avoidable costs?

Q27-4 Why are opportunity costs relevant when making decisions?

Q27-5 What is the proper approach to analyzing whether or not a product line should be dropped?

Q27-6 Give an example of a fixed cost that is not sunk but still irrelevant.

CHAPTER 27 COST INFORMATION AND MANAGEMENT DECISIONS

Q27-7 What factors other than cost should be considered in a product pricing decision?

Q27-8 What are the qualitative disadvantages of buying instead of making a component?

EXERCISES

LO 1,2

E27-1 Identification of Relevant Costs The Tisch Company manufactures tables. In the past, they produced their own metal angle brackets that were used in the production of tables. Char Reid, the chief financial officer of Tisch, initiated an investigation to determine if it may be cheaper to buy the part rather than to make it themselves. Identify which of the following items are relevant to her decision by stating that the item is relevant or irrelevant.

  a. The original cost of the bracket machine.
  b. The cost of buying the brackets.
  c. Variable factory overhead.
  d. Salvage value of the bracket machine.
  e. Space created from no longer manufacturing brackets.
  f. Material used in manufacturing brackets.
  g. The salary of the president of Tisch Company.
  h. Available capacity.
  i. The quality of the bracket manufactured.
  j. The quality of the bracket purchased.
  k. Fixed factory overhead.
  l. Shipping costs incurred in buying the bracket.
  m. Material and labor to manufacture the bracket.
  n. Depreciation on the bracket machine.
  o. A contract with the labor union.

LO 1,2

E27-2 Identification of Relevant Costs The Teller Company manufactures porcelain dinnerware along with other products. Don Lyon, the controller of Teller Company, wants to determine whether to drop the fancy dinnerware product line. Identify which of the following items are relevant to his decision.

  a. The original cost of the machinery used to manufacture the fancy dinnerware.
  b. The reduction in labor cost.
  c. Depreciation of the machinery used to manufacture the fancy dinnerware.
  d. The president's salary.
  e. The floor space used by the fancy dinnerware manufacturing equipment.
  f. The fancy dinnerware production manager's salary.
  g. Estimated salvage value of the fancy dinnerware manufacturing equipment.
  h. The cost of retraining personnel to use in another part of the company.
  i Material used in manufacturing the fancy dinnerware.
  j. Electricity used to manufacture the dinnerware.
  k. Fixed overhead allocated to fancy dinnerware.

LO 1

E27-3 Additional Processing Decision Electronic World has decided to discontinue manufacturing its Electronic Elite mobile telephone. Currently, the company has a number of partially completed phones on hand. To date, the company has spent $189 per unit to manufacture these phones. Another manufacturer is interested in purchasing the partially completed phones for $235 per unit. On the other hand, if Electronic World completes the phones, they can sell them for $495 per unit. To complete the mobile telephones, Electronic World will incur $30 of additional material, $55 of direct labor, $29 of variable overhead and $150 of allocated fixed overhead, all stated on a per unit basis. The allocated overhead relates primarily to depreciation of plant and equipment. Determine if Electronic World should complete the mobile telephones by preparing a differential analysis of further processing.

LO 1

E27-4 Make or Buy Decision Hot Dip Corporation produces whirlpool tubs for the home. In the past, Hot Dip manufactured their own pumps to power the water jets. Hot Dip has found that 40% of the pumps have burned out within the warranty period, causing them to incur large warranty costs. Because of the difficulty of manufacturing the pumps, Hot Dip investigated the possibility of purchasing the pumps from a reputable manufacturer rather than making the pumps themselves. The outside manufacturer agreed to pay any warranty costs caused by the pumps. It costs $83.75 to manufacture each pump which includes an allocation of $17.25 of fixed overhead. Also, Hot Dip has spent an average of $22.00 repairing each pump returned. Hot Dip can purchase pumps for $79.50, not including freight of $3.00 per pump. During 19X1, Hot Dip plans to sell 12,800 whirlpool tubs. Determine if Hot Dip should make or buy the pumps and the amount of cost savings of the best alternative by preparing a differential cost analysis.

LO 1,2

E27-5 Dropping a Product Line Computer Warehouse sells computer hardware and computer furniture. Because computer furniture requires a lot of floor space, the president of Computer Warehouse is considering discontinuing sales of computer furniture. The following monthly costs relate to operating the store.

Store rent	$2,100
Utilities	880
Insurance	320
Cleaning	250
Total	$3,550

The monthly costs are allocated by floor space. It was determined that 70% of cleaning costs and 10% of the insurance and utilities could be saved if the furniture line is discontinued. Also, $3,500 of additional hardware could be sold with a cost of goods sold of $1,400 if the furniture line is discontinued. In the past, $5,300 of furniture and $11,000 of hardware were sold per month with cost of goods sold of $2,915 and $4,400, respectively. Determine if Computer Warehouse should discontinue the furniture line and the financial benefit of the best alternative.

LO 3

E27-6 Production Constraints Power Vac produces two models of vacuum cleaners. It takes 3 machine hours to produce the regular model and 4 machine hours to produce the deluxe model. There is a total of 1,200 machine hours available. Determine the maximum feasible contribution margin for each model given the following price and cost data applicable to the two models.

	Regular Model	*Deluxe Model*
Selling price	$85.20	$125.00
Variable costs	61.50	99.00
Contribution margin	$23.70	$26.00

LO 5

E27-7 Full-Cost Pricing Garth Incorporated produces Globes and uses full cost pricing. Each globe has the following standard costs:

Direct material	$9.50
Direct labor	6.75
Variable overhead	8.85
Fixed cost	3.40

Determine the selling price if Garth desires a markup on full cost of: (a) 10%, (b) 25%, (c) 30%, and (d) 40%.

LO 4

E27-8 Special Orders Stuckie Manufacturing produces industrial glue. Each gallon of glue has the following standard cost:

Direct material	$ 3.50
Direct labor	1.25
Variable overhead	2.25
Fixed overhead	3.65
Total standard cost	$10.65

Box's unlimited has offered to purchase 5,000 gallons for $9.50 per gallon. Stuckie normally sells the glue for $14.25. Determine the net benefit or (loss) to Stuckie if the special order is accepted.

PROBLEM SET A

LO 1,2

P27-1A Complex Make or Buy Decision Breath-Away is a new mouthwash in a small spray container to be manufactured by Hy-Gene Corporation. The product will be sold to wholesalers and large drugstore chains in packages of 30 containers for $18.00 per package. Management allocates $200,000 of fixed production overhead costs to Breath-Away. The manufacturing cost per package of Breath-Away for expected production of 100,000 packages is:

Direct material per package	$ 6.50
Direct labor per package	3.50
Overhead per package (fixed and variable)	3.00
Total per package	$13.00

Hy-Gene has contacted packaging suppliers to determine if it would be better to buy the spray container rather than manufacture it. The lowest quote for the spray containers was $1.75 per 30 bottles. It is estimated that purchasing the sprayers from a supplier would save 10% of direct materials, 20% of direct labor, and 15% of variable overhead. Hy-Gene's manufacturing space is highly constrained. By purchasing the spray containers, Hy-Gene will not have to lease additional manufacturing space that is estimated to cost $15,000 per year. If the spray containers are purchased, Hy-Gene estimates that one supervisory position can be eliminated. Salary plus benefits for this position are $32,500 per year.

REQUIRED:

a. Calculate the variable overhead per package.
b. Prepare a differential cost analysis of the make or buy decision.
c. Should Hy-Gene make or buy the sprayer?

LO 1,2,3

P27-2A Additional Processing Decision With Production Constraints Mega Chemical produces Zilcron and a new and improved version called Flypex, along with other products. Flypex, which sells for $13.50 per gallon is manufactured from Zilcron plus additional ingredients. It takes 20 minutes to manufacture a gallon of Zilcron and an additional 10 minutes to manufacture a gallon of Flypex. Zilcron sells for $8.55 per gallon. The cost per gallon of manufacturing Zilcron and the additional costs to manufacture Flypex are as follows:

	Zilcron	*Additional Cost of Flypex*
Material	$2.25	$ .90
Labor	1.80	1.75
Variable overhead	2.60	1.10
Fixed overhead	1.75	3.95

Both products have been successful and demand for Zilcron and Flypex is strong. However, Mega's other products are also in demand and Mega is approaching full capacity. Since it takes longer to manufacture Flypex, the vice president of production is trying to determine if Flypex should continue to be manufactured.

REQUIRED:

Which product makes the largest contribution to company profit given a capacity constraint measured in terms of production time?

LO 1,2,3   P27-3A   **Dropping a Product Line**   Esoteric Electronics, a high-end consumer electronics specialist, has three product lines: audio, video, and laser discs. Common costs are allocated by percentage of sales. The income statement for Esoteric Electronics is as follows:

Esoteric Electronics
Product Line Income Statement
For the Year Ended December 31, 19X1

	Audio	Video	Laser Discs
Sales	$118,000	$96,000	$73,000
Cost of goods sold	70,800	52,800	60,100
Gross margin	$ 47,200	$43,200	$12,900
Other variable costs	2,500	3,100	1,100
Contribution margin	$ 44,700	$40,100	$11,800
Direct fixed costs	$ 4,200	$ 2,100	$ 2,600
Common fixed costs	17,700	14,400	10,950
Total fixed costs	$ 21,900	$16,500	13,550
Net income	$ 22,800	$23,600	$ (1,750)

Since the profit on laser discs is negative, the owner of Esoteric Electronics is considering discontinuing their sale.

REQUIRED:

a. Determine the impact on profit of dropping laser discs.
b. Discuss the potential qualitative effects of discontinuing the sale of laser discs.

LO 3   P27-4A   **Sales Mix With Constrained Resources**   Jeff Choi, the chief financial officer of Fibers Unlimited, is reviewing the profitability of the three products sold in the carpet division. The division manager prepared the following summary of the products.

	Economy	Standard	Deluxe
Selling price per yard	$9.50	$13.25	$19.00
Variable cost per yard	$5.00	$7.50	$9.25
Fixed cost per yard	$3.00	$4.00	$5.00
Yards produced annually	21,000	16,000	10,000
Total machine hours used	3,150	3,360	3,300

REQUIRED:

a. Calculate the number of machine hours required to produce each yard.
b. Determine the contribution margin per yard for each product.
c. Determine the contribution margin per machine hour for each product.
d. Suppose only 3,000 machine hours are available. Which product should be produced?

LO 3,4

P27-5A **Special Order with Production Constraints** Cheap Skates produces inexpensive ice skates which are primarily marketed through discount department stores and sporting goods stores. It takes 0.50 machine hours to manufacture each pair of skates. During the current year, the factory is expected to produce 45,000 pairs which entails the factory producing at 90% of capacity. The standard costs of a pair of skates are as follows:

Direct material (1.5 lbs x $4.00)	$ 6.00
Direct labor (0.4 hours x $6.00)	2.40
Variable overhead (0.4 hours x $9.00)	3.60
Fixed costs (0.4 hours x $11.00)	4.40
Total costs	$16.40

Ice Rinks of America offered Cheap Skate the one-time opportunity to sell them 4,500 pairs of skates at $12.00 per pair.

REQUIRED:

a. Calculate the impact the order will have on Cheap Skates' net income.
b. Determine if Cheap Skates should accept the special order if it were for 7,500 pairs of skates.

PROBLEM SET B

LO 1,2

P27-1B **Complex Make or Buy Decision** Goopy-Glue is a new non-toxic glue in a bottle to be manufactured by Stickum Corporation. The product will be sold to wholesalers and large hardware stores in packages of 25 bottles for $21.00 per package. Management has determined that $120,000 of fixed production overhead costs should be allocated to Goopy-Glue. The cost per package of Goopy-Glue for expected production of 80,000 packages is:

Direct material per package	$ 7.00
Direct labor per package	4.50
Overhead per package (fixed and variable)	4.00
Total per package	$15.50

Stickum has contacted packaging suppliers to determine if it would be better to buy the bottle rather than manufacture it. The lowest quote for the bottles was $2.85 per 25 bottles. It is estimated that purchasing the bottles from a supplier would save 15% of direct materials, 10% of direct labor, and 20% of variable overhead. Stickum's manufacturing space is highly constrained. By purchasing the bottles, Stickum will not have to lease additional manufacturing space that is estimated to cost $12,000 per year. If the bottles are purchased, Stickum estimates that two supervisory positions can be eliminated. Salary plus benefits for each position are $18,500 per year.

REQUIRED:

a. Calculate the variable overhead per package.
b. Prepare a differential cost analysis of the make or buy decision.
c. Determine if Stickum should make or buy the bottles.

LO 1,2,3

P27-2B **Additional Processing Decision With Production Constraints** Fiberific produces Nyloron and a new and improved version called Superon, along with other products. Superon, which sells for $10.80 per meter is manufactured from Nyloron plus additional ingredients. It takes 10 minutes to manufacture a meter of Nyloron and an additional 5 minutes to manufacture a meter of Superon. Nyloron sells for $6.80 per meter. The cost per meter of manufacturing Nyloron and the additional costs to manufacture Superon are as follows:

	Nyloron	Additional Cost of Superon
Material	$1.80	$0.70
Labor	1.44	1.40
Variable overhead	2.08	0.90
Fixed overhead	1.75	3.15

Both products have been successful and demand for Nyloron and Superon is strong. However, Fiberific's other products are also in demand and Fiberific is approaching full capacity. Since it takes longer to manufacture Superon, the vice president of production is trying to determine if Superon should continue to be manufactured.

REQUIRED:

Which product makes the largest contribution to company profit given a capacity constraint measured in terms of production time?

LO 1,2,3

P27-3B **Dropping a Product Line** Music Village has three product lines: records, compact discs, and cassettes. Common costs are allocated by percentage of sales. The income statement for Music Village is as follows:

Music Village
Product Line Income Statement
For the Year Ended December 31, 19X1

	Compact Discs	Cassettes	Records
Sales	$47,200	$38,400	$29,200
Cost of goods sold	27,800	22,600	23,100
Gross margin	$19,400	$15,800	$ 6,100
Other variable costs	1,500	1,300	700
Contribution margin	$17,900	$14,500	$ 5,400
Common fixed costs	$ 2,100	$ 2,100	$ 1,900
Allocated fixed costs	7,080	5,760	4,380
Total fixed costs	$ 9,180	$ 7,860	$ 6,280
Net income	$ 8,720	$ 6,640	$ (880)

Since the profit on records is negative, the owner of Music Village is considering discontinuing their sale.

REQUIRED:

a. Determine the impact on profit of dropping records.
b. Discuss the potential qualitative effects of discontinuing the sale of records.

LO 3

P27-4B **Sales Mix With Constrained Resources** Martha Lopez, the chief financial officer of Grasses Galore, is reviewing the profitability of the three products sold in the sod division. The division manager prepared the following summary of the products.

	Fescue	Bermuda	St. Augustine
Selling price per yard	$1.90	$2.65	$3.40
Variable cost per yard	$1.00	$1.50	$1.45
Fixed cost per yard	$0.60	$0.80	$1.00
Yards produced annually	4,200	3,200	2,580
Total machine hours used	630	672	860

REQUIRED:

a. Calculate the number of machine hours required to produce each yard.
b. Determine the contribution margin per yard for each product.
c. Determine the contribution margin per machine hour for each product.
d. Suppose only 3,000 machine hours are available. Which product should be produced?

LO 3,4

P27-5B **Special Order with Production Constraints** Subtracto Corporation produces inexpensive calculators which are primarily marketed through discount department stores and discount drug stores. It takes 0.10 machine hours to manufacture each calculator. During the current year, the factory is expected to produce 225,000 calculators which entails the factory producing at 90% of capacity. The standard costs of a calculator are as follows:

Direct material (0.2 lbs x $4.00)	$0.80
Direct labor (0.1 hours x $5.00)	0.50
Variable overhead (0.1 hours x $14.00)	1.40
Fixed costs (0.1 hours x $24.00)	2.40
Total costs	$5.10

Clearance Stores offered Subtracto the one-time opportunity to sell them 14,500 calculators at $3.25 each.

REQUIRED:

a. Calculate the impact the order will have on Subtacto's net income.
b. Determine if Subtracto should accept the special order if it were for 30,000 calculators.

CRITICAL THINKING AND COMMUNICATING

C27-1 The Tennis Pro Shop handles four lines of products that include rackets, clothes, shoes, and tennis balls. Because of intense competition from discount stores, tennis balls are sold at variable cost and at a loss if fixed costs are included. However, the other product lines are all profitable. Because of the lack of profitability, Boris Evert (the store manager) asked Chris Becker (the owner) if they should discontinue the sale of tennis balls. Boris argued that the space and selling effort could be applied to the other product lines. Chris Becker vehemently objected, and told Boris he is not to discontinue the sale of tennis balls.

REQUIRED:

Decide if the Tennis Pro Shop should carry tennis balls and support your decision.

C27-2 Monroe Nurseries provides wholesale plants and shrubs to retail nurseries in the greater Cleveland area. Cromwell Construction proposed that Monroe supply a very large order of shrubs so that Cromwell could landscape an entire housing development. The price Cromwell was willing to pay was greater than Monroe's variable cost but less than the full cost. This price is also less than the price Monroe charges its regular customers.

REQUIRED:

Write a memo to the owner of Monroe Nurseries explaining the qualitative considerations that should be considered if the special order is accepted.

CHAPTER 28

Capital Budgeting Decisions

After several years of operating a successful charter business, Steve Wilson, president of Island Air, thought it was time to add to his "fleet" of three, 7-passenger aircraft. "Look," he explained to his chief accountant, Ellen Smith, "with another plane, we can service 3,000 additional passengers a year. At an average fare of $200, that's $600,000!"

"But don't forget," Ellen pointed out, "a new plane will cost around $1,000,000; operating costs will be nearly $400,000 per year; and after five years, that $1,000,000 plane will only be worth $500,000. It's not clear that buying another plane is a good business decision."

In this chapter, we extend the discussion of decision making to include decisions requiring an investment in long-lived assets. The goal of the chapter is to provide you with the tools to solve problems like the one Steve Wilson faces.

LEARNING OBJECTIVES

1. Define capital expenditure decisions and capital budgets.
2. Evaluate investment opportunities using the net present value approach.
3. Evaluate investment opportunities using the internal rate of return approach.
4. Calculate the depreciation income tax shield and explain why depreciation is only important in investment analysis because of income taxes.
5. Use the payback period and the accounting rate of return methods to evaluate investment opportunities.
6. Explain why managers may concentrate erroneously on the short-run profitability of investments rather than their net present values.
7. Explain how the internal rate of return is calculated when there are uneven cash flows. (Appendix 28A)

CAPITAL BUDGETING DECISIONS

LO 1 Define capital expenditure decisions and capital budgets.

Individuals make "investments" in their homes, automobiles, major appliances, furniture, and other long-lived assets. Companies must also make investments in long-lived assets. Examples of some common investment decisions are presented in Illustration 28-1. In each example, a firm considers making an investment in one or more assets that will affect the firm's operations for several years.

ILLUSTRATION 28-1 Common Investment Decisions

1. A firm of architects considers buying a computer-aided design system.
2. A restaurant considers buying a new refrigeration system.
3. A moving company considers replacing its old fleet of trucks with new diesel-powered trucks.
4. A bottling company considers opening a new plant in Texas.
5. An accounting firm considers purchasing a microcomputer for preparation of client reports.
6. A furniture manufacturer considers purchasing a new lathe.
7. A car repair company considers purchasing the building it currently rents.
8. A grain processor considers converting a coal-powered boiler to natural gas.
9. A newspaper considers buying a new printing press.
10. A computer company considers purchasing patent rights to an operating system.

Investment decisions are extremely important because they have a major, long-term effect on a firm's operations. For example, when Mazda decided to build some of its cars in Flat Rock, Michigan, it made an investment in additional productive capacity that will affect its labor and transportation costs for many years to come. U.S., rather than Japanese, workers supply labor to build the cars; therefore, labor costs are largely determined by business conditions in the United States rather than those in Japan. Transportation costs are greatly reduced because Mazda can ship by rail directly from Michigan to various U.S. cities rather than from the West Coast (after a long trans-Pacific crossing). The investment decisions of small companies are also extremely important. Consider a small print shop that decides to make an investment in a computerized printing machine. The machine's cost may represent 50% or more of the company's total assets. Also, the cost savings from the investment in new technology may

CHAPTER 28 CAPITAL BUDGETING DECISIONS

make the difference between the company being a solid competitor in its market versus being on the verge of financial failure.

Investment decisions involving the acquisition of long-lived assets are often referred to as **capital expenditure decisions** because they require expenditure of capital (company funds) to acquire additional resources. Alternatively, investment decisions are called **capital budgeting decisions**. Most firms carefully analyze the potential projects in which they may invest. The process of evaluating the investment opportunities is referred to as *capital budgeting*, and the final list of approved projects is referred to as the **capital budget**.

EVALUATING INVESTMENT OPPORTUNITIES TIME VALUE OF MONEY APPROACHES

Crucial to capital budgeting decisions is an understanding of the *time value of money*. In evaluating an investment opportunity, you must know not only *how much* cash is received from (paid for) an investment, but also *when* the cash is received (paid). The time value of money concept states that it is better to receive a dollar today than to receive a dollar next year or any other time in the future. The reason, of course, is that you can invest the dollar received today so that at the end of the year it amounts to more than a dollar.

In an investment decision, a company invests money today in the hopes of receiving more money in the future. Obviously, one would not invest money in a project unless the total amount of funds received in the future exceeded the amount of the original investment. But, by *how much* must the future cash flows exceed the original investment? Since money in the future is not equivalent to money today, we need to develop a way of converting future dollars into their equivalent current or present value. The method developed to equate future dollars to current dollars is referred to as **present value analysis**. Present value techniques were explained earlier in the text in connection with the valuation of long-term debt. In this section, we present two approaches for evaluating investments that take into account the time value of money: the *net present value method* and the *internal rate of return method*.

The Net Present Value Method

LO 2
Evaluate investment opportunities using the net present value approach.

The first step in using the net present value method is to identify the amount and time period of each cash flow associated with a potential investment. Investment projects have both cash inflows (which are positive) and cash outflows (which are negative). The second step is to discount the cash flows to their present values using a required rate of return. How to estimate the required rate of return will be discussed later. For now, you should simply assume that the required rate of return is the minimum return top management wants to earn on investments. The third and final step is to evaluate the net present value.

The sum of the present values of all cash flows (inflows and outflows) is the **net present value** (NPV) of the investment. If zero, the NPV implies that the investment is generating a rate of return exactly equal to the required rate of return. Thus, management should undertake the investment. If the NPV is positive, management should also undertake the investment because it is generating a rate of return that is greater than the required rate of return. On the other hand, management should not accept investment opportunities that have negative NPVs because their rates of return are less than the required rates of return. A graphical presentation of the NPV approach to evaluating investments is presented in Illustration 28-2.

ILLUSTRATION 28-2 NPV Approach to Evaluating Investments

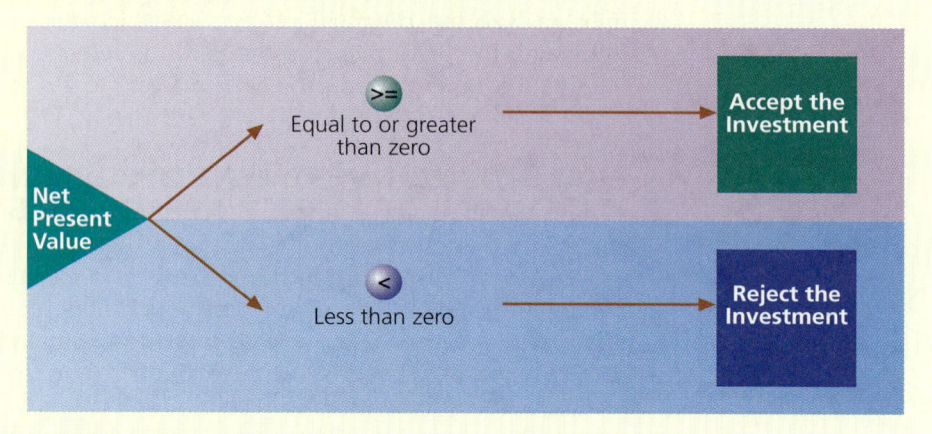

An Example of the NPV Approach. Suppose an auto repair shop considers purchasing automated paint spraying equipment. The company estimates that the equipment will last 5 years, save $2,000 annually in paint wasted in the current manual spraying operation, and reduce labor costs by $20,000. The equipment's estimated maintenance costs are $1,000 per year. The equipment costs $70,000 and has an expected residual value of $5,000. If the required rate of return is 12%, should the company invest in the new equipment?

The cash flows related to the investment opportunity are presented on the time line in Illustration 28-3. In analyzing the cash flows, we make the assumption that all cash inflows and outflows (other than the cash outflow of $70,000 for purchasing the equipment) occur at the end of a year. To simplify analysis, managers commonly make this assumption, which is unlikely to introduce significant error even though cash flows actually take place throughout the year (not just at year-end).

Consider the $70,000 cash outflow due to purchasing the spraying equipment. Note that the present value factor associated with the $70,000 purchase price is 1.0000. Because this amount is to be spent immediately, it is already expressed in terms of its present value. Now, consider the cash flows in Year 1. In this year, the net cash inflow is $21,000. The present value factor for an amount received at the end of Year 1 using a 12% rate of return is .8929. (See Table 1 in Appendix C, Present Value of $1.) Multiplying the present value factor by the cash inflow of $21,000 indicates that the present value of the net cash inflow in Year 1 is $18,751. The net present value of the investment in spraying equipment is found by summing the present values of the cash flows in each year. This amounts to $8,538. Since the net present value is positive, the company should purchase the equipment.

In the problem, the $20,000 labor savings, the $2,000 paint savings, and the $1,000 maintenance expense are identical in each of the five years. Thus, the net amount of $21,000 can be treated as a five-year annuity in calculating the present value. This treatment is presented in Illustration 28-4. The present value factor, using a 12% rate of return, for an annuity lasting five years is 3.605. (See

ILLUSTRATION 28-3 Evaluation of Automated Paint Spraying Equipment

Time Period	Present 0	Year 1	Year 2	Year 3	Year 4	Year 5
Cash Flow:						
Purchase Price	$(70,000)					
Labor Saving		$20,000	$20,000	$20,000	$20,000	$20,000
Paint Saving		2,000	2,000	2,000	2,000	2,000
Maintenance		(1,000)	(1,000)	(1,000)	(1,000)	(1,000)
Salvage Value						$5,000
Total Cash Flow	$(70,000)	$21,000	$21,000	$21,000	$21,000	$26,000
PV Factor	1.000	.8929	.7972	.7118	.6355	.5674
Total	$(70,000) +	$18,751 +	$16,741 +	$14,948 +	$13,346 +	$14,752 = $8,538

Table 2 in Appendix C, Present Value of Annuity of $1.) Multiplying this factor by the $21,000 annuity indicates a present value of $75,705. The present value of the $5,000 residual value in Year 5 is calculated using a factor from the Present Value of $1 table. Note that the total net present value, $8,542, is $4 more than the amount calculated in Illustration 28-3. The $4 difference is due to rounding in development of the present value tables.

ILLUSTRATION 28-4 Evaluation of Automated Paint Spraying Equipment Using Present Value of an Annuity Approach

Item	Cash Flow	Present Value Factor	Present Value
Purchase price	$(70,000)	1.0000	$(70,000)
Labor, paint, and maintenance	21,000	3.6050	75,705
Residual value	5,000	.5674	2,837
		Net present value	8,542

LO 3

Evaluate investment opportunities using the internal rate of return approach.

The Internal Rate of Return Method

The internal rate of return method is an alternative to net present value for evaluating investments possibilities.[1] Like net present value, it takes into account the time value of money. The **internal rate of return** (IRR) is the rate of return that equates the present value of future cash flows to the investment outlay. If the IRR of a potential investment is greater than the required rate of return, management should undertake the investment. The IRR approach to evaluating investments is presented in Illustration 28-5.

Consider a simple case where someone invests $100 to yield $60 at the end of Year 1 and $60 at the end of Year 2. What rate of return equates the two-year, $60 annuity to $100? Recall that when we performed present value analysis for annuities, we multiplied an annuity value factor by the annuity to solve for a present value. That is:

Present Value = Annuity Value Factor × Annuity

---

[1]The internal rate of return method is also referred to as the *time-adjusted rate of return* method.

ILLUSTRATION 28-5 IRR Approach to Evaluating Investments

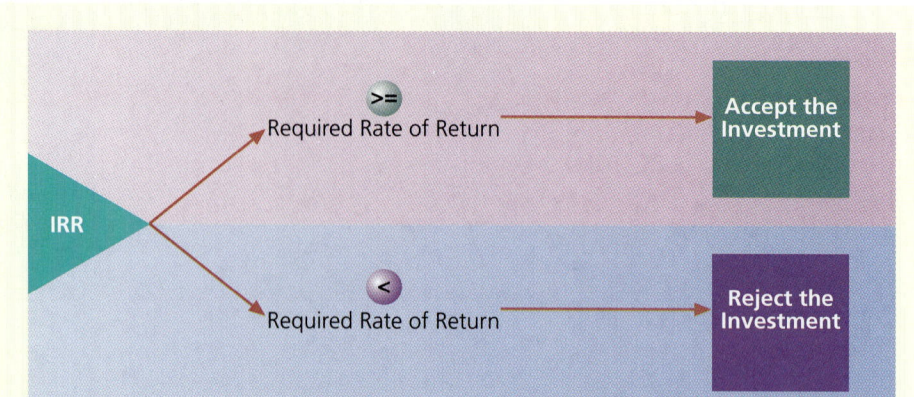

In the current case, we set the present value equal to the initial outlay for the investment. Then, we can solve for the annuity value factor and use it to look up the rate of return implicit in the investment.

$$\text{Annuity Value Factor} = \frac{\text{Cost of Investment}}{\text{Annuity Amount}}$$

With a $100 cost and a $60 annuity, the investment's annuity value factor is 1.667.

$$1.667 = \frac{\$100}{\$60}$$

Since the $60 is to be received in each of two years, we use the annuity table (Table 2 in Appendix C) to look up the internal rate of return. In the row in Table 2 for 2 periods, we find an annuity value factor of 1.668 (very close to 1.667) in the column for a 13% rate of return. Thus, the IRR on this investment is approximately 13%. If the required rate of return is 13% or less, then the investor should undertake the investment.

You can gain insight into the IRR by using it to calculate the net present value of the project. If we evaluated the project using a 13% required rate of return, what would be the net present value? The answer is *zero* since the internal rate of return equates the present value of future cash flows to the investment outlay.

Item	Cash Flow	Present Value Factor	Present Value
Cash flow	$ 60	1.668	$100.08
Initial investment	$(100)	1.000	(100.00)
		Difference (due to rounding)	$ .08

Summary of Net Present Value and Internal Rate of Return

While both the net present value and the internal rate of return methods take into account the time value of money, they differ in their approach to evaluating investment alternatives. In using net present value, management should

INSIGHTS INTO ETHICS

Henry Spellman, vice president of operations for Union Manufacturing, is preparing a presentation for the board of directors. Henry hopes to convince the board that the company should invest in a highly mechanized production line that makes extensive use of robotics. As part of his presentation, Henry will present a net present value analysis of the potential investment in equipment. In preparing this analysis, Henry discovers that the present value of the cash flows directly attributable to the investment is a negative $25,000.

Henry feels that investing in an automated production line is essential if the company is to remain competitive over the next ten years. However, the NPV doesn't capture the strategic importance of the new technology. If he "fudges" the operating expenses in his analysis, he will be able to show that the project has a positive NPV.

Should Henry "fudge" the numbers in the NPV analysis if this is the only way he can convince the board to make an investment decision that Henry feels is in the long-run interest of company? Explain.

---

undertake any investment with a zero or positive net present value. In using the internal rate of return method, management should undertake any investment with an internal rate of return equal to or greater than the required rate of return.[2]

ESTIMATING THE REQUIRED RATE OF RETURN

In the problems presented, we simply stated a required rate of return that could be used to calculate an investment's net present value or that could be compared to an investment's internal rate of return. In practice, management must estimate the required rate of return. Under certain conditions, the required rate of return should be equal to the cost of capital for the firm.

The **cost of capital** is the weighted average of the costs of debt and equity financing used to generate capital for investments. The cost of debt arises because the firm must pay interest to individuals, to banks, and to other companies that lend it money. Essentially, the cost of equity is the return shareholders demand for the risk they bear in supplying capital to the firm. Estimating the cost of capital, especially the cost due to equity capital, is a challenge even to sophisticated financial managers. Because of this difficulty, many managers take a judgmental approach to determine the required rate of return following the general principle that the more risky the investment, the higher the required rate of return.

FURTHER CONSIDERATION OF CASH FLOWS

To be useful in investment analysis, both the net present value and the internal rate of return methods require a proper specification of cash flows. It is particu-

---

[2]Under some circumstances, the net present value and the internal rate of return methods may be inconsistent with one another in evaluating the desirability of an investment opportunity. This potential problem is discussed in introductory texts on financial management.

larly important to remember that *only cash inflows and outflows, not revenues and expenses*, are discounted back to present value. Thus, if a firm expects a sale to occur in Period 1 but does not anticipate the collection of cash from the sale until Period 2, the cash flow it discounts back to present value is a Period 2 cash flow even though the related revenue will be recorded in Period 1. Likewise, if a firm anticipates a cash payment in Period 1 to purchase an asset, and records related depreciation in Periods 1 through 5, it uses only the Period 1 cash outflow in the net present value analysis. Depreciation is a legitimate business cost, but it does not require a cash outflow in the period in which it is recorded. Present value analysis is concerned only with cash flows.

Cash Flows, Taxes, and the Depreciation Income Tax Shield

LO 4
Calculate the depreciation income tax shield and explain why depreciation is only important in investment analysis because of income taxes.

In all of the examples given, we ignored the effect of income taxes on cash flows. However, tax considerations play a major role in capital budgeting decisions, and we discuss them here. If an investment project generates taxable revenue, cash inflows from the project will be reduced by the taxes that the firm must pay on the revenue. Likewise, if an investment project generates tax-deductible expenses, cash inflows from the project will be increased by the tax savings resulting from the decrease in income taxes payable.

We previously stated that depreciation is not relevant in a present value analysis of an investment opportunity because it is not a cash flow. While depreciation does not *directly* affect cash flow, it *indirectly* affects cash flow because it reduces the amount of tax a company must pay. That is, it acts to shield income from taxes. The term **depreciation income tax shield** is used to refer to the tax savings resulting from depreciation.

As an example, suppose a firm considers producing and selling a new product. Production of the product will require an investment in equipment costing $100,000. Each year, the company expects sales to amount to $70,000 and expenses (other than depreciation on the equipment) to amount to $40,000. Depreciation calculated on a straight-line basis for the expected 10-year life of the equipment is $10,000 per year. The company has a 40% tax rate.[3] Assume the company collects revenue in the period earned and pays expenses in the period incurred. Thus, net income and cash flows related to the investment are as follows:

Revenue		$70,000
Less: Operating expenses other than depreciation	$40,000	
Depreciation	10,000	50,000
Income before taxes		$20,000
Income taxes (40% tax rate)		8,000
Net income		$12,000
Add back: Depreciation		10,000
Cash flow each period		$22,000

Note that the firm deducts depreciation to arrive at income before taxes and thus reduces the amount of income taxes it must pay. However, depreciation is

---

[3] Our discussion and examples assume a 40% tax rate. This assumption ignores complexities in tax rates and rules in practice which may change from year to year. However, the assumption allows us to more clearly convey the essential role of taxes in investment decisions.

not itself a cash outflow. Therefore, the firm must add back depreciation to net income to arrive at its cash flow.

Because the project is fairly risky, the company has set a required rate of return of 16%. The net present value calculation for the investment under consideration is presented in Illustration 28-6. Note that because the amounts of revenue, expense, and tax are the same each year, we can work with the net amount and treat it as a 10-year annuity with a required rate of return of 16%. Since the net present value is a positive $6,326, the firm should undertake investment in the equipment.

ILLUSTRATION 28-6 NPV Analysis Taking Taxes Into Account

Item	Cash Flow	Present Value Factor	Present Value
Initial investment	$(100,000)	1.000	$(100,000)
Revenue	$70,000		
Operating expenses (other than depreciation)	(40,000)		
Taxes	(8,000) 22,000	4.833	106,326
Net present value			$ 6,326

The fact that depreciation reduced taxes had a significant effect on the value of the investment project. With depreciation of $10,000 and a 40% tax rate, the firm saves $4,000 in taxes each year due to depreciation. The present value of this "tax shield" over 10 years at 16% is $19,332 ($4,000 x present value factor of 4.833). Thus, it is apparent that without the tax shield afforded by depreciation, the investment would not have a positive net present value and would not be worth undertaking.

Adjusting Cash Flows for Inflation

An additional topic that must be addressed in estimating the cash flows of investments is how to handle inflation. During the 1970s and early 1980s, we experienced double-digit inflation in the U.S. High rates of inflation are still common in many foreign countries. Thus, it may be quite important to consider inflation when estimating the cash flows associated with investment opportunities. Inflation can be taken into account by multiplying the current level of cash flow by the expected rate of inflation. For example, if an investment is expected to yield a cash flow in Period 1 of $100 and the rate of inflation is expected to be 5% per year in the foreseeable future, then a reasonable estimate of the cash flow would be $105 (i.e., $100 x 1.05) in Period 2, $110.25 (i.e., $105 x 1.05) in Period 3, $115.76 in Period 4, etc. Financial journals publish estimates of inflation, and some firms that specialize in economic forecasts provide them for a fee.

If inflation is ignored in net present value analysis, firms may reject many worthwhile investment opportunities. Current rates of return for debt and equity financing already include estimates of future inflation. For example, when they estimate that inflation will be high, banks charge higher rates of interest on loans to companies. Suppose a company uses its current costs of debt and equity financing (which are high because a high rate of inflation is expected) to determine its required rate of return. Now, if the company does not take inflation into account in estimating future cash flows, the cash flows will be relatively low, while the required rate of return will be relatively high. The result may be that suitable projects will appear to have negative net present values.

SIMPLIFIED APPROACHES TO CAPITAL BUDGETING

LO 5 Use the payback period and the accounting rate of return methods to evaluate investment opportunities.

Companies often use the net present value and the internal rate of return methods to evaluate capital projects. Since the 1960s, their use has increased greatly. However, many companies continue to use other, more simple, approaches to evaluating capital projects. Two of these approaches, the *payback period method and the accounting rate of return method*, are discussed in this section. As you will see, both of these methods have significant limitations in comparison to net present value and internal rate of return.

Payback Period Method

The **payback period** is the length of time it takes to recover the initial cost of an investment. Thus, if an investment opportunity costs $1,000 and yields cash flows of $500 per year, it has a payback period of 2 years. If an investment costs $1,000 and yields cash flows of $300 per year, it has a payback period of 3-1/3 years. All things equal, a company would like to have projects with short payback periods.

One approach to using the payback method would be to accept investment projects that have a payback period less than some specified requirement. However, this can lead to extremely poor decisions. For example, suppose a company has two investment opportunities both costing $1,000. The first investment yields cash flows of $500 per year for 3 years and has a payback period of 2 years. The second investment yields no cash flows in the first two years but has cash flows of $1,000 in the third year and $4,000 in the fourth year. Thus, it has a payback period of 3 years. Obviously, the second investment is preferable. However if the company has a 2-year payback requirement, it would select the first investment and reject the second. The problem is that the payback method *does not take into account the total stream of cash flows* related to an investment. It only considers the stream of cash flows up to the time the investment is paid back. Thus, in this example, the payback period method ignores the $4,000 cash flow in the fourth year of the second investment.

A further limitation of the payback method is that it *does not consider the time value of money*. Consider two investments that both cost $1,000. The first investment yields cash flows of $700 in the first year, $300 in the second year, and $300 in the third year. Thus, it has a payback of 2 years. The second investment yields cash flows of $300 in the first year, $700 in the second year, and $300 in the third year. Thus, it also has a payback of 2 years. While both investments have the same payback (implying they are equally valuable), the first investment is really more favorable because the $700 cash inflow is received in the first year rather than in the second year. In fact, the first investment has an internal rate of return of 17%, while the second investment has an internal rate of return of only 14%.

While the payback method has significant limitations, some companies may find it useful, particularly if they have cash flow problems. Companies with cash flow problems may need to focus on investments that quickly return cash in order to avoid bankruptcy.

Accounting Rate of Return

The **accounting rate of return** equals the average after-tax income from a project divided by the average investment in the project.

$$\text{Accounting Rate of Return (ARR)} = \frac{\text{Average Net Income}}{\text{Average Investment}}$$

Companies can use the accounting rate of return to evaluate investment opportunities by comparing their accounting rates of return to a required accounting rate of return. The primary limitation of this approach is that, like the payback method, it ignores the time value of money. For example, a firm that has a cost of capital of 15% and a 40% tax rate considers two investment alternatives. Both alternatives require investments in equipment costing $100,000 and generate cash flows for two years as indicated in Illustration 28-7. Both investments are identical except that, while both have total revenue over two years of $180,000, Project 1 has $90,000 of revenue in the first year, while Project 2 has $70,000. In the second year, Project 1 has $90,000 of revenue, while Project 2 has $110,000. Illustration 28-7 presents the net incomes and cash flows of the two alternatives for the two years. We assume the firm collects all revenue items in the period earned and pays all expense items (other than depreciation) in the period incurred. Thus, the difference between net income and cash flow is simply the amount of depreciation.

ILLUSTRATION 28-7 Net Income and Cash Flow Data for Alternative Projects

	Project 1	*Project 2*
Year 1		
Revenue	$90,000	$ 70,000
Less: Operating expenses other than depreciation	20,000	20,000
Depreciation	50,000	50,000
Income before taxes	$20,000	$ 0
Taxes	8,000	0
Net income	$12,000	$ 0
Add back: Depreciation	50,000	50,000
Cash flow	$62,000	$ 50,000
Year 2		
Revenue	$90,000	$110,000
Less: Operating expenses other than depreciation	20,000	20,000
Depreciation	50,000	50,000
Income before taxes	$20,000	$ 40,000
Taxes	8,000	16,000
Net income	$12,000	$ 24,000
Add back: Depreciation	50,000	50,000
Cash flow	$62,000	$74,000

Based on the information, it is easy to calculate the accounting rate of return for each project as indicated in Illustration 28-8.

ILLUSTRATION 28-8 Comparison of ARRs for Alternative Projects

$$\text{Accounting Rate of Return (ARR)} = \frac{\text{Average Net Income}}{\text{Average Investment}}$$

$$\text{ARR for Project 1} = \frac{(\$12{,}000 + \$12{,}000) \div 2}{\$100{,}000 \div 2} = .24$$

$$\text{ARR for Project 2} = \frac{(\$0 + \$24{,}000) \div 2}{\$100{,}000 \div 2} = .24$$

Both have identical accounting rates of return of 24%, indicating that the two projects are equally desirable. However, when we take into account the time value of money, it is clear that Project 1 is more desirable than Project 2. As indicated in Illustration 28-9, using a cost of capital of 15%, the net present value of project 1 is $793.40, while Project 2 has a negative net present value of $568.60. Thus, taking into account the time value of money, Project 1 is an acceptable investment, while Project 2 is not acceptable.

ILLUSTRATION 28-9 NPV Comparison of Alternative Projects

Project 1

Time Period	Cash Flow	Present Value Factor	Present Value
0	$(100,000)	1.0000	$(100,000.00)
1	62,000	.8696	53,915.20
2	62,000	.7561	46,878.20
		Net present value	$ 793.40

Project 2

Time Period	Cash Flow	Present Value Factor	Present Value
0	$(100,000)	1.0000	$(100,000.00)
1	50,000	.8696	43,480.00
2	74,000	.7561	55,951.40
		Net present value	$ (568.60)

CONFLICT BETWEEN PERFORMANCE EVALUATION AND CAPITAL BUDGETING

LO 6
Explain why managers may concentrate erroneously on the short-run profitability of investments rather than their net present values.

In some companies, managers may be discouraged from using present value techniques for evaluating investments because of the way their own performance is evaluated. The reason for this is that some investments result in high amounts of depreciation in early years. In these early, start-up years, revenues may be quite low, resulting in low profits or even losses. However, revenues in later years may be large enough to ensure that the investments have positive net present values. If managers know that job performance is evaluated in terms of reported accounting income, they may fear being fired because of low initial profits. If this is the case, managers would likely ignore the fact that a project had a positive net present value and concentrate, instead, on reported income.

Suppose a manager considers producing a new product that requires an investment of $1,000,000 in equipment. Depreciation on the equipment will be recorded using the straight-line method. Based on a 10-year life, depreciation will be $100,000 per year. The product is not expected to sell well in the early years. (For example, expected first year revenue is only $40,000). However, by the end of the seventh year, expected revenue is up to $700,000 per year. In addition to depreciation, the company will incur $40,000 of other expenses each year. The company has a 10% required rate of return. Illustration 28-10 is a net present value analysis of the investment.

The net present value of the investment is $26,998, indicating that the manager should undertake the project. However, will the manager be motivated to do what is in the best interest of the company? Note that the project shows a

ILLUSTRATION 28-10 Net Present Value Analysis of New Product[1]

	Year 1	Year 2	Year 3	Year 4	Year 5
Revenue	$ 40,000	$ 60,000	$100,000	$150,000	$200,000
Less: Operating expenses other than depreciation	40,000	40,000	40,000	40,000	40,000
Depreciation	100,000	100,000	100,000	100,000	100,000
Net income	$(100,000)	$ (80,000)	$ (40,000)	$ 10,000	$ 60,000
Add back: Depreciation	100,000	100,000	100,000	100,000	100,000
Cash flow	$ 0	$ 20,000	$ 60,000	$110,000	$160,000

	Year 6	Year 7	Year 8	Year 9	Year 10
Revenue	$ 300,000	$400,000	$400,000	$400,000	$400,000
Less: Operating expenses other than depreciation	40,000	40,000	40,000	40,000	40,000
Depreciation	100,000	100,000	100,000	100,000	100,000
Net income	$ 160,000	$260,000	$260,000	$260,000	$260,000
Add back: Depreciation	100,000	100,000	100,000	100,000	100,000
Cash flow	$ 260,000	$360,000	$360,000	$360,000	$360,000

Time Period	Cash Flows	Factor for 10%	Present Value
0	$(1,000,000)	1.0000	$(1,000,000)
1	0	0.9091	0
2	20,000	0.8264	16,528
3	60,000	0.7513	45,078
4	110,000	0.6830	75,130
5	160,000	0.6209	99,344
6	260,000	0.5645	146,770
7	360,000	0.5132	184,752
8	360,000	0.4665	167,940
9	360,000	0.4241	152,676
10	360,000	0.3855	138,780
Net present value			$ 26,998

[1]Note that the example is simplified and ignores taxes. Therefore, there is no depreciation tax shield. Also, the example assumes the company collects revenue in the period earned and pays other expenses in the period incurred.

substantial loss in each of the first three years. The manager may fear that this will reflect badly on his or her performance, perhaps leading to dismissal. If this is the case, the manager may opt to pass up this valuable investment opportunity. The solution to this potential problem is to make sure managers realize that, if they approve projects with positive net present values that lower reported income in the shortrun, evaluations of their performance will take the expected *future* benefits into account. Managers must be confident that their performance will be evaluated with respect to the firm's long-run profitability, or they will not take a long-run perspective in evaluating capital projects.

INTERNATIONAL PERSPECTIVES

EVALUATING CAPITAL PROJECTS: COMPARISON OF PRACTICES IN THE U.S., KOREA, AND JAPAN

Are approaches to evaluating capital projects the same in different countries? A survey comparing practices in the U.S., Korea, and Japan reveals interesting similarities and differences. One survey question asked companies to rate the role of intuition in evaluating investments. Only 5% of Japanese companies indicated that intuition was extremely important or very important while the percentage was 25% in the U.S. and 22% in Korea. Thus, it appears that qualitative factors taken into account in a manager's intuition, are less important in Japan.

Respondents in all three countries considered the payback method to be important with 71% of U.S. companies, 88% of Japanese companies and 75% of Korean companies rating payback as an extremely or very important criterion for justifiying investment in capital projects. A surprising result is the low percentage of Japanese companies who consider the net present value (NPV) approach to be a useful technique for evaluating capital projects. Only 28% of the Japanese companies rated NPV as extremely or very important while the percentages in the U.S. and Korea were 60% and 64%.

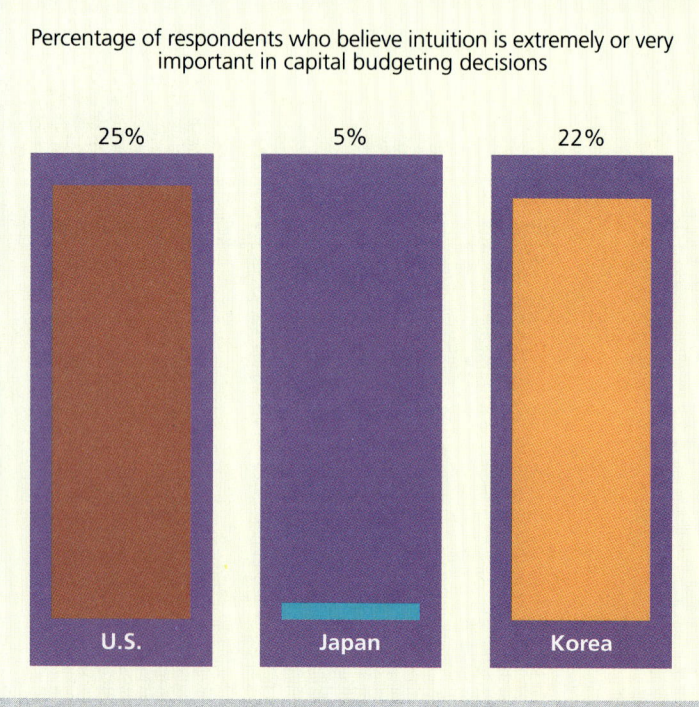

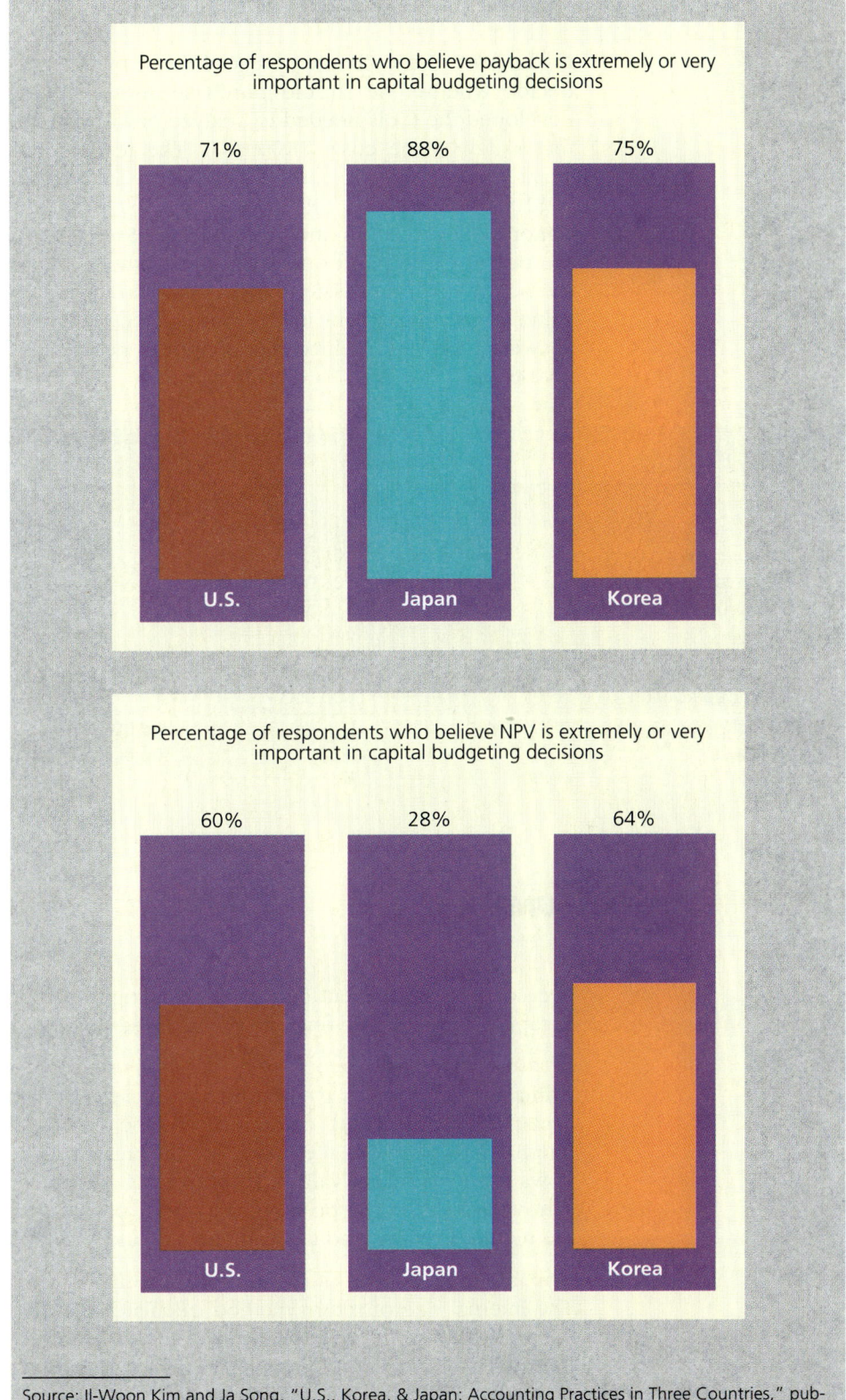

Source: Il-Woon Kim and Ja Song, "U.S., Korea, & Japan: Accounting Practices in Three Countries," published in *Management Accounting* (August 1990), pp. 26–30, copyright by the Institute of Management Accountants, Montvale, N.J.

ISLAND AIR REVISITED

At the start of the chapter, Steve Wilson, president of Island Air, was trying to decide whether he should purchase another plane. At this point, we have developed the tools needed to analyze problems like the one Steve faces. Recall that a new plane costs $1,000,000. The residual value of the plane after five years will be $500,000, and annual depreciation using the straight-line method is $100,000. Revenue will increase by $600,000 per year, and operating costs (ignoring depreciation and taxes) will be $400,000. Revenue will be collected in the period earned and operating costs, other than depreciation, will be paid in the period incurred. Assume the income tax rate is 40%. What is the net present value of the investment in the plane if the required rate of return is 10%? The answer is ($82,990). Since the amount is negative, Island Air should reject the investment.

Item		Cash Flow	Present Value Factor	Present Value
Purchase price		$(1,000,000)	1.0000	$(1,000,000)
Revenue	$600,000			
Less: Operating expenses other than depreciation	400,000			
Deprecation	100,000			
Income before income taxes	$100,000			
Income taxes	40,000			
Net income	$ 60,000			
Add back: Depreciation	100,000			
Annual cash flow		160,000	3.7910	606,560
Residual value		500,000	.6209	310,450
			Net present value	$ (82,990)

SUMMARY

Define capital expenditure decisions and capital budgets. Capital expenditure decisions are investment decisions involving the acquisition of long-lived assets. A capital budget is the final list of approved acquisitions.

Evaluate investment opportunities using the net present value approach. Two primary methods for evaluating investment opportunities, which take into account the time value of money, are the net present value method and the internal rate of return method. The net present value method reduces all cash flows to their present values. If the sum of the present values (i.e., the net present value) is zero or positive, the return on the investment equals or exceeds the required return, and the company should make the investment.

Evaluate investment opportunities using the internal rate of return approach. The internal rate of return method calculates the rate of return that equates the percent value of future cash flows to the initial investment. If this rate of return is equal to or greater than the required rate of return, then investment is warranted.

Calculate the depreciation income tax shield and explain why depreciation is only important in investment analysis because of income taxes. In analyzing cash flows for a net present value analysis or an internal rate of return analysis, remember that depreciation is not a cash flow. However, the tax savings generated by depreciation is relevant to the analysis. The tax savings due to depreciation is referred to as the depreciation income tax shield.

Use the payback period and the accounting rate of return methods to evaluate investment opportunities. The payback method evaluates capital projects in terms of how quickly the initial investment is recovered by future cash inflows. The accounting rate of return method evaluates capital projects in terms of the ratio of average after-tax accounting income to the average investment. Both of these methods' major limitation is that they ignore the time value of money.

Explain why managers may concentrate on the short-run profitability of investments rather than their net present values. From a theoretical standpoint, managers should evaluate investment opportunities using the net present value method or the internal rate of return method. However, in some cases, projects with a positive net present value or with an internal rate of return greater than required may have a negative effect on short-run income. While these projects may be quite valuable to the firm's long-run success, managers may not approve them because they fear that their own job performance will receive negative evaluations if short-run income is reduced.

LO 7
Explain how the internal rate of return is calculated when there are uneven cash flows.

APPENDIX 28-A: THE INTERNAL RATE OF RETURN WITH UNEQUAL CASH FLOWS

In the chapter, the use of the IRR method is presented for the case where cash flows are equal each year. For cases where cash flows are not equal, the approach presented in the chapter cannot be implemented because we cannot divide the initial investment by a single cash flow annuity to yield an annuity value factor. Instead, we must estimate the internal rate of return and use the estimate to calculate the net present value of the project. If the net present value is greater than zero, the estimate of the internal rate of return should be increased. If the net present value is less than zero, the estimate should be decreased. By estimating the internal rate of return in this trial-and-error fashion, it is possible to arrive eventually at the actual internal rate of return.

Suppose a company considers changes in its production process that will involve purchasing several pieces of equipment costing a total of $120,000. The changes are expected to yield cost savings of $49,500 in Year 1, $45,000 in Year 2, $35,000 in Year 3, $22,000 in Year 4 and $19,600 in Year 5.

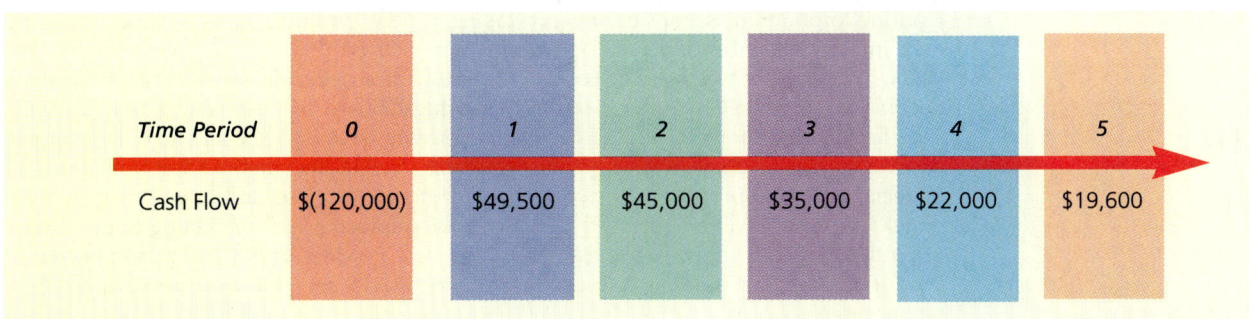

The company wants to evaluate the potential project in terms of its internal rate of return. Since the cash flows are fairly large in relation to the initial investment, a reasonable "guess" as to the internal rate of return might be 14%. However, when we use 14% to calculate the net present value of the investment as in Illustration 28-11, we see that the present value is a positive $4,880. Thus, the true internal rate of return is greater than 14%. As a next approximation, we can try 18%. However, with this rate of return, the present value is a negative $4,514. This indicates that our second estimate of the internal rate of return was too high. At this point, we know that the internal rate of return is somewhere between 14% and 18%. Thus, as a further attempt, we might try 16%. The net present value using a rate of 16% is $26. This is sufficiently close to zero to conclude that the internal rate of return is approximately 16%. If management believes that a return of 16% is sufficient, then the company should go ahead with the project.

ILLUSTRATION 28-11 Calculating the IRR When Cash Flows Are Unequal

Time Period	Cash Flows	14%		18%		16%	
		Factor for 14%	Present Value	Factor for 18%	Present Value	Factor for 16%	Present Value
0	$(120,000)	1.0000	$(120,000)	1.0000	$(120,000)	1.0000	$(120,000)
1	49,500	0.8772	43,421	0.8475	41,951	0.8621	42,674
2	45,000	0.7695	34,268	0.7182	32,319	0.7432	33,444
3	35,000	0.6750	23,625	0.6086	21,301	0.6407	22,425
4	22,000	0.5921	13,026	0.5158	11,348	0.5523	12,151
5	19,600	0.5194	10,180	0.4371	8,567	0.4761	9,332
		Total	4,880		$ (4,514)		$ 26

It may appear that estimating the internal rate of return by using a trial-and-error approach is difficult and presents a significant obstacle to using the IRR approach. Actually, this is not the case. Many spreadsheet programs for microcomputers and even some pocket calculators contain functions that easily estimate the internal rate of return of a project. The user simply inputs the cash flow information and the IRR is calculated automatically.

REVIEW PROBLEM

Horton Corporation is considering producing a new product, Super Goop. Marketing data indicate that the demand for Super Goop will be 15,000 units per year for five years. The product will be produced in a section of an existing factory that is currently not in use. To produce Super Goop, Horton must buy a machine that costs $250,000. The machine has an expected life of 5 years and will have no residual value. Horton will depreciate the machine over 5 years using the straight-line method for both tax and financial reporting purposes. Horton has a tax rate of 30%. It is anticipated that no additional fixed costs will be incurred as a result of producing and marketing Super Goop, other than $22,200 annually for advertising the new product. Super Goop is expected to sell for $21 per unit and variable production cost is $15 per unit. Horton has a required rate of return of 14%.

REQUIRED:

a. Compute the net present value.
b. Compute the internal rate of return.
c. Compute the payback period.
d. Compute the accounting rate of return.

SOLUTION:

Planning and Organizing Your Work

1. Determine cash flow for each period by calculating after-tax income and adding back depreciation expense.
2. Apply present values to the annual cash flows and the initial investment to determine the net present value.
3. Divide the investment by the annual cash flows to determine the present value of an annuity table factor.
4. Look up the table factor in the present value of an annuity table to determine the internal rate of return.
5. Determine the payback period by dividing the initial investment by the annual cash flows.
6. Calculate the accounting rate of return by dividing the average net income by the average investment.

(a) *Compute the net present value.*

The net income and cash flows related to the investment are as follows:

Revenue ($21 x 15,000)		$315,000
Less: Production expenses ($15 x 15,000)	$225,000	
Advertising expense	22,200	
Depreciation expense (250,000 ÷ 5 years)	25,000	272,200
Income before taxes		$ 42,800
Taxes (30% tax rate)		12,840
Net income		$ 29,960
Add back: Depreciation		50,000
Cash flow each period		$ 79,960

The net present value is calculated as follows:

Item	Cash Flow	Factor	Present Value
Initial investment	$(250,000)	1.000	$(250,000)
Cash flow each period for 5 years	79,960	3.433	274,503
Net present value			$ 24,503

Since the net present value is positive, Super Goop should be produced.

(b) *Compute the internal rate of return.*

Present value factor = cost of investment ÷ annual cash flow
Present value factor = $250,000 ÷ $79,960 = 3.127

Use the annuity table (Table 2 in the Appendix C) to look up the internal rate of return. In the row in Table 2 for 5 periods we find a present value factor of 3.127 in the column for a 18% rate of return. Since the rate of return exceeds the required rate of return of 14%, the Super Goop should be produced.

(c) *Compute the payback period.*

The payback period for even cash flows can be calculated as follows:

Payback period = cost of investment ÷ annual cash flow
Payback period = $250,000 ÷ $79,960 = 3.127 years

(d) *Compute the accounting rate of return.*

ARR = average net income ÷ average investment
ARR = $29,960[1] ÷ ($250,000 ÷ 2) = 24%

---
[1]See calculation in NPV analysis above.

KEY TERMS

accounting rate of return, *1117*
capital budget, *1109*
capital budgeting decision, *1109*
capital expenditure decision, *1109*
cost of capital, *1113*
depreciation income tax shield, *1114*
internal rate of return, *1111*
net present value, *1109*
payback period, *1116*
present value analysis, *1109*

SELF-QUIZ

LO 1 1. Which of the following is *not* a common investment decision?
   a. Building a new factory.
   b. Accepting a special order.
   c. Purchasing a new piece of equipment.
   d. Purchasing a computer system.

LO 2 2. List the two factors about cash flows you need to know when evaluating investment alternatives using time value of money approaches.

LO 2 3. Which of the following is *not* a true statement about the net present value method?
   a. It uses time value of money concepts.
   b. The result is computed by calculating the present value of the inflows minus the initial investment.
   c. It is consistent with generally accepted accounting principles.
   d. It requires the user to know a required rate of return.

LO 3 4. Which of the following is *not* a true statement about the internal rate of return method?
   a. It uses time value of money concepts.
   b. It equates the present value of future cash flows to the investment outlay.
   c. It yields a rate of return that can be compared to a required rate.
   d. It will lead to the same investment decisions as the accounting rate of return.

LO 3 5. True or False? When the internal rate of return exceeds the required rate of return the investment should be rejected.

LO 3 6. Depreciation expense is only relevant to a capital budgeting decision because of _____.

LO 3 7. Which of the following is true about the cost of capital?
   a. It is the weighted average of the costs of debt and equity financing.
   b. It is the interest rate of borrowing an additional $1 of debt.
   c. It is easy to estimate.
   d. It is important to know when calculating the payback of an investment.

LO 4 8. True or False? If inflation is ignored in net present value analysis, many worthwhile investment opportunities may be rejected.

LO 5 9. Which of the following is *not* a limitation of the payback period method?
   a. It is difficult to calculate.
   b. It does not take into account the total stream of cash flows related to an investment.
   c. It does not consider the time value of money.
   d. It ignores the timing of cash flows.

LO 5 10. State the formula for calculating the accounting rate of return.

SOLUTIONS TO SELF-QUIZ
1. b   2. how much cash is received or paid, when the cash is received (paid)   3. c   4. d   5. false   6. taxes   7. a   8. true
9. a   10. ARR = average net income ÷ average investment

CHAPTER 28 CAPITAL BUDGETING DECISIONS

QUESTIONS

Q28-1 What is a capital expenditure?

Q28-2 Why it is important to include time value of money concepts when making capital budgeting decisions?

Q28-3 What are the two approaches for evaluating investments that take into account the time value of money?

Q28-4 How do net present value and internal rate of return differ in their approach to evaluating investment alternatives?

Q28-5 Why do managers often take a judgmental approach to determine the required rate of return rather than using the cost of capital?

Q28-6 How are cash flows affected as a result of the tax consequences of depreciation?

Q28-7 What are the advantages of evaluating projects using the net present value and internal rate of return methods instead of the payback and accounting rate of return methods?

Q28-8 Why do managers often concentrate on the short run profitability of investments rather than their net present values?

Q28-9 (Appendix) How is the internal rate of return (IRR) determined if there are uneven cash flows?

EXERCISES

LO 2   **E28-1**   **Determine Present Values**   Suppose you face the prospect of receiving $200 per year for the next 5 years plus an extra $500 payment at the end of 5 years. Determine how much this prospect is worth today if the required rate of return is 10%.

LO 2   **E28-2**   **Determine Present Values**   Juanita Martinez is ready to retire and she has a choice of three pension plans. Plan A provides for the immediate cash payment of $100,000. Plan B provides for the payment of $10,000 per year for ten years and the payment of $100,000 at the end of year 10. Plan C will pay $20,000 per year for 10 years. Juanita Martinez desires a rate of return of 8%. Determine the present value of each plan and select the best one.

LO 2   **E28-3**   **Calculate the Net Present Value**   An investment that costs $10,000 will return $4,000 per year for 4 years. Determine the net present value of the investment if the required rate of return is 12%. Ignore income taxes. Should the investment be undertaken?

LO 2   **E28-4**   **Calculate the Net Present Value**   Fancy Florist is considering replacing an old refrigeration unit with a larger unit to store flowers. Because the new refrigeration unit has a larger capacity, Fancy estimates that they can sell another $6,000 of flowers a year that cost $3,500. In addition, the new unit is energy efficient and should save $950 in electricity each year. It will cost an extra $150 per month for maintenance. The new refrigeration unit costs $20,000 and has an expected life of 10 years. The old unit is fully depreciated and can be sold for an amount equal to disposal cost. At the end of 10 years, the new unit has an expected residual value of $5,000. Determine the net present value of the investment if the required rate of return is 14%. Should the investment be undertaken? Ignore income taxes.

LO 2   **E28-5**   **Choosing Among Alternative Investments**   Walker Shoe Corporation is considering investing in one of two heeling machines that attach heels to shoes. Machine A costs $50,000 and is expected to save the company $15,000 for six years. Machine B costs $75,000 and is expected to save the company $20,000 for six years. Determine the net present value for each machine and which machine should be purchased if the required rate of return is 10%. Ignore income taxes.

LO 3   **E28-6**   **Calculate the Internal Rate of Return**   An investment that costs $79,100 will return $14,000 per year for 10 years. Determine the internal rate of return of the investment and whether or not to make the investment if the required rate of return is 18%. Ignore income taxes.

LO 4   **E28-7**   **Calculate the Net Present Value with Taxes**   Smokey Salmon Corporation is contemplating the purchase of a new smoker. The smoker will cost $21,000 but will create additional revenue of $15,500 per year for 7 years. Additional costs other than depreciation will equal $8,000 per year. The smoker has an expected life of 7 years at which time it will have no residual value. Smokey uses the straight-line method of depreciation for tax purposes. Determine the net present value of the investment if the required rate of return is 12% and the tax rate is 40%.

LO 5   **E28-8**   **Calculate the Payback Period**   The Lower Valley Wheat Cooperative is considering the construction of a new silo. It will cost $41,000 to construct the silo. Determine the payback period if the expected cash inflows are $5,000 per year.

LO 5   **E28-9**   **Calculate the Accounting Rate of Return**   The Deaton Company is considering the purchase of a new service vehicle for $20,000. It is expected that this vehicle will increase net income by $7,000 a year for 5 years. The vehicle will be depreciated over a five-year period using straight-line depreciation with no residual value. Determine the accounting rate of return of the new service vehicle.

PROBLEM SET A

LO 2,5   **P28-1A**   **Net Present Value, Payback, and Accounting Rate of Return with Even Cash Flows**   Walter Leland, the owner of Quality Motors, is considering the addition of a paint and body shop to his automobile dealership. The construction of the building and the purchase of the necessary equipment is estimated to cost $678,000 and will be depreciated over 10 years using the straight-line method. The building and equipment have zero estimated residual value at the end of 10 years. Leland's required rate of return for this project is 10%. The shop is expected to generate $195,000 in revenues for 10 years. Ignore income taxes. The annual cost of operating the paint and body shop is as follows:

Item	Cash Flow
Materials	$(18,000)
Labor	(53,000)
Direct overhead	(17,000)
Miscellaneous	(4,500)

REQUIRED:

a. Determine the net present value of investing in the paint and body shop.
b. Determine if the project should be undertaken.
c. Calculate the payback period of the investment.
d. Calculate the accounting rate of return.

LO 2   **P28-2A**   **Choosing Among Alternative Investments With Uneven Cash Flows**   Clean-M-Up Corporation, a chain of dry cleaning stores, has the opportunity to invest in one of two new dry-cleaning machines. Machine A has a 4-year expected life and a cost of $43,000. It will cost an additional $4,500 to have the machine delivered and installed and the expected residual value at the end of 4 years is $3,200. Machine B has a 4-year expected life and a cost of $73,000. It will cost an additional $5,000 to have the machine delivered and installed and the expected residual value at the end of 4 years is $5,200. Clean-M-Up has a required rate of return of 14%. Ignore income taxes. Additional cash flows related to the machines are as follows:

Machine A

Item	Year 1	Year 2	Year 3	Year 4
Labor saving	$21,000	$21,000	$21,000	$21,000
Power saving	1,300	1,300	1,300	1,300
Chemical saving	2,900	2,900	2,900	2,900
Maintenance	(1,000)	(1,300)	(1,600)	(2,500)
Miscellaneous	(2,200)	(2,700)	(3,200)	(3,700)

Machine B

Item	Year 1	Year 2	Year 3	Year 4
Labor saving	$29,000	$29,000	$29,000	$29,000
Power saving	1,900	1,900	1,900	1,900
Chemical saving	3,200	3,200	3,200	3,200
Maintenance	(1,200)	(1,400)	(1,600)	(2,700)
Miscellaneous	(2,300)	(2,800)	(3,500)	(3,800)

REQUIRED:

a. Determine the net present value of investing in machine A.
b. Determine the net present value of investing in machine B.
c. Determine which machine should be purchased (if any).

LO 2,4

P28-3A **Net Present Value and Tax Effects** On Time Charters plans to expand operations by acquiring another aircraft. They have a bid of $828,000 from an airplane manufacturer to provide a 12-passenger commuter aircraft. The airplane has an expected life of 8 years with an expected residual value for financial reporting and tax purposes of $62,000. On Time has a tax rate of 40% and uses straight-line depreciation for tax purposes. The required rate of return is 12%. The following annual cash flows relate to the investment in the new aircraft.

Item	Cash Flow
Passenger revenues	$263,000
Labor cost	(54,000)
Fuel cost	(15,800)
Maintenance cost	(26,700)
Miscellaneous cost	(3,500)

REQUIRED:

a. Determine the net present value of investing in the airplane if taxes are ignored.
b. Determine the net present value of investing in the airplane considering taxes.

LO 2,4,5

P28-4A **Comprehensive Capital Budgeting Problem** Clayton Corporation is considering producing a new product, Autodial. Marketing data indicate that the demand for Autodial will be 35,000 units per year for five years. The product will be produced in a section of an existing factory that is currently not in use. To produce Autodial, Clayton must buy a machine that costs $300,000. The machine has an expected life of 4 years and will have an ending residual value of $20,000. Clayton will depreciate the machine over 4 years using the straight-line method for both tax and financial reporting purposes. Clayton has a tax rate of 30%. It is anticipated that no additional fixed costs will be incurred as a result of producing and marketing Autodial, other than $129,500 annually for advertising the new product. Autodial is expected to sell for $35 per unit and direct production costs (including depreciation of the new machine) are $27 per unit. The required rate of return is 14%.

REQUIRED:

a. Compute the net present value.
b. Compute the payback period.
c. Compute the accounting rate of return.

P28-5A Internal Rate of Return with Uneven Cash Flows (Appendix) Luigi's Pizza Parlor is considering the purchase of another pizza oven. The oven will cost $39,503 including installation and is expected to last 5 years. The oven will be depreciated using the straight-line method. The cash flows associated with the extra oven are as follows:

Item	Year 1	Year 2	Year 3	Year 4	Year 5
Revenue	$15,000	$16,000	$18,000	$19,000	$20,000
Power	(1,200)	(1,200)	(1,300)	(1,300)	(1,400)
Labor	(2,200)	(2,200)	(2,400)	(2,400)	(2,600)
Ingredients	(2,100)	(2,100)	(2,200)	(2,200)	(2,200)
Residual value					4,100

REQUIRED:

a. Calculate the internal rate of return for the pizza oven. (Hint: Try a range of rates between 12% and 18%.)
b. Determine if Luigi's should invest in the pizza oven if the required rate of return is 15%.

PROBLEM SET B

P28-1B Net Present Value, Payback, and Accounting Rate of Return with Even Cash Flows Dana Walentsky, the owner of Ritzy Yachts, is considering the addition of a dry dock facility to his yacht dealership. The construction of the building and the purchase of the necessary equipment is estimated to cost $585,000 and will be depreciated over 15 years using the straight-line method. The dry dock and equipment have zero estimated residual values at the end of 15 years. Walentsky's required rate of return for this project is 12%. The dry dock is expected to generate $195,000 in revenues for 15 years. Ignore income taxes. The annual cost of operating the dry dock is as follows:

Item	Cash Flow
Materials	$(26,000)
Labor	(47,000)
Direct overhead	(13,500)
Miscellaneous	(5,500)

REQUIRED:

a. Determine the net present value of investing in the dry dock.
b. Determine if the project should be undertaken.
c. Calculate the payback period of the investment.
d. Calculate the accounting rate of return.

P28-2B Choosing Among Alternative Investments With Uneven Cash Flows Kar Klean Corporation, a chain of automated car washes, has the opportunity to invest in one of two new machines. Machine A has a 4-year expected life and a cost of $153,000. It will cost an additional $6,500 to have the machine delivered and installed and the expected residual value at the end of 4 years is $12,000. Machine B has a 4-year expected life and a cost of $161,000. It will cost an additional $7,000 to have the machine delivered and installed and the expected residual value at the end of 4 years is $15,000. Kar Klean has a required rate of return of 12%. Ignore income taxes. Additional cash flows related to the machine are as follows:

Machine A

Item	Year 1	Year 2	Year 3	Year 4
Labor saving	$51,000	$52,000	$54,000	$55,000
Power saving	3,300	3,300	3,400	3,400
Detergent saving	4,100	4,200	4,200	4,400
Maintenance	(4,000)	(4,300)	(5,600)	(5,500)
Miscellaneous	(5,200)	(5,700)	(4,200)	(5,700)

Machine B

Item	Year 1	Year 2	Year 3	Year 4
Labor saving	$54,000	$55,000	$56,000	$58,000
Power saving	3,800	3,800	3,900	3,900
Detergent saving	4,200	4,300	4,300	4,500
Maintenance	(4,400)	(4,700)	(6,000)	(5,900)
Miscellaneous	(5,100)	(5,800)	(4,100)	(5,800)

REQUIRED:

a. Determine the net present value of investing in machine A.
b. Determine the net present value of investing in machine B.
c. Determine which machine should be purchased (if any).

LO 2,4

P28-3B **Net Present Value and Tax Effects** Airport Shuffle plans to expand operations by acquiring another bus. They have a bid of $157,000 from a bus manufacturer to provide an 80-passenger bus. The bus has an expected life of 6 years with an expected residual value for financial reporting and tax purposes of $19,000. Airport Shuffle has a tax rate of 40% and uses straight-line depreciation for tax purposes. The required rate of return is 10%. The following annual cash flows relate to the investment in the new bus.

Item	Cash Flow
Passenger revenues	$ 78,000
Labor cost	(21,000)
Fuel cost	(6,300)
Maintenance cost	(5,900)
Miscellaneous cost	(1,300)

REQUIRED:

a. Determine the net present value of investing in the bus if taxes are ignored.
b. Determine the net present value of investing in the bus considering taxes.

LO 2,4,5

P28-4B **Comprehensive Capital Budgeting Problem** Denton Corporation is considering producing a new product, Electroduck Call. Marketing data indicate that the demand for Electroduck Call will be 15,000 units per year for six years. The product will be produced in a section of an existing factory that is currently not in use. To produce Electroduck Call, Denton must buy a machine that costs $190,000. The machine has an expected life of 6 years and will have an ending residual value of $10,000. Denton will depreciate the machine over 6 years using the straight-line method for both tax and financial reporting purposes. Denton has a tax rate of 40%. It is anticipated that no additional fixed costs will be incurred as a result of producing and marketing Electroduck Call, other than $48,500 annually for advertising the new product. Electroduck Call is expected to sell for $30 per unit and the direct production costs (including depreciation of the new machine) are $22 per unit. Denton's required rate of return is 12%.

REQUIRED:

a. Compute the net present value.
b. Compute the payback period.
c. Compute the accounting rate of return.

LO 2,7

P28-5B Internal Rate of Return with Uneven Cash Flows (Appendix) Athena's Greek Restaurant is considering the addition of another dining room. The dining room will cost $55,837 and is expected to last 5 years, which is when the restaurant's lease expires. The addition will be depreciated using the straight-line method. The cash flows associated with the addition are as follows:

Item	Year 1	Year 2	Year 3	Year 4	Year 5
Revenue	$23,000	$25,000	$28,000	$29,000	$30,000
Power	(1,400)	(1,400)	(1,600)	(1,700)	(1,900)
Labor	(3,100)	(3,100)	(3,400)	(3,600)	(3,600)
Food	(5,200)	(5,700)	(6,100)	(6,200)	(6,400)
Residual value					3,100

REQUIRED:

a. Calculate the internal rate of return for the dining room. (Hint: Try a range of rates between 12% and 18%.)
b. Determine if Athena's should invest in the dining room if the required rate of return is 15%.

CRITICAL THINKING AND COMMUNICATING

C28-1 Amanda Li is the manager of the Communications Division of United Conglomerate Corporation. Her bonuses and promotions are based on accounting income. Amanda was trying to decide between two alternative capital investments. The following information was tabulated by Amanda's assistant.

	Project A	Project B
Net present value	$107,000	$32,000
Internal rate of return	19%	11%
Expected life	10 years	10 years
Payback	4 years	1.5 years

Amanda decided to choose Project B.

REQUIRED:

a. Why did Amanda select Project B?
b. Which project should Amanda have selected and why?
c. How could United Conglomerate encourage Amanda to select Project A?

C28-2 Grinders International manufactures a large variety of industrial grinders. Grinders has always used payback and accounting rate of return to evaluate their capital investments. You have just been promoted to corporate controller and you believe that net present value should be used as the primary method to evaluate capital projects.

REQUIRED:

Write a memo to Stan Kawalski, the president of Grinders International, explaining why the net present value method should be used.

CHAPTER 29

Control of Decentralized Organizations

Brian Adams, president and chief operating officer, rose to address the board of directors of Action Industries. "As you all know," he began, "last year we split the company into two divisions—the Tool Division and the Auto Parts Division. We gave Steve Carson, the vice president of Tools, and Ann Harris, the vice president of Auto, a lot of responsibility and the authority to run these operations independently. And, I think our strategy has paid off. Steve and Ann have been able to respond quickly to market opportunities, and the result is a 25 percent increase in corporate income."

Brian then compared the performance of the two divisions using the following financial information:

Action Industries
Comparison of Divisions

	Tool Division	Auto Parts Division	Corporate
Total assets as of 12/31/X0	$25,000,000	$10,000,000	$35,000,000
Profit in 19X0	3,000,000	1,500,000	4,500,000
Total assets as of 12/31/X1	30,000,000	11,000,000	41,000,000
Profit in 19X1	3,855,000	1,760,000	5,615,000
Increase in income	855,000	260,000	1,115,000
Percentage increase	29%	17%	25%

"In summary," Brian concluded, "the Tool Division had the largest income in 19X1 ($3,855,000 vs. only $1,760,000 for the Auto Parts Division). Further, the Tool Division had increased income by 29%, while the Auto Parts Division had an increase of 17%. In the coming year, we will be expanding and investing in equipment for both operations.

I suggest, however, that since the Tool Division is more profitable, we should focus our attention on that operation and budget more funds for its expansion."

At this point, Alister Hurd, the founder and chairman of the board of Action Industries, spoke up. "Brian, I agree we made a good decision when we decentralized and formed the two divisions. However, I don't think that in comparing the two operations we should focus solely on income or the increase in income. After all, the Tool Division is much larger than the Auto Parts Division. We're comparing apples to oranges if we don't make some sort of size adjustment."

"You've got a good point there," Brian responded. He turned to Peter Dunn, the controller of the company. "Pete, any suggestions on how we can compare the two divisions?" Pete assured Brian and the rest of the board that, after the lunch break, he would have just the information they were needing.

As firms increase in size and complexity, business segments or subunits are organized. The managers of these segments must be granted decision-making authority for the firm to function effectively. Firms that grant substantial decision-making authority to the managers of segments are referred to as **decentralized organizations**. Most firms are neither one hundred percent centralized nor one hundred percent decentralized. Decentralization is a matter of degree. To the extent that more decision-making authority is delegated to subunit managers, a firm is more decentralized. Action Industries is a decentralized organization in that substantial decision-making authority has been given to Steve and Ann, the managers of the two divisions. In this chapter, we examine the way subunits in a decentralized organization may be formed. We also illustrate how a company can use accounting information to control the behavior of subunit managers. The goal is to ensure that subunit managers make decisions that are in the best interest of the entire firm. We also discuss how to compare the profitability of two divisions. This discussion addresses the specific problem Action Industries faces.

LEARNING OBJECTIVES

1. List and explain the advantages and disadvantages of decentralization.
2. Identify cost centers, profit centers, and investment centers.
3. Calculate and interpret return on investment (ROI).
4. Calculate and interpret residual income (RI).
5. Discuss the use of market price, variable costs, full cost plus profit, and negotiation in setting transfer prices.
6. Explain how companies can use market-based transfer prices to treat service centers as profit centers.

LO 1
List and explain the advantages and disadvantages of decentralization.

WHY FIRMS DECENTRALIZE

Firms decentralize for a number of reasons. A primary reason is that subunit managers have *better information* than top management and these managers can *respond more quickly* to changing circumstances. Consider an electronics firm that has two primary divisions: a Copier Division and a Camera Division. Division managers report to top management responsible for both divisions. As shown in Illustration 29-1, each division operates in a unique environment.

ILLUSTRATION 29-1 Firm and Subunit Environments

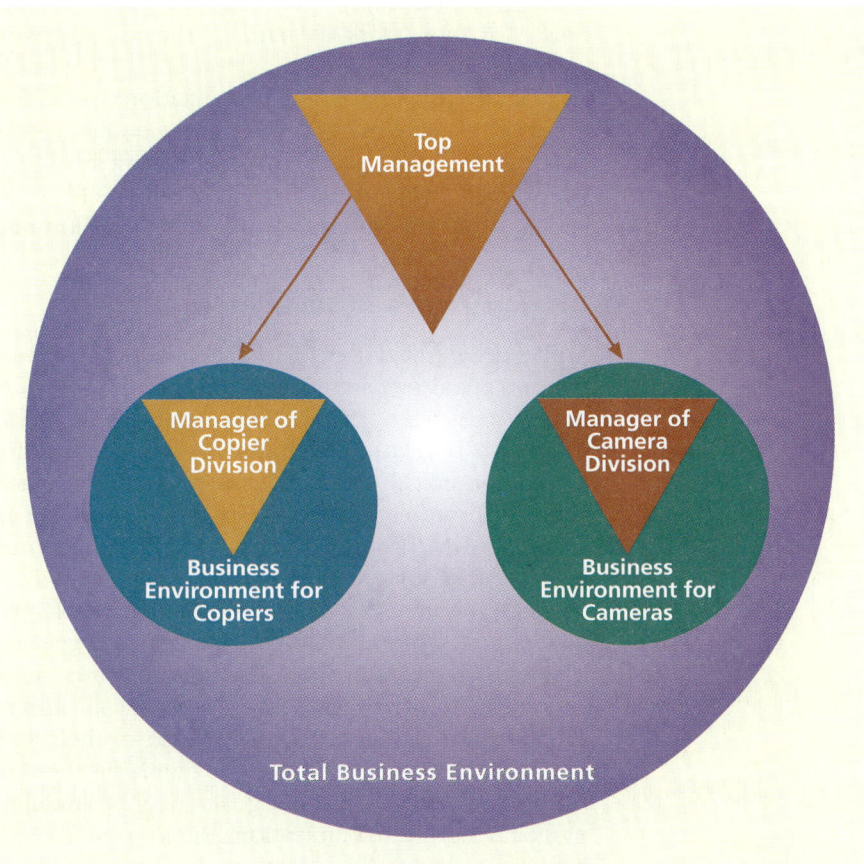

Competition, customer needs, and the supply of workers and raw materials are different for each of these product lines. Suppose a new personal copier is to be introduced in the coming year, and managers must make a pricing decision. Who has better information as to what will be an appropriate price to charge—the manager of the Copier Division or top management? Because of his or her daily involvement with the market for copiers, the manager of the Copier Division probably has a better understanding of how the market will react to a particular price. If this is the case, then the divisional manager should make the pricing decision which will further enhance the decentralization of the electronics firm.

Suppose the manager of the Camera Division learns that a supplier of camera lenses is facing excess capacity and is willing to supply the division with lenses at a bargain price. In a decentralized organization, the manager can react quickly to this opportunity and increase the profitability of both the division and the firm. However, if the firm is more centralized, the manager of the division may have to present the facts to top management who will then make the decision as to whether the lenses should be purchased. This is a more time-consuming process, and by the time top management makes a decision the supplier may no longer have excess capacity. Worse, other camera companies may have taken advantage of the situation and have gained a competitive edge.

Some firms decentralize because they believe managers who are given significant decision-making authority are *more motivated* and work harder than do managers in centralized organizations. If managers are given broad decision-making responsibility, they are thought to identify so strongly with their subunits that they work as hard as they would work if they actually owned the business.

Finally, decentralized organizations provide excellent *training* for future top-level executives. Managers in decentralized organizations are accustomed to making important decisions and taking responsibility for their actions. Thus, when high-level positions in the firm need to be filled, the firm has a ready supply of managers with the required decision-making experience.

Disadvantages of Decentralization

While decentralization has several beneficial features, it may create problems. One potential problem is that decentralization may result in a costly *duplication of activities*. For example, two subunit managers may each decide to develop their own purchasing department when one purchasing department would be more economical. Or, each major subunit may have a separate sales force when a single, coordinated sales force would be more effective.

A second problem with a decentralized organization is that managers of subunits may take actions to achieve their own goals, which may be incompatible with the goals of the company as a whole. This problem is referred to as a *lack of goal congruence*. An example of a goal congruence problem is "empire building." Some managers derive substantial satisfaction from running a large subunit (their empires). Perhaps this satisfaction comes from impressing friends and business associates with the size of their staff and the size of the facilities under their control. However, maximizing the size of the subunits, which satisfies the managers' personal goals, may be incompatible with the overall company goal of profit maximization. Bigger operations are not necessarily more profitable operations. To control goal congruence problems in decentralized organizations, companies evaluate the performance of subunits. As we will see later in this chapter, the evaluation process should encourage managers of subunits to take actions that are in the interest of the company as a whole. That is, performance evaluation should encourage managers to behave as if their own personal goals were congruent with the goals of the company as a whole.

 HISTORICAL PERSPECTIVES

DECENTRALIZATION IN CORPORATE AMERICA

Long before the rest of Corporate America made "empowerment" a management buzzword, Johnson and Johnson was practicing it. As early as the 1930s, longtime Chairman Robert Wood Johnson pushed the idea of decentralization. Believing that smaller, self-governing units were more manageable, quicker to react to their markets, and more accountable, the son of a J&J co-founder encouraged managers to operate independently. The J&J approach "provides a sense of ownership and responsibility for a business that you simply cannot get any other way," says chief Executive Ralph S. Larsen.

Source: Joseph Weber, "A Big Company That Works," Business Week, (May 4, 1992) p. 124.

A summary of the advantages and disadvantages of decentralization is presented in Illustration 29-2.

ILLUSTRATION 29-2 Summary of Advantages and Disadvantages of Decentralization

Advantages of Decentralization

1. Better information leading to superior decisions.
2. Faster response to changing circumstances.
3. Increased motivation of managers.
4. Excellent training for future top-level executives.

Disadvantages of Decentralization

1. Costly duplication of activities.
2. Lack of goal congruence.

RESPONSIBILITY ACCOUNTING AND DECENTRALIZATION

The discussion of cost allocation in an earlier chapter introduced the topic of *responsibility accounting*, a technique that holds managers responsible for costs and revenues that they can control. This idea should play a prominent role in the design of accounting systems used to evaluate the performance of managers in a decentralized organization. To implement responsibility accounting in a decentralized organization, management must first trace costs and revenues to the organizational level where they can be controlled.

For example, consider the information presented for the Jones Tool Co. in Illustration 29-3. Jones Tool Co. produces a variety of small tools in two plants: an Eastern plant and a Western plant. Each plant has a plant manager who is responsible for operations. Currently, two production shifts are run daily and individuals with the title of *production supervisor* supervise the work. A vice president of manufacturing is responsible for production in both the Eastern and Western plants. The illustration indicates, in a simplified setting, how implementation of responsibility accounting would suggest that costs be accumulated for assessing the performance of the production supervisors, the plant managers, and the vice president of manufacturing. Only labor costs and material costs are traced to the individual shift supervisors. This follows because at Jones Tool Co., the production supervisors make numerous decisions that affect the amount of labor and material costs incurred. However, plant overhead costs are not traced to the supervisors because they are not involved in decisions that affect the amount of overhead incurred at each plant. Overhead costs, however, are traced to the individual plant managers who can control overhead costs. The manager of the Eastern plant is responsible for $500,000 of labor costs ($300,000 from the first shift and $200,000 from the second shift), $400,000 of material costs ($250,000 from the first shift and $150,000 from the second shift), and $600,000 of overhead costs incurred in the Eastern plant.

The vice president of manufacturing is responsible for all costs incurred at both the Eastern and Western plants. Therefore, all production costs are traced to the vice president. For example, the overhead costs traced to the vice president are $1,400,000, which include $600,000 from the Eastern plant and $800,000 from the Western plant.

ILLUSTRATION 29-3 Tracing Costs to the Organizational Level Where They Can Be Controlled

	Eastern Plant			Western Plant		
Controllable by supervisor on Shift 1 at Eastern plant	Labor cost Material cost Total	$ 300,000 250,000 $ 550,000	Labor cost Material cost Total	$ 400,000 350,000 $ 750,000	**Controllable by supervisor on Shift 1 at Western plant**
Controllable by supervisor on Shift 2 at Eastern plant	Labor cost Material cost Total	$ 200,000 150,000 $ 350,000	Labor cost Material cost Total	$ 300,000 250,000 $ 550,000	**Controllable by supervisor on Shift 2 at Western plant**
Controllable by Eastern plant manager	Labor cost Material cost Overhead Total	$ 500,000 400,000 600,000 $1,500,000	Labor cost Material cost Overhead Total	$ 700,000 600,000 800,000 $2,100,000	**Controllable by Western plant manager**
Controllable by vice president of manufacturing			Labor cost Material cost Overhead Total	$1,200,000 1,000,000 1,400,000 $3,600,000	

Responsibility accounting also implies that if one segment of a business causes another segment to incur costs, the costs should be assigned to the operation that causes them to be incurred. For example, suppose the consumer credit department of a bank engages in promotional activities that result in the bank's central printing department incurring $10,000 of costs to print a promotional brochure. Since the manager of consumer credit made the decision that caused the incurrence of the cost, responsibility accounting suggests that the $10,000 cost be traced to his or her department.

Identify cost center, profit centers, and investment centers.

COST CENTERS, PROFIT CENTERS, AND INVESTMENT CENTERS

Business segments are identifiable collections of related resources and activities.[1] A segment may be a department, a subsidiary, or a division. Business segments are sometimes referred to as **responsibility centers**, which are organizational units responsible for the generation of revenue or for the incurrence of costs. Responsibility centers are typically classified as either cost centers, profit centers, or investment centers.

Cost Centers

A **cost center**, a type of business segment, has responsibility for controlling costs, not for generating revenue. Most service departments (e.g., machine maintenance, janitorial services, and computer services) would be classified properly as cost centers. The managers of these departments are responsible for

---

[1]"Statement on Management Accounting Number 2," *Management Accounting Terminology* (National Association of Accountants, June, 1983).

making sure that their services are provided at a reasonable cost to the company, but they typically do not have responsibility for generating firm revenue. Production departments also may be classified as cost centers. As an example, consider a department that assembles electronic components into micro- computers. The manager of the assembly department certainly is responsible for making sure that the computers are assembled at the lowest cost consistent with acceptable quality standards. However, the manager probably has little input into how the computers will be marketed and what price will be charged for them. Because the manager has little direct control over the quantity sold or the price charged, the assembly department would be considered a cost center.

A common approach to controlling cost centers is to compare their actual costs to standard or budgeted costs. If variances from standard are significant, management should investigate the cost center's activities to determine if costs are out of control or, alternatively, if cost standards need to be revised.

Profit Centers

A **profit center**, another type of business segment, has responsibility for generating revenue as well as for controlling costs. Consider our earlier example of the electronics firm that has a Copier Division and a Camera Division. Each of these divisions could be classified as profit centers because each has responsibility for generating revenue through sales and controlling costs associated with producing and marketing its products.

Because both revenue and costs (the two elements that determine income) are under the control of the profit center manager, the performance of the profit center can be evaluated in terms of profitability. Evaluation in terms of profitability is extremely useful because it motivates managers to focus their attention on ways of maximizing profit center profitability.

Companies use a variety of methods to evaluate the profitability of profit centers. Income earned in the current year may be compared to an income target or budget. Or, income earned may be compared to income earned in the prior year. Some firms evaluate profit centers using **relative performance evaluation**, which involves evaluating the profitability of each profit center relative to the profitability of other, similar profit centers. For example, the Chicken King Company operates ten fast-food restaurants in a major Midwestern city. Each outlet (restaurant) is treated as a profit center because it is responsible for generating revenue (sales of chicken sandwiches, sodas, ice cream, etc.) and for controlling costs (food costs, labor, heat and light, etc.). If each outlet is *reasonably* similar in terms of size, appearance, and menu, comparing the income earned by each outlet to the income earned by other outlets may be a useful means of assessing the effectiveness of outlet managers.

Investment Centers

An **investment center**, still another type of business segment, has responsibility for generating revenue, controlling costs, and investing in assets. Because it has responsibility for revenue, costs, and investment, an investment center has responsibility for earning income consistent with the amount of assets invested in the segment. Most divisions of a company can be treated as either profit centers or investment centers. If the division manager can significantly influence decisions affecting investment in divisional assets, the division should be considered an investment center. If the division manager cannot influence investment decisions, the division should be considered a profit center. Subsidiaries generally are treated as investment centers.

Investment center managers generally play a major role in determining the level of inventory, the level of accounts receivable, and the investment in equipment and other assets the investment center holds. Thus, it seems reasonable to hold them responsible for earning a return on these assets. However, while investment center managers play a major role, they generally are not given complete autonomy in making investments in assets. Typically, central management has final approval of all major investments. Guidelines may be set such that investment center managers must have approval for all investments greater than some specified dollar amount (e.g., investments greater than $200,000) but may make their own decisions for smaller amounts (e.g., investments less than or equal to $200,000) unless the total exceeds a total budget amount.

EVALUATING INVESTMENT CENTERS

Approaches to evaluating investment centers are discussed in the following sections. Two approaches are presented: return on investment and residual income.

Return on Investment

LO 3
Calculate and interpret return on investment (ROI)

One of the primary tools for evaluating the performance of investment centers is **return on investment (ROI)**. ROI is calculated as the ratio of investment center operating income to investment in assets. **Operating income** is usually defined as income from continuing operations before interest and taxes.[2]

$$\text{ROI} = \frac{\text{Operating Income}}{\text{Total Assets}}$$

Thus, if investment center operating income is $200,000 and total assets of the investment center (the investment) are $2,000,000, ROI would be 10%.[3] DuPont (known then as The Du Point Powder Company) developed the idea of evaluating performance using ROI in the early part of the twentieth century. It has now gained widespread acceptance.[4]

ROI has a distinct advantage over income as a measure of performance. It focuses managers' attention not only on income (the numerator of ROI), but also on investment (the denominator of ROI). Suppose two business units earn the same income—$100,000. A performance measure based solely on income would rate the two units as equally successful. However, suppose the first business unit required an investment in assets of $1,000,000, while the second busi-

---

[2]This measure of income is useful because it facilitates comparisons of investment centers without the added complication of considering their tax rates and the effect of financing the investment center with debt (resulting in interest expense) as opposed to equity.

[3]Exactly how ROI is calculated varies from company to company. Some use total assets to measure investment as suggested above. Others use net assets (i.e., total assets minus total liabilities) or operating assets. The amount of investment is sometimes calculated as the average investment in assets, and sometimes it is taken to be the end of period value. Some companies use net income of the investment center rather than operating income. These various alternative measures cannot be explained in any depth in an introductory text. Cost accounting textbooks can be consulted for a more complete treatment.

[4]See Chapter 4, H. Thomas Johnson and Robert S. Kaplan, *Relevance Lost: The Rise and Fall of Management Accounting* (Harvard Business School Press, 1987.)

ness unit required only $500,000. The second unit has performed much better than the first because it required only half the investment to earn the same level of income. This allows the company to invest the funds not required by the second unit in another project and to earn additional income. Note that, unlike income, ROI does not rate the two units as equally successful. The first unit has an ROI of only 10%, while the second unit has a much higher ROI of 20%.

Some companies break ROI down into two components: margin and turnover.

$$\underset{\text{Margin}}{\frac{\text{Operating Income}}{\text{Revenue}}} \times \underset{\text{Turnover}}{\frac{\text{Revenue}}{\text{Total Assets}}} = \frac{\text{Operating Income}}{\text{Total Assets}} = \text{ROI}$$

Margin is the ratio of operating income to revenue, while *turnover* is the ratio of revenue to total assets. Breaking ROI into these components clearly indicates to managers that they can improve ROI in two ways. Managers can take actions to improve the income earned on each dollar of sales (i.e., increase the margin), or they can take actions to generate more sales for each dollar of total assets (i.e., increase turnover).

Evaluating Investment Centers and Managers with ROI

We must be careful to distinguish between using ROI in decisions involving expanding or contracting investment centers and using ROI to evaluate the performance of investment center managers. Suppose a company has three investment centers with the following ROIs:

Investment Center 1:	7%
Investment Center 2:	15%
Investment Center 3:	20%

Based on these ROIs, it appears that if the company has limited dollars to spend on assets for investment centers, it would be wiser to invest those dollars in Investment Center 3. After all, the ROI indicates that the center earns $.20 of income for every dollar invested. On the other hand, it may be a good idea to abandon Investment Center 1 since it earns only $.07 for every dollar invested. While the ROI of Investment Center 1 may indicate that additional investment is not wise, the relatively low ROI does not necessarily imply that the manager of Investment Center 1 has performed poorly. Suppose Investment Center 1 has historically had an ROI of only 5%. Under a new manager, the ROI has risen to 7%. Should the company give this manager an unfavorable evaluation simply because the investment center has the lowest ROI? The answer is no. While we may believe that a 7% ROI is not high enough to warrant additional investment, the manager has done well in improving the performance of the investment center.

Problems with Using ROI

A major problem with ROI is that investment in assets is typically measured using historical costs. Recall that under historical cost, the carrying amount (also called *book value*) of total assets is affected by depreciation of plant and equipment. As assets become fully depreciated, the measure of investment becomes very low and ROI becomes quite large. This makes comparison of investment centers using ROI quite difficult.

Consider two investment centers that are alike in all respects, except Investment Center 1 was started five years ago and its investment in fixed assets is substantially depreciated. Investment Center 2 was started in the current year. Both earn exactly the same level of income, which is $100,000. As indicated in Illustration 29-4, the ROI of Investment Center 1 is 29.41%, while the ROI of Investment Center 2 is 23.81%. The difference of 5.6% is due to the fact that the fixed assets of Investment Center 1 are substantially depreciated. Thus, the investment base of Investment Center 1 is much lower than the investment base of Investment Center 2. However, suppose additional funds became available to invest in either of the two business segments. Would Investment Center 1 earn a higher return than Investment Center 2 on the incremental investment? While Investment Center 1 has the highest ROI, the two business segments are identical in all respects except for the age of their equipment. Thus, we would probably be indifferent as to where the funds were invested since we would expect both segments to generate the same income with the funds. The point is that using ROI to rank the attractiveness of investment centers can be difficult if the remaining useful lives of the depreciable assets are very different.

ILLUSTRATION 29-4 Comparison of Investment Centers Affected by Carrying Value of Property and Equipment

	Investment Center 1		Investment Center 2	
Income		$100,000		$100,000
Investment:				
Cash		$ 20,000		$ 20,000
Accounts receivable		70,000		70,000
Inventory		150,000		150,000
Plant and equipment:				
Cost	$200,000		$200,000	
Less: Accumulated depreciation	100,000		20,000	
Carrying amount of equipment		100,000		180,000
Total investment		$340,000		$420,000
Return on investment (ROI)		29.41%		23.81%

Some critics of ROI have suggested that undue emphasis on ROI may lead managers to delay the purchase of modern equipment needed to stay competitive. Old equipment has a low carrying value because it is substantially depreciated. Thus, the denominator of ROI (total assets) is low and ROI is high. If new equipment is purchased, it may significantly raise the level of investment and reduce ROI. If managers are evaluated in terms of ROI, they may fear that the decline in ROI will lead to low ratings of their job performance. In situations like this, managers may fail to purchase equipment that is needed for the company's long-run success.

In an earlier chapter, we recommended that investment alternatives should be evaluated in terms of their net present values. Managers should undertake investment opportunities with positive net present values, while they should reject those with negative net present values. However, if their performance is evaluated using ROI, managers may *not* be motivated to invest in projects with

INSIGHTS INTO ETHICS

Delta Laboratories is a division of Banner Products Corporation. As manager of the division, Harold Johnson knows that investing in new equipment is a good business decision. However, he also knows that the investment will reduce his division's ROI and possibly have a negative effect on how top management at Banner views his performance.

When making the investment decision, is it ethical for Harold to consider how it will impact his performance evaluation? Or, should he simply concentrate on what is in the best interest of the shareholders of Banner Products?

positive net present values. The reason is that, in the short run, projects with positive net present values may have low levels of income and correspondingly low ROIs. If evaluated in terms of ROI, managers will be quite concerned about how ROI will be affected by additional investments. The result is that managers may consider the effect on ROI instead of net present value in evaluating investment alternatives.

A related problem with ROI is that managers of investment centers with high ROIs may be unwilling to invest in assets that will earn a return that is satisfactory to central management if that return is less than the current ROI. As illustrated in the next section, this problem can be minimized through the use of residual income.

Before turning to a discussion of residual income, recall the situation presented at the start of the chapter where Brian Adams, president of Action Industries, was presenting an evaluation of the company's two divisions: the Tool Division and the Auto Parts Division. Brian concluded that since the Tool Division is more profitable, the company should focus attention on that operation and budget more funds for its expansion. Do you agree? As you now know, Brian ignored the relative size of the two divisions, which is taken into account in the calculation of ROI. The ROI of the Tool Division is only 12.85%, but the ROI of the Auto Division is 16.00%. Thus, it appears that the Auto Division may be able to earn a higher return, and the company should perhaps focus on expanding its operations.

LO 4
Calculate and interpret residual income (RI).

Residual Income

Another measure of investment center performance is residual income. **Residual income (RI)** is the investment center's operating income in excess of that required for the level of its assets. To calculate residual income, management must first specify its required rate of return. The **required rate of return** is the rate of return that a company believes *should be* earned on investments. A formula for calculating residual income is:

$$\text{Residual Income of Investment Center} = \text{Investment Center Operating Income} - (\text{Required Rate of Return} \times \text{Investment Center Assets})$$

Consider an investment center that has operating income of $200,000 and total assets of $1,500,000. The company has specified a required rate of return of 10% for investment centers. In this case, residual income is calculated as:

$$\text{Residual Income of Investment Center} = \text{Investment Center Operating Income} - (\text{Required Rate of Return} \times \text{Investment Center Assets})$$

$$\$50{,}000 = \$200{,}000 - (10\% \times \$1{,}500{,}000)$$

While the investment center had operating income of $200,000, the company required the investment center to have a minimum return of 10%. Taking into account the level of investment, the investment center should have operating income of at least $150,000 (10% of investment center assets of $1,500,000). Thus, the investment center has residual income of $50,000.

Using residual income to evaluate investment center managers can minimize one of the problems of ROI. Managers of investment centers with relatively high ROIs may be unwilling to invest in assets that will earn a reasonable return, *if that return is less than the current ROI*. Consider an investment center that has operating income of $125,000 and total assets of $500,000. Thus, its ROI is 25%. Suppose the manager of the investment center considers a project that will require an additional investment in assets of $100,000 and will increase income by $16,000. Further, suppose the company's central management believes a return of 10% is acceptable for the investment center. Should the investment center manager invest in the project? *Yes*. The project will yield a return of 16%, which is greater than the required return of 10%. However, will the manager be willing to make the investment? Perhaps not. The investment will lower the already high ROI of 25% to 23.5% as illustrated below:

	Without New Project	With New Project
Operating income	$125,000	$141,000
Investment	$500,000	$600,000
ROI	25%	23.5%

On the other hand, if the investment center manager is evaluated in terms of residual income, the manager will be motivated to invest in the new project. The reason is that the new project has a higher rate of return (16%) than the required rate of return (10%). Whenever this is the case, residual income will be increased. In the example, residual income increases from $75,000 to $81,000.

	Without New Project	With New Project
Operating income	$125,000	$141,000
Investment	$500,000	$600,000
Required return	10%	10%
Required income	$50,000	$60,000
Residual income	$75,000	$81,000

While residual income is an intriguing concept, it is not as widely used as ROI. Some top-level managers note that stockholders and financial analysts evaluate companies using ROI. These managers believe that the evaluation of investment center managers should be consistent with the way these parties evaluate the company as a whole. Therefore, they are reluctant to use residual income as a measure of performance. Also, residual income shares some of the limitations of ROI. Like ROI, residual income requires a measure of investment in assets. Historical cost accounting is used to measure the asset base in residual income calculations as well as in calculations of ROI. To the extent that using historical cost information results in misleading ROI calculations, it will also result in misleading residual income calculations.

Perhaps the most significant limitation of residual income is that it cannot be used to compare investment centers. Generally, large investment centers will be able to generate a much higher level of residual income than will small investment centers, even if their return on invested assets is lower. Consider the situation where Investment Center 1 has operating income of $100,000 and total assets of $500,000, while Investment Center 2 has operating income of $360,000 and total assets of $3,000,000. The required rate of return is 10%. As indicated in Illustration 29-5, Investment Center 1 is generating a return on invested assets of 20%, while Investment Center 2 is only generating a return of 12%. However, Investment Center 2 has a higher level of residual income ($60,000 versus $50,000). The reason, of course, is that Investment Center 2 has a much larger asset base than does Investment Center 1. In spite of the fact that Investment Center 2 has the larger residual income, if a company invested additional funds, it would probably earn the highest return in Investment Center 1.

ILLUSTRATION 29-5 Limitations in Using Residual Income to Compare Investment Centers

	Investment Center 1	Investment Center 2
Operating income	$100,000	$360,000
Investment	$500,000	$3,000,000
ROI	20%	12%
Required return	10%	10%
Required income	$50,000	$300,000
Residual income	$50,000	$60,000

TRANSFER PRICING

LO 5
Discuss the use of market price, variable costs, full cost plus profit, and negotiation in setting transfer prices.

In many cases, profit or investment centers "sell" goods or services to other profit or investment centers within the same company. For example, a university print plant may sell printing services to other university departments. As another example, consider a car manufacturing company that has one division producing cars and another division producing a variety of auto and marine batteries. Most likely the Car Division will use auto batteries the Battery Division produces. The price used to value internal transfers of goods is referred to as a **transfer price**. If the Battery Division transfers 10,000 batteries to the car division at a transfer price of $15, the battery division will have revenue of $150,000. However, this revenue is only recognized for internal reporting purposes. For external financial reporting purposes, a company cannot recognize revenue on the sale of goods between responsibility centers within the firm because the revenue has not been realized. For financial reporting purposes, a company realizes revenue when it sells goods or services to customers outside the firm. Sales within a company are not "arm's-length" transactions. Without this restriction, companies could inflate sales and income by engaging in numerous unnecessary internal sales transactions.

Opportunity Costs and Transfer Prices

In practice, companies take a number of different approaches to setting transfer prices. The primary alternatives they practice are transfer prices based on: (1) market price, (2) variable cost, (3) full cost plus profit, and (4) negotiated price. These alternatives are discussed in the following sections. Which transfer price is most appropriate depends on the circumstances. What companies desire is a transfer price that will motivate division managers to make good decisions that maximize the firms' income. The transfer price that motivates the best decisions is the *opportunity cost of producing an item and transferring it inside the company to the buying division*. Recall that an opportunity cost is the foregone benefit or increased cost of selecting one alternative over another. Opportunity costs as transfer prices will be explained below.

Market Price as the Transfer Price

In some cases, the producing division transfers a product internally to a buying division and also sells the same product outside the firm. For example, the Battery Division of the car manufacturing company may sell batteries to various auto supply companies and also "sell" batteries internally to the Car Division. When the company or division sells a product outside the firm, that market price can be used as the transfer price. The external market price is an excellent internal transfer price because it allows both the buying division and the selling division to be treated as stand-alone, independent companies. Generally, both the buying and the selling divisions perceive market prices as fair and reasonable. The buying division cannot complain that the transfer price is too high because it represents the same price it would have to pay in the open market. Likewise, the selling division cannot complain that the transfer price is too low because it is the same price it receives in the open market.

In some cases, the selling division has cost savings from selling its product internally to the buying division rather than selling it externally. This may be due to reduced shipping costs if the buying division is close to the selling division. Advertising costs may also be lower, and production costs may be reduced if the selling division finds it easier to schedule production for internal sales versus production for external sales. If cost savings exist, the selling division should reduce the market price by the cost savings to arrive at the transfer price.

For example, suppose the Processor Division of Tectron Manufacturing Co. produces a micro-processor that it sells to a large number of companies at a market price of $300 each. The Computer Division of Tectron produces personal computers that utilize the micro-processor the Processor Division produces. By selling the micro-processor internally, the Processor Division saves approximately $2 per unit in shipping costs, $.50 per unit in advertising costs, and $1 per unit in manufacturing costs. In this case, a reasonable transfer price would be $296.50 (i.e., $300 market price − $3.50 cost savings).

Market price	$300.00
Savings due to reduced shipping costs	2.00
Savings due to reduced advertising costs	.50
Savings due to reduced manufacturing costs	1.00
Adjusted transfer price	$296.50

Market Price and Opportunity Cost

We have suggested that the best transfer price should be the *opportunity cost of producing an item and transferring it to the buying division*. When a market price exits, it is a good transfer price because it equals the opportunity cost. Suppose the Sweet Company is composed of two divisions. The Syrup Division produces corn syrup, and the Candy Division produces a variety of candies using corn syrup as a sweetener. The Syrup Division can sell corn syrup to outside buyers for $8 per gallon. If the Syrup Division uses the market price as a transfer price for sales of corn syrup to the Candy Division, it will set the transfer price at $8. However, is $8 the opportunity cost of transferring the corn syrup from the Syrup Division to the Candy Division? Since an opportunity cost is the foregone benefit or increased cost of selecting one alternative over another, what benefit is foregone by transferring corn syrup internally? The answer: the $8 that could have been earned by selling the corn syrup externally is foregone when the product is transferred to the Candy Division. Thus, the opportunity cost equals the market price of the transferred product.

Suppose one gallon of syrup is used to produce every 10 pounds of rock candy the Candy Division manufactures. The rock candy sells for $50 for a 10-pound container. Variable costs are as follows:

10-Pound Container	
Variable production cost, excluding corn syrup	$43
Transfer price of corn syrup	8
Total variable cost per container	$51

In this situation, the Candy Division has a negative contribution margin of $1 per 10-pound container and would not be willing to produce rock candy. Suppose the Candy Division argues that if the Syrup Division reduced the transfer price of corn syrup to $5 (the variable cost of producing corn syrup), then its variable costs would only be $48 and rock candy would have a positive contribution margin. Should the Syrup Division lower the transfer price? The answer is *no*. The Syrup Division's income and the Sweet Company's total income would be reduced if the Candy Division was subsidized by a transfer price lower than the market price. If the Candy Division cannot earn a profit by paying a transfer price equal to what it would pay if it had to purchase the syrup in the open market, then Sweet Company should consider eliminating the division.

The effect on the company's contribution margin of lowering the transfer price and transferring the syrup inside to the Candy Division is presented in Illustration 29-6. If the transfer price is the market price of $8, the Candy Division will not find production of rock candy to be profitable. Thus, the Candy Division will not demand syrup, and the Syrup Division will sell all syrup in the marketplace. In this case, the Syrup Division earns $3 of contribution margin on every gallon of syrup, the Candy Division earns no contribution margin, and the contribution margin of the company as a whole is $3. However, if the Syrup Division transfers syrup to the Candy Division at a transfer price of $5, the Syrup Division will earn no contribution margin because the transfer price equals its variable costs of producing the syrup. However, for each gallon of syrup the Candy Division can produce a 10-pound container of rock candy that sells for $50. The Candy Division will have $43 of variable costs, in addition to the $5 transfer price it must pay for each gallon of syrup. Thus, the Candy Division will earn a contribution margin of $2. The contribution margin to the company will also be $2 because the Syrup Division will have a contribution margin of zero.

Note that while the Candy Division is certainly better off with a transfer price of $5, the Syrup Division is worse off, and the company as a whole is worse off by $1 for each gallon of syrup transferred at the $5 transfer price.

ILLUSTRATION 29-6 Analysis of Lowering the Transfer Price Below the Market Price

Sell Syrup at Market Price

Contribution Margin of Syrup Division per Gallon of Syrup		Contribution Margin of Candy Division per 10-Pound Container		Contribution Margin of Company
Selling price	$8		0	
Variable costs	5		0	
Contribution margin	$3		0	$3*

Transfer Syrup to Candy Division at $5

Contribution Margin of Syrup Division per Gallon of Syrup		Contribution Margin of Candy Division per 10-Pound Container		Contribution Margin of Company
Transfer price	$5	Selling price	$50	
Variable costs	5	Own variable costs	43	
Contribution margin	$0	Transfer price	5	
		Contribution margin	$ 2	$2*

*Note that a gallon of syrup is required to produce a 10-pound container of candy. Thus, a gallon of syrup is equivalent to a 10-pound container of candy.

Variable Costs as the Transfer Price

When, the transferred product is unique, the producing division may not sell it in an open market. Obviously, no market price exists, and the division must choose some other transfer price. The variable costs of producing the transferred good may be the best choice of transfer price in this situation. The reason for selecting the variable costs of production as the transfer price is that it conveys accurate opportunity cost information. When no external market exists, the opportunity cost of producing and selling an item internally is simply the variable costs of producing that item.[5] Each time it produces an additional unit, the company must incur additional costs equal to the variable costs of production.

When it knows the opportunity cost of the transferred product, the buying division can make well-informed decisions. For example, suppose the buying division considers a special order from a customer. To produce the product, the buying division must use a component that another division of the firm (the selling division) will supply. Suppose the buying division will incur variable production costs, excluding the transfer price, of $50 per unit. Further, suppose the variable costs of producing the component are $25. What is the minimum price that the buying division could accept for the special order? The answer is $75, which is equal to the $50 of variable costs the buying division incurs and the $25 of variable costs the selling division incurs. Any price above $75 will increase the overall contribution margin of the company and its income.

However, suppose the selling division sets the transfer price at an amount greater than its variable costs. For example, suppose it sets the transfer price at

---

[5]This assumes that the selling division has excess capacity. If not, the opportunity cost must include the income lost on items that cannot be produced when capacity is used to produce goods for internal transfer.

$40. In this case, the manager of the buying division will perceive that the minimum acceptable selling price for the special order is $90, not $75. The $90 equals the $40 transfer price the selling division pays for each unit plus the other variable costs the selling division incurs that are equal to $50. The manager of the buying division would turn down the special order at prices between $75 and $90 at a definite loss of income for the company as a whole. In not knowing the real opportunity cost of production, the buying division manager may make poor decisions.

Full Cost Plus Profit as the Transfer Price

A very significant problem with using variable costs as the transfer price is that the selling division cannot earn a profit on production of the transferred product. In fact, if the transfer price equals the variable costs and if there are any fixed production costs, the selling division will have a loss equal to the amount of fixed costs. Thus, division managers may not find variable costs acceptable as transfer prices. For this reason, many companies add a profit margin to the full cost of an item and use the resulting amount as the transfer price.

For example, suppose the variable costs of producing an item for internal sale to a buying division is $100 per unit. Further, the producing division expects 1,000 units will be transferred in the coming year and its fixed costs will amount to $200,000 per year. Assume the fixed costs relate primarily to depreciation of equipment. Thus, they are fixed and sunk. The full cost per unit is $300 ($100 variable cost + $200 fixed cost). At a transfer price of $300, the selling division will just break even on the internal transfer. However, if the company utilizes a transfer pricing policy such that the transfer price equals the full cost plus 10%, the transfer price will be $330. Thus, the selling division will earn income of $30 on each item produced.

While full cost plus profit may be more acceptable as a transfer price to division managers, the information conveyed by the transfer price may not measure the opportunity cost of producing the transferred product. As we saw earlier, this can result in decisions that do not maximize the profitability of the whole company. Suppose the buying division must incur $400 of variable costs, in addition to the costs the selling division incurs. The market price for the item the buying division produces is $690. The buying division will not continue producing the product unless it makes a positive contribution toward covering its fixed costs. With a transfer price of $330, the contribution margin the buying division faces is a negative $40 (i.e., $690 selling price − $400 variable costs − $330 transfer price). Thus, the buying division will be inclined to drop the product. However, the product does, in fact, make a positive contribution to firm income. The selling price of $690 is greater than the variable costs of both the buying division ($400) and of the selling division ($100) by $190. Thus, the company as a whole will actually be better off by $190 for each unit it sells.

	Transfer Price Equals Full Cost Plus Profit	Transfer Price Equals Variable Costs
Selling price of final product	$690	$690
Less: Variable costs of the buying division, except for the transfer price	(400)	(400)
Transfer price	(330)	(100)
Contribution margin of buying division	$ (40)	$190

Negotiated Transfer Prices

As discussed at the start of this chapter, one benefit of decentralization is that managers who are delegated significant decision-making responsibility tend to be highly motivated. To encourage the sense of autonomy, some companies allow division managers to negotiate transfer prices. The subunit managers then face the same situation as an independent business that must negotiate a price for specialized items. However, the resulting transfer price may reflect the relative negotiating skill of the subunit managers and fail to reflect the underlying opportunity cost associated with producing a good and transferring it internally.

Service Centers Turned Into Profit Centers with Transfer Prices

LO 6 Explain how companies can use market-based transfer prices to treat service centers as profit centers.

Earlier in this chapter we noted that most service centers (e.g., janitorial services and computer services) are treated as cost centers and are controlled by comparing their actual costs to budgets. However, some companies treat service centers as profit centers. They accomplish this by assigning transfer prices that value the services these centers provide to other segments of the business. Attributing both revenue and expenses to their service centers, companies can calculate income and treat their service centers as profit centers. Companies have implemented this approach because they believe that evaluation in terms of income (rather than just cost) improves the efficiency of service center operations.

The transfer price companies typically use is an estimate of what the services would cost if they were purchased externally. Thus, transfer prices are based on market prices. For example, suppose the computer services department provides computer support to three operating departments at Jones Tool Company. The computer services department keeps track of how many hours of central processing unit (CPU) time is required for processing each department's work. In September, CPU time required for the three departments is:

	CPU Time in Hours
Department 1	100
Department 2	200
Department 3	150
Total	450

If the market value of similar computer services is estimated to be $50 per CPU hour, then Jones Tool could use $50 as the transfer price for computer services. With $50 as a transfer price, the computer services department would have $22,500 of revenue (i.e., 450 hours x $50). Of course, Jones Tool would not include this revenue in the annual income statement because it represents internal sales transactions between units of the same company. However, Jones Tool would include the revenue in the performance report of the computer services department. If the computer services department incurred $20,000 of expenses during the month of September, then it would have income of $2,500 for the month.

Companies must exercise care in treating service centers as profit centers. The approach works best when both the service centers and the departments that utilize their services are allowed to obtain or sell services externally. For example, if a user department believes that the $50 per CPU hour the computer services department charges is too high, the user should be allowed to obtain computer services externally at a lower price. Also, if Jones Tool holds the computer services department responsible for earning income, it should allow the department to sell its services to buyers willing to pay the highest price, even if those buyers are outside the company. It would not be appropriate to hold service center managers responsible for earning income and then restrict their opportunities for earning income to internal sales only. As a general rule, the more closely a service center resembles an autonomous business, the more appropriate it is to treat the service center as a profit center.

Transfer Prices and Income Taxes in an International Context

When goods are transferred between profit centers in different countries, the income tax situations in these countries may create incentives for relatively high or relatively low transfer prices. For example, suppose the tax rate in Country A is 10%, while the tax rate in Country B is 40%. Holding everything else constant, this creates an incentive to have high transfer prices when goods are transferred from a profit center in Country A to a profit center in Country B. With this approach, the profit center in Country A will have relatively high income (which is taxed at a low rate), and the profit center in Country B will have relatively low income (which is taxed at a high rate). Thus, overall taxes of company income for the two profit centers will be reduced. If goods were to be transferred from a profit center in Country B to a profit center in Country A, there would be an incentive for a relatively low transfer price. The Internal Revenue Service in the United States and the taxing authorities in other countries are aware of these incentives and try to make sure that transfer prices are not unreasonably high or low in response to the incentives created by differences in income tax rates between countries.

SUMMARY

List and explain the advantages and disadvantages of decentralization.
Decentralization may lead to better information, faster responses to changing circumstances, and better motivation for managers. Decentralized organizations also may provide excellent training for future top-level executives. On the other hand, decentralization may lead to costly duplication of activities and problems of goal congruence.

INTERNATIONAL PERSPECTIVES

DODGING U.S. CORPORATE INCOME TAXES WITH HIGH TRANSFER PRICES

Economic advisors of President Clinton have alleged that some Japanese companies charge their U.S. subsidiaries high prices for the parts shipped from their factories in Japan. The U.S. subsidiaries avoid showing a profit within the U.S. and tax revenues are shifted back to Japan. Clintonites estimate that the loss from transfer pricing abuses runs up to $15 billion yearly.

Source: Paul Magnusson, "Why Corporate Nationality Matters," *Business Week* (July 12, 1993), p. 142.

Identify cost centers, profit centers, and investment centers. Managers of cost centers are responsible only for controlling costs. Managers of profit centers are responsible for generating revenue as well as for controlling costs. Investment center managers are responsible for generating income and for the level of assets used to generate income.

Calculate and interpret return on investment (ROI). Return on investment is calculated as the ratio of investment center operating income to investment center assets. Operating income is income before interest and taxes.

Calculate and interpret residual income (RI). Residual income equals an investment center's operating income in excess of that required for the level of its assets.

Discuss the use of market price, variable costs, full cost plus profit, and negotiation in setting transfer prices. If available, a market price is the best transfer price. If no market price exists, variable costs are a potential measure of the opportunity cost of producing the transferred good. However, use of variable costs will not allow the selling division (the subunit that produces the transferred item) to earn income. Thus, many managers do not find variable costs to be an acceptable transfer price. Some firms use full cost plus profit as a transfer price. While managers may find this more acceptable, it does not measure the opportunity cost of producing the transferred item; and managers may make poor decisions from using transfer prices based on full cost plus profit. Finally, some firms allow subunit managers to negotiate transfer prices.

Explain how companies can use market-based transfer prices to treat service centers as profit centers. Service centers (e.g., janitorial services and computer services) that are normally treated as cost centers can be treated as profit centers if the company can determine a market value transfer price for the services they provide. Treatment as profit centers may be appropriate if service centers are allowed to *market* their services externally, and if internal users are allowed to *purchase* the services externally.

REVIEW PROBLEM

Watch-While-You-Sleep Alarm Company manufactures, sells, and installs residential alarm systems. The alarm systems include smoke and heat detection, motion detection, and window and door movement detection. They include high decibel internal and external alarms and automatic 911 dialing. Production is done in a single factory building with the completed units transferred to a storeroom located in the same building as the sales and installation departments and the administrative offices. Chin Hui, the company president, designed the original units which have remained basically unchanged. The company has operated successfully since 19X3. Chin, concerned that profits were not as high as they should be, divided the operation into two divisions at the end of 19X6. The Production Division operates the factory and the Sales/Installation Division works from the administrative building. Transfers of product to inventory are made at wholesale market price. As of the end of 19X8, the following data were made available for analysis.

Watch-While-You-Sleep Alarm Company
Divisional Data for 19X7 and 19X8

	Production Division	Sales/ Installation
Revenues, 19X7	$3,600,000	$10,600,000
Revenues, 19X8	5,200,000	12,400,000
Total assets (net) 12/31/X7	1,200,000	1,120,000
Total assets (net) 12/31/X8	1,400,000	1,125,000
Net income 19X7	240,000	420,000
Net income 19X8	320,000	510,000
Taxes 19X7	120,000	210,000
Taxes 19X8	150,000	312,000
Interest expense 19X7	25,000	4,000
Interest expense 19X8	35,000	2,000

REQUIRED:

a. Calculate operating income (before interest and taxes) for both divisions in 19X7 and 19X8.
b. Calculate the return on investment for both divisions to reflect margin and turnover in 19X7 and 19X8.
c. Calculate the residual income for both divisions in 19X7 and 19X8, assuming a required rate of return of 25%.
d. Mark Holland, the manager of the Sales/Installation Division, has suggested that since his division has a much higher return and requires a much lower investment, the company should consider phasing out the production unit and purchasing the alarm systems. Evaluate his idea.

SOLUTION:

(a) *Calculate operating income for both divisions for 19X7 and 19X8.*

	Production Division	Sales/ Installation
Net income, 19X7	$240,000	$420,000
Taxes, 19X7	120,000	210,000
Interest, 19X7	25,000	4,000
Income from operations before income and taxes	$385,000	$634,000
Net income, 19X8	$320,000	$510,000
Taxes, 19X8	150,000	312,000
Interest expense, 19X8	35,000	2,000
Income from operations before income and taxes	$505,000	$824,000

(b) *Calculate return on investment for both divisions, 19X7 and 19X8.*

$$\text{Margin} \times \text{Turnover} = \text{Return on Investment}$$

$$\frac{\text{Operating Income}}{\text{Revenue}} \times \frac{\text{Revenue}}{\text{Total Assets}} = \frac{\text{Operating Income}}{\text{Total Assets}}$$

Production Division:

19X7:

$$\frac{\$385,000}{\$3,600,000} \times \frac{\$3,600,000}{\$1,200,000} = \frac{\$385,000}{\$1,200,000}$$

$$.10694 \times 3.0 = .3208$$

19X8: $$\frac{\$505,000}{\$5,200,000} \times \frac{\$5,200,000}{\$1,400,000} = \frac{\$505,000}{\$1,400,000}$$

.09712 x 3.71429 = .3607

Sales/Installation Division:

19X7: $$\frac{\$634,000}{\$10,600,000} \times \frac{\$10,600,000}{\$1,120,000} = \frac{\$634,000}{\$1,120,000}$$

.05981 x 9.46429 = .5661

19X8: $$\frac{\$824,000}{\$12,400,000} \times \frac{\$12,400,000}{\$1,125,000} = \frac{\$824,000}{\$1,125,000}$$

.06645 x 11.02222 = .7324

(c) *Calculate residual income for both divisions, 19X7 and 19X8*

$$\text{Investment Center Operating Income} - \left(\text{Required Rate of Return} \times \text{Investment Center Asset}\right)$$

Production Division:

19X7	$385,000	− (.25 x $1,200,000) =	$85,000
19X8	$505,000	− (.25 x $1,400,000) =	$155,000

Sales/Installation Division:

19X7	$634,000	− (.25 x $1,120,000) =	$354,000
19X8	$824,000	− (.25 x $1,125,000) =	$542,750

(d) *Discuss the option of phasing out the production unit and purchasing the alarm systems.*

Both divisions of the company have done very well. Both reflect significant increases in their ROI and RI figures. These indicate improvement over the preceding year. The fact that residual income exists, and has increased over 19X7, indicates that the returns are greater than the minimum established by corporate management. The Sales/Installation Division manager's suggestion would imply that the same resources now employed in the Production Division could be invested at a higher return in the Sales/Installation Division. This is not necessarily true. There is no indication of production holding back the sales and installation activities. Finally, the whole issue of production versus purchasing the alarm systems involves many factors not included in this problem. Product quality, product availability, and future opportunities associated with each option would have to be considered. It is quite possible that the alarm company would elect to retain the manufacturing operation because of the opportunities associated with manufacturing capabilities, as well as increased quality control and product availability.

KEY TERMS

business segments, *1140*
cost center, *1140*
decentralized organizations, *1136*
investment center, *1141*
operating income, *1142*
profit center, *1141*
relative performance evaluation, *1141*
required rate of return, *1145*
residual income (RI), *1145*
responsibility center, *1140*
return on investment (ROI), *1142*
transfer price, *1147*

SELF QUIZ

LO 1 1. Which of the following is *not* a reason for having decentralized organizations?
   a. Better information at the local level leads to superior decisions.
   b. Goal congruence is enhanced.
   c. Quicker response to changing circumstances.
   d. Increased motivation of managers.

LO 1 2. Which of the following is an advantage to having decentralized organizations?
   a. Suboptimization through local goals in decisions.
   b. Tendency toward empire building.
   c. Provides a training ground for future top executives.
   d. Goal congruence is impaired.

LO 1 3. Which of the following is most indicative of a decentralized organization?
   a. The physical facilities of the firm are widely dispersed geographically.
   b. The organization is divided into several operating divisions.
   c. Accounting is performed, in part, in the several operating divisions.
   d. The entity grants substantial decision making authority to the heads of each of its several operating divisions.

LO 1 4. Identify which of the following should *not* be used to evaluate the performance of a plant manager in a decentralized organization:
   a. Direct labor expense in the manager's plant.
   b. Depreciation expense on equipment the manager authorized.
   c. Variable overhead expenses in the manager's plant.
   d. Fixed overhead allocated by the central office.

LO 1 5. Responsibility accounting suggests that a cost should be charged against a department other than the one actually incurring the costs, for:
   a. Costs incurred for overhead in a production department.
   b. Costs incurred by a department for services provided to another department.
   c. Costs incurred for direct labor in a production department.
   d. None of the above.

LO 2 6. Identify which of the following is *not* a cost center.
   a. An accounting department.
   b. A production department.
   c. A retail sales outlet.
   d. A maintenance department.

LO 2 7. An investment center is responsible for:
   a. Investing in assets.
   b. Controlling costs.
   c. Generating revenues.
   d. All of the above.

LO 2 8. A profit center is responsible for all of the following except:
   a. Investing in assets.
   b. Controlling costs.
   c. Generating revenues.
   d. None of the above.

LO 2 9. A cost center is responsible for which of the following?
   a. Investing in assets.
   b. Controlling costs.
   c. Generating revenues.
   d. None of the above.

LO 2 10. Which of the following is a responsibility center?
   a. Cost center.
   b. Profit center.
   c. Investment center.
   d. All of the above.

LO 3 11. Return on investment is calculated as:
   a. Revenue ÷ Total assets.
   b. Operating income ÷ Total assets.
   c. Operating income ÷ Revenue.
   d. None of the above.

LO 2 12. Cost centers are evaluated by:
   a. Variance analysis.
   b. Relative performance evaluation.
   c. Return on investment.
   d. Residual income.

LO 3 13. Profit centers are evaluated using:
   a. Variance analysis.
   b. Income budgets or targets.
   c. Return on investment.
   d. Residual income.

LO 3 14. Investment centers are evaluated by which of the following?
   a. Variance analysis.
   b. Relative performance evaluation.
   c. Return on investment.
   d. Residual income.
   e. Both c and d.

LO 3 15. One drawback to the use of return on investment in evaluating investment centers and managers is:
   a. Income from continuing operations before interest and taxes may be easily misstated by management.
   b. Operating income does not take into account the other gains and losses which may have occurred.

c. The historical cost method and depreciation method may provide a misleading asset basis for the denominator.
d. None of the above.

LO 3 16. Which of the following is a problem in using return on investment to evaluate managers?
   a. Managers could elect not to invest in projects yielding less than current ROI.
   b. Managers could elect not to invest in projects yielding less than the minimum rate of return.
   c. Managers' morale may suffer from being evaluated.
   d. None of the above.

LO 4 17. Identify which of the following is *not* a part of the calculation of residual income.
   a. Operating income.
   b. Total assets.
   c. Required rate of return.
   d. Market rate of interest.

LO 4 18. One drawback to the use of residual income in evaluating investment centers and managers is:
   a. Income from continuing operations before interest and taxes may be easily misstated by management.
   b. Operating income does not take into account the other gains and losses which may have occurred.
   c. It does not offer a good comparison of investment centers in a number of circumstances.
   d. None of the above.

LO 4 19. In comparing investment centers:
   a. Return on investment can be greater because of older, more depreciated assets.
   b. Residual income often does not provide a good basis of comparison.
   c. Both a and b.
   d. None of the above.

LO 5 20. When a ready market exists, the best transfer price will probably be the:
   a. Market price.
   b. Variable cost.
   c. Full cost plus profit.
   d. Negotiated transfer price.

SOLUTIONS TO SELF-QUIZ
1. b   2. c   3. d   4. d   5. b   6. c   7. d   8. a   9. b   10. d   11. b   12. a   13. b   14. e
15. c   16. a   17. d   18. c   19. c   20. a

QUESTIONS

Q29-1 List four advantages frequently occurring because of decentralization of an entity's operations.

Q29-2 List two disadvantages normally associated with the decentralization of an entity's operations.

Q29-3 Discuss how decentralization of an entity's operations is a matter of degree rather than an absolute condition.

Q29-4 Discuss how decentralization can improve the motivation of managers.

Q29-5 What is empire building?

Q29-6 How could costly duplication of activities occur in a decentralized operating environment?

Q29-7 How does a decentralized operating environment provide an excellent training ground for future top-level executives?

Q29-8 Discuss goal congruence and how it impacts the decision to decentralize.

Q29-9 Explain how responsibility accounting is implemented.

Q29-10 Under the concept of responsibility accounting, discuss what is done when one segment causes another segment to incur costs.

Q29-11 Distinguish between cost centers, profit centers, and investment centers.

Q29-12 Discuss business segments and how they relate to responsibility centers.

Q29-13 What is the formula for return on investment?

Q29-14 What is the formula for residual income?

Q29-15 Identify two ways of evaluating investment centers.

CHAPTER 29 CONTROL OF DECENTRALIZED ORGANIZATIONS 1159

Q29-16 Explain the advantages of using market value as a transfer price.

Q29-17 Discuss the advantages and disadvantages of using variable cost as a transfer price.

Q29-18 Explain why a division manager might want to use full cost plus profit as the transfer price.

Q29-19 Describe the disadvantage of using negotiated transfer prices.

Q29-20 In an international context, transfer price will be set at a high dollar amount when:
a. The goods are moving from a high tax economy to a low tax economy.
b. The goods are moving from a low tax economy to a high tax economy.
c. The goods are moving to an economy with taxes comparable to the those in the sending economy.
d. None of the above.

EXERCISES

LO 1

E29-1 Why Firms Decentralize Malcort Corporation is a manufacturer of automobile bumpers and is highly centralized in its decision making. The four operating divisions are located in Atlanta, St. Louis, Detroit, and Los Angeles, each serving the large automobile manufacturers in its area. Discuss some advantages that might be gained by Malcort if it grants a greater degree of autonomy to each of its four plants in the form of decentralization.

LO 1

E29-2 Disadvantages of Decentralization Marke Products has three operating divisions. They have been operating under a highly decentralized model for several years. Top management has allowed the three managers near autonomy in operating over that time period, but is now very concerned that depreciation and other overhead costs have grown significantly faster than in other firms within the industry. Discuss possible decisions by the division managers which could account for the higher than average costs.

LO 1,2

E29-3 Responsibility Accounting and Decentralization Rutland Manufacturing Company has two operating divisions, Shaping and Joining, both of which are cost centers. They are nearing the end of the first year of decentralized operation. Describe how responsibility accounting could be implemented in the two divisions to provide a control mechanism.

LO 2,3

E29-4 Cost Centers and Profit Centers Melrose Tool Company manufactures several lines of tools in two geographically separated plants that operate as cost centers, and feed their output into a finishing plant, a profit center, which polishes, packages, and sells the tools. As the management of Melrose finds it easier to control the one profit center than either of the two cost centers, you have been asked how they could convert the two cost centers to profit centers. Write a brief explanation to Melrose's management.

LO 2

E29-5 Profit Centers and Investment Centers Brunswick Tents has two operating divisions that operate as profit centers. Top management has found the high degree of autonomy given the managers has resulted in performance at a level even better than hoped for and they now want to shift further responsibility to the two divisions. This would involve scaling down some of the activities at the corporate office, which is also appealing to management. Identify activities that might be shifted to the two operating divisions which would in essence convert them from profit centers to investment centers.

LO 3

E29-6 Evaluating Investment Centers, ROI Lowery Mill is a division of Mharum, Inc., operating as an investment center. The mill reported income of $250,000 after taxes of

$150,000 and interest expense of $100,000. The assets totaled $4,000,000 with accumulated depreciation of $2,500,000. Calculate the return on investment for Lowery Mill.

LO 4   **E29-7**   **Evaluating Investment Centers, RI**   Modern Mill is an investment center and a division of Abacus Manufacturing. The mill reported income of $300,000 after taxes of $250,000, and interest expense of $100,000. The assets of the plant totaled $3,500,000 with accumulated depreciation of $1,000,000. Abacus has established a required rate of return of 20% of assets. Calculate the residual income of Modern Mill.

LO 3,4   **E29-8**   **Evaluating Investment Centers, ROI Versus RI**   Vassian Valves operates two investment centers of approximately the same size. Use the following information to compare the two centers under return on investment and residual income and comment on the results.

	Commercial Valves	*Residential Valves*
Operating income (before taxes and interest)	$1,200,000	$1,600,000
Total assets net of accumulated depreciation	6,000,000	7,500,000
Required rate of return	16%	16%

LO 5   **E29-9**   **Transfer Pricing, Market Price**   The market price of a sub-assembly produced in the Brockton plant is used as the transfer price charged to the Boston plant. Explain why the managers of both plants will tend to support such a transfer price in the absence of any special cost savings to the Brockton plant resulting from intra-company sales.

LO 2,5   **E29-10**   **Transfer Pricing, Variable Cost**   The variable cost of a sub-assembly produced in the Amherst plant is used as the transfer price charged to the Winston plant. The manager of the Amherst plant is very concerned that the operation of the plant always reports a loss. Explain to the Amherst plant manager why the corporation finds it advantageous to use variable cost as the transfer price and why it would not affect the method under which the plant's operation is evaluated.

LO 5   **E29-11**   **Transfer Pricing, Full Cost Plus Profit**   Four Seasons Paint Company has a plant that manufactures containers used by their paint-producing plants. Margaret Tignor, the manager of the container plant, has been operating this cost center for several years. The containers are transferred to paint plants at variable cost. She has approached the corporate executive committee concerned that her plant is the only one in the corporate group which is not a profit center and that it may affect the evaluation of her performance compared with other plant managers. She suggests that containers be transferred from her plant at full cost plus a ten percent profit. Discuss the disadvantages to the corporate group of treating this cost center as a profit center under this option.

LO 6   **E29-12**   **Turning Service Centers into Profit Centers**   Roberta McCoy, the manager of the vehicle maintenance service department for a large distribution and delivery company, has indicated a desire for some degree of autonomy in operating the service unit. She proposes billing each operating unit served using labor rates and part prices comparable to local repair shops. Discuss how this proposal could benefit the business.

PROBLEM SET A

LO 1,2   **P29-1A**   **Decentralization, Cost Centers, Profit Centers**   Gutierrez Guttering Company manufactures metal and plastic guttering for use in both commercial and residential construction. Production occurs in two separate plants. Distribution is from a central warehouse

CHAPTER 29 CONTROL OF DECENTRALIZED ORGANIZATIONS

through a central sales office. Both production plants are currently treated as cost centers with the budgets prepared in close consultation with the central office and variance analysis as the control mechanism.

REQUIRED:

a. Explain how budgets and variance analysis provide a means of controlling cost.
b. Describe how the plants could be treated as profit centers in a decentralized model and the advantages of such a change.
c. Explain what control mechanisms would be available in a decentralized model operating as profit centers.

LO 3

P29-2A Return on Investment, Effect of Depreciation The manager of the Baldwin Corporation has heard that the ROI as a measure of effectiveness for investment centers will be distorted as assets age. The following data are available:

Total facility assets (gross)	$4,000,000
Operating income for the period before interest and taxes	900,000

REQUIRED:

Calculate the return on investment for Baldwin assuming the assets are:
a. 20% depreciated.
b. 50% depreciated.
c. Explain the difference in the results of a and b.

LO 3

P29-3A Evaluating Investment Centers, Return on Investment Gammon Company produces game machines in two plants for casinos. Each plant functions as an investment center serving different geographical regions. Data for the year of 19X8 are as follows:

	Reno Plant	*Atlantic Plant*
Total assets at plant	$1,900,000	$2,600,000
Accumulated depreciation on plant assets	800,000	500,000
After tax income	400,000	450,000
Tax on income	280,000	320,000
Interest expense	120,000	180,000
Revenue for the period	3,800,000	4,200,000

REQUIRED:

a. Calculate the return on investment for the Reno plant for 19X8, showing both the margin and the turnover ratios.
b. Calculate the return on investment for the Atlantic plant for 19X8, showing both the margin and the turnover ratios.

LO 3,4

P29-4A Evaluating Investment Centers, Residual Income Aphid Pest Control Corporation manufactures ecologically safe chemicals to control plant pests in its Due East plant. Plant fertilizers are produced in its Due West plant. Management is trying to compare the results of the Due East plant and the Due West plant. Both plants were built in the mid 80's and are approximately the same size.
Consider the following data:

	Due East Plant	*Due West Plant*
Reported income after taxes and interest	$ 400,000	$ 300,000
Taxes on income	280,000	210,000
Interest expense	30,000	20,000
Total assets (net)	1,600,000	1,520,000

REQUIRED:

a. Calculate the residual income for the Due East plant assuming a required rate of return of 20%.
b. Calculate the residual income for the Due West plant assuming a required rate of return of 20%.
c. Comment on the relative performance of the two plants.

LO 5

P29-5A **Transfer Pricing, The Alternatives** MacAllin Wool Products manufactures kilts and other Scottish wear from imported woolen yarns. The yarns are woven into tartan patterns in one plant and the various articles of clothing are cut and sewn in two other plants. Currently, the goods are transferred from the weaving plant to the sewing plants at full cost. The managers of the sewing plants have expressed concern that the weaving plant is inefficient and the prices which they pay for the yard goods are excessive compared to goods available on the open market. The weaving plant manager, on the other hand, has complained that the sewing plants reflect a profit which is used to justify salary increases to the sewing plants above that received by the weaving plant.

REQUIRED:

a. Discuss four possible transfer prices which could be reasonably used in the company.
b. Select and defend one of the four transfer prices from the standpoint of dealing with the objections of both the weaving and sewing managers.

LO 6

P29-6A **Turning Service Centers into Profit Centers with Transfer Prices** The City of Portal operates a plumbing and electrical maintenance department which is charged with maintaining all water and electric service functions in buildings owned by the city. Marie Esposito, the manager of the service department, is concerned that many of the service calls are strictly nuisance calls which would be avoided if the departments using the various facilities were billed for the services at regular plumbing and electrical rates. She cites examples of numerous calls for defective electrical outlets which turn out to be unplugged equipment, burned out light bulbs in lamps which could easily be changed by the users, and drains plugged up by coffee grounds. She suggests that her department could in fact function effectively with fewer employees if the city would establish the department as a profit center.

REQUIRED:

a. Discuss how the plumbing and electric maintenance department could be set up as a profit center.
b. Discuss how the plumbing and electric maintenance department could be set up as an investment center.

PROBLEM SET B

LO 1,2

P29-1B **Decentralization, Cost Centers, Investment Centers** The Century Steel Company mines coal for use in steel-making operations. The coal is mined in West Virginia and shipped to Century's three steel foundries located in the east.

REQUIRED:

Discuss the options Century might consider to generate accounting information which can be used to evaluate and control the mining operation.

LO 3

P29-2B **Return on Investment, Effect of Depreciation** Aaron Gest Inc. has two divisions that operate as profit centers. Division 1 and Division 2 have the same dollar total cost of assets, but Division 1 assets are 6 years old and Division 2 assets are only 3 years old. Both divisions reported income of $120,000 after taxes of $80,000 and interest expense of $60,000. Cost of facilities at gross historical cost (10 yr. life and no residual value) were $1,000,000 for each division.

REQUIRED:

a. Calculate the return on investment for Division 1.
b. Calculate the return on investment for Division 2.
c. Explain the effect the different ages of the assets have on the ROI for the two divisions.

LO 3   P29-3B   **Evaluating Investment Centers, Return on Investment** Markwatt Manufacturing produces transformers and generators for electric utility companies. Production occurs in two operating divisions, the Transformer Division and the Generator Division, which are investment centers. The following data are from the first quarter of 19X7.

	Transformer Division	Generator Division
Total assets at division	$6,000,000	$10,000,000
Accumulated depreciation on plant assets	600,000	1,200,000
After tax income	500,000	850,000
Tax on income	320,000	510,000
Interest expense	400,000	550,000
Revenue for the period	6,000,000	9,000,000

REQUIRED:

a. Calculate the return on investment for the Transformer Divison for 19X7, showing both the margin and the turnover ratios.
b. Calculate the return on investment for the Generator Divison for 19X7, showing both the margin and the turnover ratios.

LO 3,4   P29-4B   **Evaluating Investment Centers, Residual Income** The Happy Gardener Seed Company grows seeds in two facilities. The Grass Seed plant is located in Long Creek, South Carolina and the Plant Seed plant is located in Havre, Montana. Both plants have an extensive investment in enclosed propagation facilities to avoid the intrusion of unwanted seed strains into the process. Both plants are relatively new. The following information is from the accounting records of the two plants.

	Grass Seed	*Plant Seed*
Total revenue	$1,140,000	$1,600,000
Net income	250,000	280,000
Tax expense	180,000	195,000
Interest expense	40,000	60,000
Total assets (net)	2,070,000	2,100,000

REQUIRED:

a. Calculate the residual income for the Grass Seed plant given a required rate of return of 18%.
b. Calculate the residual income for the Plant Seed plant given a required rate of return of 18%.
c. Identify further analyses which could be performed.

LO 5   P29-5B   **Transfer Pricing, The Alternatives** MacAbee Modern Parts produces automotive replacement parts in two plants. The Stamping plant stamps all of the parts from metals appropriate for the product and transfers the parts to the Finishing plant, which deburrs the parts, bores, threads, polishes and paints as required. Twenty percent of the production is sold to other finishers outside the corporate group and eighty percent are transferred to the Finishing plant. The corporate offices set the transfer price based on the variable costs incurred in the Stamping plant. Corporate management has had second thoughts about the transfer price selected. They believe that the Stamping plant might operate more efficiently if another transfer pricing policy were established.

REQUIRED:

a. Discuss briefly alternative transfer prices which could be considered in view of the concerns of corporate management.
b. Suggest and defend your choice of a transfer pricing method.

P29-6B Turning Service Centers into Profit Centers with Transfer Prices Johnson Medical Center has a computer assistance group whose job is to solve computer problems in Johnson's fifteen administrative offices. The chief financial officer of Johnson is concerned because the cost of the computer assistance group has increased dramatically in the last three years. The senior employee of the computer assistance group, Mary Pelton, contends that the administrative offices have made unreasonably high demands for computer support and, to meet their demands, she has had to expand her staff. Mary points to a recent case where an administrative office requested assistance because a computer was malfunctioning—the problem turned out to be an unplugged machine.

Currently, the computer assistance group is treated as a cost center and user offices are not charged for services rendered by the group.

REQUIRED:

a. Why are the administrative offices "overusing" the services of the computer assistance group?
b. Recommend one or more solutions to the problem using transfer prices to charge for computer assistance.

CRITICAL THINKING AND COMMUNICATING

C29-1 Raz Corporation, a regional metal products company, has historically functioned in a centralized environment. The new chairperson of the board of directors is considering the implementation of some degree of decentralization of the operations. There are five operating plants. Four produce individual products which are sent to a central warehouse for distribution and the fifth produces components which are used in the other four. All five plants and the warehouse are located within five miles of the Middleground Community.

REQUIRED:

Prepare a letter to the chairperson of the board which explains the advantages and disadvantages of decentralization and includes descriptions of cost centers, profit centers, and investment centers as possible models for implementation.

C29-2 Santoriello Electric, S.A., an electric utility in a Central American country burns coal for generating power. The entity has acquired a high sulphur coal mine in central Tennessee and will ship the coal to its power generation facility via rail to northern Mexico and then by tractor trailer to its plant. In planning for profits, they found that they must file federal income tax returns in the U. S. at an average rate of 35% on the profits of the coal mine. The domestic tax rate for the power facility is 15%.

REQUIRED:

What steps may Santoriello take to minimize its total tax burden and thereby maximize its profits? What legal and ethical considerations should enter into the decision?

APPENDIX A   Present and Future Value Tables

TABLE A-1 Present Value of $1 Due in *n* Periods

	1.00%	1.25%	1.50%	1.75%	2.00%	3.00%	4.00%	5.00%	6.00%	7.00%	8.00%	9.00%	10.00%	12.00%	14.00%	15.00%
1	0.9901	0.9877	0.9852	0.9828	0.9804	0.9709	0.9615	0.9524	0.9434	0.9346	0.9259	0.9174	0.9091	0.8929	0.8772	0.8696
2	0.9803	0.9755	0.9707	0.9659	0.9612	0.9426	0.9246	0.9070	0.8900	0.8734	0.8573	0.8417	0.8264	0.7972	0.7695	0.7561
3	0.9706	0.9634	0.9563	0.9493	0.9423	0.9151	0.8890	0.8638	0.8396	0.8163	0.7938	0.7722	0.7513	0.7118	0.6750	0.6575
4	0.9610	0.9515	0.9422	0.9330	0.9238	0.8885	0.8548	0.8227	0.7921	0.7629	0.7350	0.7084	0.6830	0.6355	0.5921	0.5718
5	0.9515	0.9398	0.9283	0.9169	0.9057	0.8626	0.8219	0.7835	0.7473	0.7130	0.6806	0.6499	0.6209	0.5674	0.5194	0.4972
6	0.9420	0.9282	0.9145	0.9011	0.8880	0.8375	0.7903	0.7462	0.7050	0.6663	0.6302	0.5963	0.5645	0.5066	0.4556	0.4323
7	0.9327	0.9167	0.9010	0.8856	0.8706	0.8131	0.7599	0.7107	0.6651	0.6227	0.5835	0.5470	0.5132	0.4523	0.3996	0.3759
8	0.9235	0.9054	0.8877	0.8704	0.8535	0.7894	0.7307	0.6768	0.6274	0.5820	0.5403	0.5019	0.4665	0.4039	0.3506	0.3269
9	0.9143	0.8942	0.8746	0.8554	0.8368	0.7664	0.7026	0.6446	0.5919	0.5439	0.5002	0.4604	0.4241	0.3606	0.3075	0.2843
10	0.9053	0.8832	0.8617	0.8407	0.8203	0.7441	0.6756	0.6139	0.5584	0.5083	0.4632	0.4224	0.3855	0.3220	0.2697	0.2472
11	0.8963	0.8723	0.8489	0.8263	0.8043	0.7224	0.6496	0.5847	0.5268	0.4751	0.4289	0.3875	0.3505	0.2875	0.2366	0.2149
12	0.8874	0.8615	0.8364	0.8121	0.7885	0.7014	0.6246	0.5568	0.4970	0.4440	0.3971	0.3555	0.3186	0.2567	0.2076	0.1869
13	0.8787	0.8509	0.8240	0.7981	0.7730	0.6810	0.6006	0.5303	0.4688	0.4150	0.3677	0.3262	0.2897	0.2292	0.1821	0.1625
14	0.8700	0.8404	0.8118	0.7844	0.7579	0.6611	0.5775	0.5051	0.4423	0.3878	0.3405	0.2992	0.2633	0.2046	0.1597	0.1413
15	0.8613	0.8300	0.7999	0.7709	0.7430	0.6419	0.5553	0.4810	0.4173	0.3624	0.3152	0.2745	0.2394	0.1827	0.1401	0.1229
16	0.8528	0.8197	0.7880	0.7576	0.7284	0.6232	0.5339	0.4581	0.3936	0.3387	0.2919	0.2519	0.2176	0.1631	0.1229	0.1069
17	0.8444	0.8096	0.7764	0.7446	0.7142	0.6050	0.5134	0.4363	0.3714	0.3166	0.2703	0.2311	0.1978	0.1456	0.1078	0.0929
18	0.8360	0.7996	0.7649	0.7318	0.7002	0.5874	0.4936	0.4155	0.3503	0.2959	0.2502	0.2120	0.1799	0.1300	0.0946	0.0808
19	0.8277	0.7898	0.7536	0.7192	0.6864	0.5703	0.4746	0.3957	0.3305	0.2765	0.2317	0.1945	0.1635	0.1161	0.0829	0.0703
20	0.8195	0.7800	0.7425	0.7068	0.6730	0.5537	0.4564	0.3769	0.3118	0.2584	0.2145	0.1784	0.1486	0.1037	0.0728	0.0611
21	0.8114	0.7704	0.7315	0.6947	0.6598	0.5375	0.4388	0.3589	0.2942	0.2415	0.1987	0.1637	0.1351	0.0926	0.0638	0.0531
22	0.8034	0.7609	0.7207	0.6827	0.6468	0.5219	0.4220	0.3418	0.2775	0.2257	0.1839	0.1502	0.1228	0.0826	0.0560	0.0462
23	0.7954	0.7515	0.7100	0.6710	0.6342	0.5067	0.4057	0.3256	0.2618	0.2109	0.1703	0.1378	0.1117	0.0738	0.0491	0.0402
24	0.7876	0.7422	0.6995	0.6594	0.6217	0.4919	0.3901	0.3101	0.2470	0.1971	0.1577	0.1264	0.1015	0.0659	0.0431	0.0349
25	0.7798	0.7330	0.6892	0.6481	0.6095	0.4776	0.3751	0.2953	0.2330	0.1842	0.1460	0.1160	0.0923	0.0588	0.0378	0.0304
26	0.7720	0.7240	0.6790	0.6369	0.5976	0.4637	0.3607	0.2812	0.2198	0.1722	0.1352	0.1064	0.0839	0.0525	0.0331	0.0264
27	0.7644	0.7150	0.6690	0.6260	0.5859	0.4502	0.3468	0.2678	0.2074	0.1609	0.1252	0.0976	0.0763	0.0469	0.0291	0.0230
28	0.7568	0.7062	0.6591	0.6152	0.5744	0.4371	0.3335	0.2551	0.1956	0.1504	0.1159	0.0895	0.0693	0.0419	0.0255	0.0200
29	0.7493	0.6975	0.6494	0.6046	0.5631	0.4243	0.3207	0.2429	0.1846	0.1406	0.1073	0.0822	0.0630	0.0374	0.0224	0.0174
30	0.7419	0.6889	0.6398	0.5942	0.5521	0.4120	0.3083	0.2314	0.1741	0.1314	0.0994	0.0754	0.0573	0.0334	0.0196	0.0151

TABLE A-2 Present Value of an Ordinary Annuity of $1 Per Period

	1.00%	1.25%	1.50%	1.75%	2.00%	3.00%	4.00%	5.00%	6.00%	7.00%	8.00%	9.00%	10.00%	12.00%	14.00%	15.00%
1	0.9901	0.9877	0.9852	0.9828	0.9804	0.9709	0.9615	0.9524	0.9434	0.9346	0.9259	0.9174	0.9091	0.8929	0.8772	0.8696
2	1.9704	1.9631	1.9559	1.9487	1.9416	1.9135	1.8861	1.8594	1.8334	1.8080	1.7833	1.7591	1.7355	1.6901	1.6467	1.6257
3	2.9410	2.9265	2.9122	2.8980	2.8839	2.8286	2.7751	2.7232	2.6730	2.6243	2.5771	2.5313	2.4869	2.4018	2.3216	2.2832
4	3.9020	3.8781	3.8544	3.8309	3.8077	3.7171	3.6299	3.5460	3.4651	3.3872	3.3121	3.2397	3.1699	3.0373	2.9137	2.8550
5	4.8534	4.8178	4.7826	4.7479	4.7135	4.5797	4.4518	4.3295	4.2124	4.1002	3.9927	3.8897	3.7908	3.6048	3.4331	3.3522
6	5.7955	5.7460	5.6972	5.6490	5.6014	5.4172	5.2421	5.0757	4.9173	4.7665	4.6229	4.4859	4.3553	4.1114	3.8887	3.7845
7	6.7282	6.6627	6.5982	6.5346	6.4720	6.2303	6.0021	5.7864	5.5824	5.3893	5.2064	5.0330	4.8684	4.5638	4.2883	4.1604
8	7.6517	7.5681	7.4859	7.4051	7.3255	7.0197	6.7327	6.4632	6.2098	5.9713	5.7466	5.5348	5.3349	4.9676	4.6389	4.4873
9	8.5660	8.4623	8.3605	8.2605	8.1622	7.7861	7.4353	7.1078	6.8017	6.5152	6.2469	5.9952	5.7590	5.3282	4.9464	4.7716
10	9.4713	9.3455	9.2222	9.1012	8.9826	8.5302	8.1109	7.7217	7.3601	7.0236	6.7101	6.4177	6.1446	5.6502	5.2161	5.0188
11	10.3676	10.2178	10.0711	9.9275	9.7868	9.2526	8.7605	8.3064	7.8869	7.4987	7.1390	6.8052	6.4951	5.9377	5.4527	5.2337
12	11.2551	11.0793	10.9075	10.7395	10.5753	9.9540	9.3851	8.8633	8.3838	7.9427	7.5361	7.1607	6.8137	6.1944	5.6603	5.4206
13	12.1337	11.9302	11.7315	11.5376	11.3484	10.6350	9.9856	9.3936	8.8527	8.3577	7.9038	7.4869	7.1034	6.4235	5.8424	5.5831
14	13.0037	12.7706	12.5434	12.3220	12.1062	11.2961	10.5631	9.8986	9.2950	8.7455	8.2442	7.7862	7.3667	6.6282	6.0021	5.7245
15	13.8651	13.6005	13.3432	13.0929	12.8493	11.9379	11.1184	10.3797	9.7122	9.1079	8.5595	8.0607	7.6061	6.8109	6.1422	5.8474
16	14.7179	14.4203	14.1313	13.8505	13.5777	12.5611	11.6523	10.8378	10.1059	9.4466	8.8514	8.3126	7.8237	6.9740	6.2651	5.9542
17	15.5623	15.2299	14.9076	14.5951	14.2919	13.1661	12.1657	11.2741	10.4773	9.7632	9.1216	8.5436	8.0216	7.1196	6.3729	6.0472
18	16.3983	16.0295	15.6726	15.3269	14.9920	13.7535	12.6593	11.6896	10.8276	10.0591	9.3719	8.7556	8.2014	7.2497	6.4674	6.1280
19	17.2260	16.8193	16.4262	16.0461	15.6785	14.3238	13.1339	12.0853	11.1581	10.3356	9.6036	8.9501	8.3649	7.3658	6.5504	6.1982
20	18.0456	17.5993	17.1686	16.7529	16.3514	14.8775	13.5903	12.4622	11.4699	10.5940	9.8181	9.1285	8.5136	7.4694	6.6231	6.2593
21	18.8570	18.3697	17.9001	17.4475	17.0112	15.4150	14.0292	12.8212	11.7641	10.8355	10.0168	9.2922	8.6487	7.5620	6.6870	6.3125
22	19.6604	19.1306	18.6208	18.1303	17.6580	15.9369	14.4511	13.1630	12.0416	11.0612	10.2007	9.4424	8.7715	7.6446	6.7429	6.3587
23	20.4558	19.8820	19.3309	18.8012	18.2922	16.4436	14.8568	13.4886	12.3034	11.2722	10.3711	9.5802	8.8832	7.7184	6.7921	6.3988
24	21.2434	20.6242	20.0304	19.4607	18.9139	16.9355	15.2470	13.7986	12.5504	11.4693	10.5288	9.7066	8.9847	7.7843	6.8351	6.4338
25	22.0232	21.3573	20.7196	20.1088	19.5235	17.4131	15.6221	14.0939	12.7834	11.6536	10.6748	9.8226	9.0770	7.8431	6.8729	6.4641
26	22.7952	22.0813	21.3986	20.7457	20.1210	17.8768	15.9828	14.3752	13.0032	11.8258	10.8100	9.9290	9.1609	7.8957	6.9061	6.4906
27	23.5596	22.7963	22.0676	21.3717	20.7069	18.3270	16.3296	14.6430	13.2105	11.9867	10.9352	10.0266	9.2372	7.9426	6.9352	6.5135
28	24.3164	23.5025	22.7267	21.9870	21.2813	18.7641	16.6631	14.8981	13.4062	12.1371	11.0511	10.1161	9.3066	7.9844	6.9607	6.5335
29	25.0658	24.2000	23.3761	22.5916	21.8444	19.1885	16.9837	15.1411	13.5907	12.2777	11.1584	10.1983	9.3696	8.0218	6.9830	6.5509
30	25.8077	24.8889	24.0158	23.1858	22.3965	19.6004	17.2920	15.3725	13.7648	12.4090	11.2578	10.2737	9.4269	8.0552	7.0027	6.5660

TABLE A-3 Future Value of $1 Due in n Periods

	1.00%	1.25%	1.50%	1.75%	2.00%	3.00%	4.00%	5.00%	6.00%	7.00%	8.00%	9.00%	10.00%	12.00%	14.00%	15.00%
1	1.0100	1.0125	1.0150	1.0175	1.0200	1.0300	1.0400	1.0500	1.0600	1.0700	1.0800	1.0900	1.1000	1.1200	1.1400	1.1500
2	1.0201	1.0252	1.0302	1.0353	1.0404	1.0609	1.0816	1.1025	1.1236	1.1449	1.1664	1.1881	1.2100	1.2544	1.2996	1.3225
3	1.0303	1.0380	1.0457	1.0534	1.0612	1.0927	1.1249	1.1576	1.1910	1.2250	1.2597	1.2950	1.3310	1.4049	1.4815	1.5209
4	1.0406	1.0509	1.0614	1.0719	1.0824	1.1255	1.1699	1.2155	1.2625	1.3108	1.3605	1.4116	1.4641	1.5735	1.6890	1.7490
5	1.0510	1.0641	1.0773	1.0906	1.1041	1.1593	1.2167	1.2763	1.3382	1.4026	1.4693	1.5386	1.6105	1.7623	1.9254	2.0114
6	1.0615	1.0774	1.0934	1.1097	1.1262	1.1941	1.2653	1.3401	1.4185	1.5007	1.5869	1.6771	1.7716	1.9738	2.1950	2.3131
7	1.0721	1.0909	1.1098	1.1291	1.1487	1.2299	1.3159	1.4071	1.5036	1.6058	1.7138	1.8280	1.9487	2.2107	2.5023	2.6600
8	1.0829	1.1045	1.1265	1.1489	1.1717	1.2668	1.3686	1.4775	1.5938	1.7182	1.8509	1.9926	2.1436	2.4760	2.8526	3.0590
9	1.0937	1.1183	1.1434	1.1690	1.1951	1.3048	1.4233	1.5513	1.6895	1.8385	1.9990	2.1719	2.3579	2.7731	3.2519	3.5179
10	1.1046	1.1323	1.1605	1.1894	1.2190	1.3439	1.4802	1.6289	1.7908	1.9672	2.1589	2.3674	2.5937	3.1058	3.7072	4.0456
11	1.1157	1.1464	1.1779	1.2103	1.2434	1.3842	1.5395	1.7103	1.8983	2.1049	2.3316	2.5804	2.8531	3.4785	4.2262	4.6524
12	1.1268	1.1608	1.1956	1.2314	1.2682	1.4258	1.6010	1.7959	2.0122	2.2522	2.5182	2.8127	3.1384	3.8960	4.8179	5.3503
13	1.1381	1.1753	1.2136	1.2530	1.2936	1.4685	1.6651	1.8856	2.1329	2.4098	2.7196	3.0658	3.4523	4.3635	5.4924	6.1528
14	1.1495	1.1900	1.2318	1.2749	1.3195	1.5126	1.7317	1.9799	2.2609	2.5785	2.9372	3.3417	3.7975	4.8871	6.2613	7.0757
15	1.1610	1.2048	1.2502	1.2972	1.3459	1.5580	1.8009	2.0789	2.3966	2.7590	3.1722	3.6425	4.1772	5.4736	7.1379	8.1371
16	1.1726	1.2199	1.2690	1.3199	1.3728	1.6047	1.8730	2.1829	2.5404	2.9522	3.4259	3.9703	4.5950	6.1304	8.1372	9.3576
17	1.1843	1.2351	1.2880	1.3430	1.4002	1.6528	1.9479	2.2920	2.6928	3.1588	3.7000	4.3276	5.0545	6.8660	9.2765	10.7613
18	1.1961	1.2506	1.3073	1.3665	1.4282	1.7024	2.0258	2.4066	2.8543	3.3799	3.9960	4.7171	5.5599	7.6900	10.5752	12.3755
19	1.2081	1.2662	1.3270	1.3904	1.4568	1.7535	2.1068	2.5270	3.0256	3.6165	4.3157	5.1417	6.1159	8.6128	12.0557	14.2318
20	1.2202	1.2820	1.3469	1.4148	1.4859	1.8061	2.1911	2.6533	3.2071	3.8697	4.6610	5.6044	6.7275	9.6463	13.7435	16.3665
21	1.2324	1.2981	1.3671	1.4395	1.5157	1.8603	2.2788	2.7860	3.3996	4.1406	5.0338	6.1088	7.4002	10.8038	15.6676	18.8215
22	1.2447	1.3143	1.3876	1.4647	1.5460	1.9161	2.3699	2.9253	3.6035	4.4304	5.4365	6.6586	8.1403	12.1003	17.8610	21.6447
23	1.2572	1.3307	1.4084	1.4904	1.5769	1.9736	2.4647	3.0715	3.8197	4.7405	5.8715	7.2579	8.9543	13.5523	20.3616	24.8915
24	1.2697	1.3474	1.4295	1.5164	1.6084	2.0328	2.5633	3.2251	4.0489	5.0724	6.3412	7.9111	9.8497	15.1786	23.2122	28.6252
25	1.2824	1.3642	1.4509	1.5430	1.6406	2.0938	2.6658	3.3864	4.2919	5.4274	6.8485	8.6231	10.8347	17.0001	26.4619	32.9190
26	1.2953	1.3812	1.4727	1.5700	1.6734	2.1566	2.7725	3.5557	4.5494	5.8074	7.3964	9.3992	11.9182	19.0401	30.1666	37.8568
27	1.3082	1.3985	1.4948	1.5975	1.7069	2.2213	2.8834	3.7335	4.8223	6.2139	7.9881	10.2451	13.1100	21.3249	34.3899	43.5353
28	1.3213	1.4160	1.5172	1.6254	1.7410	2.2879	2.9987	3.9201	5.1117	6.6488	8.6271	11.1671	14.4210	23.8839	39.2045	50.0656
29	1.3345	1.4337	1.5400	1.6539	1.7758	2.3566	3.1187	4.1161	5.4184	7.1143	9.3173	12.1722	15.8631	26.7499	44.6931	57.5755
30	1.3478	1.4516	1.5631	1.6828	1.8114	2.4273	3.2434	4.3219	5.7435	7.6123	10.0627	13.2677	17.4494	29.9599	50.9502	66.2118

TABLE A-4 Future Value of an Ordinary Annuity of $1 Per Period

	1.00%	1.25%	1.50%	1.75%	2.00%	3.00%	4.00%	5.00%	6.00%	7.00%	8.00%	9.00%	10.00%	12.00%	14.00%	15.00%
1	1.0000	1.0000	1.0000	1.0000	1.0000	1.0000	1.0000	1.0000	1.0000	1.0000	1.0000	1.0000	1.0000	1.0000	1.0000	1.0000
2	2.0100	2.0125	2.0150	2.0175	2.0200	2.0300	2.0400	2.0500	2.0600	2.0700	2.0800	2.0900	2.1000	2.1200	2.1400	2.1500
3	3.0301	3.0377	3.0452	3.0528	3.0604	3.0909	3.1216	3.1525	3.1836	3.2149	3.2464	3.2781	3.3100	3.3744	3.3396	3.4725
4	4.0604	4.0756	4.0909	4.1062	4.1216	4.1836	4.2465	4.3101	4.3746	4.4399	4.5061	4.5731	4.6410	4.7793	4.9211	4.9934
5	5.1010	5.1266	5.1523	5.1781	5.2040	5.3091	5.4163	5.5256	5.6371	5.7507	5.8666	5.9847	6.1051	6.3528	6.6101	6.7424
6	6.1520	6.1907	6.2296	6.2687	6.3081	6.4684	6.6330	6.8019	6.9753	7.1533	7.3359	7.5233	7.7156	8.1152	8.5355	8.7537
7	7.2135	7.2680	7.3230	7.3784	7.4343	7.6625	7.8983	8.1420	8.3938	8.6540	8.9228	9.2004	9.4872	10.0890	10.7305	11.0668
8	8.2857	8.3589	8.4328	8.5075	8.5830	8.8923	9.2142	9.5491	9.8975	10.2598	10.6366	11.0285	11.4359	12.2997	13.2328	13.7268
9	9.3685	9.4634	9.5593	9.6564	9.7546	10.1591	10.5828	11.0266	11.4913	11.9780	12.4876	13.0210	13.5795	14.7757	16.0853	16.7858
10	10.4622	10.5817	10.7027	10.8254	10.9497	11.4639	12.0061	12.5779	13.1808	13.8164	14.4866	15.1929	15.9374	17.5487	19.3373	20.3037
11	11.5668	11.7139	11.8633	12.0148	12.1687	12.8078	13.4864	14.2068	14.9716	15.7836	16.6455	17.5603	18.5312	20.6546	23.0445	24.3493
12	12.6825	12.8604	13.0412	13.2251	13.4121	14.1920	15.0258	15.9171	16.8699	17.8885	18.9771	20.1407	21.3843	24.1331	27.2707	29.0017
13	13.8093	14.0211	14.2368	14.4565	14.6803	15.6178	16.6268	17.7130	18.8821	20.1406	21.4953	22.9534	24.5227	28.0291	32.0887	34.3519
14	14.9474	15.1964	15.4504	15.7095	15.9739	17.0863	18.2919	19.5986	21.0151	22.5505	24.2149	26.0192	27.9750	32.3926	37.5811	40.5047
15	16.0969	16.3863	16.6821	16.9844	17.2934	18.5989	20.0236	21.5786	23.2760	25.1290	27.1521	29.3609	31.7725	37.2797	43.8424	47.5804
16	17.2579	17.5912	17.9324	18.2817	18.6393	20.1569	21.8245	23.6575	25.6725	27.8881	30.3243	33.0034	35.9497	42.7533	50.9804	55.7175
17	18.4304	18.8111	19.2014	19.6016	20.0121	21.7616	23.6975	25.8404	28.2129	30.8402	33.7502	36.9737	40.5447	48.8837	59.1176	65.0751
18	19.6147	20.0462	20.4894	20.9446	21.4123	23.4144	25.6454	28.1324	30.9057	33.9990	37.4502	41.3013	45.5992	55.7497	68.3941	75.8364
19	20.8109	21.2968	21.7967	22.3112	22.8406	25.1169	27.6712	30.5390	33.7600	37.3790	41.4463	46.0185	51.1591	63.4397	78.9692	88.2118
20	22.0190	22.5630	23.1237	23.7016	24.2974	26.8704	29.7781	33.0660	36.7856	40.9955	45.7620	51.1601	57.2750	72.0524	91.0249	102.4436
21	23.2392	23.8450	24.4705	25.1164	25.7833	28.6765	31.9692	35.7193	39.9927	44.8652	50.4229	56.7645	64.0025	81.6987	104.7684	118.8101
22	24.4716	25.1431	25.8376	26.5559	27.2990	30.5368	34.2480	38.5052	43.3923	49.0057	55.4568	62.8733	71.4027	92.5026	120.4360	137.6316
23	25.7163	26.4574	27.2251	28.0207	28.8450	32.4529	36.6179	41.4305	46.9958	53.4361	60.8933	69.5319	79.5430	104.6029	138.2970	159.2764
24	26.9735	27.7881	28.6335	29.5110	30.4219	34.4265	39.0826	44.5020	50.8156	58.1767	66.7648	76.7898	88.4973	118.1552	158.6586	184.1678
25	28.2432	29.1354	30.0630	31.0275	32.0303	36.4593	41.6459	47.7271	54.8645	63.2490	73.1059	84.7009	98.3471	133.3339	181.8708	212.7930
26	29.5256	30.4996	31.5140	32.5704	33.6709	38.5530	44.3117	51.1135	59.1564	68.6765	79.9544	93.3240	109.1818	150.3339	208.3327	245.7120
27	30.8209	31.8809	32.9867	34.1404	35.3443	40.7096	47.0842	54.6691	63.7058	74.4838	87.3508	102.7231	121.0999	169.3740	238.4993	283.5688
28	32.1291	33.2794	34.4815	35.7379	37.0512	42.9309	49.9676	58.4026	68.5281	80.6977	95.3388	112.9682	134.2099	190.6989	272.8892	327.1041
29	33.4504	34.6954	35.9987	37.3633	38.7922	45.2189	52.9663	62.3227	73.6398	87.3465	103.9659	124.1354	148.6309	214.5828	312.0937	377.1697
30	34.7849	36.1291	37.5387	39.0172	40.5681	47.5754	56.0849	66.4388	79.0582	94.4608	113.2832	136.3075	164.4940	241.3327	356.7868	434.7451

GLOSSARY

The chapter in which the word first appears or is uniquely defined is indicated in parentheses.

A

Ability to bear costs (24): The notion in cost allocation that the allocation base should result in more costs being allocated to products, services, or departments that are more profitable.

Accelerated Cost Recovery System (ACRS) (10): The rules for depreciation for income tax purposes.

Accelerated depreciation methods (10): A group of depreciation methods that result in depreciation expense that is higher in the earlier years but is lower during the later years of a plant asset's estimated useful life.

Account (2): A subclassification of the accounting equation used for storing and summarizing information about transactions that affect a particular element of the business's financial position.

Accountability (l): The process by which individuals and groups demonstrate to others that they have properly or effectively discharged their responsibilities.

Account analysis (23): An analysis in which the accountant uses his or her professional judgment to classify costs as either fixed or variable.

Account balance (2): The balance at the end of the period consisting of the beginning balance plus increases during the period minus decreases during the period.

Accounting (l): The process of systematically and selectively capturing financial data, recording these data, summarizing them, and preparing statements that communicate to decision makers relevant information about economic entities, transactions, and events.

Accounting controls (6): Controls implemented by management to ensure that accounting reports are reliable.

Accounting cycle (2): The sequence of procedures accountants follow to complete the financial accounting process, consisting of analyzing transactions, recording transactions to journals, posting journal entries to ledger accounts, recording adjusting entries, preparing the financial statements, and closing all temporary accounts.

Accounting entity concept (1): The concept that the accounting process focuses on specific, separate economic entities.

Accounting equation (1): The equation that governs the relationship among the three accounting elements expressed as assets equal liabilities plus owner's equity.

Accounting period (3): The period of time for which a business determines net income.

Accounting period concept (1): The concept that financial statements or other reports should be prepared at regular intervals such as every month, quarter, or year.

Accounting rate of return (28): The average after-tax income from a project divided by the average investment in the project.

Accounting system (6): An organization of physical facilities, personnel, equipment, documents, records, and procedures designed to provide relevant information and to accomplish accounting control objectives.

Accounts payable (1): Amounts owed to suppliers for goods and services purchased on credit.

Accounts receivable (1): Payments due from customers for products or services previously provided on a credit basis.

Accounts receivable subsidiary ledger (6): The ledger containing an individual account for each credit customer.

Accrual basis of accounting (3):
Revenues are recorded in the period that they are earned, and expenses are recorded in the period that they are incurred.

Accrued expenses (3): Incurred but unpaid expenses.

Accrued revenue (3): Revenue earned by a business but not yet received.

Accumulated depreciation (3, 10): The cumulative depreciation of the assets since they were acquired; a valuation (contra-asset) account.

Acid-test ratio (7): Liquid current assets divided by current liabilities.

Activity-based costing (ABC) (21): A method of assigning overhead costs to products using a number of different allocation bases.

Adjusted trial balance (3): A trial balance prepared after posting the adjusting entries.

Adjusting entries (3): Those entries needed to adjust the accounts to their proper balances to conform with GAAP for purposes of preparing appropriate financial statements.

Administrative controls (6): All controls implemented by management that are not accounting controls.

Allocation base (21): The measure of activity used to calculate an overhead rate.

Allowance for uncollectible accounts (8): A valuation account representing the cumulative amount of past sales that a business estimates to be uncollectible but has not written off.

Allowance method (8): A method of accounting for accounts receivable in which the business anticipates and estimates uncollectible accounts to be recognized as uncollectible accounts expense in the period of sale.

Amortization (11): The process of allocating the cost of intangible assets to the periods benefited by the asset.

Annuity (17): Any series of equal payments to be paid or received at the ends of a series of fixed periods.

Annuity due (17): Any series of equal payments to be paid or received at the beginnings of a series of fixed periods.

Annuity value (17): The present value of an annuity of $1 equal to the sum of the present values of each of the individual $1 amounts received at the end of each of a specified number of periods in a $1 annuity.

Application controls (6): Controls over the inputs, outputs, and processing logic of a particular accounting computer application.

1169

Application programs (6): Sets of computer instructions to accomplish specific tasks such as word processing, databases, and spreadsheets.

Appropriation of retained earnings (16): A restriction on the amount of retained earnings available for dividends.

Articles of incorporation (15): A contract between the corporation and the state which incorporators submit to states to obtain a charter.

Assets (1, 13): Probable future economic benefits owned or controlled by a business as a result of past transactions or events.

Asset utilization ratios (19): A group of ratios that assess a business's ability to efficiently use assets to generate long-run profitability.

Attainable standard (26): Standards that take into account the possibility that a variety of circumstances may lead to costs that are greater than ideal.î

Authorized shares (15): The number of shares of stock a corporation can issue.

Automated clearing house (7): A electronic system for the transfer of funds between banks.

Available-for-sale securities (16): Long-term investments in stocks and bonds that are not held to maturity or held for short-term trading. Such securities generally are accounted for by the market method.

Avoidable costs (27): Costs that can be avoided if a company takes a particular action.

B

Balance sheet (1): The financial statement that communicates a business's financial position at a specific point in time.

Balance sheet approach (8): A method for estimating uncollectible accounts expense in which a business accrues estimated uncollectible accounts expense based on its past experience with the percentage of accounts receivable that are estimated to be uncollectible.

Bank card (8): Card that permit a customer to purchase goods on credit, while the merchant receives immediate cash payment.

Bank charges (7): Various charges made by the bank reducing the amount in a customer's bank account for such things as check printing, service fees, and NSF items.

Bank reconciliation (7): A schedule that adjusts the company's cash balance and the balance on the bank statement until they each equal the correct amount of cash as of a given date.

Bank statement (7): A statement prepared by the bank showing the activity in the depositor's bank account for a month.

Bearer or coupon bonds (17): Bonds that have detachable coupons that are redeemed for interest payments with the issuer or the issuer's agent. The bearer (owner) of the bonds surrenders them when they mature in exchange for payment of the principal amount.

Bondholders (17): The creditors or lenders who purchase bonds.

Bond indenture (17): A document containing all the debt's terms and conditions.

Bonds (17): Debt securities.

Bonds held to maturity (17): In accounting for long-term investments, a classification of bonds in which no gains or losses are recorded until the bonds are sold. To qualify, the business must have a positive intent and ability to hold the bonds to maturity.

Bookkeeping (l): The mechanical and clerical aspects of the accounting process.

Book value (15): The common stockholders' equity in the corporation's net assets determined by dividing the stockholders' equity by the sum of the number of shares outstanding and the number of shares subscribed.

Break-even point (23): The number of units a company must sell to earn a zero profit.

Budget committee (25): The group responsible for preparing budgets.

Budgeted balance sheet (25): A planned (or pro forma) balance sheet prepared from the amounts in the master budget.

Budgeted income statement (25): An income statement for a future period prepared from the amounts in the master budget.

Budgets (20, 25): Formal documents that quantify a company's plans for achieving its financial goals.

Budget variances (25): Differences between budgeted and actual amounts.

Businesses (l): Private organizations operated to earn profits for their owners.

Business risk (19): The risk associated with the nature of the business and the markets in which it operates.

Business segments (29): Identifiable collections of related resources and activities.

Bylaws (15): Specific rules adopted by the board of directors to govern the corporation's conduct.

C

Canceled checks (7): Paid checks that have been stamped or perforated by the bank at the time of payment.

Capital acquisitions budget (25): The budget for capital assets.

Capital assets (10): Tangible productive assets owned by a business that are useful for more than one year and are acquired to be used in the business's operations, not to be resold.

Capital budget (28): The final list of approved capital expenditures developed after the potential projects have been analyzed.

Capital budgeting decisions (28): Investment decisions involving the acquisition of long-lived assets.

Capital expenditure decisions (28): Investment decisions involving the acquisition of long-lived assets.

Capital expenditures (10): Those expenditures subsequent to the acquisition that extend the plant asset's useful life beyond its original useful life or those expenditures that enhance the asset's efficiency or effectiveness.

Capitalizing retained earnings (16): The process of transferring an amount from retained earnings to contributed capital resulting from such events as a stock dividend.

Capital leases (17): Long-term leases that involve the lessee's acquisition of at least some significant ownership rights and obligations, in addition to the use of the assets over the term of the lease.

Carrying amount (10): An amount representing the undepreciated cost of a plant asset as of the balance sheet date.

Cash basis of accounting (3): Revenues are recorded only in the period that cash payments are received from customers; and expenses are recorded only in the period that cash payments are made.

Cash control systems (7): Systems designed to provide adequate control of both cash receipts and cash disbursements.

Cash disbursements journal (6): The special journal used to record payments to suppliers and service providers and other cash outflows.

Cash equivalents (18): Temporary investments of excess cash in short-term, highly liquid securities.

Cash receipts journal (6): The special journal used to record cash received from customers and other cash inflows.

Cause and effect (24): A relationship in which the allocation base used results in costs being allocated to cost objectives that caused the costs to be incurred.

Charities (1): Private organizations that are operated not for profit but for humanitarian purposes.

Charter (15): A document required by state governments to establish a corporation.

Chart of accounts (2): A list of all account names and account numbers used by a business.

Check register (7): The special journal used to record all checks written.

Classified balance sheet (4): A balance sheet that presents the assets and liabilities arranged in certain customary groupings, such as current assets; long-term investments; property, plant, and equipment; and intangible assets.

Closing temporary accounts (4): The process of transferring temporary account balances to owners' capital.

Common costs (27): Costs incurred for the common benefit of all product lines.

Common-size financial statements (19): Financial statements whose numerical amounts are re-expressed as percent of an important summary figure.

Common stock (15): The residual ownership interest of the common stockholders in the corporation's net assets.

Comparability (13): The quality of financial statement information that enables users to identify similarities in and differences between two businesses or within a single business between two or more periods.

Complete set of financial statements (18): Consists of income statement, balance sheet, retained earnings statement, and statement of cash flows.

Compound interest (17): Interest earned or paid on principal and previous interest amounts.

Comprehensive income (13): The change in equity of a business during a period from transactions and other events and circumstances from nonowner sources.

Computer-controlled manufacturing systems (21): Highly automated manufacturing systems that use computers to control equipment and generally increase the flexibility and accuracy of the production process.

Computer hardware (6): All of the computer system's mechanical and electronic components.

Computer software (6): Sets of instructions that control the computer hardware's operations and direct it to perform computational and other logical tasks.

Conceptual Framework (13): A coherent system of interrelated objectives and fundamentals that can lead to consistent standards and that prescribes the nature, function, and limits of financial accounting and financial statements developed by the FASB.

Conservatism (13): A modifying convention that deals with uncertainty by requiring accountants to use the least optimistic estimate in presenting financial statements.

Consistency (13): The quality of financial statement information that means using the same accounting methods for a business from period to period.

Consolidated financial statements (16): Financial statements prepared as though the parent and subsidiary were one corporation.

Contingent liabilities (8, 12): Potential obligations that depend on the outcome of future events to determine whether the business must pay.

Contributed capital (15): The stockholders' claim to the corporation's net assets due to the purchase of the corporation's capital stock.

Contribution approach (27): An approach to pricing that basically suggests that a company should accept any order as long as it has a positive contribution margin.

Contribution margin (23): The difference between the selling price and variable costs per unit.

Contribution margin ratio (23): The contribution margin per unit divided by the selling price.

Control (6, 16): Steps taken by management to ensure that goals are achieved, only necessary costs are incurred, activities are conducted in accordance with management's policies, assets of the business are safeguarded, and financial reports are reliable. Also, when one corporation owns a majority of another corporation's voting stock.

Control account (6): The general ledger account that relates in total to the details contained in a particular subsidiary ledger.

Controllable cost (20, 24): A cost that a manager can influence by the decisions he or she makes.

Controllable overhead variance (26): The difference between the amount of overhead that would be included in a flexible budget for the actual level of production and the actual amount of overhead.

Conversion costs (22): The total costs of labor and overhead.

Co-ownership of partnership property (14): Property invested by partners in a partnership becomes the partnership's property and is owned jointly by all of the partners.

Copyrights (11): Exclusive right granted by the federal government to creative works for the lifetime of the creator plus 50 years.

Corporation (1, 15): A legal entity separate from its owners created when a state government grants a charter.

Cost allocation (24): The process of assigning indirect costs.

Cost basis (11): In exchanges of assets, the carrying amount of the old asset plus the cash payment.

Cost/benefits convention (13): A modifying convention that requires that information presented in financial statements should provide benefits to the users that exceed the costs of preparing and using the information.

Cost center (29): A business segment responsible for controlling costs, not for generating revenues.

Cost driver (21): The activity that corresponds to a particular cost pool.

Cost-effective (6): A requirement of efficient accounting systems in which the benefits must outweigh the costs.

Cost method (16): A method used to account for investments in stocks where the investor is unable to exert significant influence on the investee company's decisions and where market prices for the stock are not available. Under this method, the investment is initially recorded at cost and is carried at cost until the securities are sold.

Cost objective (24): The object of cost allocation.

Cost of capital (28): The weighted average of the costs of debt and equity financing used to generate capital for investments.

Cost of goods available for sale (9, 20): The cost of the beginning inventory plus the cost of purchases during the year, including transportation costs. Also, the sum of the beginning balance in finished goods plus the cost of goods manufactured.

Cost of goods manufactured (20): The cost of items that have been completed in the current accounting period.

Cost of goods purchased (5): Net purchases plus transportation-in.

Cost of goods sold (5): The total purchase costs of the goods the business provides to customers for the period.

Cost of goods sold ratio (5): Cost of goods sold divided by net sales.

Cost per equivalent unit (22): The sum of the cost in beginning work in process and the cost incurred in the current period divided by the sum of the units completed and the equivalent units in ending work in process.

Cost pool (21, 24): A group of overhead costs based on the major activity that create them. Also, a grouping of individual costs whose total is allocated using one allocation base.

Cost principle (1, 19): Requires that the amounts of assets and liabilities recorded in the accounting records should be the amounts paid (or promised to be paid) for the assets when acquired or the amounts received for the liabilities when incurred.

Cost-volume-profit (C-V-P) analysis (23): An analysis of how profits change when a company's volume changes.

Credit (2): The right side of a T-account.

Credit balance (2): An account balance which occurs when the sum of credits exceeds the sum of debits.

Credited (2): Recording an amount on the right side of a T-account.

Credit memorandum (7): A document reporting an increase in the bank account.

Cumulative preferred stock (15): A type of preferred stock that allows preferred stockholders an annual stated amount of dividends before the common stockholders can receive any dividends. The right to receive the dividend does not expire if the board of directors fails to declare dividends in a given year. Instead, the right to receive the preferred dividends carries over to future years.

Current assets (4): Cash and assets that the business reasonably expects to sell, consume, or convert into cash within one year or within one operating cycle, whichever is longer.

Current liabilities (4, 12): Those obligations due within one year or within one operating cycle, whichever is longer, and that must be satisfied by paying cash, providing other current assets, or incurring other current liabilities.

Current ratio (4): Current assets divided by current liabilities.

Current value (10): The amount that the asset could be sold for at its current age and in its current condition.

D

Days-purchases-in-payables (12): Accounts payable divided by purchases times the days in the period.

Days-sales-in-receivables (8): Accounts receivable divided by credit sales times days in the period.

Debit (2): The left side of a T-account.

Debit balance (2): An account balance which occurs when the sum of debits exceeds the sum or credits.

Debited (2): Recording an amount on the left side of a T-account.

Debit memorandum (7): A document reporting a decrease in the bank account.

Debt-equity ratio (17): Total liabilities divided by total stockholders' equity.

Decentralized organizations (29): Firms that grant substantial decision-making authority to the managers of segments.

Decision usefulness (13): The primary qualitative characteristic of financial statement information that requires the information to be useful in making investment, credit, and other decisions.

Declaration date (15): The date that the board of directors declares the dividend and is legally bound to pay the dividend on a stated payment date.

Defined-benefit pension plan (12): A plan that promises employees specific retirement benefits based on their lengths of service and their level of earnings.

Defined-contribution pension plan (12): A plan in which the employer sets aside a specific amount each pay period for each employee, based on the employee's level of earnings.

Deflation (19): General decreases in prices.

Demand notes (8): Promissory notes that are due at any time the payee or holder in due course presents them for payment.

Denominations of bonds (17): The amounts that appear on the face of the bonds, also referred to as par values, face values, principal amounts and maturity values.

Depletion (11): The process of allocating the cost of natural resources to the periods benefited by the assets.

Deposits-in-transit (7): Deposits made and recorded by the business but not received by the bank in time to appear on the current bank statement.

Depreciable cost (10): The cost of the plant asset minus the estimated residual value.

Depreciation (10): The process of allocating the cost of the assets to the periods benefited from the services they provide.

Depreciation expense (3): The expense that recognizes the expiration of portions of the total lifetime usefulness of plant assets.

Depreciation income tax shield (28): The tax savings resulting from depreciation.

Depreciation schedule (10): A schedule showing the allocation of depreciation expense over the plant asset's useful life.

Differential costs and revenues (27): Cost of revenue items that differ among alternatives.

Direct cost (20): A cost that is directly traceable to a product, activity, or department.

Direct costing (23): An alternative to full costing in which only variable production costs are included in inventory. All fixed production costs are treated as period costs.

Direct labor (20): All labor that is directly traced to items produced.

Direct material (20): All materials and parts that are directly traced to items produced.

Direct method (18): A method of presenting cash flows from operating activities showing major classes of cash receipts and cash payments and their sum.

Direct method of allocating costs (24): The allocation of service department costs to production departments but not to other service departments.

Direct write-off method (8): A method of accounting for uncollectible accounts in which accounts receivable and customers' accounts are credited and Uncollectible Accounts Expense is debited when amounts owed are deemed to be uncollectible. The method is not acceptable under GAAP, but is acceptable under the Internal Revenue Code.

Discount (8, 17): When notes or bonds are sold for less than face or maturity value, the discount is the difference between the selling price and the face or maturity value.

Discounting a note (8): The process of selling or assigning a note.

Dissimilar assets (11): In accounting for exchanges of plant assets, assets that serve different functions.

Distributions to owners (1, 13): Decreases in the equity of a business resulting from transferring assets, rendering services, or incurring liabilities by the business to owners.

Dividend payout (16): Dividends per share divided by earnings per share.

Dividends (1, 15): Distributions by corporations to its stockholders.

Dividends in arrears (15): The undeclared dividends on cumulative preferred stock from previous years.

Dividend yield (16): Dividends per share divided by the market price per share.

Double-declining-balance method (10): A method of depreciation that allocates depreciation expense by multiplying the asset's carrying amount by 200% of the straight-line rate.

Double-entry rule (1): Each change in an element of the accounting equation must be matched by at least one change that has an equal, but opposite, effect.

Double taxation of corporations (15): The fact that corporations pay tax on their pre-tax earnings and stockholders must include dividends (distributions of a corporation's after-tax earnings) in taxable income.

E

Earnings per share (EPS) (15): The ratio of net income available to the common stockholders to the number of shares of common stock outstanding.

Economic entities (I): Any entity that carries on economic activities such as buying or selling products or providing or consuming services.

Effective interest rate (17): The interest rate at which the present value of all the payments due on a bond equal the proceeds of issuing the bond.

Electronic funds transfers (7): A system that manages the transfer of cash electronically, rather than by coins, currency, or checks.

Elements of financial statements (13): Classes of items included in financial statements as defined by the FASB.

Employee benefits (12): Benefits such as insurance and pension plans provided to employees as part of their compensation.

Employee earnings record (12): A record of the individual employee's earnings, withholdings, and deductions for each payroll period and often cumulatively from the beginning of the year.

Employer payroll expense register (12): A special journal used to record all the payroll expenses, other than the employees' gross wages and salaries expense.

Equity (13, 24): The residual interest in the assets of an entity that remains after deducting its liabilities. In a business, the equity is the ownership interest. Also, the notion in cost allocation that suggests that the allocation base should result in allocations that are perceived to be fair.

Equity method (16): A method used to account for long-term investments in another company's stock that is large enough that the investor is able to exert significant influence on the investee company's operating and financial policies. Under this method, the investment is initially recorded at cost, and the investor recognizes in its net income the earning of income by the investee.

Equivalent units (22): Partially completed units expressed as a comparable number of whole units.

Estimated liabilities (12): Liabilities whose exact amounts will not be known until future events occur.

Estimated net realizable value (9): Estimated selling price less the estimated costs of disposing of the merchandise.

Estimated residual value (estimated salvage value) (10): Either the estimated net proceeds if the plant asset is sold or the trade-in value if the plant asset is traded in on a replacement asset.

Estimated useful life (10): The estimated period of time that the business can use the plant asset in the business.

Exchange rate (16): The value of one currency expressed in terms of another currency.

Expenses (1, 13): Decreases in net assets caused by the revenue-producing activities during a specific period. Outflows or other using up of assets or incurrences of liabilities from delivering or producing goods, rendering services, or carrying out other activities that constitute the entity's ongoing major or central operations.

Extraordinary items (19): Items that create gains or losses but are not normal parts of doing business and are not expected to repeat themselves in the foreseeable future.

F

Face amount (8): The amount stated on a bond or promissory note as the principal amount due at maturity.

Feedback value (13): A characteristic of relevance that information should be able to improve decision makers' capabilities to predict by providing feedback about earlier expectations.

Financial accounting (I): An area of accounting that specializes in the processes and principles used to prepare financial statements.

Financial auditing (I): An independent investigative activity through which public accountants lend credibility to the financial statements or other representations of economic entities.

Financial position (1): The relationship among assets, liabilities, and owner's equity.

Financial ratios (19): Numerical statistics that represent important relationships between financial statement amounts.

Financial risk (19): The risk incurred when a business uses debt financing.

Financial statement analysis (19): The art of systematically utilizing (1) financial statement data, (2) ratios and other statistics calculated from financial statement data, and (3) information related to the financial statements to answer questions about a business and to make predictions about its future.

Financial statements (1): Standardized reports prepared by organizations for use by outsiders such as owners and prospective owners of a business, lenders, customers, and creditors.

Finished goods inventory (20): The cost of goods that are completed and ready to sell.

First-in, first-out (FIFO) (9): A method of assigning cost to the ending inventory assuming that the cost of the units in ending inventory consists of the costs of the most recent units purchased.

Fiscal year (3): The specific twelve-month accounting period a business adopts.

Fixed assets (10): Tangible productive assets owned by a business that are useful for more than one year and are acquired to be used in the business's operations, not to be resold.

Fixed costs (20, 23): Those costs that do not change when there are changes in business activity.

Flexibility (6): An accounting system objective that requires the system to support new decisions without needing major modifications.

Flexible budget (25): A budget that is adjusted for the actual level of activity.

Flexible manufacturing systems (21): Manufacturing systems configured so that machines easily can be adjusted to produce a number of different products or variations of standard products.

Foreign currency transaction (16): A transaction that calls for settlement in a currency other than the U.S. dollar.

Franchise (11): A legal agreement in which one party grants the exclusive right to another party to market a product or provide a service within a designated geographical area.

Full cost (21): Product cost information that reflects the total cost of manufacturing a product.

Full cost pricing (27): A cost-based approach to pricing in which the cost marked up is the full cost of an item, including fixed and variable costs.

Full term (17): The total time between the date the bond can first be issued and the date it matures.

G

Gains (13): Increases in equity from peripheral or incidental transactions of an entity and from all other transactions and other events and circumstances affecting the entity except those that result from revenues or investments by owners.

General and administrative expenses (5): Expenses that do not relate directly to the selling function.

General controls (6): Controls oriented toward organizing the data processing function and protecting computer equipment and related documents, files, etc.

General journal (2): A chronological listing of transactions.

General ledger (2): A collection of all the business's accounts.

Generally Accepted Accounting Principles (1): Professional standards to which the financial statements published and distributed by U.S. businesses must conform.

General price changes (19): The general trend in prices in the economy as a whole, in a major sector of the economy, or in a region of the country.

Going-concern assumption (3, 13): In the absence of evidence to the contrary, the assumption that the business will continue to operate indefinitely.

Goods in transit (9): Items of merchandise in the possession of a carrier, such as a trucking, railroad, or airline company.

Goodwill (11, 16): The business's ability to generate earnings at a higher rate than is normal for the industry in which the business operates. Goodwill is only recorded when an entire business or a major portion of a business is purchased. Also, the excess of cost over the fair value of the net assets.

Government accounting (1): A category of accounting consisting of the same activities as private accounting—but performed in cities, counties, and state and federal agencies.

Governments (1): Public organizations formed to supply essential public services to the citizenry and to the state.

Gross pay (12): Total salary or wages of an employee for a period.

Gross profit (5): The difference between net sales and the cost of goods sold.

Gross profit method (9): A method of estimating inventories for interim financial statements using a cost of goods sold to sales ratio.

Gross profit ratio (5): Gross profit divided by net sales.

Gross sales (5): The sum of the prices of all goods a business sells in a period.

H

High-low method (23): A method of estimating fixed and variable cost components in which a straight line is fitted to the data points representing the highest and lowest levels of activity.

Holder in due course (8): The buyer of a negotiable promissory note having equal or greater rights than the original payee.

Horizontal analysis (19): Analysis of the rates of change across periods in the components of a particular financial statement.

I

Ideal standard (26): Standards developed under the assumption that no obstacles to the production process will be encountered.

Implicit principal payment (17): The amount by which an installment payment reduces the principal amount owed on a note, determined by subtracting the interest component from the total payment.

Improvements (10): A subsequent expenditure that makes a plant asset more efficient or effective, but does not necessarily extend the asset's useful life.

Income persistence (19): The tendency for a component of income to continue in future periods under steady-state (no change) assumptions.

Income quality (19): The degree to which management does not exercise or does not have the opportunity to manipulate the firm's income to paint an optimistic picture of ongoing income.

Income statement (1): The financial statement that communicates the revenues, expenses, and net income of a business for a period of time.

Income statement approach (8): A method in which a business accrues and estimates uncollectible accounts expense based on its past experience with average collections per dollar of credit sales.

Income Summary (4): A temporary account to which all revenue and expense accounts are closed.

Independent auditor's report (19): A report prepared by an independent auditor for the purpose of issuing an opinion whether financial statements fairly present what they are supposed to present in all material respects in conformance with GAAP.

Indirect costs (20): A cost that either is not directly traceable to a product, activity, or department or is not worth tracing.

Indirect labor costs (20): All labor costs that are not directly traced to items produced.

Indirect materials (20): All materials and parts that are not directly traced to items produced.

Indirect method (18): A method of presenting cash flows from operating activities the begins with net income and shows the adjustments necessary to determine cash flows from operating activities.

Indirect (net) method (8): A method of reporting the effect of uncollectible accounts on the balance sheet in which accounts receivable are reported net of the allowance for uncollectible accounts.

Inflation (19): General increases in prices.

Installment loan (17): A loan that is repaid with a series of equally spaced payments of a constant amount.

Installment method (13): A method of recognizing revenue from an installment sale where each receipt of cash is considered to consist of a recovery of part of the cost of the goods sold and part of the gross profit from the sale used when there is significant uncertainty about whether the cash will be collected.

Intangible assets (4, 11): Noncurrent assets that have no physical substance such as patents, copyrights, franchises, and trademarks.

Interest (8): The expense a borrower incurs and the revenue or income a lender earns for the use of the money owed in fixed-amount agreements such as promissory notes.

Interest-bearing note(8): A debt instrument that expressly states an interest rate to be applied to the face amount of the note.

Interest method of amortization (17): A method of amortization in which interest expense is determined by applying the implicit interest rate to the bond's carrying value and amortization of premium or discount is the difference between interest expense and interest paid.

Interest rate (8): The percentage rate that applies to the face amount of the note.

Interim financial reports (3): Financial statements for a period less than a year.

Internal audit (l): An investigation by accountants of an economic entity designed to determine whether: employees and departments conform to management (or government) policies; functions in the organization are performed at reasonable cost; and a department or division is fully meeting its goals and objectives.

Internal rate of return (28): The rate of return that equates the present value of future cash flows to the investment outlay.

Inventory turnover (9): The rate at which inventory passes through a business.

Inventory turnover ratio (9): Cost of goods sold divided by average inventory.

Investment center (29): A business segment responsible for generating revenue, controlling costs, and investing in assets.

Investments by owners (1, 13): Increases in equity of a business resulting from transfers to it other entities of cash or other assets from entities that wish to obtain or increase their ownership interests.

Issuer of bonds (17): An entity that borrows by issuing debt securities called bonds.

J

Job (21): An individual product or batch of which a company needs cost information.

Job cost sheet (21): A form used to accumulate the cost of producing the item or items ordered.

Joint costs (24): The costs of the common inputs to be allocated to two or more products.

Joint products (24): Two or more products that always arise from common inputs.

Journal entry (2): The recording of one event or transaction in the general journal.

Journalizing (2): The process of recording a transaction.

Just-in-time (JIT) system (21): A manufacturing system designed to minimize inventories of raw materials and work in process.

L

Labor efficiency variance (26): The difference between the standard labor hours allowed for the number of units produced and the actual number of labor hours worked times the standard labor wage rate.

Labor rate variance (26): The difference between the standard and actual wage rates times the actual number of labor hours worked.

Large stock dividend (16): A stock dividend that is greater than 20-25% of the outstanding shares.

Last-in, first-out (LIFO) (9): A method of assigning cost to the ending inventory assuming that the cost of the units in ending inventory consists of the costs of the earliest units purchased.

Legal capital (15): The minimum amount of contributed capital for the number of shares issued.

Leverage (19): The effect of using debt financing to complement owner's capital to provide the necessary funds to operate a business.

Liabilities (1, 12, 13): Probable future sacrifices or economic benefits arising from present obligations of a business to transfer assets or provide services to other entities in the future as a result of past transactions or events.

Like-kind exchanges (11): Exchanges of similar plant assets for which no taxable gain or loss may be recognized.

Limited life (14): The characteristic of a partnership that any event or act that terminates the partnership agreement terminates the partnership.

Limited partnership (14): A form of partnership in which the general partner has unlimited liability, but the limited partners are liable only for the amount of their investment in the partnership.

Liquidity (4): The expected length of time needed to convert an asset into cash.

Liquidity ratios (19): A group of ratios that assess a business's ability to meet its current obligations as they come due.

Long-term investments (4): Assets a business does not expect to sell or collect within one year or within the operating cycle, whichever is longer.

1175

Losses (13): Decreases in equity from peripheral or incidental transactions of an entity and from all other transactions and other events and circumstances affecting the entity except those that result from expenses or distributions to owners.

Lower-of-cost-or-market rule (9): Reporting inventories at market value when the market value has fallen below cost.

Lump-sum allocation (24): Allocations of fixed costs in which predetermined amounts are allocated regardless of changes in the level of activity.

M

Majority interest (16): When a company owns more than 50% of another company's voting stock.

Maker of a note (8): The party who makes a written promise to pay.

Management by exception (20, 25): Managers investigate departures (or variances) from the plan that appear to be exceptional; they do not investigate minor departures (or variances) from the plan.

Managerial accounting (l, 20): An area of accounting that specializes in preparing information for use by managers in making decisions about the current and future activities of economic entities.

Market value (15): The price at which investors can sell and purchase assets, such as shares of stock.

Manufacturing costs (20): All costs associated with the production of goods.

Manufacturing overhead (20): The costs of all manufacturing activities other than direct material and direct labor.

Margin of safety (23): The difference between the expected level of sales and break-even sales.

Master budget (25): A comprehensive planning document that incorporates a number of individual budgets.

Matching principle (2, 13): The accounting principle that states that expenses incurred to produce products and services should be recognized in the same period that revenues from those products and services are recognized.

Material difference (17): Amount of an error or omission in financial statements that could alter the decision of a qualified and informed individual who takes the care to analyze the financial statements.

Materiality (8, 13): The amount of error or incorrectness in a set of financial statements that could change a decision of a knowledgeable user of financial statements. A modifying convention that involves judgments about whether errors and omissions in financial statements are of sufficient size to cause the financial statements to be misleading.

Material price variance (26): The difference between the standard and actual prices per unit of material times the actual quantity of material used.

Material quantity variance (26): The difference between the standard quantity of material allowed for the number of units produced and the actual quantity of material used times the standard price of the material.

Maturity value of a note or bond (8): The amount to be paid when the note or bond is due.

Measurement (13): To assign a numerical amount to the information that is recognized in the accounts.

Merchandise inventory (5): A merchandising business's stock of goods available for sale as of a particular point in time.

Merchandise inventory card (9): A record in both quantities and costs of the beginning inventory of each item, purchases of the item, and sales of the item.

Minority interest (16): Other stockholders when one investor owns more than 50% of the voting stock in a subsidiary.

Mixed costs (23): Costs that contain both variable and fixed cost elements.

Modified Accelerated Cost Recovery System (MACRS): The most current rules for depreciation for income tax purposes.

Modifying conventions (13): Constraints on the application of accounting principles adopted by the accounting profession.

Monetary measurement concept (1): The concept that the focus of accounting is on business events, resources, and obligations that can be expressed in money terms.

Mutual agency (14): The characteristic of a partnership that makes each partner an agent of the partnership, and is therefore able to enter into binding agreements on behalf of the partnership.

N

Natural resources (11): Wasting assets such as oil, gas, mineral deposits, and stands of timber.

Negotiable promissory note (8): An debt instrument that the original payee can sell readily to collect cash earlier than the due date of the note.

Net book value (10): An amount representing the undepreciated cost of a plant asset as of the balance sheet date.

Net income (1, 3): The excess of revenues over expenses for a period.

Net loss (3): The excess of expenses over revenues for a period.

Net pay (12): Gross pay minus withholdings and deductions.

Net present value (28): The sum of the present values of all cash flows.

Net purchases (5): Purchases less purchases returns and allowances and purchases discounts.

Net sales (5): The total amounts a business receives or expects to be collected for the period's sales of merchandise to customers expressed as gross sales less sales returns and allowances and sales discounts.

Neutrality (13): A characteristic of reliability that means that in choosing an accounting method, there is freedom from bias towards a pre-determined result.

Noncontrollable costs (20): A cost that a manager cannot influence.

Noncumulative preferred stock (15): A type of preferred stock that allows preferred stockholders a stated amount of dividends before the common stockholders can receive any dividends. However, if no dividend is declared for a year, the preferred stockholders right to receive dividends for that year lapses.

Noncurrent liabilities (long-term liabilities or long-term debts) (4, 12): Those obligations due in more than one year or more than one operating cycle, whichever is longer, from the balance sheet date.

Noninterest-bearing note (8): A debt instrument that does not state an interest rate to be applied to the face amount of the note.

Non-like-kind exchanges (11): Exchanges of dissimilar plant assets for which a taxable gain or loss is recognized.

Nonmanufacturing costs (20): All costs that are not associated with the production of goods.

Non-negotiable promissory note (8): A debt instrument that does not satisfy the legal conditions for negotiability.

Nonparticipating preferred stock (15): A type of preferred stock in which the stock certificate limits the dividends on preferred stock to the stated amount.

No-par value stock (15): Stock issued without a par value.

Not-for-profit (15): An entity organized to conduct business with some other purpose than earning a profit, such as charities, educational institutions, and certain medical organizations.

NSF checks (7): Checks that the banks that they are drawn on refuse to pay for lack of funds in the maker's accounts.

O

Objectives of financial statements (13): Objectives developed by the FASB to provide broad guidelines for financial statements prepared by businesses.

Off-balance-sheet financing (17): Any scheme or system through which a business effectively acquires or retains property rights in assets for future payments without showing the assets or the related liabilities on its balance sheet.

Operating cycle (4, 12): The average period of time between committing resources to providing goods or services and collecting cash from customers.

Operating expenses (5): All the expenses of running the business for a period other than the cost of goods sold.

Operating income (29): Income from continuing operations before interest and taxes.

Operating leases (17): Short-term or long-term leases that involve strictly renting assets for use in the lessee's business. No special rights or privileges are acquired, and the lessor bears all of the risks of ownership.

Operating systems (6): Fundamental programs that tell the computer how to coordinate the parts of the system.

Opportunity costs (27): The values of benefits foregone by selecting one decision alternative over another.

Organization costs (15): Costs incurred in forming a corporation.

Outstanding checks (7): Checks that a business has issued and recorded but which have not be presented to the bank for payment.

Overapplied overhead (21): The difference between the debits and credits to Manufacturing Overhead if actual overhead is less than the amount of overhead applied.

Overhead allocation (21): The process of assigning manufacturing overhead to specific jobs and recording overhead in various accounts.

Overhead allocation rate (21): Estimated overhead costs divided by the estimated quantity of the allocation base.

Overhead applied (21): The amount of overhead assigned to jobs.

Overhead volume variance (26): The difference between the amount of overhead applied to production at the standard and the amount of overhead included in the flexible budget.

Owner's equity (1): The residual interest owners have in the business's assets after deducting the liabilities.

P

Paid-In Capital in Excess of Par (15): The account used to record the difference between the par value of the stock and the selling price when the selling price is greater than the par value.

Parent corporation (16): The investor company who is able to control the investee.

Participating preferred stock (15): A type of preferred stock in which the stockholder has the right to participate in dividends in excess of the stated amount in certain circumstances.

Partnership (1, 14): An association of two or more persons to carry on a business as co-owners.

Partnership agreement (14): The agreement between two or more persons that governs their association as partners and constitutes a contract that creates that partnership.

Par value (15): The amount printed on the stock certificate and established by the corporation's charter. The par value of the stock issued determines the corporation's legal capital.

Patents (11): The exclusive right granted by the federal government to use the product or process for a period of 17 years.

Payback period (28): The length of time it takes to recover the initial cost of an investment.

Payee (8): The party to whom money is owed.

Payment date (15): The date that the corporation actually pays the dividends that have been previously declared by the board of directors.

Payroll register (12): A special journal used to record employees' gross wages, withholdings, deductions, and net pay.

Percentage-of-completion method (13): A method that recognizes revenue for long-term construction contracts by dividing the total estimated cost by the cost incurred in the current period and multiplying the resulting percentage by the total revenue on the project.

Percent-change financial statements (19): Conventional financial statements with changes and percents of changes added.

Percent utilization of a line of credit (12): Loan balance divided by the maximum available loan.

Performance reports (20, 25): Reports comparing the budget with the actual results that shows budget variances.

Period (term, duration) of a note (8): The length of time for which the promissory note is in effect.

Period costs (20): Costs identified with accounting periods rather than with goods produced.

Periodic inventory method (5): A method of accounting for inventory in which the balance in Merchandise Inventory is updated at the end of the accounting period as a result of taking a physical inventory.

Perpetual inventory method (5): A method of accounting for inventory in which the costs of purchases and the cost of goods sold are recorded on a daily, or even a continuous, basis.

Petty cash fund (7): A fund used to make small cash payments.

Petty cash receipts (7): Documents providing evidence of disbursements made from the petty cash fund stating the purpose of the payments, the amounts, the dates, and other pertinent information.

Physical inventory (5): A process of physically counting all goods of each kind in the merchandise inventory as of a particular date, assigning costs to them and calculating an inventory balance.

Plant assets (plant and equipment, or property, plant, and equipment) (10): Tangible productive assets owned by a business that are useful for more than one year and are acquired to be used in the business's operations, not to be resold.

Point-of-sale systems (7): Computer-based cash receipts systems that allow customers to transfer funds immediately from their bank accounts to the merchant's bank account at the time of a sale.

Pooling-of-interests method (16): A method of accounting for business combinations in which the acquired company's net assets are reported in the consolidated financial statements at their book values immediately preceding the combination. This method is used for combinations that involve the exchange of common stock.

Post-closing trial balance (4): A trial balance prepared immediately after closing.

Posting (2): The process of recording transactions in the general ledger accounts.

Predetermined overhead rate (21): The estimated level of allocation base divided by the estimated total overhead cost.

Predictive value (13): A characteristic of relevance that the information should help users form predictions about the outcomes of events.

Preemptive right (15): The right of common stockholders to purchase additional shares before the shares are offered for sale to others.

Preferred stock (15): Generally nonvoting stock, entitling the stockholder to certain preferences relative to those of common stockholders.

Premium (17): When bonds are sold for more than face value, the premium is the difference between the face value and the selling price.

Present value (17): The amount that a rational person would accept now in exchange for the right to receive an amount in the future.

Present value analysis (28): The method developed to equate future dollars to current dollars.

Private accounting (I): A broad category of accounting consisting of all accounting activities required to meet the information needs of private-sector managers and of outside users such as prospective owners and lenders.

Privately-owned corporation (15): Corporations whose shares are held by a relatively few number of owners. The shares are not traded on stock exchanges.

Product costing systems (21): An integrated set of documents, ledgers, accounts, and accounting procedures used to a measure and record the cost of manufactured products.

Production cost report (22): An end-of-the-month report for a process costing system that provides reconciliations of units and costs as well as the details of the cost per equivalent unit calculations.

Product costs (20): Costs assigned to goods produced.

Profitability ratios (19): A group of ratios that assess a business's ability to earn a profit in the future.

Profit center (29): A business segment responsible for generating revenue as well as for controlling costs.

Profit margin (3): The amount of net income as a percent of revenues, stated as net income divided by revenues.

Promissory note (4, 8): A written promise by one party to pay a specified amount of money, usually with interest, to another party on a specified date at a specified place.

Property, plant, and equipment (4): The long-lived assets that the business uses to sell and/or manufacture a product or to provide a service.

Proprietorship (1): A business owned by an individual.

Proxy (15): A legal document giving an agent power to cast a stockholder's votes at stockholders' meetings.

Public accounting (I): A category of accounting in which accountants provide professional accounting services to individuals, businesses, government units, and other entities for fees.

Publicly-owned corporation (15): Corporations whose shares are publicly traded on stock exchanges.

Purchase allowances (5): Adjustments to the amount owed for goods resulting from minor deficiencies in the goods.

Purchase discounts (5): Reductions in amounts owed to encourage early payments.

Purchase method (16): A method of accounting for business combinations in which the acquired company's assets and liabilities are reported at their fair values on the date of the business combination, with any excess of the cost over the fair value of the net assets reported as goodwill.

Purchase order (7): A formal offer to buy goods sent to the supplier after it has been properly authorized.

Purchase requisition (7): A request to purchase needed goods prepared by the person responsible for maintaining the stock on hand.

Purchase returns (5): A reduction in the amount owed because flawed or unacceptable goods are returned to the supplier.

Purchases journal (6): The special journal used to record purchases of merchandise and supplies.

Q

Qualitative characteristics (13): Characteristics of decision-useful financial statement information consisting of primary and secondary qualities.

Quick ratio (7): Liquid current assets divided by current liabilities.

R

Rate of return on owner's equity (1): Net income divided by average owners' equity.

Raw materials inventory (20): The cost of materials on hand that are used to produce a company's products.

Realization principle (2): The accounting principle that revenues should be recognized in the period they are earned if they either are collected in cash or they will be collected from customers in the future.

Receiving report (7): A document containing evidence of the quantities and condition of goods actually received from suppliers completed by employees who physically receive goods on the business's behalf.

Recognition (13): The recording of effects of events and transactions formally in the accounts as assets, liabilities, revenues, expenses, etc.

Recognize (2): To record in an account.

Reconciling the bank statement (7): The process of verifying the balance in the cash account against the bank balance of cash by taking into account appropriate adjustments to both balances.

Record date (15): The date the board of directors designates for determining who owns what number of shares of stock and, therefore, who is entitled to receive the dividend.

Redemption (call) price (15): The amount specified on some preferred stock at which the corporation may redeem the shares.

Registered bonds (17): Bonds issued in the buyer's name and recorded by the issuer in a bond register.

Registrar (15): The person or business who is responsible for transferring the corporation's stock.

Regression analysis (23): A statistical technique that uses all available data points to estimate the intercept and the slope of a cost equation.

Relative benefits (24): The notion in cost allocation that the allocation base should result in more costs being allocated to the cost objectives that benefit most from incurring the cost.

Relative performance evaluation (29): The evaluation of profitability of profit centers relative to the profitability of other, similar profit centers within the company.

Relative sales value method (24): A method of allocating joint costs in which the allocation is based on the relative sales values of the products at the split-off point.

Relevance (13): A primary qualitative characteristic of financial statement information that requires the information to be capable of making a difference in a decision.

Relevant costs (27): The only cost items managers need to consider when analyzing decision alternatives because they differ among alternatives.

Relevant range (23): The range of activity for which estimates and predictions are likely to be accurate.

Reliability (13): A primary qualitative characteristic of financial statement information that assures that the information is reasonably free from error or bias and faithfully represents what it intends to represent.

Remittance advice (7): A document attached to a check that notifies the payee of the purpose of the payment. Also, a duplicate invoice sent by the payee that may be returned with payment and serves the same purpose.

Repairs (10): Ordinary and routine revenue expenditures to maintain the plant asset in good working condition.

Replacements (10): Nonroutine, capital expenditures that extend a plant asset's useful life beyond its original estimated useful life.

Representational faithfulness (13): A characteristic of reliability that requires a high degree of correspondence between financial statement numbers and the assets, liabilities, transactions, and events those numbers intend to represent.

Required rate of return (29): The rate of return that a company believes should be earned on investments.

Research and development (11): The search for and the application of knowledge to new products or processes.

Reserve funds (19): Consist of dispensable assets, arranged but unused sources of credit, and untapped sources of new credit and equity capital. Reserve funds represent the margin of protection a business has against sudden financial distress.

Residual income (29): The investment center's operating income in excess of that required for the level of its assets.

Responsibility accounting system (24): A system of accounting that traces revenues and costs to organizational units and individuals with related responsibility for generating revenue and controlling costs.

Responsibility centers (29): Organizational units responsible for the generation of revenue or for the incurrence of costs.

Retail method (9): A method of estimating inventories for interim financial statements using a cost to retail ratio for the goods available for sale.

Retained earnings (15): The cumulative net income of a corporation less the cumulative dividends paid to stockholders from the beginning of the corporation's life.

Return on investment (29): Operating income divided by total assets.

Return on total assets (10): The sum of net income and interest expense divided by total assets.

Revenue expenditures (10): Those expenditures that merely maintain the plant asset's usefulness and keep it functioning at its original capacity.

Revenues (1, 13): Increases in net assets that result directly from providing products or services to customers during a specific period. Inflows or other enhancements of assets of a business or settlement of its liabilities from delivering or producing goods, rendering services, or other activities that constitute the entity's ongoing major or central operations.

Reversing entry (4): An entry that is exactly the opposite of an adjusting entry made at the end of the preceding accounting period.

S

Sales allowance (5): A reduction in the price given because merchandise is partially flawed.

Sales discounts (5): Reductions in payments to induce early payments.

Sales journal (6): The special journal used to record credit sales transactions.

Sales return (5): A refund given to the customer when merchandise previously purchased is returned.

Scattergraph (23): A graph of costs at various activity levels.

Selling expenses (5): Expenses directly related to storing, handling, displaying, selling, and shipping or delivering products to customers.

Separation of incompatible duties (7): An accounting control which divides the responsibility for various duties among employees to reduce the opportunity for dishonesty.

Sequential method of allocating costs (24): The allocation of service department costs that considers the fact that service departments make use of each other's services.

Serial bonds (17): Bonds issued under indentures that specify that certain subsets of the total issue of bonds are due at different maturity dates.

Short-term, revolving lines of credit (12): A bank's commitment to advance funds on demand to a borrower up to a limit and for a specific period.

Similar assets (11): In accounting for exchanges of plant assets, assets that serve the same function.

Slack (25): Amounts managers may add into budgets to assure that budgeted costs can be easily achieved.

Slide (2): An error that results from adding or dropping one or more zeros from a number.

Solvency ratios (19): A group of ratios that assess a business's ability to generate sufficient cash to meets its obligations.

Special journals (6): Substitutes for the general journal used to record particular classes of transactions.

Specific identification method (9): A method of assigning costs to the ending inventory by tracking the actual physical flow of units during the period.

Specific price changes (19): Changes in the prices of particular goods or services, irrespective of general trends.

Split-off point (24): The stage of production when individual products are identified.

1179

Stable-dollar assumption (13, 19): The assumption that the U.S. dollar is a reasonably constant unit of measure and that, even though prices change, assets, liabilities, revenues, and expenses are still recorded and reported in the financial statements according to the cost principle.

Standard cost (26): The cost that management believes should be incurred to produce a good or service under anticipated conditions.

Standard cost variance (26): The difference between the standard cost and the actual cost.

Stated, nominal, or coupon rate (17): The interest rate stated in the bond indenture.

Stated value (15): A corporation's legal capital if the corporation assigns a value to no-par value stock.

Statement of cash flows (1, 18): A financial statement that displays a business's cash receipts and cash disbursements for a period according to categories of business activities—operating activities, financing activities, and investing activities.

Statement of owner's equity (1): The financial statement that reflects the effect of owners' equity of net income, owner's investments, and owner's withdrawals for a period of time.

Statement of partners' capital (14): The statement of owner's equity for a partnership.

Static budget (25): A budget that is not adjusted for the actual level of activity.

Straight-line method (10): A method of depreciation that allocates an equal amount of depreciation expense to each period in the asset's estimated useful life.

Straight-line rate (10): 100% divided by the estimated useful life.

Stock certificate (15): A document providing evidence of ownership of shares in a corporation.

Stock dividend (16): When a company issues common stock to its own common stockholders without receiving any assets in return.

Stockholders (15): The owners of the corporation.

Stockholders' ledger (15): A subsidiary ledger containing the information about stock ownership.

Stock split (16): A method of reducing the market price per share accomplished by replacing the outstanding shares with a multiple number of the shares previously outstanding.

Stock subscription (15): A sale of shares of stock in which the purchaser agrees to pay a specified price for the shares at some future date(s).

Subsidiary corporation (16): The investee controlled by the parent corporation.

Subsidiary ledgers (6): Sets of ledger accounts that contain the details of balances in individual general ledger asset, liability, and owner's equity accounts.

Sum-of-the-years'–digits method (10): A method of depreciation that allocates depreciation expense by multiplying the asset's depreciable cost by a fraction for each year.

Sunk costs (27): Costs incurred in the past and are irrelevant to present and future decisions.

Supplier's invoice (7): The supplier's billing document containing descriptions, quantities shipped, prices of goods, the total amount owed, and the terms of credit.

System flowcharts (6): Symbolic representations of systems.

T

T-account (2): The simplest representation of an account resembling the letter T and consisting of the account title, the left (debit) side and the right (credit) side.

Temporary accounts (4): Accounts that are closed at the end of the accounting period.

Term bonds (17): Bonds issued under indentures that specify that all the bonds are due at the same date.

Term to maturity (12, 17): The period of time until a liability must be paid. The time remaining before a bond matures.

Timeliness (6,13): An objective of accounting systems that requires that information be supplied with sufficient lead time to permit management to assimilate and use it in the decision at hand. A characteristic of relevance that requires information to be available to the user before it loses its capacity to influence decisions.

Time periods assumption (13): The assumption that the life of a business can be divided into a series of equal time periods.

Time tickets (21): Forms completed by workers to keep track of the amount of time spent on each job.

Total quality management (TQM) (21): Programs designed to insure high-quality products that involve listening to customers' needs, making products right the first time, reducing defective products, and encouraging workers to improve their production processes continuously.

Trademarks (trade names) (11): Words, symbols, or other devices that identify or distinguish a product or a business. If registered with the federal government, exclusive right may be granted to use the trademark or trade name for a period of 20 years.

Trading securities (17): Bonds and equity securities that are purchased and held for resale in the near future.

Transaction (I): A voluntary exchange between economic entities, typically involving a sale/purchase of products or services that changes an economic entities' financial position.

Transfer agent (15): The person or business who is responsible for transferring the corporation's stock.

Transfer price (29): The price used to value internal transfers of goods.

Transferred-in costs (22): The cost a prior processing department incurs and transfers to the next processing department.

Transposition error (2): The reversal of two digits during the process of recording the number.

Treasury stock (16): Reacquired shares of previously issued stock.

Trial balance (2): A list of debits and credits from the general ledger accounts used to test the equality of debits and credits.

U

Unadjusted trial balance (3): A trial balance prepared before posting the adjusting entries.

Uncollectible accounts expense (8): The estimated portion of a period's credit sales that a business ultimately will not collect from customers.

Uncollectible-accounts-as-a-percent-of-credit sales (8): Uncollectible accounts expense divided by credit sales.

Underapplied overhead (21): The difference between the debits and credits to Manufacturing Overhead if actual overhead is greater than the amount of overhead applied.

Unearned revenue (3): Payment received in advance of delivering the goods or performing the services.

Unitized fixed cost (24): Fixed costs stated on a per unit basis.

Units-of-production method (10): A method of depreciation that allocates depreciation expense to the time periods based on the plant asset's output.

Unlimited liability (14): The characteristic of a partnership that holds each partner personally liable for all partnership liabilities.

Useful life of an asset (3): The period of time the business estimates it can use the asset in its operations.

V

Valuation account (contra-asset account) (3, 10): An account that reduces another account to its correct balance for presentation in the financial statements. For example, Accumulated Depreciation is the valuation account for the related plant asset account.

Variable costing (23): An alternative to full costing in which only variable production costs are included in inventory. All fixed production costs are treated as period costs.

Variable costs (20, 23): Those costs that increase or decrease in response to increases or decreases in business activity.

Verifiability (13): A characteristic of reliability that results from a high degree of agreement among independent measurers.

Vertical analysis (19): Analysis of the percentage composition of the components of a particular financial statement for a particular year.

Voucher (7): The document on which relevant data about an obligation to pay are summarized for approval, recording, and payment under a voucher system.

Voucher system (7): An integrated control system in which adequate support documents (vouchers) are prepared for all acquisitions and expenditures.

W

Weighted-average cost method (9): A method of assigning costs to the ending inventory based on the average cost per unit, which consists of the combined cost of the beginning inventory and the purchases made during the year.

"What-if" analysis (23): An examination of the results of various courses of action.

Withdrawals (1): Distributions by proprietorships or partnerships.

Work in process inventory (20): The cost of goods that are only partially complete.

Z

Zero base budgeting (25): A method of budget preparation that requires each department to justify budgeted amounts at the start of each budget period, even if the amounts were supported in prior budget periods.

INDEX

A

Account analysis
    def., 939
Accounting rate of return
  as method for capital budgeting, 1117
  def., 1117
Accounts
  and job order costing, 867
  cost flows through, 905
  flow of product costs in, 842
  recording standard costs in, 1067
Accrual basis of accounting
  and taxation, 1174
Activity-based costing (ABC)
  and multiple overhead rates, 874
  approach, 998
  comprehensive example, 999
  def., 874
  problems of using only measures of production volume to allocate overhead, 997
  relating cost pools to products using, 998
Allocating joint costs, 989
  illus., 990
  physical quantity approach, 991
  relative sales value method of, 990
Allocating overhead
  problem of using only measures of production volume in, 997
Allocating service department costs, 985
  direct method, 985
  direct method, *illus.*, 986
  sequential method, 986
  sequential method, *illus.*, 987
Allocation base
  ability to bear costs as a way of selecting, 985
  cause-and-effect relationship necessary for, 984
  def., 874
  equity as a way of selecting, 985
  for overhead, 874
  relative benefits as a way of selecting, 985
  selecting, 984
Alternative minimum tax, 1183
Attainable standards
  def., 1055

Avoidable costs
  def., 1085
  summary of, 1089

B

Balance sheet
  budgeted, 1034
  product costs on, 841
Break-even point
  def., 945
  illus., 946
Budgetary control, 1035
  budget variances and, 1035
  performance reports and, 1035
Budget committee
  def., 1024
Budgeted balance sheet
  def., 1034
  illus., 1034
Budgeted income statement
  def., 1029
  illus., 1031
Budgeting
  zero base, 1025
Budget planning process
  budgetary control, 1035
  static and flexible budgets, 1036
  use of computers in, 1035
Budgets
  def., 834, 1023
  developing, 1024
  for planning, 834
  master, 1025
  role of, in performance evaluations, 1025
  standard costs and, 1054
  use of computers in, 1035
  use of, in planning and control, 1024
Budget time period, 1025
Budget variances
  def., 1035
  investigating, 1037
Business segments
  def., 1140

C

Capital acquisitions budget
  def., 1031
  illus., 1031
Capital budget
  def., 1109

Capital budgeting
  accounting rate of return, 1117
  conflict between performance evaluations and, 1118
  decisions, 1108
  decisions, *def.*, 1109
  internal rate of return method of evaluating opportunities for, 1111
  net present value method of evaluating opportunities for, 1109
  payback period method, 1116
  simplified approaches to, 1116
Capital expenditure decisions
  and income taxation, 1178
  def., 1109
Capital gains and losses
  and income taxation, 1180
Cash basis of accounting
  and income taxation, 1173
Cash flows
  adjusting for inflation, 1115
  and evaluating investment opportunities, 1113
Cash receipts and disbursements budget, 1031
  illus., 1033
C corporations
  taxation of, 1169
Common costs
  def., 1087
Computer-controlled manufacturing systems
  def., 880
Computers
  use of, in budget planning process, 1035
Contribution approach to pricing
  def., 1094
Contribution margin
  approach to multiproduct analysis, 949
  calculation of, 947
  def., 947
Contribution margin ratio
  approach to multiproduct analysis, 949
  calculation of, 947
  def., 947
Controllable costs
  and responsibility accounting, 991
  def., 848, 992

1182

Controllable overhead variance
　calculating, 1061
　def., 1061
　reconciling to total overhead variance, 1061
Conversion costs
　def., 905
Cost allocation
　arbitrary, 992
　def., 979
　determining the cost objectives, 982
　forming cost pools for, 983
　lump-sum allocations, 994
　problems with, 991
　process of, 982
　purposes of, 980
　selecting allocation base for, 984
　to encourage evaluation of services, 982
　to provide "full cost" information, 981
　to provide information for decision making, 980
　to reduce frivolous use of common resources, 981
　unitized fixed costs in, 994
Cost behavior
　common patterns, 936
　of variable costs, 937
Cost centers
　def., 1140
Cost classifications
　for manufacturing firms, 839
　for planning, evaluation, and decision making, 846
Cost drivers
　common activities associated with, 999
　def., 874
　examples of, 875
　relating cost pools to products using, 998
Cost estimation methods, 939
　account analysis, 939
　high-low method, 941
　regression analysis, 944
　scattergraph approach, 941
Cost information
　emphasis on, for managerial accounting, 838
Costing systems
　job-order, 867
　process costing, 867
　types of, 866
Cost objectives
　def., 983
　determining, 982
　illus., 983
Cost of capital
　def., 1113
Cost of goods available for sale
　def., 845
Cost of goods manufactured
　def., 842

illus., 843
　statement of, 844
Cost of goods sold
　flow of costs in job order system, 873
　illus., 844
　recording in accounts, 1069
Cost of services, 846
Cost per equivalent unit
　applying, 909
　calculating, 908
　def., 908
Cost pools
　def., 874, 983
　examples of, 875
　forming, 983
　overhead rates using, *illus.*, 996
　too few, 995
　using cost drivers to relate to products to, 998
Costs
　allocating service department, 985
　avoidable, 1085
　common, 1087
　controllable, 848, 991
　fixed, 846, 937
　full, 865
　flow of, 873
　direct, 848
　indirect, 848
　mixed, 937
　noncontrollable, 848
　product, 866
　variable, 846, 936
Cost transferred out, 910
Cost-volume-profit (C-V-P) analysis
　assumptions of, 951
　break-even point, 945
　contribution margin, 947
　def., 936
　margin of safety, 947
　profit equation, 946
　"what-if" analysis, 948

D

Decentralized organizations
　advantages of, 1136
　and responsibility accounting, 1139
　def., 1136
　disadvantages of, 1138
Decision making, 836
　cost allocation provides information for, 980
　cost classifications for, 846
　product costs and, 866
　qualitative considerations in, 1094
Deferred-payment contract
　def., 1175
Depreciation
　income tax shield, *def.*, 1114
Differential analysis
　of further processing decision, *illus.*, 1084

of make or buy decision, *illus.*, 1085
　single-column format for, 1086
Differential costs
　additional processing decision, 1082
　def., 1082
　summary of, 1089
Differential revenues
　additional processing decision, 1082
　def., 1082
Direct costing
　def., 953
Direct costs
　def., 848
Direct labor
　def., 840
　in process cost system, 906
　time tickets to record, 870
Direct labor budget, 1028
　illus., 1029
Direct labor variances, 1058
　labor efficiency variance, 1058
　labor rate variance, 1058
　reconciliation of, *illus.*, 1064
　reconciling, 1059
Direct material
　def., 839
　in process cost system, 906
　material requisition form to request, 869
　on job cost sheet, 869
Direct material purchases budget, 1027
　illus., 1028
Direct method
　of allocating service department costs, *def.*, 985
Double taxation of corporations
　def., 1169
Dropping a product line, 1087
　analysis of, *illus.*, 1088

E

Equivalent units
　cost per, 908
　def., 908
Evaluation
　cost classifications for, 846
　performance reports used for, 835
　process, *illus.*, 835
　of services, 982
Exchange rate
　performance reports for, 835

F

Financial accounting
　differences between managerial accounting and, 837
　similarities between managerial accounting and, 838
Financial reporting
　and product costs, 866

1183

Financial statements
  comparison of merchandising and manufacturing firms, 845
Finished goods inventory
  def., 842
  flow of costs in job order system, 873
  recording in accounts, 1069
Fixed costs
  behavior, *illus.*, 938
  def., 847, 937
  unitized, 994
Flexible manufacturing systems
  def., 881
Flexible budgets
  def., 1036
  performance evaluation with, *illus.*, 1037
Full cost
  cost allocation to provide, 981
  def., 865
  plus profit as transfer price, 1151
Full cost pricing
  approach, *illus.*, 1092
  def., 1092

H

High-low method
  as method of cost estimation, 941
  def., 941
  illus., 943

I

Ideal standards
  def., 1055
Income statement
  budgeted, 1029
  presentation of product costs, 843
  showing cost of goods sold, 844
  variable costing, 953
Income tax allocation, 1176
Income taxes
  and capital expenditure decisions, 1178
  and method of accounting decision, 1172
  and transfer prices, 1153
  aspects of business decisions, 1165
  for C corporations, 1169
  form of business decision, 1165
  for partnerships, 1169
  for S corporations, 1169
  for sole proprietorships, 1165
Indirect costs
  def., 848
Indirect labor
  def., 840
Indirect material
  def., 840
Inflation
  adjusting cash flows for, 1115
Installment method
  and income taxation, 1175

Internal rate of return
  approach to evaluating investments, *illus.*, 1112
  calculating when cash flows are unequal, *illus.*, 1124
  def., 1111
  method of evaluating investment opportunities, 1111
  summary of, 1112
  with unequal cash flows, 1123
Investment centers
  def., 1141
  evaluating, 1142
Investment opportunities
  evaluating, using the time value of money, 1109

J

Job cost sheet
  direct material cost on, 869
  illus., 869
Job-order costing systems, 867, 869
  and financial statement accounts, 867
  differences between process costing systems and, 904
  flow of costs in, *illus.*, 868
Jobs
  allocating overhead, 873
  def., 867
  how manufacturing costs are traced to, *illus.*, 873
  product costs related to, *illus.*, 867
  tracing costs to, 872
Joint costs
  allocating, 989
  def., 989
Joint products
  def., 989
Just-in-time (JIT) manufacturing
  def., 880

L

Labor
  direct, 840
  indirect, 840
  recording costs in accounts, 1068
Labor efficiency variance
  def., 1058
  reconciling to total labor variance, 1059
Labor rate variance
  def., 1058
  reconciling to total labor variance, 1059
Lump-sum allocations
  as problem in cost allocation, 994
  def., 994

M

Make or buy decisions, 1083
Management behavior
  in budget planning process, 1038

Management by exception
  and standard cost variances, 1066
  def., 836, 1038
Managerial accounting
  def., 833
  differences between financial accounting and, 837
  emphasis on future, 837
  emphasis on nonmonetary information, 837
  evaluation, 834
  introduction to, 834
  planning, 834
  similarities between financial accounting and, 838
Manufacturing costs
  def., 839
  direct labor, 840
  direct material, 839
  manufacturing overhead, 840
  traced to jobs, *illus.*, 873
Manufacturing environment
  and product costing systems, 879
  changes in, 879
  computer-controlled, 880
  flexible manufacturing systems, 881
  just-in-time (JIT), 880
  total quality management (TQM), 881
Manufacturing firms
  comparison of financial statements for merchandising and, 845
  cost classifications of, 839
Manufacturing overhead, 871
  allocating to jobs, 873
  common types of, 840
  def., 840
  in process cost system, 906
  overhead allocation rate for, 872
  recording costs in accounts, 1068
Manufacturing overhead budget, 1029
  illus., 1029
Marginal tax rate
  def., 1167
Margin of safety
  def., 947
Market prices
  and opportunity costs, 1148
  as transfer prices, 1147
Master budget
  budgeted balance sheet, 1034
  budgeted income statement, 1029
  capital acquisitions budget, 1031
  cash receipts and disbursements budget, 1031
  def., 1025
  direct labor budget, 1028
  direct materials purchases budget, 1027
  manufacturing overhead budget, 1029
  production budget, 1026

1184

sales budget, 1026
selling and administrative expense budget, 1029
Materials
 direct, 839
 indirect, 840
 recording costs in accounts, 1067
Material price variance
 calculating, 1057
 def., 1057
 reconciling to total material variance, 1057
Material quantity variance
 calculating, 1057
 def., 1057
 reconciling to total material variance, 1057
Material requisition form
 def., 869
 illus., 870
Material variances
 material price variance, 1057
 material quantity variances, 1057
 reconciliation, *illus.*, 1063
 reconciling, 1057
Merchandising business
 comparison of financial statements for manufacturing firms and, 845
Mixed costs
 behavior, *illus.*, 938
 def., 937
Multiproduct analysis, 949
 contribution margin approach, 949
 contribution margin ratio approach, 949

N

Negotiated transfer prices, 1151
Net present value
 analysis of new product, *illus.*, 1119
 approach to evaluating investments, *illus.*, 1110
 def., 1109
 evaluating investment opportunities using, 1109
 summary of, 1112
Noncontrollable costs
 def., 848
Nonmanufacturing costs
 def., 840
 general and administrative costs, 840
 selling costs, 840

O

Operating income
 def., 1142
Opportunity costs
 and market prices, 1148
 and transfer prices, 1147
 illus., 1086
 summary of, 1089

Overapplied overhead
 def., 878
Overhead allocation base
 selecting, 874
Overhead allocation rate, 873
 calculating, 874
 def., 872
 selecting base, 874
Overhead applied
 def., 872
 overapplied, 878
 underapplied, 878
Overhead rates
 and activity-based costing, 874
 multiple, 874
 predetermined, 877
 using one versus two cost pools, *illus.*, 996
Overhead variances, 1059
 controllable overhead variance, 1061
 overhead volume variance, 1059
 reconciliation of, *illus.*, 1065
 reconciling, 1061
Overhead volume variance
 calculating, 1059
 def., 1059
 interpreting, 1060
 reconciling to total overhead variance, 1061

P

Partnerships
 taxation and, 1169
Payback period method
 approach to capital budgeting, 1116
 def., 1116
Performance evaluation
 conflict between capital budgeting and, 1118
 relative, 1141
 role of budgets in, *illus.*, 1025
Performance reports
 def., 835, 1035
 for budgetary control, 1035
 for evaluation, 835
 illus., 836
Period costs
 def., 841
Permanent differences
 in income tax allocation, 1176
Planning
 budgets used for, 834, 1024
 cost classifications for, 846
 process, *illus.*, 835
Predetermined overhead rates
 calculating, 877
 def., 877
Present value analysis
 def., 1109

Pricing decisions, 1092
 contribution approach to, 1092
 full cost pricing, 1092
Process costing systems, 867
 basic steps in, 911
 differences between job-order costing systems and, 904
 product and cost flows, 904
Product constraints
 decisions involving, 1090
Product cost information
 financial reporting and, 866
 managerial decision making and, 866
Product costing system
 and changes in the manufacturing environment, 879
 def., 865
 job-order, 867
 process costing, 867
Product costs
 balance sheet presentation of, 841
 def., 841
 financial reporting and, 866
 flow in accounts, 842, 905
 flow in accounts, *illus.*, 843
 managerial decision making and, 866
 income statement presentation of, 843
 in process costing systems, 904
 related to jobs, *illus.*, 867
Product flows
 in process costing systems, 904
 through departments, 904
Production budget, 1026
 illus., 1027
Production cost report
 def., 911
 illus., 912
 reconciliation of costs, 911
 reconciliation of units, 911
Profit centers
 def., 1141
 using transfer prices to turn service centers into, 1152
Proprietorship
 taxation and, 1165

R

Raw material inventory, *def.*, 841
Regression analysis
 def., 944
 illus., 944
Relative performance evaluation
 def., 1141
Relative sales value method
 def., 990
 of allocating joint costs, 990
Relevant costs
 def., 1082
Relevant range
 def., 944
 illus., 945

Required rate of return
  estimating, 1113
Residual income
  calculating, 1145
  def., 1145
Responsibility accounting system
  and controllable costs, 991
  and decentralization, 1139
  and variances, 1067
  def., 992
Responsibility centers
  def., 1140
Return on investment (ROI)
  calculating, 1142
  def., 1142
  evaluating investment centers and managers with, 1143
  problems with, 1143

S

Sales budget, 1026
  illus., 1027
Scattergraph
  approach to cost estimation, 941
  def., 941
  illus., 942
Schedule of cost of goods manufactured
  illus., 844
S corporations
  taxation of, 1169
Selling and administrative expense budget, 1029
  illus., 1030
Sequential method of allocating service department costs
  def., 987
  illus., 987
Service centers
  turned into profit centers using transfer prices, 1152
Service departments
  allocating costs, 985
  direct method of allocating costs, 985
  direct method of allocating costs, *illus.*, 986
  sequential method of allocating costs, 986
  sequential method of allocating costs, *illus.*, 987

Split-off point
  def., 989
  illus., 990
Standard costs
  and budgets, 1054
  def., 1054
  development of, 1055
  recording in accounts, 1067
Standards
  attainable, 1055
  ideal, 1055
Standard cost variance
  def., 1056
  investigation of, 1065
Static budgets
  def., 1036
  performance evaluation with, *illus.*, 1036
Sunk costs
  def., 1083
  summary of, 1089

T

Taxes
  and capital budgeting decisions, 1114
Temporary differences
  in income tax allocation, 1177
Time tickets
  def., 870
  illus., 871
Total quality management (TQM)
  def., 881
Tracing costs
  to the organizational level where they can be controlled, 1140
Transfer pricing
  and income taxes in an international context, 1153
  def., 1147
  full cost plus profit as the, 1151
  market price and, 1148
  negotiated, 1151
  opportunity costs and, 1147
  service centers turned into profit centers with, 1152
  variable costs as the, 1149
Transferred-in cost, 913
  def., 905
  in process cost system, 906
  production cost report showing, *illus.*, 914

U

Underapplied overhead
  def., 878
Unit costs
  calculating, 907
  equivalent units, 908
Unitized fixed costs
  def., 994

V

Variable costing
  benefits of for internal reporting, 957
  def., 953
  effect of, 954
  income statement, 953
Variable costs
  as transfer prices, 1149
  behavior, *illus.*, 937
  def., 846, 936
Variance analysis
  and responsibility accounting, 1067
  closing accounts in, 1069
  direct labor variances in, 1058
  general approach to, 1056
  material variances in, 1057
  overhead variances in, 1059

W

"What-if" analysis
  change in selling price, 948
  def., 948
Work in process inventory
  def., 842
  flow of costs in job order system, 873

Z

Zero base budgeting
  def., 1025